# Understanding Health and Social Care

## An Introductory Reader

edited by
Margaret Allott and Martin Robb

The Open
University

in association with
The Open University

SAGE Publications
London • Thousand Oaks • New Delhi

SAGE Publications Ltd
6 Bonhill Street
London EC2A 4PU

SAGE Publications Inc
2455 Teller Road
Thousand Oaks, California 91320

SAGE Publications India Pvt Ltd
32, M-Block Market
Greater Kailash – I
New Delhi 110 048

**British Library Cataloguing in Publication data**

A catalogue record for this book is available from the
British Library

ISBN 0 7619 5685 9
ISBN 0 7619 5686 7 (pbk)

**Library of Congress catalog card number 97–062172**

Typeset by Mayhem Typesetting, Rhayader, Powys
Printed in Great Britain by The Cromwell Press Ltd,
Trowbridge, Wiltshire

# Contents

Acknowledgements      viii

Introduction      1
*Celia Davies and Martin Robb*

**SECTION 1   Accounts of Care and Caring**      7

Introduction      7
*Jan Walmsley*

1   Anthology: Voices from the Institutions      9
*Joanna Bornat*

2   The Insider Researcher      26
*Howard Mitchell*

3   A 'Tangled Web' of Emotions      36
*Val Hollinghurst*

4   Caring in Families: a Case Study      40
*Jan Walmsley*

5   Snowballs and Acorns: Medicine by Impact      48
*Tom Heller*

6   Nursing Practice and the Lived
Experience of Illness      56
*P. Benner and J. Wrubel*

**SECTION 2   Where Care Takes Place**      59

Introduction      59
*Sheila Peace*

7   The Persistent Image      62
*R.A. Parker*

8   Total Institutions      70
*K. Jones and A.J. Fowles*

9   Losing Your Home      75
*A. Norman*

10   The Physical World                                          80
     *D. Willcocks, S. Peace and L. Kellaher*

11   Black Perspectives on Residential Care                      91
     *Black Perspectives Sub-Group*

12   The Shifting Concept of Community                          104
     *Marjorie Mayo*

**SECTION 3   Models of Care: Challenge and Change**            111

     Introduction                                               111
     *Celia Davies and Martin Robb*

13   Striking Balances: Living with Parkinson's Disease         114
     *Ruth Pinder*

14   The New Obstetrics: Science or Social Control?             123
     *Lesley Doyal*

15   Listening and Life-History Work                            130
     *John Killick*

16   Approaches to Reminiscence                                 139
     *Joanna Bornat*

17   From Group Meeting to Therapeutic Group                    145
     *Bernadette Duffy and Brian McCarthy*

18   Housing Primary Health Care in the Community               155
     *Lyn Fisk*

19   Creating a Space for Absent Voices: Disabled Women's
     Experience of Receiving Assistance with Daily Living
     Activities                                                 163
     *Jenny Morris*

20   Carers and Professionals – the Carer's Viewpoint           171
     *Annie Bibbings*

21   'He's our child and we shall always love him' – Mental
     Handicap: the Parents' Response                            182
     *Robina Shah*

22   The Cloak of Professionalism                               190
     *Celia Davies*

23   Principles of Empowerment                                  198
     *Marian Barnes and Alan Walker*

**SECTION 4   When Care Goes Wrong**                            209

     Introduction                                               209
     *Hilary Brown*

24   Towards an Explanation of the Corruption of Care        212
     *Julia Wardhaugh and Paul Wilding*

25   Bedroom Abuse: the Hidden Work in a Nursing Home        230
     *Geraldine Lee-Treweek*

26   Body Care and Learning To Do for Others                236
     *Jocelyn Lawler*

27   Child Protection: Messages from Research               246
     *Dartington Social Research Unit (HMSO)*

28   Elder Abuse and the Policing of Community Care          258
     *Simon Biggs*

**SECTION 5   Contexts of Care: Policies and Politics**    263

     Introduction                                           263
     *Celia Davies*

29   Becoming Consumers of Community Care: Households
     within the Mixed Economy of Welfare                    266
     *John Baldock and Clare Ungerson*

30   The Medical/Social Boundary                            272
     *Julia Twigg*

31   Working on the Front Line: Risk Culture and Nursing in
     the New NHS                                            279
     *Ellen Annandale*

32   Learning Disabilities: a Service in Jeopardy           287
     *R. Hadley and R. Clough*

33   Evaluating Market Principles in Health Care            295
     *Linda J. Jones*

34   Principles of Reform                                   302
     *David Marsland*

35   Alternative Futures                                    306
     *Roger Hadley and Roger Clough*

Index                                                      311

# Acknowledgements

The editors and publishers wish to thank the following for permission to use copyright material.

Marian Barnes, Alan Walker and The Policy Press for material from (1996) 'Consumerism versus Empowerment: a Principled Approach to the Involvement of Older Service Users', *Policy and Politics*, 24(4). Blackwell Publishers Ltd for material from Ellen Annandale (1996) 'Working on the Front Line: Risk Culture and Nursing in the New NHS', *Sociological Review*, 94(3): 416–51. Blackwell Science Ltd for material from Lyn Fisk (1996) 'Housing Primary Health Care in the Community', in R. Bryar and B. Bytheway (eds) *Changing Primary Health Care: the Teamcare Valleys Experience*. Cambridge University Press for material from Julia Twigg (1997) 'The Medical/Social Boundary', *Journal of Social Policy* 26(2): 211–32. Cassell plc for material from R. Hadley and R. Clough (1991) *Care in Chaos*. Centre for Policy on Ageing for material from A. Norman (1980) 'Losing Your Home' in *Rights and Risk*. Churchill Livingstone for material from Joanna Bornat (1996) 'Approaches to Reminiscence' in I. Norman and S. Redfern (eds) *Mental Health Care for Elderly People*. Generations Review for material from Geraldine Lee-Treweek (1994) 'Bedroom Abuse: The Hidden Work in a Nursing Home', *Generations Review*, 4(1); and Simon Biggs (1996), 'Elder Abuse and the Policing of Community Care', *Generations Review*, 6(2). Herefordshire Mind Association for material from ex-patients and staff (1995), *Boots On! Out!*, pp. 55–7. HMSO for material from R.A. Parker (1988), 'The Persistent Image' in Ian Sinclair, *Residential Care: The Research Reviewed*; Dartington Social Research Unit (1995), *Studies in Child Protection: Messages from Research*; and Black Perspectives Sub-group (1993), 'Black Perspectives on Residential Care' in NISW, *Residential Care: Positive Answers*. Margot Jefferys (1996) for material from her paper 'Objectives and Obstacles: Recollections of Some of the Pioneers of Geriatric Medicine' given at the Oral History Society Annual Conference, Birkbeck College, London. Little Brown for material from Fred Fever (1994), *Who Cares: Memories of a Childhood in Bernardo's*. Macmillan Press Ltd and Rutgers for material from Lesley Doyal (1995) *What Makes Women Sick? Gender and the Political Economy of Health*; and Linda Jones (1994) *The Social Context of Health and Health Work*. Macmillan Press Ltd, Basingstoke and St Martins Press,

Incorporated for material from Marjorie Mayo (1994), *Communities and Caring: the Mixed Economy of Welfare*; and D. Marsland (1996), *Welfare or Welfare State?* Mencap Northern Division, Harrogate, for material from David Barron (1996) *A Price to be Born*, pp. 58–60. The National Children's Bureau for material from Robina Shah (1992) *The Silent Minority: Children with Disabilities in Asian Families*. Northcote House for material from Maggie Potts and Rebecca Fido (1991) '*A Fit Person to be Removed': Personal Accounts of Life in a Mental Deficiency Institution*, p. 17; and Steve Humphries and Pamela Gordon (1992) *Out of Sight: The Experience of Disability 1900–1950*, pp. 90–1. Nursing Times for material from Celia Davies (1996) 'Cloaked in a Tattered Illusion', *Nursing Times*, 92(45); and 'A New Vision of Professionalism', *Nursing Times*, 92(46). Pearson Professional for material from Jocelyn Lawler (1991) *Behind the Screens: Nursing, Somology and the Pattern of the Body*. QueenSpark Books for material from Mary Adams (1995) *Those Lost Years*. Routledge for material from Peter Townsend (1962) *The Last Refuge: A Survey of Residential Homes and Institutions for the Aged in England and Wales*, pp. 4–5; Val Hollinghurst (1985) 'A Tangled Web of Emotions' in A. Briggs and J. Oliver (eds) *Caring Experiences of Looking After Disabled Relatives*; K. Jones and A.J. Fowles (1984) *Ideas on Institutions*; D. Willcocks, S. Peace and L. Kellaher (1987) 'The Physical World', in *Private Lives in Public Places*; Ruth Pinder (1988) 'Striking Balances: Living with Parkinson's Disease', in R. Anderson and M. Bury (eds) *Living with Chronic Illness*; and Annie Bibbings (1994) 'Carers and Professionals – the Carer's Viewpoint' in A. Leathard, *Going Interprofessional*. Joseph Rowntree Foundation for material from J. Baldock and C. Ungerson (1994) *Becoming Consumers of Community Care: Households within the Mixed Economy of Europe*. Sage Publications for material from Julia Wardhaugh and Paul Wilding (1993) 'Towards an Explanation of the Corruption of Care', *Critical Social Policy*, 37: 4–31. Sholom Glouberman and King's Fund for material from Sholom Glouberman (1990) *Keepers: Inside Stories from Total Institutions*, pp. 91–2. Stanley Thornes (Publishers) Ltd for material from Peter Nolan (1993) *A History of Mental Health Nursing*, pp. 108 and 111. Waltham Forest Oral History Workshop for material from Ernest (Tom) Atkins, *One Door Closes Another Opens: a Personal Experience of Polio*, pp. 39–41. Whiting and Birch Ltd for material from Bernadette Duffy and Brian McCarthy (1993) 'From Group Meeting to Therapeutic Group', *Groupwork*, 6(2): 152–62.

Every effort has been made to trace all the copyright holders, but if any have been inadvertently overlooked the publishers will be pleased to make the necessary arrangement at the first opportunity.

# Introduction

*Celia Davies and Martin Robb*

We would all like to live healthy, happy lives, but none of us can achieve that entirely independently. Each of us relies at some time on support, guidance or practical assistance from others: in helpless infancy, during the explorations of childhood, over the turmoil of adolescence, lying ill in bed at home or in hospital, or adjusting to chronic illness, disability or old age. And most of us, at times, find ourselves supporting and caring for others, as a parent, a partner or spouse; a daughter or son, as a volunteer answering a help-line, or as a paid worker in health or social care settings.

What does it feel like to be on the receiving end of care provision, or to be an 'informal carer' caring for others, unpaid, at home, or to work in contemporary health and social care services? Where should care take place – in the home, or in institutions, or in the wider community? How can care be organized so that service users feel valued and involved in decisions about their own health and welfare? How can abuse be prevented, both in informal settings and in institutions? Should existing care services remain the responsibility of the public sector, or is there a case for reducing dependence on the state? These questions are brought into the open in this volume, and the reader will gain a sense of how they have been debated and discussed.

This book is distinctive in at least two senses. First, there are already a number of other books in existence which deal with issues surrounding the financing, organization and administration of care services. This book does not attempt to duplicate them, or to consider in any detailed way the party political issues that currently surround care. What it does do, in a way that is not adequately represented in the current literature, is to connect the day-to-day experience of caring and being cared for, with new ideas and ways of thinking about health and social care. By juxtaposing the voices of service users with insight from academic debate and research, it links policy to practice and theory to experience in a tangible way. The book is also unusual in the way it cuts across the conventional divide between health care and social care, and in its attempt to provide material that will be relevant to, for example, nurses, health visitors and therapists on the one hand, and on the other hand social workers, residential and home carers, and others engaged in work with children, and with older and disabled people.

The articles and accounts included in the book have been selected to provide a deliberately broad and wide-ranging introduction to some of the key issues and debates in contemporary health and social care. We have set out to include up-to-date research findings and academic debates, alongside accounts from 'front-line' workers and carers, and those on the receiving end of care. We have been very aware of the sheer diversity of settings and roles in care work, and have chosen material that we hope will be of relevance both to health care workers and to those involved in social care or social work; to unpaid or informal carers and users of services, as well as those with a professional caring role. Throughout, we have sought to include a wide range of views, paying particular attention to voices and perspectives that are often ignored or suppressed – such as those of service users, or disabled or older people, or members of minority ethnic groups.

## Research on care and caring

Traditionally, caring has been seen as a private matter, something taken for granted, not of interest for public policy in the way that education, disease, poverty or unemployment are. Since around the mid-1970s there has been a rise of interest on the part both of researchers and campaigning organizations in the subject of care. Who does it, what it entails, how it is supported or not supported by wider social institutions, are some of the questions that have been asked. One result is a growing amount of evidence, built up through surveys and often through detailed interviews on the situation of unpaid carers in the home (see e.g. EOC, 1980; Nissel and Bonnerjea, 1982; Charlesworth et al., 1984; Ungerson, 1987; Lewis and Meredith, 1988; Twigg, 1992; Twigg and Atkin, 1994). Much of this work focused on the 'plight of carers' and the 'burden of care'. It showed that caring, willingly taken on and built on a good relationship between carer and cared-for, can be a deeply rewarding experience in which intimacy and mutual appreciation grows. But it also demonstrated powerfully that caring can mean a relentless daily grind taking a physical and mental toll: isolation, resentment at loss of income, status and social contact through work and a sense that there is no support. Care, at first given willingly, can deteriorate; families can resent the loss of the wife and mother to the role of daughter caring for an elderly parent, and carer and cared-for can be locked in hopelessness and guilt. It was in part in reaction to some of these negative research findings, as well as to the lobbying of campaigning organizations such as the Carers National Association, that the Carers (Recognition and Services) Act 1995 was passed, giving legal status and rights to carers for the first time.

This initial wave of research on caring was undoubtedly of immense importance in putting carers and caring on to the map of social policy. Much of the impetus at this time came from feminists and from the newly established Equal Opportunities Commission, able to raise the contradiction between governments who both supported opportunities for women in the workplace and also argued for more 'community care', apparently locking women into obligations to family and kin (see especially Finch and Groves, 1980). Academics were also stimulated to ask why caring slipped through the net of study in disciplines such as psychology and sociology. A series of what are now seen as classic writings demanding new perspectives emerged (Stacey, 1981; Graham, 1983; Waerness, 1987; Dalley, 1988). But it soon became apparent that this new work about care was deeply controversial.

This first wave of work had emphasized the burden of care, neglecting the extent to which care was undertaken willingly and found to be rewarding. It had concentrated on the carer, almost entirely neglecting the perspective of the other party to the relationship – the person being cared for. And among the carers, it had focused attention on women, not men, on adults not young carers and on white and often middle-class carers, rather than ethnic minority carers and those from working-class backgrounds. One of the strongest criticisms has come from the Independent Living Movement in the field of disability. Jenny Morris's chapter in this collection, written from the point of view of women with physical disabilities, argues that the views of those being cared for have been eclipsed – what women with disabilities often want is not 'care' that renders them passive and dependent, but the right to buy assistance so that they can live their lives as they want to and take part in caring for others. This line of argument about rights has recently been extended to a consideration of how the debate about young carers might be framed differently (Keith and Morris, 1995).

There is at least some truth in the charge that, however important it had been, early work on caring was the product of white, middle-class, anti-family feminists. An important start has been made on reassessing the first wave and devising new work to respond to criticisms (Bytheway and Johnson, forthcoming). It is also true, however, that the first phase of work challenged government policy and laid bare the implications for women of a demand that more care should happen in 'the family' or 'the community'. The wider debate here – how to strengthen the family, how to promote the return of a community spirit – can be seen cynically as cost-cutting, and as aiming at the removal of hard-won services, but it is also (as some of the final contributors to this book indicate) about the kind of society that we are trying to foster and the place of caring in it. Caring straddles the public and the private worlds. How much of a place it should have in each and how to accord it the value it deserves is an important and ongoing debate.

While the majority of health and social care is carried out on an unpaid basis in the home, there is nonetheless also a substantial paid workforce in the care sector. Readers of this book will appreciate how far in the past 'care' became 'control', especially in the large, long-stay institutions. Regimentation, routinized care, physical and mental cruelty and abuse by those paid to care are, sadly, not always things of the past, as some of our excerpts make clear. At the same time, there are many developments aimed at understanding how care can go wrong, improving care regimes and identifying and supporting good practice. A further factor for those who work in the care sector has been the prevalence of a medical model of care and a belief that care can be achieved by a 'technical fix'. While much health 'care' can be a technical matter of diagnosis and skills in administering the relevant dosage, surgical technique or therapeutic regime, and much social 'care' can be a matter of the practicalities of wound care, continence regimes and so on, the old joke about writing TLC (tender loving care) on the prescription testifies to the importance of caring. Nurses in particular have struggled with the difficulty of putting caring into words, teaching it and organizing for it in care settings. *The Primacy of Caring*, an at once scholarly and anecdotal volume, became an instant classic in the world of nursing when it was published in 1989 (Benner and Wrubel, 1989). The concept of 'emotional labour' too has proved valuable, where the visible and tangible work that nurses, care assistants and others do can seem to be trivial tasks, or even no tasks at all – just spending time with someone (Hochschild, 1983; James, 1989, 1992). In the rational world of work, it is curing that has high status and caring can easily become devalued.

## Using the book

The book has been designed to be used by a variety of groups of readers, and in several different ways. Students on a wide range of courses in health and social care, whether at undergraduate or pre-degree level, should find the articles and accounts included here an invaluable aid to their studies. We anticipate that general readers with an interest in care matters – whether they are paid workers, volunteers, informal carers, or users of services – will find material here that will deepen their understanding, and help them to link their personal experiences to wider debates. The book is also a set text for the Open University course Understanding Health and Social Care (K100), which offers a broad undergraduate-level grounding in the knowledge, understanding and skills needed in caring work of many kinds.

The book sets out to be accessible to newcomers to the field, and assumes no previous knowledge or experience of the topics covered. It is intended primarily as a resource, to be dipped into and used for reference, rather than read straight through. However, it can be read section by section, and the editorial introductions serve as a guide to the reader who wishes to do this. We hope that the book will open up areas of knowledge and interest that readers will want to take forward, perhaps by following up the references provided at the end of chapters.

The book is divided into five sections, each of which includes a selection of readings on a particular topic or theme. The introduction to each section provides an overview of its contents, draws attention to links between the chapters in the section, and often adds a broader context. One of the key themes of the book is the value of the perspectives and experiences of service users, and the book opens, in Section 1, with a selection of accounts by those involved in care provision, whether as carers or cared-for. Section 2 looks at the ways in which the experience of caring, or of being cared for, is to some extent shaped by the setting or environment in which it takes place, whether this is the family home, an institution, or the wider community. In Section 3 we step back from the everyday experience of care to look at some of the ways in which care has been conceptualized, with a particular emphasis on themes of participation and user involvement. Much media coverage of care matters has focused on cases of abuse in care settings, and this sensitive topic is investigated in Section 4 of the book. The final section places care in its wider political context, exploring some of the important policy changes of recent years and their impact on care services, as well as suggesting ways in which policy may change in the future.

This book has grown out of debates and discussions within the K100 course team at the Open University. Course team members have gathered together a wide range of material for the course as a whole, and the editors have made a selection from that material for this volume. Members of the team have also helped in the editing and preparation of the articles, and in drafting introductions to the different sections of the book (these contributions are signalled by the names at the foot of the relevant page). Besides the editors, other course team members involved in preparing the book have been Joanna Bornat, Hilary Brown, Celia Davies, Roger Gomm, Andy Northedge, Sheila Peace and Jan Walmsley. Tanya Hames and Jan Smith provided secretarial support. Special thanks are due to Celia Davies for her contribution to the overall editing process, and finally to the authors of the articles and accounts reproduced here for allowing their work to be used.

## References

Benner, P. and Wrubel, R. (1989) *The Primacy of Caring: Stress and Coping in Health and Illness*. Menlo Park, CA: Addison-Wesley.

Bytheway, B. and Johnson, J. (forthcoming) 'The social construction of "carers"', in A. Symonds and A. Kelly (eds), *The Social Construction of Care in the Community*. London: Macmillan.

Charlesworth, A., Within, D. and Durie, A. (1984) *Carers and Services: a Comparison of Men and Women Caring for Dependent Elderly People*. Manchester: EOC.

Dalley, G. (1988) *Ideologies of Caring*. Basingstoke: Macmillan.

Equal Opportunities Commission (1980) *The Experience of Caring for Elderly and Handicapped Dependants, a Survey Report*. Manchester: EOC.

Finch, J. and Groves, D. (1980) 'Community care & the family: a case for equal opportunities?', *Journal of Social Policy*, 9(4): 487–514.

Graham, H. (1983) 'Caring: a labour of love', in J. Finch and D. Groves (eds), *A Labour of Love: Women's Work and Caring*. London: Routledge & Kegan Paul.

Hochschild, A. (1983) *The Managed Heart: Commercialization of Human Feeling*. Berkeley: University of California Press.

James, N. (1989) 'Emotional labour: skill and work in the social regulation of feelings', *Sociological Review*, 37(1): 15–42.

James, N. (1992) 'Care = organization + physical labour + emotional labour', *Sociology of Health and Illness*. 14(4): 488–509.

Keith, L. and Morris, J. (1995) 'Easy targets: a disability rights perspective on the "children as carers" debate', *Critical Social Policy*, 44/45, 36–57.

Lewis, J. and Meredith, B. (1988) *Daughters Who Care*. London: Routledge.

Nissel, M. and Bonnerjea, L. (1982) *Family Care of the Handicapped Elderly: Who Pays?* London: PSI.

Stacey, M. (1981) 'The division of labour revisited or overcoming the two Adams', in P. Abrams, R. Deem, J. Finch and P. Rock (eds), *Practice and Progress: British Sociology 1950–1980*. London: Allen & Unwin.

Twigg, J. (ed.) (1992) *Carers: Research and Practice*. London: HMSO.

Twigg, J. and Atkin, K. (1994) *Carers Perceived: Policy and Practice in Informal Care*. Buckingham: Open University Press.

Ungerson, C. (1987) *Policy is Personal: Sex, Gender and Informal Care*. London: Tavistock.

Waerness, K. (1987) 'On the rationality of caring', in A.S. Sassoon (ed.), *Women and the State: the Shifting Boundaries of Public and Private*. London: Unwin Hyman.

# SECTION 1

# ACCOUNTS OF CARE AND CARING

Care is about people. Whatever policies, structures and financing arrangements are in place, the litmus test of care is how it is experienced by individuals – caregivers and those who are cared for. It is for this reason that the first section of this reader consists of accounts of care from the front line. The selection of readings spans care at home, care in hospitals, care in long-stay institutions, and care in places in between. There are accounts by workers and patients remembering the past or reflecting on the present, alongside accounts from researchers reporting from direct observation of care in some of its many guises. The first account was written in 1909, the last in 1997, just before the book went to press. What they have in common is that each gives direct insight into the individual experience of care and caring. No claim is made that they are representative, but they offer the reader some idea of the sheer range of people involved in care, of places where care takes place, and of emotions that care evokes.

Section 1 begins with an anthology of accounts of institutional life, gathered together by Bornat. It opens with two excerpts from Peter Townsend's classic *The Last Refuge*. By exposing the aridness of life in institutional care for old people, this book played a part in changing ideas about how and where care should be provided. As community care policies led to the closure of the kinds of long-stay hospitals and asylums described by Townsend, a need emerged for residents and staff alike to record the reality of a way of life that was disappearing.

This selection of accounts of institutional care is followed by Howard Mitchell's article, 'The insider researcher'. His story of being an insider researching the history of Lennox Castle hospital shows that finding out the 'truth' about what life was like in just one institution is not straightforward.

As institutions closed, so care in the community became the norm. The next set of accounts gives just a glimpse of the sheer diversity of what health and social care in the community means. Care in the community depends on the hard work of many people. Of these, numerically the largest group is unpaid (or informal) carers. Estimates suggest there were around 7 million of them in the UK in 1996. Val Hollinghurst's account is one of 'coming to terms with the tangled web' of her own emotions, the transition from being a teacher, lay magistrate and mother of two sons to being a 'carer'. Few accounts by carers illustrate so well that caring can be about both love *and* labour. Jan Walmsley's 'Caring in families: a case study' is the story of another unpaid carer, Lynne. But Lynne was also a woman with learning disability, and the combination of a sick father and a disabled daughter created rather an unusual set of circumstances.

The last two accounts in Section 1 take us back to health care in one-to-one settings. Tom Heller's 'Snowballs and acorns' provides a contemporary perspective from a professionally qualified caregiver, a GP. He presents an all too vivid picture of the inside story of general practice today, belying the popular image of the serene doctor dispensing prescriptions in the surgery. Medicine, in his account, is far from the rational scientific activity many people like to believe in. Good nursing, too, can often be about more than technical competence. When cure is not possible, it may be tempting to feel helpless, but Benner and Wrubel's case study, drawn from a highly influential American text, is a good example of how just 'being with' someone in pain, and understanding it as their lived experience, is an important part of the repertoire of the caregiver.

Jan Walmsley

# 1

# Anthology: Voices from the Institutions

*compiled by Joanna Bornat*

The chapter that follows is a collection of excerpts from a range of publications. At first sight, they may seem quite disparate. These are accounts from visitors, a social worker, a woman with learning disability, a man disabled by polio as a child, another who was born blind, a Barnado's boy, mental health nurses, a hospital cleaner and a doctor. These 'voices' are first-hand accounts from people who have, in some way and at some stage in their life, lived or worked in those large institutions which used to be so dominant in health and social care. The fact that they come from such a wide range of groups of people and from different social backgrounds is evidence perhaps of the pervasiveness of the institutional solution to care and support not so very long ago.

However, this anthology has been drawn together with some specific reasons in mind. These accounts are almost all drawn from past experience. As such, they present the reader with insights into a tradition of institutional life which has largely, though not quite, disappeared. Some of the accounts – those from Townsend, Potts and Fido, Nolan, Glouberman and Jefferys – were collected as part of an investigation, by researchers whose interests were to reconstruct and understand the logic and culture of institutions. Others, from Dora Mountford, David Barron, Mary Adams, Ernest (Tom) Atkins and the hospital cleaner were published, some at the individual's own instigation, as personal accounts of institutional life. Their urge was to witness, to testify about experience which might otherwise go unrecorded.

Perhaps most important of all, this is not an anthology of victims' voices. These are accounts which illustrate the resilience and thoughtfulness of people, some of whom spent a large part of their lives in conditions that denied individuality and that were often inhumane. Strikingly, this was true for both workers and inmates.

**1** Peter Townsend, sociologist and social reformer, wrote a trenchant attack on institutional care for frail older people which signalled the beginning of rethinking of care in the 1960s. The two accounts here are from his book, *The Last Refuge*, published in 1962. The first quotes from a report of visits to workhouses by members of the Royal

Commission on the Poor Laws of 1909. The second is from his own account of lives he observed 50 years later in the 1950s.

The inmates, over 900 in number, were congregated in large rooms, without any attempt to employ their time or cheer their lives. There was a marked absence of any human interest . . . It could not be better described than as a 'human warehouse'. The dormitories, which in some cases accommodated as many as 60 inmates, were so full of beds as to make it impossible to provide chairs, or to walk, except sideways, between them. [. . .] The . . . 'Home' which we visited in the afternoon seemed to us defective in every particular . . . The rooms were low, ill-lighted, and hopelessly overcrowded. The men were, in many cases, lounging in the bedrooms, there being no chairs except in the dining-hall, and there was a total absence of books or newspapers – as far as we saw – and it is impossible to conceive a more dismal and hopeless asylum for age. The administration consists of but two officers for 268 inmates. The officer in charge, however, stated that they had no difficulty in enforcing such discipline as was necessary. The only outdoor space available for the inmates was an asphalted roof yard, some 35 feet by 25 feet, up so many flights of stairs that a large proportion of inmates were unable to mount it.

The impression was grim and sombre. A high wall surrounded some tall Victorian buildings, and the entrance lay under a forbidding arch with a porter's lodge at one side. The asphalt yards were broken up by a few beds of flowers but there was no garden worthy of the name. Several hundred residents were housed in large rooms on three floors. Dormitories were overcrowded, with ten or twenty iron-framed beds close together, no floor covering and little furniture other than ramshackle lockers. The day-rooms were bleak and uninviting. In one of them sat 40 men in high-backed Windsor chairs, staring straight ahead or down at the floor. They seemed oblivious of what was going on around them.

The sun was shining outside but no one was looking that way. Some were seated in readiness at the bare tables even though the midday meal was not to be served for over an hour . . . I was told, in justification of their inactivity, that 'although they sit and vegetate they have company. They can see other people. That's better than solitude at home in one room. They're less lonely here.' Yet I noticed isolated persons sitting alone in a wash-room, standing in a corridor and one looking out of the staircase window weeping silently. In the day-rooms there was little conversation.

\* \* \*

**2**  Dora Mountford trained as a social worker in the 1930s and in an account which she published herself, locally, describes some early approaches to care in the community with some patients at a large psychiatric hospital on the outskirts of south London.

The boarding-out work took up a good deal of my time. The first patient I boarded out was Connie, a young woman of 36 years who had been in the hospital for 18 years. She was a case of simple schizophrenia and had made quite a good recovery, although she was rather vacant at times. She was a good ward-worker. She looked plump and comfortable and she was good natured. She had no relatives to go out to.

I found a working-class mother of a family in south-east London whose daughter had died the previous year. This daughter was very brilliant and beautiful and the mother thought she would like to take someone to replace her. She had applied to take a child, but was not considered suitable for this. She had a grown-up son and a working-class husband who was out a large part of the time.

Connie was, in a way, a slight disappointment to her I think, but they got on well enough. She lectured Connie quite a lot about her shortcomings and when I went to visit there, Connie would tell me about this a bit. When I visited boarded-out patients I always insisted on seeing them separately for a time and then seeing the person who looked after them separately and then getting them together to smooth out any difficulties.

After she had been there for a year, I moved her to a house in a more leafy suburb. There was a mother with two small girls and a husband who was an artist and was at home all the time. They wanted a new maid to look after their children and home and agreed to have Connie on trial for a time. She went there and was dressed resplendently in a blue dress and white apron; she looked very competent. She adored the little girls and took them out every day and usually came back with some small toy she had bought them out of her own money although she was only paid seven-and-sixpence a week at first.

After she had been there for about six months, these people took her over completely and paid her wages themselves. I often saw Connie, because these people were my friends and I used to stay there a lot for weekends. This all went on very successfully. They made allowances for her shortcomings and were quite fond of her.

I do not know what happened eventually because during the Second World War the friends moved away to their seaside cottage and I had other matters on hand and lost touch with them. But I expect that Connie would end up at a ripe old age in an old people's home, or something like that.

Another patient that I boarded successfully was a nurse who had been in the hospital for eight years; who sat about unoccupied and looking rather depressed but was rational and quite pleasant when spoken to. Not far away from where the friends who took Connie lived, I found a fairly elderly lady who lived alone and was lonely. She welcomed the idea of a companion. The nurse went there and settled down without the slightest of difficulty. These two women got on well together.

One of the doctors at the hospital said to me one day, 'I suppose there must be something in this boarding-out plan; there was that nurse who had been here for eight years – I thought she would be back again in a few days; but she went, and we have never heard of her since.'

I boarded out two deaf patients, one completely deaf and the other nearly completely deaf, with a woman who was herself very deaf but could hear a little. This woman had a large comfortable house and had her old mother living there and a young niece, who went out to work. The two deaf patients were also very happy but at first they complained because, although they were extremely well fed, they were not given a cup of tea after their midday dinner. But when the deaf lady realized what a lot this meant to them, she provided them with a kettle and a teapot and they made their own tea.

The most depressing thing in my work was the poverty and unemployment of the people. I always carried this with me in my mind and could not be quite as happy as I would like because I could not find work for them. Unemployment pay was small and did not last long and people had to manage on the old Poor Law relief. They had to attend the Relieving Officer's premises and wait about for small stipends.

One of our first voluntary patients in the Old Hospital was a very nice man, aged about 40, who had been unemployed, but had then worked in the kitchen of a large hotel. He earned £2 a week and his food but he lived at home with his charming young wife and two small girls. That was all the money they had to live on.

One evening when he left the hotel he was stopped at the door and searched and two eggs were found in his pockets which he was taking home for his two little girls, out of the vast store of eggs and luxuries in the hotel. The police were sent for and he was promptly arrested and charged with theft. By the time he appeared in the court he was in such a state of depression and agitation that he was advised to go into hospital for six months and this he agreed to do. So he came to the Old Hospital.

I visited his wife and children in a small council house in a pleasant housing estate not many miles from the hospital. It was clean and tidy and the little girls were well cared for but I do not know how they managed to live. The mother told me that they were always asking her about the two little Princesses, Elizabeth and Margaret Rose, who were the same age as her two daughters and who were talked about a great deal and whose pictures were in the newspapers. These two little girls were always saying 'Do they have this? Do they have that?' thinking up all the luxuries which they could not have for themselves. The mother said that drove her crazy, although she was not at all a crazy type of person.

Another sad case was that of a mother who was brought into the hospital in a state of mental confusion and depression. She had two small children, a boy and a girl, and a nice husband who worked as a temporary porter on the railway. He earned £3 a week out of which they had to pay their rent and live, which they could not really do. The mother became ill and was examined by a doctor who found her to be grossly undernourished because for some time she had been giving all the food to her husband and children. The husband had not realized this. She soon began to recover in the hospital with proper food and medication. In those days the railways were not nationalized and the Railwaymen's Union was very weak. The doctors at the hospital were very concerned about this state of affairs. It worried me more than anybody, because I felt that I ought to be able to find him a better job or persuade the railways to pay him more but none of this happened.

* * *

3  Maggie Potts and Rebecca Fido interviewed patients at Meanwood Park Hospital in Leeds as part of an investigation into the history of institutional care for people with learning disability. Many of the women, like Sally, had stories to tell about their lives before coming into hospital which raised questions about how they came to be admitted in the first place.

Sally worked in a mill from leaving school until she was 19 years old.

> When I worked in 'mill and I were only getting 35 shilling and I said to the overlooker, 'Can I have some more money?' and he said, 'No, you can't.' He said, 'You can take your cards and clear out!'

She was admitted to The Park towards the end of the war. The Park seems to have been used as a kind of bogeyman in her parents' attempt to restrict her.

> I was brought there 'cos I wouldn't get up for 'mill. And me mother put me there 'cos I wouldn't do as I were told. Me mother weren't too keen on me, but me father were different altogether. He used to spoil me and me mother were 'opposite.
> Well, how it started because she saw me at 'pictures with a boy and she came spying on me and she saw me and said if you don't come back home wi' me you're off to The Park. So she did it, she got me here. That's the place where they punish you if you're naughty!
> If she hadn't put me to The Park, we might've been married. I never saw him again. I think that were awful! I were just getting on nice and then me mother put

me there. That were 'first time I'd seen him at the pictures and he said, 'We'll go for some fish and chips when we go.' And I didn't get them!

I knew what were going to happen when she said, 'If you don't come home you're going to The Park.' So I said, 'Well, I'll go home.' But she still got me there.

\* \* \*

**4**  Mary Adams spent all her life in convents and was only able to leave shortly before she died. Her account illustrates the mixed emotions which institutional care could evoke, at the time, and in recall. Her story was published by Queen Spark Books of Brighton, which specializes in publishing the writing of local people.

We had instructions every month about our behaviour and how to behave, and many a time the residents had to be shown up as a bad example if they broke silence, also because some of them used to run away with boys. Times seemed very Victorian then. We were punished if we did not do our work right. One of the punishments was to kneel in the middle of the dining room, at the top of the room so that everyone could see us, for our meals. I was often one of those. I remember I used not to clean my wellingtons after a day's work on the farm. As I had been several times warned what would happen, eventually I had to spend three whole meals on my knees with the dirty wellingtons tied around my neck.

I had a feeling of guilt and shame, also I felt so embarrassed to have everyone staring at me as though I had committed a mortal sin. I felt that it was very unjust at the time and wished I could have stuck up for my rights, but I was too scared to say anything as I would have been the worse off for it. I always cleaned my wellingtons after that.

Whenever I was punished I always felt a sense of shame and I was very frightened. Whenever I was caught doing something wrong I lived in a fog of fear until I came face to face with the person I was reported to. Then, even though I was punished, wherever I went all through my life it was a relief when my wrongdoing was out in the open. When I think of it now I have a good laugh, because it seems so ridiculous to be punished for such small things. I used to cry about it, but now I have toughened up. The sisters loved us so much that they punished us for our own good, but if you had any problems they were kindness itself. When Mother died they went out of the way to console me and so they did to everyone else.

\* \* \*

**5**  Ernest (Tom) Atkins spent much of his early life in orthopaedic hospitals for children after he was disabled by polio. He tape-recorded his memories of disability for a local history group and the account was subsequently published with support from his local authority.

One was exploring the world of Brookfield and its environs, and very interesting environs they were really. My home was a very working-class home, typical of the 1920s in which I was born. The childhood I experienced was to be, apart from it being subjected to the disabling effects of polio, in some respects almost a middle-class experience of childhood. Experiences which were not vouchsafed my contemporaries, experiences which were not incarcerated inside Brookfield Hospital. Because we had these acres to explore, to get around, wide acres. We had the companionship of a dog, a donkey [and] numerous chickens were always kept on the establishment. It's rather an interesting experience, the seasons beginning with the hatching of these rather fluffy creatures in their boxes, going through until they were introduced to the actual hen-house. Some time or other they appeared upon our table.

We had several acres to get around and believe you me we did get around. There were various bath chairs which we purloined as our own. Those that had been there the longest had the most clout. There was a very strict pecking order, this was a matter of precedence by tradition. There were various favourite bath chairs in the wards [in] which those of us who needed them used to get around. I don't quite remember how I used to traverse the far-flung spots which were really inaccessible to wheelchairs. I imagine I used to crawl. Because we used to have dens. A den consisted of purloined pieces of wood, bits and pieces of carpet and the sort of things kids have seen as treasure. We made a little shelter under trees from which we used to play games in the long grass. Yes I must have done a fair bit of crawling. There's no way you are going to be left out of the fun.

As far as we were concerned there was nowhere off limits officially, with the exception of porter-cum-handyman, Cripps. I should think he was the only part of Brookfield which we didn't have an 'open sesame' to. Which is a great pity really because he had all sorts of treasures there which we would have loved for building our dens. The only time we could get hold of these was if he was misguided enough to leave them lying outside the perimeter. Those of them I describe as the runners would go down, swoop, run and take it up to the far end of the area where we kept our bits of treasure for our dens. I wasn't one of them, I was the lookout and the spotter, who would spy a suitable piece of material and say, 'Look what's there. I'll keep cavey.' [. . .]

We were off armed with our nets, a tin probably of fish paste sandwiches and a jug of lemonade and attempt to catch tiddlers from the lake. Of course this was when one realized one was not free. We were free within the perimeters of the hospital. We became conscious of other children who came from you know not where. Obviously by the nature of our circumstance, [they] would stare at us and probably pass on and go away. But we would stay as a collective. And you realized that they came from somewhere and that there was somewhere beyond. This tended to give a feeling of yearning to be beyond the immediate area of daily experience. So that was a nostalgic moment, I suppose, remembering home. [. . .]

I think one felt one was missing out. If we went to any public place, when we went fishing we were aware that there were other people around us and they were going elsewhere. We were all going back to one place and continue to go back. I can remember for instance going to the cinema. That was an adventure piling into the back of a van and being taken to the Regal, Highams Park. I can still remember the film I went to see. That's how many times I went to the cinema in those days. I saw a film called *The Whip*, and *Journey's End*. But when the lights went up and there were other people. They were not all going together, they were going their various ways separately as you saw them come out. So yes, one did have these moments. I think they call it depression these days.

* * *

6 David Barron has written more than one account of his exceptional life and we only have space for a brief excerpt here. His misfortunes began as a young boy, orphaned and fostered with a cruel and abusive foster mother. The account included here is taken from the point in his story when, as a teenager, he somehow came to be placed in a large mental handicap hospital.

To take one example, there was the selling of bread crusts. A patient with whom I became friendly had the misfortune to be without teeth, which meant he could not eat the corners of his two regular slices of bread supplied for breakfast and tea. Cutting the corners off each of the slices he sold two crusts for a halfpenny and four for a penny. I was only given a halfpenny a week so it was not very long before I was up to the eyeballs in debt. I just could not settle for two crusts a week and my friend was so tight he would not even part with one crust for nothing in spite of the fact I was his friend. All I got from him were the same old repeated refusals. No money, no crusts. 'Come on, David. You will have to pay up or I will stop giving you my crusts,' he would say. In spite of his pleas he had to wait a long time before I was able to settle up with him. In fact, he had to wait a few years before I was in sight of getting straight with him. Come to think of it, I do not think I ever did because by the time my money went up sufficiently enough to pay him for all the crusts I ate he had unfortunately passed away.

Apart from the bread-crust bargaining, other patients were selling practically all their meals in some form or another, and it was this that the wily superintendent was trying to stamp out, but he had a hard job on his hands and he knew it. There were all sorts of ways in which patients could make themselves a lot of money on the side. Those who stood to make the most were those who worked in the main kitchen.

A kitchen worker could easily smuggle bread and cake out when they finished work at night to sell in the dormitory in exchange for money or cigarettes. I was myself tempted on several occasions by pieces of cake and the temptation was often too great for me to resist, even though I left myself wide open to be severely punished if caught. Not only did I leave myself wide open to be punished by the authorities if caught with any cake but I also had the problem of not being able to pay for it once it was received. By then, of course, it would be too late because I ate the cake without stopping to think what the consequences might be. As it turned out, I need not have felt too worried because there was very little the patients who gave me the cake could do about it for fear of being found out. At worst, they could make my life unpleasant by bullying but that did not bother me unduly. Bullying was something I had grown to accept as part of my everyday life. The cake was well worth a bit of extra bullying. [. . .]

I was about to sample my first bit of freedom, if that is what you could call it. On Sunday morning I was going to see outside the grounds for the first time since I was admitted. At 9.30 a.m. prompt we all had to leave our wards, and make our way round to the main drive where we had to line up in twos ready for inspection. It proved to be a long process and no wonder. There were nearly 450 patients in the line and some of these had their shoes on the wrong feet. It was no fault of theirs, poor souls. Then there were some who had not put their ties on and some who had not put them on properly. Others, like myself, had failed to clean their shoes or comb their hair. The superintendent ticked me off for failing to attend to these proprieties before moving on to find some patient who had not fastened their shoelaces. This was hardly surprising for many did not have any laces in them to fasten, but it did not improve the superintendent's temper one bit. He wanted everything to be just right before we left the institution and he did not care how long it took. I imagine we must have stood for at least half an hour, and considering we had five and a half miles' walk ahead of us I do not think it was fair of him to delay us so long. In fact, I was all in before we even set off. That was a lad who had not yet reached his 14th birthday, so try and think what it must have been like for the other patients of 30 and upwards. Mind you, it could well have been that they took it better than I did because they were used to it. I suppose they had covered that route so often that they could have walked the whole stretch blindfold. The time would come when I would be able to do the same.

The route in question was Kirk Hammerton, Green Hammerton and Whixley, the three villages we had to walk through although the pace we went at made it more appropriate to call it a crawl and that is precisely what I did. There was this walk I called 'The Whixley Crawl' and there was another name I thought up for it, 'The Chain Gang', and the reason for this is about to be explained. Aye, I know it is not the type of thing which should be joked about but as far as it concerned me then, it was stark reality. Being a mere child I could see the funny side of it, just like any other child would have done, but when I think about it now that was an ordeal we should never have had to undergo. I am sure the superintendent could have found some other way for us to be taken for our Sunday walks round the villages instead of making us a mass public spectacle for all the villages to see. I suppose it was all right for the lower-grade patients. To those poor souls it was just a part of their way of life, and they had no way of knowing that we were the laughing stock of the villages, but the more upgraded patients like myself could sense the public's ridicule, not that we could do anything about that. On the other hand, some villagers were very sympathetic towards us, as I was to find out for myself when I grew up. The reason for nicknaming our Sunday morning stroll 'The Chain Gang' was simply due to the way we were taken out. As I said earlier, we all had to form up in twos until the superintendent was satisfied with his inspection. Giving the attendant in charge the OK to be off, we would then move away with four attendants walking alongside. One would be at hand at the head of the line, one in the middle, and two bringing up the rear.

* * *

7   It was in the spirit of testifying to a cruel and insensitive regime that Ted Williams recalled his time at the Manchester Road School for the Blind in the 1920s. His account was one of several collected for a television series on the experience of disability between 1900 and 1950 and later published as a book.

One of the prevalent methods of caning was on the hand. Blind people, of course, are very dependent on their hands and fingers but I suffered a stroke hard across the fingers quite often. And believe you me it used to hurt. Well, that for quite a while left the hand really numb and dead and we used to have to wait before we could even think about looking at a braille book, until the numbness wore off. One particular teacher used to delight in punishing us in the maths lesson. We all had little arithmetic frames with sharp points sticking up to denote certain numbers to us. Now, if the teacher was trying to instil a sum into our heads and we couldn't get it she would clamp her hands on the backs of our fingers on these points and press them down and say, 'Can't you feel? Can't you feel?' And this again meant our fingers would be dead for a good time afterwards and any braille reading was impossible. The punishment that the teachers used to concentrate on though was Coventry. At the smallest offence you could be put into Coventry. Now, that meant that you must not speak, except to a teacher, for the period they stated. And what made it worse the other children must not speak to you, otherwise they got the same punishment. Many's the time when I was caught for speaking out of turn or bumping into another boy in line and that was that – 'Williams, was that you? You can have two days in Coventry.' Once I was punished for something that two of us had done and the other boy got off. Part of my punishment was Coventry and in spite of myself, everywhere I went I were saying, 'It's beastly unfair, it's unfair.' And a teacher heard me so I got punished again for talking and my Coventry was extended. Another day's silence for me. Well, I was a bit of a loner and I could take refuge in reading and more or less studying and making poetry up, and I would get in a corner of a desk in the playroom and keep myself to myself. But to some of the children, who were the merry kind of boys and who couldn't read, then a time in Coventry was absolutely dreadful. That punishment was the one we hated most: imagine as a blind person, being shut off from your main way of getting about and communicating, it was worse then getting the cane for us boys.

\* \* \*

8   Fred Fever was a 'Barnardo's boy' whose account highlights the effect of uniformity on his developing identity as a young teenager 'in care'.

To get new clothes you had to have some money in your clothing allowance, a set [amount of] money allocated to an individual annually by Barnardo's. The amount varied according to your age: the older you got, the higher your clothing allowance. There were two major restrictions: first, you always had to have a member of staff with you when you bought new clothes, and secondly, you could only purchase your clothes from one particular shop. . . .

I disliked going to Cracknall's and being virtually forced into buying unfashionable clothes. I never looked forward to having new clothes – all it meant was more confrontation. The fact that 'they' dictated what clothes you could buy and where you bought them made the whole experience very unenjoyable. The clothes from Cracknall's made the boys from Highbroom stand out – we looked so dated in our Cracknall Groovers. This added notoriety was something we could well have done without.

\* \* \*

**9**   Peter Nolan's study of the history of mental health nursing brought him into contact with nurses whose professional careers went back to earlier regimes of nurse management and patient care. Two nurses' experiences are included here.

I started mental nursing in 1947. I was given a cubicle at the end of a dormitory. When it was decided that I was useful, I was given a room. The last meal was at 4 p.m.; the lights were put out at 10 o'clock and we were up at 5.30 a.m. The charge nurses were in complete control of their wards and nobody ever challenged them. Many of them spoke in a bullying way to patients; they were arrogant and always spoke down to junior staff. They were men who were familiar with violence from the war. I was a coward – I should have done something about what I saw, but those to whom I would have had to complain were part of the same system. Patients who were beaten were seen by the medical superintendent who invariably accepted the account of the incident given by the charge nurse which was always untrue.

The first charge nurse I worked with came from a family of attendants. He stood well over six feet tall. He walked in a deliberate and purposeful way and everyone knew he was in charge. When he entered the day-room, a sudden silence would descend on the place and all eyes turned towards him. He had a presence that I have never encountered in anyone else. If there was ever a fight among patients, he would stand by the door of the day-room and in a calm tone of voice mention the names of those involved and instantly the fight would cease. He would hold the offenders with his eye for five or ten minutes afterwards. I never saw him resort to violence; I would also say that the patients were not afraid of him. They respected him and they trusted him. They knew he was in charge.

* * *

**10**   Sholom Glouberman interviewed nurses, following up Goffman's study of the 'total institution'. In this excerpt, he recorded a registered nurse working on a long-stay ward in a psychiatric hospital.

We have one charge nurse in the two wards, and she has 62 patients altogether. There are only two nurses working on each side, for 30 or 32 patients. So the most staff there are for 62 patients is four, five, or some days there will be six.

We start work at 8 a.m. We take the reports from the night staff and then the charge nurse makes the assignments. She delegates the work: giving baths, morning care, and then supervising those patients who are really capable of doing things on their own. So between 8.30 and 10 you give your morning care. Then everyone has to leave their room and the rooms are closed and some of the patients go to occupational therapy. Only around 10 patients are supposed to stay here. This is an open ward, so most of our patients come and go as they please. . . .

I have a hard time to treat them like persons, like regular persons. Some of the patients have talents, like they can play piano and we have a piano here. We have some patients who can play the harmonica. Almost half of them just participate in their own ways. It's up to the staff to let them participate and function at their own capacities. Up until 11 they're having their rest or coffees, and then at 11 it's medication time. And then someone goes down to the cafeteria and gets the lunch trays for the patients who can't go downstairs by themselves. At 11.30 one staff goes with the patients for lunch and the other stays on the ward. Between 12.30 and 2 the rooms are opened for the patients so they can rest. The patients who work in the OT room usually leave by 1.30 and we close the doors of the rooms again at 2 o'clock. The others sit in the day-room and watch TV. After our break at 2, we see who leaves the ward to go to other supervised activities.

* * *

**11** 'The cleaner' is from a collection of accounts from ex-patients and staff at a hospital which has since gone through a closure programme. As with some of the other voices, her recall of institutional life brings a mixed message of individual deprivation coupled with collective support.

## The cleaner

I was a student at art college and needed to supplement my student days. I saw an advert asking for domestics at St Mary's. I thought I'd go for it and was taken on. The interview was virtually done over the phone.

I'd had no experience of working with people with mental health problems. A friend of mine had been in a small psychiatric hospital and I had visited him, but I'd never visited such a large institution as St Mary's.

My preconception of loony bins, as I called them, was based on Hitchcock films; mad people with axes – that was the distorted impression I had. They were just nutters, totally crazy, and you had to be careful of them. They were scary; they could do anything because they were mad. I think a lot of people had similar ideas to mine about mental patients.

I hadn't known what to expect. I just thought it would be an interesting experience. I was looking forward to working as a domestic as a novelty, especially in a psychiatric hospital – and with women. I had an open mind.

I talked a lot to the patients, nurses and got to know everyone. As a domestic I seemed to have a different relationship with patients than a nurse; they were someone in authority I suppose. That barrier was broken down so I was on a more even level with everybody.

I really enjoyed the experience. More than anything I enjoyed chatting to the patients. It was a new experience; I was comfortable with them.

People had heavy mental health problems, but it was *their* problem. There was no feeling that they were going to hit you or be aggressive, or even shout at you. You could see that some of them were going through hell. Most of the patients were pretty drugged up; some were zombified, actually. Just walked around, woodenly, expressionless, devoid of human spark. That was really sad.

Some of the patients were going through a lot of heaviness and turmoil. I could feel that and it didn't make me feel good. I'd try and console them. It wasn't my job but, as time went on, I'd become more involved with patients themselves.

I made friends with some of the patients. Some people I couldn't communicate with at all. Some didn't actually verbally communicate with anybody.

The first week I was here I sat down and chatted with a patient for half an hour. Afterwards I asked one of the other domestics how long the patient had been at St Mary's and she said, 'About 25 years – but he's one of the staff!' He seemed pretty weird. He was very humorous but quite distorted.

I felt that the psychiatrists and consultants were clever people. The staff were very amusing. Their humour was really off-beat. Sometimes my interactions with patients were quite bizarre. I had some pretty surreal conversations. We might talk about something which a particular individual had been doing before they came into St Mary's; something like chickens. They'd believe that there were actually chickens around. Sometimes I joined in and went along with it and other times I would challenge them. I felt really sorry for some of the patients.

There were different atmospheres on different wards. It depended not necessarily on the patients but sometimes on the staff. Some of them had been here a long time. Personally, I feel that working in one place, especially a psychiatric hospital, is detrimental to one's health.

A chap had died and was lying on a bed where I was cleaning. It felt really odd. I kept looking at him.

I feel that if you're with the same people on the same ward, for say 10 years, you become stale and lose the energy you had at the start.

If you were moved around, it would be a new experience and you'd get to know new people. I felt some nurses were really 'into it' whereas for others it was just a job, and they weren't adding anything to the situation. It was an easy option with no fresh challenges. It seemed to result in an uncaring attitude to the work and there was a staleness around. Added to this was the sensation of the place being run down, few new patients coming in and the patients were long-term, chronically mentally ill people who wouldn't recover.

Generally speaking the experience was good, positive, beneficial. The job itself was monotonous but was secondary to my experience; I was much more interested in the people. I think that's what started the ball rolling with me and mental health. I seem to have some sort of affinity with people on the outside, on the fringe: that don't necessarily fit into mainstream society. Several nurses thought I'd make a good nurse and encouraged me to consider it. It was a foundation for future work.

My experiences at St Mary's were an important part of my development as a caring person. As a cleaner I was able to get an overview of the whole hospital. I really felt that I was part of a family at St Mary's.

The closure of St Mary's was being talked about for 15 years and there were very few new staff taken on while I was there. Half the wards were unoccupied. Most of the patients were elderly – psychogeriatrics. They thought they were going to be here till they died. One chap used to walk the corridors. He used to say to me, 'I don't have to go home, do I? You have to go home but I live here.' He'd been there most of his life; he was 60.

My previous assumption about large psychiatric hospitals was that they were bad because people became dependent and lost their self-worth, but I actually found it was more like being in a family. Reading the transcripts of ex-patients about their experiences here also reinforced my feeling that their time here was beneficial.

The most surprising aspect [. . .] is that I expected people to recall their experiences in a negative way. I thought they would see it as a prison, but the overriding impression has been positive.

\* \* \*

**12** Margot Jefferys and two colleagues obtained personal reminiscences of the conditions experienced by older people admitted to chronic illness long-stay wards in the 1950s. The following extract records the situation encountered in Bradford in 1953 by one of the first appointees to the new medical specialism of geriatrics. This account matches almost exactly our first two extracts in terms of content and, in the case of Peter Townsend's own observations, in terms of period.

So I had to look after these 750 patients in seven hospitals single-handed. When I went round they had had absolutely no notes. They had a sort of card on which was written particulars for identification, and what their father had been and what their religion was, but as for medical notes there was nothing at all.

And these chronic sick wards, so-called, were of a very tumble-down nature. Three of them were single-storey buildings made of match-boarding. And they had four ranks of patients. Forty-eight patients per ward, anyway, down each side of the ward near the windows, and then in the middle there were two ranks head to head all the way down the middle. The light wasn't good, the plumbing was absolutely deplorable and the roofs leaked. . . . And before I got there they said 'There's a new physician coming, he'll want good, sound, safe beds.' So they equipped two of the four wards with deep cot-sided metal bedsteads like children's cots only 6 foot 6 inches long with high sides which clattered as you put them up and down, and they imagined that I was going to keep my patients in these for ever! And they said 'They'll at least be safe!'

Well, this really wasn't good enough, particularly since the temperature in the ward – I suppose this was midwinter – had fallen to something like 35 degrees Fahrenheit. And one patient died that night, and it so happened that the young house physician I had helping me, who had been a paratrooper and was a tough egg said, 'I'm going to certify this case as dying of neglect.' So I said, 'Hang on a minute' and rang the secretary of the Bradford A Group and said 'We've got a case here which is going to be certified as dying of neglect.' He said, 'Oh my God, stop him doing that! Give me 10 minutes and I'll be back to you.' So 10 minutes later I was rung up by the chairman of the Group saying 'It'll be dreadful for the reputation of the Group if this man is certified as having died of neglect. Can't you stop that?' And I said, 'I might be able to persuade this young man, but my conditions for doing so are that you put men on the roof and make it watertight, that you put a steam heating pipe up and down the ward and that you do so in the next 24 hours.' And he said, 'Right doctor, I will do that.' And he did. But this was sheer blackmail and we had quite often to use these sorts of methods to get proper care, basic care, even temperature and leaking roofs for elderly people in those days.

## Sources

1  Townsend, Peter (1962) *The Last Refuge: A Survey of Residential Homes and Institutions for the Aged in England and Wales.* London: Routledge & Kegan Paul.
2  Montford, Dora (1987) *'With Malice Aforethought': the Journal of a Scientific Social Worker.* London: ILEA Fleet Community Centre. pp. 45–50.

3  Potts, Maggie & Fido, Rebecca (1991) *'A Fit Person To Be Removed': Personal Accounts of Life in a Mental Deficiency Institution.* Plymouth: Northcote House. p. 17.
4  Adams, Mary (1995) *Those Lost Years.* Brighton: QueenSpark Books. p. 35.
5  Atkins, Ernest (Tom) (1994) *One Door Closes Another Opens: a Personal Experience of Polio.* London: Waltham Forest Oral History Workshop. pp. 39–41.
6  Barron, David (1996) *A Price to be Born.* Harrogate: Mencap Northern Division. pp. 58–60.
7  Humphries, Steve and Gordon, Pamela (1992) *Out of Sight: The Experience of Disability 1900–1950,* Plymouth: Northcote House. pp. 90–1.
8  Fever, Fred (1994) *Who Cares? Memories of a Childhood in Barnardo's.* London: Warner Books. pp. 120–1.
9  Nolan, Peter (1993) *A History of Mental Health Nursing.* London: Chapman and Hall. pp. 108, 111.
10  Glouberman, Sholom (1990) *Keepers: Inside Stories from Total Institutions.* London: King Edward's Hospital Fund for London. pp. 91–2.
11  Ex-Patients and Staff (1995) *Boots On! Out! Reflections on Life at St Mary's Hospital.* Hereford: Herefordshire MIND & Logaston Press. pp. 55–7.
12  Jefferys, Margot (1996) 'Objectives and obstacles: Recollections of some of the pioneers of geriatric medicine'. Unpublished paper given at Oral History Society annual conference, London.

# 2

# The Insider Researcher

*Howard Mitchell*

As a novice, starting project work for the first time, my concept of academic research included the assumption that a necessarily detached standpoint was required in the search for objective truths. Like many, I had some hazy image of research which was based on the natural sciences; the laboratory, the white coat, the breakthrough. With the social sciences, fieldwork replaced the laboratory, but for many years the methodologies of the more established and higher-status sciences provided the template for research. With this template came the associated premise: knowledge is a neutral portrayal of fact achieved through impartial collection and analysis of data. [. . .]

My initial grasp of research and the little I had discovered of methodological theory provided me with problems concerning the area that I wanted to do my own research in.

I was no 'outsider' and I did not want to describe any 'otherness'. I was an insider to the subject area and many of the people and practices I wished to investigate. Could I be 'scientific' and objective with a subject I was so familiar with and just where and how would I address this or even acknowledge this in my work? I had no theoretical framework to apply.

## My insider status

I was born in Lennox Castle Hospital in 1955. For 23 years, several of the wards which were purpose built for patients with a mental deficiency were converted for use as a maternity unit. I grew up in the village of Lennoxtown, living 400 metres from the hospital entrance. My family were in the minority in our street in that none of us worked in 'The Castle' at that time. I could not help but be aware of the institution throughout my childhood. Sunday walks were often along the hospital drive and around part of the grounds and the staff housing. We would usually be engaged in conversation by some of the patients and the redbrick villa where I was born was pointed out.

In our block of terraced council housing the three other families consisted of:

husband and wife, both nurses at Lennox Castle;
mother, son and daughter, all Castle nurses and the father, latterly
   boiler room worker;
father (Castle van driver) and daughter (domestic worker).

This was typical of Lennox Road. If there was a house where no
member of the family had some attachment to the hospital then it was
unusual. Irate nightshift workers regularly interrupted my football
training regimes as I curled free kicks against their bedroom walls.

The children from the staff houses went to a one-room school in
nearby Campsie Glen along with those from outlying farms and communities and joined the rest of us in Lennoxtown primary in primary
five. I became close friends with one of the 'Castle kids' and spent a
few years of my adolescence around the Oval. I became party to some
of the lore surrounding the hospital and thoroughly explored the large
grounds. There were no frightening or threatening connotations
attached to the place at all for me. I would regularly cycle home from
my friend's house in the dark, through the grounds, when I was 12 and
13, with little trepidation. Major preoccupations at the time were, who
was allowed to play in the Oval – the children jealously guarded their
swings from anybody from Lennoxtown – and who owned the hospital.

My recollection of any kind of view I had about the patients who
inhabited Lennox Castle is hazy. Certainly news of escaped patients
seemed to filter down to us as children but there was no attempt in my
family to use the hospital or the patients as a means of control – no
bogeyman stories. I grew up with a benign acceptance. From any
dealings I had with the patients I took them to be talkative and
amusing. There were several individuals in the village who were
recognized as 'simple'. They stayed with their families and were subjected to varying degrees of intolerance. I did not equate them with
patients from the Castle.

For my first 19 years I lived adjacent to the institution, had been
aware of the part it played in employment for much of Lennoxtown,
had seen the separate community that was the staff housing, had had
limited contact with some of the patients, but I had little idea what
happened inside the wards. I benignly accepted the existence of the
hospital and can recall little curiosity.

Unemployed, a friend and I were ushered into starting as nursing
assistants in Lennox Castle by a friend of our families who was senior
tutor there. We commenced on the same ward on the same day and
were orientated by a nurse who was my next-door neighbour. Adjusting to working with the range of patients we encountered was
challenging. There were some with gross physical deformities, some
tiny people, some huge. From these bodies some would scream or
grunt all day and some would hold interesting conversations with us.
Some patients would tear all their clothes off, break windows and try

to run away. Some would try to sell us TVs or tape recorders they had acquired while out on pass in Glasgow. Some appeared sensible and wise. It took me many months before I had any clear idea of what mental deficiency, as it was called then, was.

Adjusting to the range of staff who we worked with was also challenging. Some seemed cruel and indifferent to the patients but most were caring and giving. All were welcoming to us initiates in their own ways. The personnel all seemed slightly eccentric in one form or other but were full of personality.

It was a culture totally different from anything that I had encountered before. I had worked in various jobs and had grown up in close proximity to the hospital and knew many of the people associated with it but the inside environment was still totally unexpected. It was shocking in many ways but also exciting and embracing. The sheer novelty of such a range of characters – both patients and staff – and the lively social life surrounding the workplace was intoxicating.

I took nurse training there and was a charge nurse for a year before leaving to do general nurse training and eventually attend university. Over the five-year period that I worked in Lennox Castle my feelings and opinions inevitably shifted. The stimulation of many new and odd acquaintances was to be replaced with a far more questioning attitude towards their behaviours and practices. I had witnessed and indulged in conduct which I was later ashamed of and was determined not to repeat or allow to be repeated.

My concerns became more focused on the needs and rights of people with learning disabilities and towards creating an environment in which these could be best met and maintained. As such I regarded the Castle as anachronistic and many of its practices and personnel corrupt. However at this point in the late 1970s it was also obvious that institutional care of this group had suffered and was suffering from gross and chronic lack of provision and recognition. Many attempts at progressive measures from well-motivated and far-sighted staff and management seemed to be met with indifference from higher levels. There was a feeling of powerlessness among the nursing staff together with a perception that there was little understanding or appreciation of their work. National press coverage of conditions and criticism of several incidents at Lennox Castle had created a poor image of the institution. Staff in the hospital felt they were more aware than anyone else of the shortcomings but were unable to change them. A group of workers who were suspicious of comment or criticism from outsiders was the result. They reasoned that only those who worked in the place could understand it.

I left with a great deal of ambivalence. I felt that perhaps the only solution to the problems of the hospital would be closure and relocation of the residents. But there remained with me a large degree of affection and respect for many of the nurses and patients. I particularly had a lot of time for some of the older men and women who had worked there for a long number of years. Their attitudes by the standards of the time were certainly out of date but this was understandable, coming from a very different era, and some of their stories about 'the old days' in the hospital were fascinating and illuminating.

## Research strategy

As an undergraduate I was familiar with the work of Paul Thompson and Trevor Lummis and was attracted to the concept of oral history providing a forum for the voices of people who had been neglected, disadvantaged or discriminated against. For postgraduate research I considered concentrating on patients who had lived in long-term institutional care, a group whose voices had rarely been heard. However, several depictions of life within these hospitals which I read all portrayed the patients as victims and the nursing staff as perpetrators of various forms of abuse and neglect. I recognized these depictions as being truthful and accurate for I had witnessed similar actions. I also knew that the total truth was not being represented. While I myself felt critical of the actions of many nursing staff and the whole concept of institutional care for those with learning disabilities, I still experienced a residual defensive stance to criticism from outsiders 'who don't understand'.

Nursing staff were seen as perpetrators but they also suffered from a lack of representation and voice. The patients were seen as victims but the nurses were in many ways victims also: victims of established practices, difficult conditions and a powerful medical presence. I did not want to be in any way an apologist for those who practised mistreatment but I did want to encompass some kind of balanced account and explore the understanding that *both* groups had of their experiences.

By concentrating on the relationship between the patients and the nurses and researching and analysing the factors which made up their separate but parallel communities and cultures I hoped to illuminate what I believe to be the core of life in the institution: the interface between the two groups. This would hopefully lend some understanding to the nature of this particular institution, and to institutions for people with learning disabilities in general.

As can be seen, I was very intimate with and emotionally attached to my area of research. This gave me many worries as to the value of the work I was doing. Was it 'real' research? Was I in some way cheating by having all this pre-knowledge and therefore pre-judgement? And how could I represent the involvement that I had experienced? Would I just ignore it and present my data and analysis from an outsider's standpoint like a proper researcher? These thoughts all clouded my early work but I got on with the task of my research processes and put these awkward bits to the side.

## Insider advantages

While the theoretical concepts of being an insider continued to cause me angst, I was experiencing some practical advantages. I was not coming cold to the subject of learning difficulties in general and had a fair knowledge of their history and related social, medical and parliamentary milestones and watersheds, and so had a fair start in background reading. Researching the local environment was also helped by the fact that I had known the librarian in Lennoxtown for a long number of years.

Possibly the area where I was most at an advantage was with informants. I started interviewing nurses whom I had known when I worked in the hospital and who were retired. I simply phoned them up, told them what I was doing and asked if I could interview them. With this group I was always made very welcome. Another set of people I interviewed were those who had worked at Lennox Castle at the same time as myself, were retired but who did not know me. I turned up at their doors and explained who I was and that I had worked in the hospital at the same time as them and again, they were all very co-operative. A third group were those who had retired before I started work and whom I did not know. They were suggested by some of the other informants. Again I knocked at their doors and explained what I was doing and told them who I was personally as well as professionally, i.e. who my mother and granny were. They were all familiar with my family, who had lived in Lennoxtown for generations. These work and family familiarities certainly eased my way into people's homes to record and set up an initial trust in me. I do not suggest that it would have been impossible for an outsider to record some of these people, but I am fairly sure that some others would not have co-operated at all. Latterly, as word circulated in the community, I was being approached in pubs by nursing staff and offered interviews.

To interview people with learning disabilities, I started in a community unit in Glasgow where ex-residents from Lennox Castle were living. I knew the nurse who was manager there personally. After obtaining consent from any relatives through the unit, I visited the residents, most of whom I knew and who knew me, and recorded the interviews on videotape.

It was only at this stage that I contacted Lennox Castle Hospital itself and asked to interview residents there and have access to documentary material. I had been reluctant to do this initially as I anticipated a rejection, probably based on my perceptions of the institution from the past. I could not have been more wrong. The hospital manager had been my immediate line manager when I worked there and he was enthusiastic and helpful. The management team and medical consultants gave me permission to interview, within the wards, residents and staff, providing they consented of course. I was also given access to hospital documentation and ledgers which were kept on site and various old documents and artefacts which were offered by various individuals. There was an obvious interest in the work that I was doing from the manager and various other staff, based, I think, on the fact that someone was acknowledging the institution and themselves as being of some social and historical significance.

Whether I would have encountered a similar attitude had I not been known, I am not sure. I suspect that there was a large degree of personal trust shown again. I should probably ask. When the manager retired he was succeeded by another acquaintance who had been brought up round the corner from me and she was equally co-operative and interested in the research. [. . .] Probably the least I can conclude is that the accommodating and supportive climate I encountered from the hospital management was partly due to my insider status and that this certainly eased and simplified my work. As an academic attached to a university, in pursuit of a legitimate research topic, I had been granted access to Greater Glasgow Health Board archives and would have expected access to any local archive material as well, but assistance, thankfully went far beyond that.

This was well illustrated when I attempted to seek permission to interview Margaret Scally. She was living in a community house after leaving Lennox Castle and the suspicion, obstruction and lack of help I initially encountered from the management of the agency responsible for her residence, brought home the difficulties that an outsider might experience.

Nursing is a profession, like others such as medicine, law or the police force, where confidentiality is instilled as part of the training and carried on in day-to-day work. Institutions for people with learning disabilities were held in very low esteem, particularly Lennox Castle which had generated criticism from many areas. People who worked there were touchy. These factors may have provided a barrier first of all to access to a nurse informant and secondly within the interview itself if there had been no shared background. I was able to gain rapport and trust through many shared factors: community, class, workplace, language – not only dialect but the language of the hospital – and certain attitudes. I was able to interview people in their own homes, which is usually conductive to a more relaxing and rewarding encounter. The questions I asked within fairly open-style interviews would be relevant, informed and sensitive given my familiarity with the subject.

When interviewing informants with learning difficulties, again I knew many of them personally from the past. I knew something of their day-to-day lives, environment, habits, preoccupations and sensitivities and the network of peers and members of staff who they were familiar with. I was used to talking to and interacting with people with disabilities, some of whom present special problems in communication and temperament. Some were shy and some were overbearing but they all, apart from one, were aware of the background that I shared with them.

### Insider disadvantages

Trust opened many doors for me as an insider. People trusted me as one of them, from the hospital management to the nursing informants. They welcomed me into their homes and workplaces partly because they knew me or my background and had confidence in me. This was a double-edged sword. What did they trust me to do and did I have a duty towards them because they had shown trust in and friendliness towards me? Would this influence me to present my data and draw conclusions in a more sympathetic manner, first of all because it was expected of me and secondly because I was aware that many of my informants wanted to read what I wrote?

My data, however, had been influenced by my insider status from the beginning. I selected who I was going to interview according to my preconceptions and contacts and while I was attempting to portray a representative cross-section of the nursing community over time there is no doubt I could have obtained a very different picture by interviewing different personnel.

While I may have gained initial rapport in my interviews and felt confident in directing informants into relevant areas, these had their downsides also. There is always a danger that an informant will fill in little detail of a subject or incident if they are aware the interviewer has similar knowledge. I found this most prevalent in trying to establish the daily routines of the nurses who usually started off describing this fine then soon said something like, 'Och you'll know yourself.' There were also many times, on reflection, when I did not ask for more detail when I should have, as I knew about what was being described or alluded to, but most would not. Perhaps sometimes I was so confident about the facets that I wanted to touch on that I did not allow the interviewee to establish the things that were most important to him or her.

Similar critical points can be made about my interviews with residents and ex-residents of Lennox Castle but further, there is the factor of my nurse–patient relationship with them. As mentioned above, many had known me in the role of nurse and all of the others except one were aware of my status. This must have influenced them in their contributions in the interviews. I would certainly have been perceived as a representative of established authority and, given the effects of years of institutionalization, their conversations might have been quite different with someone without my connotations. This factor may be partly responsible for the fact that the most free and lurid criticism of the hospital and nurses that I recorded was from an ex-patient who did not seem to grasp that I had worked there myself.

## Ethical considerations

I first interviewed three residents in one ward in Lennox Castle and went to the duty room to thank the nursing staff and say goodbye. Unexpectedly they had laid out the three sets of case notes for me to read and left me to it. I did read them and was impressed by the corroboration of accuracy of incidents and dates mentioned in the interviews. However this raised the question of whether I should make any use of the material in these notes that were available to me. Reasoning that the relationship I had formed with these people with learning difficulties as a researcher and interviewer would be challenged if I did this, I decided against it. I felt I would be going behind their backs. I also had no similar recourse to check on any of the nurses I had interviewed. This may have been poor research verification technique but I was certainly happier that way.

I also felt some uncertainty over the issue of informed consent. I had gone through 'the proper channels' in my interviews with ex- and current residents of the hospital, but many of the group were so used to accommodating requests from authority figures that there could hardly have been any refusal.

I was not particularly comfortable that some of my nurse informants wanted to and would read what I had written about them and the hospital. This was ameliorated by the knowledge that at least they would experience something tangible in return for giving their time and experience even if they might disagree with the picture I had painted and the conclusions I came to. However, the same could not be said for those with learning difficulties whom I had interviewed. I questioned if I was exploiting them and my position, as it is so easy to do, and offering them nothing in return.

## Theoretical framework

When I began research work I could not have contemplated writing the above. I would have regarded these issues as subjective, unscientific, peripheral and self-indulgent. However, along the way I did manage to discover methodological frameworks and theories which allowed me to address concerns which I initially felt would cloud and restrict the subject. In fact a burgeoning literature on the relationships between researcher and researched has placed this dynamic at the centre of the research process and raises many theoretical and ethical questions.

Facts and data are seen as only one half of a complete picture and 'the other half – how ethnography comes about as a process of perception and writing – deserves to be analysed' (Lonnqvist, 1990: 22). The 'self' has been recognized as the research instrument, dictating which research problem to tackle, which framework to utilize, what informants to give emphasis to and, as such, what goes on inside the researcher has become of the utmost importance.

> The 'self' may be 'simultaneously enabling and disabling' [. . .] but this means we have two good reasons for paying it due attention rather than dismissing it as an unfortunate, complicating factor in our work. In any case, since we cannot shed the self, we must give it a focal point in our writings. (Crick, 1992: 175)

An awareness of who reads what we write is also to the forefront. No longer can the audience be considered as fellow academics and both the subjects we research and the press have to be considered as readers, and readers who will have a reaction.

> The authors collectively ask us to re-evaluate the viability of a distinction between 'insider' and 'outsider.' They examine further the issues of ethnographic authority and the politics of representation, and demonstrate how they personally have dealt with the challenges to authority and interpretation that they have faced either during the process of field work or after the publication of the results of their research. (Brettell, 1993: 22)

Different forms of research text have also been explored and co-operative manuscripts, written by informants and researchers together, are a variation on the conventional productions. I might have attempted this with some of the interviewees with learning disabilities, had I been familiar with the concept at the time, to allow them to experience some autonomy and return.

## Conclusion

The fact that I was so much an insider initially gave me great problems in my approach to the research, although I recognized certain advantages and disadvantages which it generated. One of the biggest disadvantages which I perceived initially was how to communicate my own past experiences and address their effect on my research processes. I came to understand that, far from being a confusing problem, the discussion of my status as an insider should be central to any analysis and that this lent clarity rather than confusion to my work.

## References

Brettell, Caroline B. (ed.) (1993) *When They Read What We Write: the Politics of Ethnography*. Westport, CT: Bergin & Garvey.
Crick, Malcolm (1992) 'Ali and me: an essay on street-corner anthropology' in Okely and Callaway (eds), *Anthropology and Autobiography*. London: Routledge.
Lonnqvist, Bo (1990) 'Remembering and forgetting. Recording for posterity', *Ethnologia Scandinavica*, 20.

# 3

# A 'Tangled Web' of Emotions

*Val Hollinghurst*

One of the hardest problems I have found in caring for my mother has been coming to terms with the 'tangled web' of my own emotions: love, which naturally grows when you tend someone in need, mixed in with fear, resentment and guilt. Exhaustion and isolation made it difficult in the first stages to get anything into proportion or to make any effort to improve things.

When my mother had her stroke, four and a half years ago, I was just becoming established in my career as a teacher and a lay magistrate. After years willingly given to my family (two sons in early teens plus husband's career and home needs) it was now my turn to be a person in my own right. To find, quite literally overnight, that I had to give up the mental stimulus, the company of professionals, my ambition, to go back into the home and wash and care for my mother, was at least as horrifying to me as any more conventional redundancy.

The first six months were a nightmare. My mother's physical condition improved quite rapidly, but, to my horror, I found she had an almost total memory loss; she couldn't wash, dress, feed herself or do anything for herself, not because of the partial paralysis, but because she had forgotten how to. My mother had become my brain-damaged baby! My doctor's cheery 'You're coping marvellously. You don't need any help, do you?' was intended as a compliment, but it successfully cut me off from all sources of information and support – and without adequate information and people to talk to, fear takes over. Everyone needs help and information in the first stages if they are to do the job properly. So many of us make our own problems that wear us down later, simply because we don't understand the situation. It is no use either just asking whether the carer needs help or has any questions. I was too ignorant to ask intelligent questions or even to know what help was being offered, and I hadn't the courage to say so. It is not surprising, therefore, that I made just about all the mistakes possible. Most of these seem to be tied up in our image of what the

Originally published in A. Briggs and J. Oliver (eds) (1985) *Caring: Experiences of Looking after Disabled Relatives.* London: Routledge & Kegan Paul. pp. 15–20.

world expects of carers. I saw myself as a cross between Florence Nightingale and an early Christian martyr – nursing and caring for my mother, keeping the home spotless, washing, ironing, cooking, shopping, gardening, yet always available with a sympathetic ear and practical help for my husband and sons . . . and of course, always smiling bravely! Fortunately, my marvellous family and friends pointed out that this desire for perfection was a recipe for a nervous breakdown, and I was forced to re-examine my new role and my reactions to it – a process I have not yet completed.

To begin with I had to recognize that I am not, and never have been, perfect, and secondly that if society really does expect such perfection from us then society is wrong. Anyone who criticizes can take over for a month and discover reality the hard way. None of us are the super-human people we would like to think ourselves and *we owe it to the person we care for to look after our own well-being.* [. . .] With this and a knowledge of my own shortcomings in mind I started again. My family have learned from painful experience that I am a rotten nurse; but I am a good teacher, so why not try to teach my mother to care for herself? People do it for brain-damaged babies, so it should be easier for an adult who only has to relearn. The months of endless, patient repetition that followed were exhausting. When I could regard it as a professional job it was easier to cope, but when I remembered my once brilliant mother and watched her spending a week to do a 20-piece jigsaw puzzle I shed many a tear in private. But it was worth all the tears and anguish, because as she learned to do more and more and more for herself so her dignity as a human being returned and I can think of nothing more important than human dignity. You hear of someone who does everything for their disabled relative and society praises them – rightly if they have reached the stage where any movement or decision is impossible, but most people can learn to do *something* for themselves and it would be cruel not to allow them to make choices even if that does involve taking risks. Life is a risky business, after all. We don't wrap our children up in cotton wool and refuse to let them cross the road; we teach them to do it as safely as possible and then stand back. Why then do we try to shelter our elderly people from every wind that blows? The risk I found hardest to take was to leave my mother alone. Shopping was done in a frantic rush and all invitations out were refused. It was bad enough to risk my mother falling while I was unavoidably out, but the ultimate sin was to risk her falling *while I was enjoying myself!* Yet in the long run she gained by my occasional absences. A doctor's prescription saying 'Take time out to enjoy yourself at regular intervals' would often be much more valuable than Valium. The first time I plucked up the courage to leave my mother at lunchtime I stupidly left her a Thermos flask of hot food – not the most sensible thing for someone who could only use one hand! Yet when I rushed back, instead of disaster I was met by a triumphant mother who had gone out alone for the first time and got help from a neighbour: she wasn't going to miss her lunch! My mother's confidence grew from that day on so we both learned from my mistake. We were both becoming people in our own right instead of prisoners locked together in mutual dependency and resentment.

There was still a long way to go. Humility has never been my strong point, and I found, still find, learning to accept help very hard. I have only recently realized that by doing everything myself I was depriving my mother of new friends, faces and experiences and making her far too dependent on me. Getting her to go to clubs in the first stages, though, was even harder than persuading reluctant toddlers that school was a lovely place really. 'I'm just a burden to you' is the usual response, but my *mother* is not a burden: the *illness* is a burden that we are both fighting together. It is amazing the difference it can make in a relationship when you define things accurately. Communication is just as important between carer and cared-for, as it is between husband and wife. Elderly people often become very demanding, but how much of this is our fault because we shield them from reality? They probably don't realize that their demands are unrealistic and if we don't tell them we are encouraging them to be selfish. I now talk to my mother about my tiredness, my fears and needs and our love has increased with understanding. We don't let our children become selfish because it destroys friendship and ruins their lives in this life and the next. Do our elderly parents not have friends or an immortal soul?

Recognizing that my mother and I are still individuals and cannot live through each other has been the most important factor in freeing us from the more damaging aspects of caring/cared-for roles. Guilt is not as strong since I have acknowledged my own inadequacies and my mother's right to make her own decisions – even her own mistakes. She recently fell in the shower, and well-meaning friends and professionals said, 'You won't allow her to take a shower alone again, will you?' Note that word 'allow'. Is that why so many of our elderly people become senile, because decision-making is taken away from them in the interests of safety? I *asked* my mother whether she wanted help and she said 'no' very firmly. I hope I won't feel guilty if she falls again, but will public opinion insist that I do? It's harder standing outside the shower biting my fingernails, but as we've taken reasonable risks together our fears have decreased. Coming back into the world has also helped: fear feeds on isolation and lack of information. The Association of Carers [now Carers National Association] has also helped because there I am a person in my own rights: a carer, yes – but not *just* a carer. In our local group we discover we are not alone, and we are still people.

I have found resentment the hardest emotion to come to terms with, and every time I think I've won the battle I find little pockets of it left.

Why shouldn't I have a career as so many people assume is a woman's right these days? But if I had my career I wouldn't have so many other things that I now value. Having realized that resentment was growing inside me like a cancer I decided to fight it. If Christ could wash the disciples' feet, am I really too important to look after my mother? I have the prayer of St Francis on my kitchen wall and I am trying to live by it: 'May I seek not so much to be consoled as to console, to be loved as to love' . . . it's hard, and some people would say I'm just brain-washing myself, but the point is it works! I have reached the stage where if I had the opportunity to go back and leave the caring to someone else and take up my career I would refuse the offer! Because I've been at home, my house has become a meeting place for young people, friends of my sons, whom I would otherwise have hardly known – and what a joy their company has been. I've gained valuable insight into myself and become a stronger person; above all I've come to understand and love all my family, including my mother, more. Caring can do that to you – if you let it.

Of course I'm still afraid of the future at times and I have days when I wonder why I do it. Don't we all? Basically, though it all comes down to choice: very few of us have any real choice as to whether we care for our relatives or not; we do have a choice what to do with the very real burden caring imposes. We can wear it on our backs for everyone to see and pity us, or we can use it as a stepping stone to something better. I wear mine too frequently on my back – all that sympathy is lovely to wallow in – but when I have the courage to be positive I glimpse a freedom and happiness I thought were lost. I haven't unravelled all the 'tangled web' of emotions yet, but I'm beginning to think it is an interesting challenge. In years to come will I think I've been lucky to have that challenge?

# 4

# Caring in Families: a Case Study

*Jan Walmsley*

**Editors' introduction**

This is an extract from a study of 22 adults with learning disabilities interviewed about their experiences of care and caring. Lynne's story was the one which raised the most complex issues about being a woman, about having the label of 'learning disability' and about being both carer and cared-for.

\* \* \*

**Interview situation**

The local MENCAP secretary told me about Lynne as a woman with learning difficulties who cared for her father. A lengthy attempt to make contact followed. I was helped in this by Rita, the disability employment worker whose job was to look after people with learning difficulties in work. She tried to arrange an interview at Lynne's workplace and failed. In the end we met at the hostel near Lynne's flat. At Lynne's request Rita was to be present.

At the hostel I was introduced to the officer in charge who had known Lynne for 20 years. She told me Lynne's father, like many others, had difficulty accepting self-advocacy. Lynne's sister, she said, 'doesn't do much', and Eddie, Lynne's boyfriend had been harassed by Lynne's father: for example he would ring him up to do errands when Lynne was unavailable. Staff had stepped in to defend Eddie. All agreed that Lynne's father should not be told about the interview and helped Lynne rehearse a story about visiting a friend, as a reason for being out that evening.

From J. Walmsley (1995) 'Gender, caring and learning disability'. PhD dissertation, Open University, Milton Keynes.

**Lynne's life story as she told it**

Lynne was 43. She was nervous: 'I don't know what I'm going to say tonight.' In fact, she was reticent about the past, and the facts are briefly recounted.

She was born in L—— and once lived 'up Burley Hill'. With difficulty I obtained the information that she'd been to Fivetrees (an occupation centre opened in 1959). (The minutes of the Mental Treatment Subcommittee dated 12 September 1957 record that she was put on statutory supervision at the age of eight.) She said firmly it was a school. She later went to the centre, from where she obtained her job. Her mother died:

> I was down the Salvation Army when she died and Dad had to go up the hospital with me uncle and it was too late so someone told me down the Salvation Army. On the quiet before they gave it out . . . she'd got cancer . . . she kept falling over and I went to work.

She was unable to give any indication of when this happened. When pressed to give details she did not want to recall she changed the subject. However, it did result in her father taking over the cooking in the family, something that Rita referred to more than once when arguing that Lynne owed caring obligations to him.

The only event which was dated was her starting work:

> Been there seven years, nearly eight years . . . I wanted a job. I worked in C & A for a month's work experience and me dad said there's a factory up near where he works.

She said her social worker had found the job (though Rita said it was the officer from MENCAP Pathway, a specialist job-finding service).

**Family**

Throughout her life Lynne had lived with her family. Her mother died, her sister left home to marry, and she remained. She began the first interview by saying:

> I know I'm not very happy at home at the moment . . . I'm a bit fed up with me dad. He doesn't know where I am tonight. He thinks I'm going round a friend's. I daren't tell him.

Fear of her father, and dislike of living with him, were recurrent themes, a graphic illustration of a care relationship which was felt to be burdensome and restrictive.

It took some time to ascertain the precise nature of the tasks Lynne did for her father. Rita questioned her persistently to discover what these were. One was shopping:

> Dad writes a list out and we have to get what he wants. He likes his stew and dumplings and I don't.

Lynne handed her 'board money' to her father and he gave some back for his shopping. Money was a matter of contention:

> Well every Thursday night I usually give him me board money. I didn't this week cos I didn't draw me money out till Saturday. 'Where's me money, where's me money.' I give up. He wanted his money for shopping Friday night, I think. He didn't know we was doing it on Saturday.

Other than shopping, Lynne said her work in the home included 'cooking his dinner and washing up what I normally do'. Lynne prepared her father's dinner the night before, and left it ready for the home help to put in the oven. She had to monitor what he ate because of his diabetes: 'He's only allowed potatoes when he doesn't have stew and dumplings cos of his diet.' She peeled all the potatoes for the week on Saturday nights.

She said she spent little actual time with him:

> *Jan*: You scared of him?
> *Lynne*: I am. I'm always in me bedroom. Part from tomorrow. I goes to the club.
> *Jan*: But you don't actually spend any time with your dad?
> *Lynne*: No.
> *Jan*: Is that, do you choose not to?
> *Lynne*: I have me dinner with him. Sometimes if it's hot I have to wait for it to cool down.
> *Jan*: But you don't sit and talk to him at all?
> *Lynne*: No.
> *Jan*: Would you like to?
> *Lynne*: No, I'd rather go out.

The tensions in the relationship came to a head in between our two interviews. Rita brought the subject up, and Lynne said she'd prefer Rita to tell the story:

> The way I understand it is that Dad was having a go at Lynne and Lynne lost her temper. She was peeling the potatoes. And she waved the knife to her dad. So he told the home carer and the home carer fetched the social worker.

Lynne corroborated this and said:

> I wouldn't really do it. I was upset at work, wasn't I . . . he was going on . . . he said do something while I was peeling the potatoes . . . he [social worker] said he'd put me away next time . . . social worker said to me dad you won't be staying here, you'll be going a long way away . . . he said if I tried that again to call him, he said I won't be in L——— . . . I heard him.

This incident summed up Lynne's situation with her father, and her social worker. She felt that her father asked too much of her, that he tried to stop her going out, and that the social worker was on her father's side. It was perhaps unsurprising that she wanted to leave home. She was a single daughter at home with an invalid father, and worked a double shift, at home and at a full-time job, yet remained infantilized by her father, a view shared by staff at the hostel.

## Impact of services

Lynne's career until she got her job seems to be fairly typical of a woman of her age who was certified as ineducable, and whose family were prepared to take responsibility for her: certification, occupation centre, then training centre. There are many examples of such a life course in the records of the Mental Treatment and Mental Health subcommittees.

However, what is missing from these written accounts is the subjective meaning of such a biography. She did not mention the process of being certified. Her reference to Fivetrees Occupation Centre as a school reflects, perhaps, an attempt to normalize her situation, or possibly the well-meaning efforts of family and staff to do so. The importance of her job was reflected in the fact that this was the only event she was able or willing to date. Even the means by which she got the job was presented as a family initiative, not an intervention by MENCAP's Pathway.

Getting a job set her apart from all the people I interviewed, and made her situation uniquely complex. I examine this below.

## Identities around gender, caring and dependency

Lynne seemed to have three distinct social identities: as an employee; a woman with learning difficulties; and an unpaid carer.

Lynne talked of her work at a pharmaceuticals factory with pride. She washed her own uniform, got herself up and off to work by rising at 5.20 every morning. As an employee she spent her working day in the company of non-disabled people with minimal specialist support. The company were, according to Rita, anxious to treat Lynne like any other employee. Some interventions, such as Rita's visits, were accepted, and there had been special efforts to ensure she was well fed, and that her wages were accessible to her. But it was not sheltered employment. Lynne was expected to pull her weight, packing drugs with the other workers. She herself made reference to this.

Possibly as a consequence of her status as a working woman Lynne had more casual community contacts than many I interviewed:

> I get me money out in town now . . . . If I want a prescription I ask sometimes the library to do it for me . . . I go in the estate agents next door too, I still pop in to say hello [this was where she used to draw her wages], Thursday nights I still go down to pay me rent.

The need and the opportunity to meet people in the course of running her life seemed to give Lynne confidence in these transactions. It was an obvious benefit of her employment.

However, she remained a person with learning difficulties in many respects. She did not acknowledge this openly, but it was clear from her social contacts that she was still part of the network. Service providers lingered in Lynne's life from her days as a client. The officer in charge at the hostel where we met knew Lynne well. She had contact with professionals through Eddie, still a user of services – for example she was anticipating going out to eat with Eddie and his key worker. The one worker who currently had responsibility for Lynne was Rita. Lynne appeared to trust her, as she insisted on her being present at both interviews. Rita assumed the role of co-interviewer, and used the opportunity to pursue in some detail those areas which concerned her as disability employment officer – Lynne's diet, her health, her teeth ('I think you're having trouble with your teeth, you know. They're falling out all the time').

Lynne's leisure time was largely spent with other people with learning difficulties. She went to the club on Wednesday evenings, and on the outings organized for its members, she went to the gardening classes at the hostel. Above all, she knew people. This network, shared by Beryl and many others I interviewed, was long-standing and durable. Its significance was illustrated by an incident at the hostel. I had brought a gift for Rita and while we awaited her arrival a hostel resident tried to grab it. I could not cope with the situation, but Lynne said 'Sit down, David' and he did. Later we talked about the incident. Lynne said she'd known him from the centre and he used to talk 'but now he don't'.

Lynne was also a carer, for her the least welcome identity. This entailed relationships with a number of professionals who were there for her father. He had home aides and home care assistants coming into the home, including at weekends. It was a home care assistant who called in the social worker after the knife incident. Lynne had mixed feelings about the home care assistants:

> Sometimes Dora comes at weekends. She's all right. She does say hello to me . . . . But sometimes I just want to keep out of the home care's way and go out.

In this respect, her home was the site of someone else's care, and this compromised her autonomy within it (Gavilan, 1992).

Her caring role was most complex in relationship to the social worker. He was Asian and she claimed to be unable to understand him. There also seemed to be a greater difficulty; he was both her father's social worker and hers [. . .] and they had different and irreconcilable interests. Lynne was keen to leave home and live on her own 'before I get too old'. The social worker may have been the key person to achieve that, but their relationship was such that she could not imagine making contact with him to talk about rehousing.

It seemed that for the social worker she was part of her father's network of support, not a person with needs of her own, a classic conflict of interest.

As an adult daughter at home Lynne was under pressure to take on the role of caring for her father. This was clearly spelt out by Rita, who told Lynne that the fault in the relationship was not one sided:

> I think sometimes Dad gets cross cos you aren't doing the things you really should do. Cos you just want to go out. Am I right? It's not always Dad's fault he gets cross, is it? It's sometimes your fault . . . . Well I say to Lynne sometimes that hard as it is for her to have to have someone like Dad dependent on her to a certain extent he took care of her when she was young and helpless and needed someone and now she is grown up and able to cope in life she should help if she can.

It is a clear exposition of a commonly held view on daughterly obligations to elderly parents, though some of the language ('now she is grown up') seems inappropriate for a woman of 43.

Lynne also had a boyfriend, Eddie. She met him at the Adult Training Centre and they had been friends for 13 years. In answer to a question from Rita she said he had asked her to marry him, but she'd said no because he was too old. It was not described as a sexual relationship, but it did give both practical and affective support. He did the shopping with her and they met most days after she'd finished work. She described how he made sure she ate:

> Eddie took me straight down town to have two beefburgers. I said 'Eddie I only want one beefburger.' 'You're having two, you got to eat.'

Eddie had been banned from Lynne's flat because her father was trying to get him to run errands.

Lynne was exceptional. Beryl told me she was the only person from the centre to have got and kept a real job. But this change in status was in some ways superficial. She still did not enjoy the autonomy that having her own income might be expected to bring. Her father, according to her and others, still treated her as if she was a dependant, took 'board money' and expected her to obey him and account for her movements. She was expected by him, and others, to carry out daughterly obligations, and her wish to be an independent householder was not taken seriously. In terms of care, she was both carer and cared-for. The formal care she received was very much geared to sustaining her ability to carry out her job. Rita was responsible for overseeing her health – food, spectacles, teeth were all matters of interest to Rita. The care work Lynne did for her father was actually quite substantial, but she got little credit for it and no rewards. Her history as a woman with learning difficulties had followed her into the world of work. The consequences for Lynne were

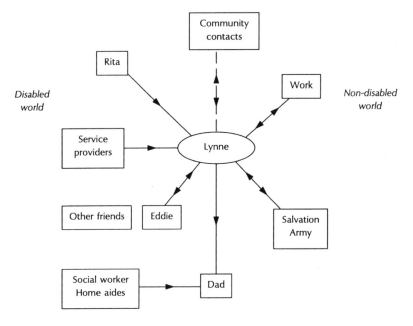

Figure 4.1

that she uncomfortably straddled two worlds, and had few of the benefits of either.

### 'Lynne' case study: issues around care and caring

Lynne is a woman with learning difficulties, a label which implies dependency and excludes her from a role as a 'carer' or a worker. But she is also:

- a woman who has a classic 'double shift': full-time work and caring duties at home;
- a daughter whom Rita sees as having an obligation to care for her dad to repay him for caring for her when she was younger;
- a single daughter at home on whom the obligation to care often falls (Lewis and Meredith, 1988);
- a full-time worker;
- a recipient of 'care' herself in a limited fashion from Rita whose role as disability employment officer has been adapted to support Lynne, and a person in whom learning disability service providers take an interest.

Her social relationships are complex (see Figure 4.1).

## What does Lynne's story tell us about 'care'?

(1)  It depends on who you ask and how you ask. Had I asked Lynne's
     father, social worker, Rita, home aides about her life I'd have got
     a very different picture. What if I'd used a questionnaire?

(2)  Care relationships change over time: 10 years earlier it would
     have been a very different picture – Lynne at a training centre,
     Mum alive, and out at work. Five years later, different again,
     maybe.

(3)  Caring services went into the household for individuals. Rita did
     not know much about Lynne's home life. She used the interview
     to find out. The social worker, home aides and care assistants
     apparently saw their role as supporting Lynne's dad, not Lynne.
     There is no evidence of a holistic approach: indeed Rita was not
     employed by Social Services at all and felt she had no leverage
     with Lynne's social worker over, for example, Lynne leaving
     home or resolving differences between her and her social worker.

(4)  There are gender issues here: would Rita have said what she did
     to a man? Class issues, also?

(5)  Lynne's views of her social worker, and her ability to com-
     municate with him, were complicated by race. She claimed to be
     unable to understand him, and was, by implication, racist.

(6)  What sorts of services might help?
     - allocating a social worker to Lynne as well as to her father;
     - Dad's social worker to act as broker between Lynne and her
       father rather than advocate for him alone;
     - a gender perspective for Rita – did she recognize her role in
       reinforcing gender stereotypes?
     - training for the home carers/aiders in working with Lynne
       rather than around her, and recognizing her contribution to
       the household;
     - someone to listen to Lynne and respond to her clearly
       articulated wish to have a home of her own;
     - a carers' support group for Lynne.

## References

Gavilan, H. (1992) 'Care in the Community: issues of dependency and control – the
  similarities between institution and home', *Generation Review*, 4(2): 9–14.
Lewis, J. and Meredith, B. (1988) *Daughters Who Care*. London: Routledge.

# 5

# Snowballs and Acorns: Medicine by Impact

*Tom Heller*

## Diad

*It's that feeling*

It's that feeling waiting for the on-call call to call
Harsh bleep connects direct to inner brain.
Turfed out of bed
When just about to make love or sleep.

Did you do the right thing
For everyone, every time?
And too much to do in any one day
Every day

Moments on the toilet interrupted
By more bleeping insistence.
Forms to fill in
And forms to order more forms.

Distant people controlling what you do
Diktats from above and demands from below.
A professional sandwich
In the middle of a packed day

Like the snatched snack
Taken huddled over the gear stick.
Ten illicit minutes between visits
In the midday side street

Hoping you won't be recognized
Like four times in Safeways
Twice at the footy
And while taking a piss at the Odeon

No numbers on the houses
Black scrawl sprayed over street names
Puddles on the floor of the tower block lift
And the illest people live furthest away, that's a fact.

Cold internal fear of blunder
Killing them dead.
Or wrong word in anger
Slipping out in a moment

You are on your own
Don't tell anyone how you feel.
They are too busy caring for others
To care about you.

Be the boss
Control the staff
Run the business
Decide everything

Your car's vandalized
The computer's stolen
A serious brick lobbed through window
Serves as a local greeting

After a day when the computer crashed
While fending off insistent, ignorant health service managers
And half the team's in tears
Home again to await the bleep's bleeping bleep

* * *

## It's great being a GP

It's great being a GP, it really is
People come and give you things
Like crystals or polished stones
Or a part of their lives

Little glimpses or great big globs
Freely given
To be savoured and nurtured
And healed if possible

They trust you to look after bits
Not shared with anyone else
Knowing you will treasure them
And be alongside them as they carry their wound

Abused and never told
Of violent relationship
Searching for sexuality
Or functions not working

Accept these gifts
Stay alongside as they go through their darkest times
And care when they come for small things
Because big assaults are shadow-lurking just behind

Chuckle at their babies
They are special
Each one a glimpse into life's purpose
With limitless potential of pink-podgy limbs

Stay with them while good things happen
Like the birth of a baby
Illness conquered
Or relationships sorted

Remain with them as disease and pain
And pus discharges from all places
For we are human
And decay until death

They let you into their homes
Like a glimpse
Into warm fleshy intimate parts
To surrender the pink internal decorations

Those few special minutes
Behind the closed door
Confessional
Crying the salty truth out loud

Rich with privilege and power.
While others have shit jobs
We are challenged
To learn about our central selves

\* \* \*

Patricia Williams, a black woman who rose from humble beginnings in the USA to become, amongst other things, the Reith Lecturer in 1997, recalls her schooldays in an all-white school in the USA where she and her sister were pelted variously with snowballs and acorns, 'I remember the change of seasons by what they threw at us' (*Guardian* 23 January 1997, G2: 4–5). And so it can seem in general practice. 'In the spring and summer they pelt us with hay fever and rashes from being out in the sun, during the autumn and winter it's colds and flu', and just about at any time of day or night a steady stream of ailments and upsets assault the tetchy doctor who may well have virtually no interest in, or answers for, these conditions.

But what of the human beings in these interchanges?

After almost exactly 11 hours at the surgery I arrive home. It has not exactly been an easy day for any of us. My marriage partner is exhausted from her day at work, and the children are under pressure from their schools and friendship groups in various ways. At least two of us are recovering from flu-like illness ourselves, and the post has brought worrying news about one of our closest friends as well as some other family matters that need our attention. As I put on the kettle the on-call pager goes bleep in my pocket. I always jump when it goes off. I have become conditioned after many years of on-call to jerk and judder into action as the particular high-pitched sound resonates, day or night. I can still get the same reaction if I am surprised when passing Pelican crossings, or even by unexpected bleeping noises on the television. I have been home for about 10 minutes. The call is from a young woman who has recently joined our list and is worried about her small child. 'I tried to get an appointment this evening, but you were full up. I don't think it will wait until the morning now. He's been having coughing bouts and gone blue four times during the day with the effort of coughing. He's not feeding either and he's starting to be sick.' The child may well need some attention. However, I know that the woman is not telling the whole truth. For various reasons there have been spare appointments at the surgery during tonight's evening session. She has waited until surgery is over so she will not be told to bring the child down, but will have the service delivered to her door. I have a choice of possible ways of reacting. I could make her and her child suffer. 'You will have to wait until the morning, and I will see him during the morning surgery.' But this option seems risky and the stories of doctors who have not visited fill the pages of the defence society's journals. Making the child wait for treatment over a further night also seems rather cruel: it is our (adult) problem not hers. I could work myself into an even more angry response: 'There were appointments for this evening, you should have brought her down then.' Would the effort of confronting the woman be more sapping than just doing the visit without making an issue of it? Would the passive acceptance of her statement indicate to her that she can treat doctors like this at any time she chooses? Why does she not see me as a human being, and the service as a potentially decent set-up trying its best in quite difficult circumstances?

What would the holistic counsel of perfection dictate? I should make this situation into a learning experience for myself and for the woman and her family. I should make sure that I understood her psychological make-up and appreciate the ways that she has been treated by authority and statutory organizations throughout her life. I should understand that her social situation is not easy. She has ended up, virtually without education, qualifications or job prospects in a draughty flat on a highly undesirable housing estate where it is hard to survive, let alone give your own children a better chance of improving their prospects than she has had. I should be prepared to explore the possibility that there are features in her individual life story that have made life especially difficult for her. She may have lost her parents at an early age, or been abused by them. No wonder she finds it hard to deal appropriately with powerful male figures who are in authority over her.

Switching quickly into biomedical gear I must also be aware of the differential diagnosis of the child she is presenting to me. Everyone is worried about meningitis since the highly publicized cases in the next town. What are the chances that this child has something serious or sinister? Going blue can be a sign of a heart defect. Have I missed this at a previous examination in our baby clinic? If the child does have an infection, am I properly set up to establish what this is? Have I got the relevant swabs and containers to send to the pathology department? Is it 'just a virus' and if so what role does any treatment have? Am I up to date with the evidence-based medicine which may give fairly full guidelines about ways of treating a whole range of conditions? Should I know what antibiotics are most likely to work if this is a chest infection, or an ear infection? And if the child is vomiting, then what is the significance of this for the diagnosis and treatment? I am aware that I am also straying into a legal minefield with many potential problems awaiting the practitioner. For what is the level of competence that I must display, and what if something does go wrong? I can easily commit sins of omission or commission, and a keen lawyer will run rings round me in the cold light of day.

The new dimension in all this is the financial juggling that will be going on in my mind. What are the costs of this transaction in monetary terms? We have just become a fundholding practice and we have a fixed, and probably diminishing, annual budget for the drugs we use, for the hospital facilities we 'purchase', and for the staff we work with. When I see this small child or other members of her family I must be aware of the cost implications of each component of their care. Although the newest antibiotics might well have a smaller risk of troublesome side effects, they may be more than six times as expensive as their routine generic equivalents. Hospital services, laboratory tests, out-patient or in-patient services all diminish our budget. If we overspend on one item of expenditure such as drugs, or hospital investigations we have to make savings in other areas, possibly sack members of staff, or restrict the innovative or preventive work that we try to do. Can we afford transactions like this? Are this family aware of the fact that they are potentially an 'expensive family', and that the cost of providing services for them far exceeds the amount that the practice is given under the current rules for looking after them? However ill they are, and whatever their needs, we are given the same amount of money to look after them. Although their flat is in a deprived area, and looks run down to any casual observer, we do not receive 'deprivation payments' because these are calculated at ward level, and the ward we serve does have some less needy areas which push the average 'deprivation score' above the level that would trigger special payments.

During the visit to the poorly child later that evening the mother, Julia, mentions that she herself has developed a serious heroin habit since being rehoused on to the estate. 'I just used pot for a while, and then someone from the other flats had some heroin and suggested that I would feel better if I smoked some. It really was great at first, but now I can't manage without it, and I'm getting into more and more debt and other sorts of trouble. Housing are on my back again, and I think the gas and electricity are about to be cut off.'

Oh dear. It is now nearly 10 o'clock at night. I have been working for over 14 hours with only the shortest break over a rushed tea at home, which was, however, long enough to remind me of my own family's needs. They need a bit of time with me, perhaps some help sorting out a few blips and concerns from their lives, but how does it compare with the problems that Julia's family has? This is the first time she has told anyone in authority about her drug problem and the way that I respond to her may be crucial for their future . . . . Does she know of my special interest in working with drug users? What signals have I given out that it may be OK to talk about her problems as well?

For some reason I often seem to have a special empathy when working with drug users, and at times I reflect why this might be.

*The tearaway I never was*: Here they are the ultimate rebels against society. I am jealous of their rebelliousness. I regret that I never quite got it together to kick against society's pricks in the uninhibited way that many of the drug misusers continue to do.

*I like the power*: If there is always a power imbalance in every consultation then how much greater is it with drug misusers as patients? I can chose to give or to refuse, alter the contract, decide whether to help them or not. Every consultation reinforces my position of authority. I control the oracle, the all-powerful pre-scription pad.

*Is it the competitive challenge against other doctors?* These people have not been helped by anyone else, nobody can do it as well as I can. Look at my skill in helping these people. I get extra status from being able to cope with this lot and here I am enjoying it.

*Is it compensation for the pleasures I do not allow myself?* What is it like to use heroin? I fantasize that it must be a great buzz. Here I am a vegetarian, non-smoking, virtual teetotaller. Why am I so tightly controlled and deny myself so many pleasures yet feel empathy with people who are defined by their reckless pleasure-seeking behaviour?

*What about sexual attraction?* Within all consultations there is a sexual element. Am I physically attracted to drug misusers more than to other people who come to see me? Is it because the attraction seems so implausible and so unlikely to be acted out, such a deep taboo, that there is some extra chemistry?

*Does it feed the voyeur in me?* There are always stories and glimpses of worlds I have never known when I talk with drug misusers. Tales of the dark side of town, parts of the city I do not know, and deeds and deals that are way beyond my comprehension. It feeds my imagination.

*Am I just bored with other parts of my work?* If one more person tells me that they have had a cough 'since Friday, no it was Saturday',

and expects me to be fascinated I shall scream. Is working with drug misusers a respite from other routines of general practice?
*Is it all about parenting?* Delicate, vulnerable people, drug misusers come for help rather like newborn or recently adopted children. Is it my job to be their parent, to protect them from bad things and to try to be a constant element in their lives? As my own children are growing, have the drug misusers become my substitute little children?

So, working with drug users has given me the opportunity to learn more about myself. But back at Julia's flat more details are emerging of the life that she has been leading:

> 'It really has been hell living here over the last few months. We can't get out of the flat at all now because some people have started to get aggressive towards me and the kids. A group of the other residents have found out that I have been using drugs and they have been shouting really vile things at me in the street. They call me "whore" and "junkie" and worse. A couple of young lads attacked me with a baseball bat and I was probably lucky to escape with my life. My toddler, Timmy, was cornered and spat at by a bunch of women only last week and I haven't dared to let him out to play since then. That is why I can't even get down to the surgery. I'm sorry to drag you out on a night like this, but I am really worried about him.'

The 'drug problem' has become worse recently on the estate. Built just after the Second World War, the estate was the proud recipient of returning heroes. They soon got jobs in the steelworks or in nearby coal mines. Their wives created decent homes for their children, who in turn worked for the local council, or on the buses, or followed their fathers into their traditional industries. Over the last 20 years though, most of these sources of 'secure' employment have ceased to exist. Only a very small minority of grown-up men have kept their jobs, and many of those who have remained as wage earners moved off the estate when they saw the writing on the wall, literally and metaphorically. The people who planned the estate unfortunately neglected to build in any communal or recreational facilities. It really is just row after row of semi-detached houses and decaying low-rise flats. The solitary row of shops is half boarded up, and graffiti and restless gangs of young people deface the neighbourhood. There is nothing to do and nowhere to go. Life choices for young people growing upon the estate are severely limited. The young women often choose to have babies at a very early age and turn their energies to the next generation in the hope of finding meaning and fulfilment. Children being born to children. The young men have even fewer options. Poorly trained in the local schools, with no real long-term job prospects they seem to have individual and collective low self-esteem and do not seem to be wanted on the domestic scene once conception has been ensured. The choices for them remain the terminal tedium of insecure, low-paid work or unemployment, madness or increasingly the escape that drugs can bring. The drugs subculture has become one of the few ways that young people can become economically active, and the attractions of this means of escape are obvious.

At the same time many of the traditional 'helping agencies' are in an accelerated state of decline. The local authority has virtually withdrawn all facilities from the area. The last youth worker has been 'redeployed' to an office job at the other end of the city, and funding priority has switched to a rival estate which had the foresight to stage some rioting a couple of years back. The Social Services department has been reorganized yet again, with the effect that only child protection cases are being followed up. The local church struggles on with a vicar shared between this estate and four others, and no real resources . . . etc. etc. The remaining agencies are the police and the doctors' surgery.

But what of Julia? She is a deviant. She has chosen to spend all her and her children's money on drugs. She has prioritized her own selfish needs as higher than paying for the gas and electricity. She has been stealing from shops and occasionally gone on trips to other towns to steal from their shops also. She may have been involved in small-scale drug dealing herself, or selling her body from time to time to pay for her next smoke. Is she the cause or the effect of the estate's decline? In any event she is an easy target for some of her neighbours, who can release some part of their aggression on her. She is a threat at many levels to whatever collective pride they can muster. What stance does the doctor take? Should I be the advocate for Julia, look after her and attempt to protect her from the community? Does the surgery become the bolt-hole for her and other 'deviants', or should the surgery go with the 'moral majority' and castigate and punish further people who have fallen on hard times?

In any event it is midnight before I return home. The lights are all off. The family have given up on me and gone to bed.

# 6

# Nursing Practice and the Lived Experience of Illness

*P. Benner and J. Wrubel*

Understanding the meaning of the illness can facilitate treatment and cure. Even when no treatment is available and no cure is possible, understanding the meaning of the illness for the person and for that person's life is a form of healing, in that such understanding can overcome the sense of alienation, loss of self-understanding, and loss of social integration that accompany illness.

A paradigm case written by Clare Hastings illustrates the worth of understanding the lived experience of the illness regardless of what other medical or nursing therapies may be available.

## Paradigm: the lived experience of the illness
## Making contact with the patient

Clare Hastings

> I had a powerful clinical experience when I was working in the rheumatology screening clinic. It changed my understanding of how nurses can affect patients even during brief encounters. This event took place in the clinic, where we see patients who are referred for evaluation and consideration for entry into research protocols. The clinic was set up so that patients spent a fair amount of time with one of the nurses, who went over why they had been referred to the clinic and orienting them to the National Institutes of Health. The setting was what is now the 'chemo room' in one of the clinics. It had several beds and a desk. It was a crowded space with not a lot of privacy.
>
> An older woman in a wheelchair came with her daughter. I remember that she had *terrible* rheumatoid arthritis. When we say 'terrible rheumatoid arthritis', we mean someone who might be presented in a textbook – one with a lot of deformities, who can't walk and is all twisted up and in pain. We talked about this patient

From P. Benner and J. Wrubel (1989) *The Primacy of Caring: Stress and Coping in Health and Illness.* Menlo Park, CA: Addison-Wesley. pp. 9–11.

later as a 'medical disaster'. She came to us after having been treated by a lot of physicians and really not having had what we would have recommended as appropriate medical therapy. She had gone through many years of what I considered almost useless suffering.

When I see patients in this kind of situation, I usually begin by asking them some background questions about why they're here, what their history is, how long they've been ill, and so on. The first thing I asked her was whether she usually used a wheelchair. Was that the way she usually got around? And that question brought a flood of expression from her. Apparently, even though I thought her extremely disabled and deformed, this was the first time she had needed to use a wheelchair. She had somehow managed to cope with all the things that arthritis means, get around her house, take care of her family, and do her job, without having to resort to the symbolic state of 'being in a wheelchair'. Right away, that put us in touch with each other, and the encounter shifted to an emotional level. We were talking about feelings right from the beginning, before I had found out much about her.

It's hard to express, but there is a sense when you feel that you are making contact with the patient – and again I don't know whether it is the way you talk about the illness, the way you approach the patient, the kinds of questions you ask, or the language you use – but somehow, patients know that you know what they are talking about, that you have seen these kinds of things before. You understand *what they are.* You have dealt with the disease and the consequences of the illness daily, and you have a thorough knowledge of it. The illness is horrible to most people, and they never talk about it to the patient, but it is an everyday thing to you, something you have dealt with, something you know about, and therefore not horrendous or awful. I could feel that between us – that contact.

I then moved into doing a physical assessment and looking at her various joints. Thinking about this later, I realized one of the ways I was able to communicate with her, really get to some of the things she felt, was just by the *way* I looked at her joints. I made distinctions about swelling, the level of inflammation, and so on. It is possible to touch a person and move the person's hand or wrist, and say: 'I can tell that this must be really painful right now', or 'It looks like you haven't been able to use this hand for a long time', or 'What is this finger doing way out here?' or 'This must be really difficult when you take a bath.' I asked her to raise her arms, and I saw that she couldn't even get them up past her shoulders. I asked: 'Does anyone help you get dressed in the morning?' Actually these are the kinds of questions I typically ask.

As we were methodically looking at her whole body, she was getting more emotional; probably she had never discussed these personal things before. Maybe the fact that her daughter was there had something to do with it. She had never really discussed anything with anyone beyond: 'This knee hurts' and 'This finger is swollen.' She had never talked about what the symptoms meant to her. She had never said: 'This means that I can't go to the bathroom by myself, put my clothes on, even get out of bed without calling for help.'

When we finished I said something like: 'Rheumatoid arthritis really has not been nice to you.' She burst into tears, and her daughter did also, and I sat there, very close to losing it myself.

She said: 'You know, no one has ever talked about it as a personal thing before, no one's ever talked to me as if this were a thing that mattered, a personal event.'

That was the significant thing about the encounter. I didn't really have much else to offer her. She ended up not being eligible for what we were doing at NIH. She had what we call 'old disease', or 'burned out rheumatoid arthritis'. The disease had wrecked her joints years ago. What she really needed was for someone to put a lot of new hardware inside her, and maybe some physical therapy, but it wasn't the kind of thing we were offering. I knew at the end of the interview that we would probably not be following her, and I had to tell her that. I gave some advice about ways she could go about getting help in the community, but that was clearly not what was significant about the event. Something really significant had happened between us, something that she valued and would carry away with her.

This was a paradigm case for Clare Hastings because it made her recognize the significance of understanding the lived experience of the illness. No one had ever *understood* what the illness meant to this woman before, and the understanding alone was a great gift, because it moved back the walls of isolation and suffering created by the disease.

# SECTION 2
# WHERE CARE TAKES PLACE

Although care is primarily a relationship between people – whether based on love, duty, obligation, service or paid labour – the nature of that relationship is inevitably influenced by the setting or environment in which it takes place. Debates about where care should take place mirror debates about the nature of the caring relationship. They are often polarized into informal or family care and the home, on the one hand, and state or formal services and institutions on the other.

'Home', the locus of the family, and to some extent the 'community', has often been viewed as a positive ideal, just as the idea of the 'institution' has been vilified. Institutional care with its roots in workhouse history still conjures up an image of large segregated settings, with austere and harsh regimes, where those without support and without means live out their lives. The Wagner Committee's review of residential care in the 1980s sought to underline the distinction between accommodation and care services, stressing that people should not have to change their residence in order to obtain services but that if they chose to do so they should sill have access to services within that community (NISW, 1988: 22–3).

Meeting such needs demands a wide range of settings in which care may be provided. It means that choice should exist. At present arguments in favour of adaptable housing or lifetime homes stand alongside residential alternatives such as sheltered housing, housing with care schemes, and small group homes. Some are seen to reinforce ideas of independent living whilst others offer residential living as a group. Diversity is beginning to emerge and yet still the worry remains: will the very existence of any form of group solution to the care needs of vulnerable people always mean that institutional care is only one step away? Do those who argue for alternatives do so from the security of their own family home? Or is that family home also a myth? After all, many of us experience a range of accommodation during our lives, so why not advocate residential living?

It is against this backdrop that the extracts featured in Section 2 of the reader should be viewed. The pieces chosen focus predominantly on institutional care and the development of residential services. They reflect a need to understand both the history of policy development and how places affect our lives. Without this understanding it becomes hard to develop alternatives. Parker's chapter is taken from the introduction to the review of research carried out for the Independent Review of Residential Care chaired by Lady Wagner in 1985. This overview provides us with an historical context. It demonstrates the way in which institutions have been used to control and segregate from society those deemed in some way deviant – the poor, the sick, the old – while at the same time acting as a deterrent. It also locates this history within its time, comparing living conditions within institutions with those of working-class people across the century. Whilst not condoning institutionalization it highlights some of the humane aspects of institutions and shows how care for the sick within hospitals became an acceptable aspect of institutional care.

Historical analysis tells us why institutions develop and persist, but we also need to understand what happens within them. One of the most influential writers in this area has been Erving Goffman, whose book *Asylums* presented a series of papers concerning the institutional process (Goffman, 1961). Here we use a summary of his work on 'total institutions' by Jones and Fowles to present his ideas. The influence of Goffman has been widespread and some would say his work has been misinterpreted. It has been used to support a view which blames the internal organization of institutions for the poor quality of life provided to some residents rather than looking at the wider structural issues (Baldwin et al., 1993). However, to understand how and where care takes place we need to explore the worlds of both policy and practice, societal and individual experience.

The importance of personal control in moving between places is central to the extract by Norman from her book *Rights and Risks*. Here the disruption of place is seen as a form of loss which can have devastating effects for those whose vulnerability leaves them without the ability to cope. The circumstances surrounding relocation can directly influence how well the individual adjusts to new surroundings and is able to maintain a sense of self. This adjustment may be compounded by their own understanding of their new environment. The work of Willcocks, Peace and Kellaher (Chapter 10) focuses on the physical environment of residential homes for older people. It makes the distinction between public and private space within homes and shows how issues of access, privacy and territory can influence the balance of power between residents and staff. Here environmental control is seen as one aspect of personal autonomy.

The extract from *Black Perspectives on Residential Care* summarizes the work of a sub-group of the Wagner Development Group set up in 1988 to take forward the recommendations of the Wagner Committee. All too often in the debate about institutional and residential care the views of minority ethnic groups have been ignored. Yet their experience has been different from that of the majority population – black children and black adults with mental health problems have higher rates of institutionalization, while older black people are less likely to live in residential settings. This extract presents us with an alternative view of residential care based on black-led projects. It makes some important statements about the experience of racism and how this can be used as a starting point for developing a holistic philosophy of care as well as exploring the relationship between residential living and community support. In looking at practical issues of caring in residential settings, it shows how people can live valued lives outside the domestic setting while remaining very much part of the black community. Perhaps there are lessons to learn here about the way in which community and care in the community have been defined.

Ideas about 'community' and the ways in which they have influenced debates about health and social care are the focus of Chapter 12, in which Mayo offers an overview of the many and various ways in which the concept of 'community' has been used, and is critical of attempts to shore up or reinstate inequalities under the guise of community initiatives.

Sheila Peace

## References

Baldwin, N., Harris, J. and Kelly, D. (1993) 'Institutionalization: why blame the institution?', *Ageing and Society*, 13(1): 69–81.

Goffman, E. (1961) *Asylums*. New York: Doubleday/Anchor.

NISW (1988) *Residential Care: a Positive Choice. Report of the Independent Review of Residential Care*. London: HMSO.

# 7

# The Persistent Image

*R. A. Parker*

The idea of institutional life has always been viewed with repugnance by a broad section of the population. This attitude has persisted despite many changes and improvements and although now it may be weakening, it nevertheless continues to be influential. Its survival has been assured by at least four forms of reinforcement: the deliberate cultivation of a repellent image; reported cases of the abuse of inmates; the enforced association and routine of institutional life, and the compulsion often associated with entry as well as with subsequent detention.

The management of destitution, and to a lesser extent madness and criminality, has dominated the history of institutions in this country. In this, the aim of the Poor Law was as much to affect the beliefs, attitudes and behaviour of working-class people generally as it was to discipline or provide for those who received its outdoor relief or entered its institutions. 'The poor law,' wrote Rose, 'was an ever-present symbol to the . . . poor of the fate to which their poverty might condemn them' (Rose, 1985: 3). The workhouse was at once the most visible and most impressive manifestation of that symbol. The similarities to the penal system are obvious. A common factor was the belief in the need for deterrence, not primarily aimed at those who were incarcerated but at the far greater number who were assumed to threaten to overwhelm the available resources or to disturb a precarious social order. However great the commitment to reformation and humane treatment, a regime fulfilling such deterrent purposes is constrained to preserve the evidence of severity, discipline and deprivation if it is both to be feared and supported by those outside (see Ignatieff, 1983).

Although the workhouse occupied such a central position in the history of the rise of the institution, comparatively few people passed through its doors. For example, in the peak year of 1871, after a prolonged period of economic depression, about a million people were getting poor relief in England and Wales: that was 4.6 per cent of the

From R.A. Parker (1988) 'An historical background', in Ian Sinclair (ed.), *Residential Care: the Research Reviewed*, London: HMSO. pp. 8–14.

population. Most of these recipients were being paid outdoor relief; only 150,000, or 0.6 per cent of the population, were in Poor Law institutions, a third of them children under 16 (Registrar-General, 1873: 13). If, as seems likely, this reflected the success of the workhouse as a deterrent, it also reflected the success of the Poor Law system as a whole in restricting the scale of its relief payments. The moralistic and inquisitorial manner in which relieving officers or the committees conducted their inquiries made any approach to the Poor Law a step to be avoided if at all possible. Uncertainty about the outcome of an application doubtless played its part as well. Given the laws of settlement (at least in England and Wales) recent arrivals in an area might well find that relief involved being returned to their union of settlement and, of course, it might also be linked with the offer of the House [i.e. the workhouse]. We do not know how many people, after having applied, refused to accept relief on these terms.

Thus fear and hatred of the workhouse have to be set within the context of Poor Law administration as a whole. Nonetheless, the workhouse represented the ultimate sanction. The fact that comparatively few people came to be admitted did not detract from the power of its negative image, an image that was sustained by the accounts that circulated about the harsh treatment and the separation of families that admission entailed. The success of 'less eligibility' in deterring the able-bodied and others from seeking relief relied heavily upon the currency of such images. Newspapers, songs and gossip, as well as orchestrated campaigns for the abolition or reform of the system, all lent support to the deliberate attempts that were made to ensure that entry to a workhouse was widely regarded as an awful fate.

Of course, the dread of the workhouse felt by the poor was not simply the product of hearsay and rumour or of exaggerated horrors. Well-documented accounts of ill-treatment, victimization, humiliation and appalling living conditions are to be found at all periods, even though views about what is excessive and intolerable have changed. Furthermore, what commissions and inquiries reported was certainly only a fraction of what was suffered in asylums, boarding schools, training ships and children's homes, as well as in workhouses and prisons. Such accounts stretch at least from the massive report produced by the committee that investigated the Andover Union and its scandals in 1846[1] to the series of inquiries into cruelty against patients in hospitals for the mentally handicapped that were conducted in the 1970s (for example DHSS, 1969). The extremes were never part of any deliberate policy; indeed, central authorities were at pains to advocate and legislate for fair and reasonable treatment. In their eyes the scandals that from time to time erupted were usually attributable to a combination of the inadequate nature of their power to control what happened locally; cruel or ignorant staff; or brutal, incompetent and weak leadership. They were seen as deplorable deviations caused by the perversity of human nature and therefore as departures from good practice that were difficult to prevent. What was less often acknowledged was that such incidents were also symptomatic of the contemporary rationales of institutions (of deterrence, punishment or reformation) or of the gap that existed between benign aims (like treatment or care) and the resources that were made available. Whether institutions were set up as cost-cutting initiatives (as were the workhouses, at least after 1834) or whether they were underfunded for the more elevated purposes that they were intended to serve, the common result was an unwillingness or inability to appoint and train sufficient staff of the right calibre.

Whether or not the reality of life in an institution accorded wholly with its popular image, what was certain was that it entailed associating with strangers in intimate surroundings and worse, the probability of thereby becoming a member of a stigmatized group. Townsend captured the essence of the first element when he described what he considered to be an inherent disadvantage of residential homes for old people.

> Individuals from diverse localities and backgrounds are brought together under one roof and are expected to share most of the events of daily life. Staff are employed and a common routine is established. The resulting 'community' is in many ways an artificial one because it does not consist of people . . . who are linked by a network of family, occupational and neighbour ties and whose relationships are reinforced by the reciprocation of services. (Townsend, 1962: 435)

Half a century before, Charles Booth had stated his belief 'that the respectable aged were deterred from entering the workhouse because they might be herded with disreputable characters' (quoted in Crowther 1981: 84). Despite the desire on the part of many administrators to separate the deserving from the undeserving and the reputable from the disreputable, the reality of institutional life has been one of enforced and uncertain association. Choice of associates has been limited and escape from the disruptive, distressing or frightening behaviour of other people well-nigh impossible.

Furthermore, the separation, often at moments of crisis, from those who were most cherished and best known was always painful, not least because it left the new inmate without established support or dependable allies. The prospect of entry to a residential establishment touches a deep-seated fear of being inescapably cast alone and defenceless amongst strangers, especially strangers whose codes are unknown but assumed to be disturbingly different from one's own. Such a basic social and psychological component of human fearfulness has played its part in sustaining the widespread negative image of institutions; but when many of the strangers who lived in them were believed to be, and indeed frequently were, members of some of the most stigmatized groups in society the fear of association took on an added dimension.

The distinction repeatedly drawn between the deserving and the undeserving in both official and charitable quarters was undoubtedly also made by members of the working class. The Royal Commission on the Aged Poor in 1895 concluded that although there was a widespread dislike among the poor of entering the workhouse they nonetheless regarded it as suitable for wastrels and ne'er-do-wells and, indeed, as much better than they deserved (*Report*, 1895: para. 97, p. xxxi). Strong conventions existed to ensure the retention of an identity distinctively separate from the 'rough' or under-class. For many working-class people admission to a workhouse (or even the need to apply for out-door relief) threatened the painstakingly constructed and carefully maintained differentiation from that level. Perhaps the most significant achievement of the Poor Law was to have provided and confirmed the lowest stratum of the many that existed within the working class. As Roberts recalls in his personal account of life in a Salford slum during the first quarter of this century: 'the workhouse paupers hardly registered as human beings at all' (Roberts, 1971: 8). They were at the bottom of a carefully graded heap and provided the means by which others, however lowly, could elevate their status. Thus, it was not simply a fear of associating with strangers that created the widespread aversion to institutions but also the fear that entry would result in a loss of status and self-respect as one became reclassified by association. This was an important weapon in the armoury of deterrence clearly revealed in the reaction of the 1895 commissioners to the proposal, made by a number of their witnesses, that in order to protect the aged but respectable poor from having to mix with objectionable people almshouses should be provided instead (*Report*, 1895: para. 128, p. xxxviii). This was considered to be unwise since it would discourage individuals from making adequate provision for their old age as well as weaken the resolve of sons and daughters to provide for their aged parents in their own homes.

Echoes of concerns about disagreeable associations are still to be heard today, albeit in the modified forms of the distaste that the elderly express for having to live alongside those who are mentally infirm; in what children in care say about being assumed to have been 'in trouble' if they live in a children's home, and in the way in which many parents of mentally handicapped children react to their off-spring being placed residentially with those whose handicaps are obviously more severe.[2] The issues of classification, the debasement of status and stigma by association have all been enduring themes in the history of institutional provision. The fact that proportionately few people have entered residential care has made it that much more likely that those who do (or who have to stay) come to be regarded – and regard themselves – as a defeated and outcast group.

The negative image of institutions has undoubtedly been reinforced by the processes of legal compulsion that have preceded much admission. Until 1930 the doors of public institutions for the treatment of the mentally disordered were closed to all but people certified as 'a lunatic, an idiot or a person of unsound mind' and ordered to be detained for care and treatment by a judicial authority. Such a requirement imposed a stigma additional to any that was associated with being in an asylum. Not only was admission dependent upon certification, but the order for commitment carried with it the prospect of its irrevocability. Decertification and release were not easily obtained. Under these circumstances it is understandable that admission was frequently deferred for as long as possible. As a result, patients were liable to arrive on the wards in particularly distressed states and without the benefit of any earlier intervention that might have mitigated their condition. Visitors to the asylums therefore saw patients in states of crisis as well as many others suffering from the adverse effects of their long residence. Moreover, many mentally handicapped people were certified and admitted alongside the mentally ill (for a general review and account of these issues see *Report*, 1926: 15–30). All these things tended to reinforce prevailing stereotypes about the uniform character of madness. Indeed, the lack of understanding of the difference between mental illness and mental handicap was superimposed upon the widespread popular assumption that mental afflictions were hereditary in nature. This made the act of certification an additionally distressing event. Relatives were upset by the public confirmation of mental weakness in the family and could feel stigmatized by their membership. In that sense certification was often experienced as a matter of family shame.

Over and above this, in the great majority of cases, certification also led to the stigma of pauperism. Unless the certified person could pay, or be paid for, as a private patient, the costs of confinement and treatment had to be borne by the Poor Law up until 1930. Many inmates therefore became certified paupers as well as certified lunatics. For many families this would have been their first encounter with the Poor Law, although there was also a steady stream of entrants to the asylums who were already in receipt of outdoor relief or who came from the workhouses. Indeed, certification as a means of establishing eligibility for admission to an asylum (renamed mental hospitals after 1930) at public expense was 'equivalent to the order for the admission of a pauper to a workhouse, and to the order and medical certificate which were required until . . . 1948 for the admission of any patient, except in an emergency, to a poor law hospital' (*Report*, 1957: 62–3). Where it differed was that it was also an authority for the detention of the patient, whether in an asylum, workhouse or elsewhere. Even though it was possible for patients to enter a mental hospital on a voluntary basis after 1930, this relaxation did not extend to the so-called mentally defective. From 1913 until the reforms of 1957 nobody could be admitted to a public mental deficiency institution without certification and the parallel authority for confinement (for discussion and details see Board of Control, 1929: Part 1).

The statistics assembled by the Royal Commission on the Law Relating to Mental Illness and Mental Deficiency (1954–7) show how extensive the elements of compulsion and detention remained in spite of the growing use of voluntary admission to mental hospitals. Although only 18 per cent of patients received into mental hospitals in 1955 were certified, about 70 per cent of all patients in hospital at the end of the year fell into that category. This was because many of them had been there a long time but also because, being detained, this population accumulated. Thus, there were some 105,000 certified patients in mental hospitals in England and Wales in 1955. Added to these were a further 58,000 in mental deficiency hospitals, making a total of 163,000 certified and detained patients – more than double the number at the turn of the century (*Report*, 1957: 318). Although the 1959 Mental Health Act eliminated the traditional use of certification, the long-term certified patients from the earlier period remained in the hospitals for some time and arrangements were continued for compulsory admission and detention under certain circumstances.

Compulsion combined with detention was not the only disquieting aspect of admission to an institution. By the end of the nineteenth century there were various laws that enabled authorities to detain those who had originally been admitted to institutions on a voluntary basis. This had been a long-standing option for boards of guardians. For example, where families were admitted to the workhouse parents could not discharge themselves unless they took their children with them and guardians could seek to have inmates certified and thus reallocated to a detained class. Moreover, in the late nineteenth century several measures were introduced that enabled organizations to detain children (who were mostly in their institutions) against the wishes of their parents. In 1889 boards of guardians were enabled by administrative procedures to assume parental rights and duties over children in their care until they were 16.[3] There was other legislation of a similar kind. Under the Custody of Children Act, 1891 not only guardians but any person or institution could acquire custody of a child in place of the parents if they had been looking after that child at their expense and the parents could not reimburse them. This was largely the outcome of intensive pressure by Barnardo but it enabled any voluntary children's society to prevent children being returned to poor parents who were not considered to be fit persons. In the same year the Reformatory and Industrial Schools Act also made it more difficult for parents to have their children back after the term of their detention had expired. Managers, under certain provisions, could override parental wishes about what should happen to a boy or girl upon discharge. This was considered to be especially valuable in arranging their emigration or employment well away from detrimental parental influences. (For further discussion of some of these issues see Parker, 1986.)

These are but examples: the important point is that there were circumstances in which admission to an institution on a voluntary basis could lead to compulsory detention which might also be accompanied by transfer to a different regime. Few people would understand the legal niceties but many would be aware that simply being in an institution could lead to steps being taken to prevent you leaving. It is difficult to assess, at different times, the full extent of compulsion and detention as correlates of institutional life; but it has been considerable. If, for example, one takes the figures in the 1931 Census, then of all the recorded inmate population (including those in prisons and hospitals but not in boarding schools) about 45 per cent would have been subject to compulsory detention (estimated from Registrar-General, 1934: 118. Table 16). Although that proportion had probably fallen to some 10 per cent by the time of the 1981 Census (mainly as a result of the abandonment of certification and an ageing population) the idea of residential establishments as places where people are confined against their will lingers on; not least, perhaps, because in practice many residents have little or no alternative. Legal compulsion may have been replaced, especially amongst the aged, by the compulsion of their circumstances. The historical association of commitment to an institution with being either mad or bad dies hard and has certainly contributed to the unfavourable view of residential provision. How could it be otherwise if one needed to be compelled to enter and stopped from leaving?

## Notes

1  *Report* (1846). See also Anstruther (1973) for a discussion of the role of *The Times* in using the official report to further the campaign against the Poor Law.
2  Page and Clark (1977). Another child in care explains that 'when you go to a new place before you've got your foot in the door they say "hey, what are you in for?"' . . . they come to me and said "what you done wrong?" Because, you know they look upon it [a children's home] as a detention centre.'
3  This provision continues to the present day in the form of Section 3 of the Childcare Act 1980.

## References

Anstruther, I. (1973) *The Scandal of the Andover Workhouse*. London: Bles.

Board of Control (1929) *Report of the Mental Deficiency Committee*. London: HMSO.

Crowther, M.A. (1981) *The Workhouse System, 1834–1929: the History of an English Social Institution*. London: Methuen.

Department of Health and Social Security (1969) *Report of the Committee of Inquiry into Allegations of Ill Treatment of Patients and Other Irregularities at the Ely Hospital, Cardiff.* CMND. 3975. London: HMSO.

Department of Health and Social Security (1971) *Report of the Farleigh Hospital Committee of Inquiry.* CMND 4557. London: HMSO.

Ignatieff, M. (1983) 'Total institutions and working classes: a review essay', *History Workshop Journal*, 15.

Page, R. and Clark, G.A. (1977) *Who Cares? Young People in Care Speak Out.* London: National Children's Bureau.

Parker, R.A. (1986) 'Childcare: the roots of a dilemma', *Political Quarterly*, 57(3).

Registrar-General (1873) *Digest of the English Census of 1871.* London.

Registrar-General (1934) *General Report of the Census, 1931.* London: HMSO.

*The Report of the Select Committee on the Andover Union* (1846) HC663Iii. London: HMSO.

*Report of the Royal Commission on the Aged Poor* (1895) Vol. 1, c. 7684. London: HMSO.

*Report of the Royal Commission on Lunacy and Mental Disorder* (1926) CMND 2700. London: HMSO.

*Report of the Royal Commission on the Law Relating to Mental Illness and Mental Deficiency, 1954–57* (1957) CMND. 169. London: HMSO.

Roberts, R. (1971) *The Classic Slum: Salford Life in the First Quarter of the Century.* Manchester: Manchester University Press.

Rose, M.E. (ed.) (1985) *The Poor and the City: the English Poor Law in its Urban Context, 1834–1914.* Leicester: Leicester University Press.

Townsend, P. (1962) *The Last Refuge: a Survey of Residential Institutions and Homes for the Aged in England and Wales.* London: Routledge & Kegan Paul.

# 8

# Total Institutions

## K. Jones and A. J. Fowles

[Erving] Goffman introduced the term 'total institution' and defined it more carefully than many of his imitators have done. A 'total institution' is 'a place of residence and work where a large number of like-situated individuals, cut off from the wider society for an appreciable period of time, together lead an enclosed, formally administered round of life' (Goffman, 1961: xiii).

Not all institutions are total institutions, though 'every institution has encompassing tendencies'; but some institutions, such as homes for the blind or the aged, mental hospitals, prisons, concentration camps, army barracks, boarding schools and monasteries or convents, are 'encompassing to a degree discontinuously greater than the ones next in line'.

Goffman's concept of the 'total institution' can be represented as follows: there is a continuum from open to closed institutions, but there is a break towards the closed end, separating off a group of closed, or nearly closed, institutions which can be described as 'total'.

In fact, both the completely open institution and the completely closed institution are abstractions. No institution is ever completely open: if it were, it would have no distinguishing characteristics at all. No institution is ever completely closed. If it were, it would die off. Open systems theory has taught us that all human systems are dependent to some extent on their immediate environment, and that they cannot survive without it. A mental hospital or prison imports staff, inmates, policy, material supplies and public reactions from the outside world; it exports staff on completion of contract, inmates on completion of stay or sentence, empirical material which may affect policy, the product of work programmes (mailbags, assembled electric switches, carpentry, scrubbing brushes, fancy paper hats, those curious toys which are made in occupational therapy, and so on), garbage, and stories of strike, threat and crisis which form the basis of public reactions. All sorts of people cross the boundary: inspectors, professional superiors, inmates' visitors, research workers, workmen,

From K. Jones and A.J. Fowles (1984) 'Goffman: the radical', in *Ideas on Institutions*. London: Routledge & Kegan Paul. pp. 12–16.

students, policemen, magistrates and others. But these considerations do not invalidate Goffman's argument about the relatively closed or 'total' institution. His contention is that this group of institutions has features in common: he qualifies it by adding that none of these features is specific to them, and that not all of the features may be found in any one of them. What he proposes is not a list of features to be identified in all cases, but a constellation of features which tend to occur in most cases, and which have some relation to each other. He is embarking on a sort of verbal cluster analysis. What he describes as a 'total institution' will probably not fit any real-life institution exactly. It is a Weberian ideal type against which the practices of real-life institutions may be measured.

It is important to clarify this definition, because the term 'total institution' has become something of a catch-phrase, and is often applied unthinkingly to particular prisons or mental hospitals. Goffman is much more scholarly than some of his imitators, and his frame of reference is precisely defined.

'Total institutions' have four main characteristics: batch living, binary management, the inmate role, and the institutional perspective.

'Batch living' describes a situation where 'each phase of the member's daily activity is carried on in the immediate company of a large batch of others, all of whom are treated alike, and required to do the same thing together'. It is the antithesis of individual living, where there are large areas of life which may be pursued on a basis of personal choice. It is characterized by a bureaucratic form of management, a system of formal rules and regulations, and a tight schedule which allows little or no free time. It allows the inmate no freedom of movement between different social groups, and no choice of companions: he lives with the same group of people, elected and defined by outside authority, 24 hours a day, without variety or respite. This is contrasted with 'a basic arrangement in modern society. . . . the individual tends to sleep, play and work in different places, with different co-participants, under different authorities, and without an overall rational plan' (Goffman, 1961: 5–6). In the institutional situation, individuals are not merely constrained by, but are violently attacked by, the system. They live under surveillance, and any infraction of the rules 'is likely to stand out in relief against the visible, constantly examined compliance of the others'.

Goffman is not clear which came first, the 'large blocks of managed people' or the staff who manage them; but 'each is made for the other'. 'Total institutions' typically consist of these two groups of people, the managers and the managed – staff and patients, prison officers and prisoners, teachers and pupils.

This is 'binary management': 'Two different social and cultural worlds develop, jogging alongside each other with points of official contact, but little mutual penetration' (ibid.: 9). The managers have power, and social distance is their weapon. They exercise this most tellingly in withholding information, so that the managed exist in 'blind dependency', unable to control their own destinies. The very fact of being an inmate is degrading: 'Staff tend to feel superior, and righteous. Inmates tend . . . to feel inferior, weak, unworthy and guilty' (ibid.: 7). Because the two groups do not and cannot know each other as individuals, they set up antagonistic stereotypes. Staff tend to see all patients or prisoners or pupils as being alike – 'bitter, secretive and untrustworthy'. The managed draw similar hostile pictures of the managers. The two groups may use a special tone of voice in talking to each other, and informal conversation and social mixing may be frowned upon by both sides.

How do ordinary people, with their own way of life and personal networks and round of activities, become inmates? Goffman thinks that this is not a process of 'acculturation', which involves moving from one culture to another, but of 'disculturation' or 'role-stripping' so powerful that the individual who is subjected to it may be rendered incapable of normal living when he returns to the community. He has been reduced from a person with many roles to a cypher with one: the 'inmate role'.

Much of this process is achieved through admission procedures, which Goffman sees as 'a series of abasements, degradations, humiliations and profanations of self' – a mortification process. Institutions are 'the forcing houses for changing persons'. To become an inmate involves a total break with the past, symbolized by the acquisition of a new name or number, uniform clothing, and the restriction or confiscation of personal possessions. All this may be done in a highly ritualized admission procedure in which the inmate may be forced to recite his life history, take a bath, possibly without privacy, and submit to weighing, fingerprinting, intrusive medical examination and head-shaving. The overt reason for these activities is administrative necessity: the real purpose is role dispossession. The bath, in particular, is a highly symbolic ritual, involving physical nakedness as the midpoint of a process of abandoning one life for another. 'The new arrival allows himself to be shaped and coded into an object that can be fed into the administrative machinery of the establishment, to be worked on smoothly by routine operation' (ibid.: 16). The new clothes are likely to be standard issue, the property of the establishment. Combined with a loss of 'personal maintenance equipment' such as combs, shaving sets or cosmetics, they create a new and humiliating appearance. The process is one of personal defacement.

As the stay is prolonged, so the loss of personal identity becomes more marked. There may be systematic violation of privacy through the practice of group or individual confession. The inmate's defences may be repeatedly collapsed by a process called 'looping' where the mere fact of defence is taken as proof of guilt (ibid.: 35–7). There may be 'indignities of speech or action' – inmates are forced to beg humbly for a glass of water or a light for a cigarette, to move or speak in a markedly deferential way indicating their lowly status. They may be beaten, or subjected to electric shock treatment, or physically contaminated – there are some particularly nasty examples drawn from concentration camps and political prisons.

Control may be kept by means of a system of rewards and punishments, petty by outside standards, but assuming Pavlovian dimensions in a situation of deprivation. Rules may not be made fully explicit. The inmate cannot appeal to them for protection, and may break them unwittingly, and be punished for it. Like Kafka's K., he exists in a half-world of guilt and apprehension. He has no privacy, no rights, and no dignity.

How does the inmate survive these attacks on his personality? Goffman suggests four types of 'secondary adjustment' (ibid.: 61–4):

1   The inmate may withdraw, cutting himself off from contact.
2   He may become intransigent, and fight the system.
3   He may, in a vivid phrase, become 'colonised', paying lip-service to the system like the inhabitant of some African or Asian country awaiting the day of independence.
4   He may become converted, genuinely accepting the institution's view of himself, and what is acceptable behaviour.

The last of these is not really survival, but a kind of personal extinction. Curiously, and on the face of it illogically, it is the only adjustment acceptable to the authorities of the institution. Any attempt by the inmate to immunize himself against the destructive forces focused on him will be seen as non-co-operation, and may be used as an excuse to detain him longer.

He may develop a 'line', a sort of edited account of how he came to be an inmate, repeated to his fellows and to anyone else who will listen with increasing self-pity. He may have a sense of 'dead and heavy-hanging time' – of life wasted, and the months or years ticking away without gain or satisfaction. Against these reactions, the authorities offer 'the institutional perspective': a view of life which denies his individual perspective and validates the institution's existence. It is promoted by such means as the house magazine, the annual party, the institutional theatrical, the open day and the sports day, which create an artificial sense of community. These formal events offer certain minor possibilities of role release for the inmate – recognized and routinized liberties, forbidden in normal circumstances, may be allowable; but the total effect is to reinforce the power of the institution, and the 'assault on the self': 'These ceremonial practices are well suited to a Durkheimian analysis: a society dangerously split into inmates and staff can through these ceremonies hold itself together' (ibid.: 109).

## Reference

Goffman, E. (1961) *Asylums*. New York: Doubleday/Anchor.

# 9

# Losing Your Home

## A. Norman

It is not sufficiently realized that the loss of one's home – however good the reasons for leaving it – can be experienced as a form of bereavement and can produce the same grief reaction as the loss of a close relative. Peter Marris in his book *Loss and Change* (1974) quotes a study of the reactions of families moved from the West End of Boston under an urban renewal scheme in which it was concluded that:

> for the majority it seems quite precise to speak of their reactions as expressions of *grief*. These are manifest in the feelings of painful loss, the continued longing, the general depressive tone, frequent symptoms of psychological or social or somatic distress, the active work required in adapting to the altered situation, the sense of helplessness, the occasional expressions of both direct and displaced anger, and the tendencies to idealise the lost place. At their most extreme, these reactions of grief are intense, deeply felt and, at times, overwhelming.
>
> Altogether about half the 250 women and 316 men studied said they had been severely depressed or disturbed for a while, and another quarter had been more mildly upset. A quarter of the women were still very depressed two years after they had moved, while a fifth had taken over six months to recover their spirits. The unhappiest exiles described their loss in similar phrases to the bereaved: 'I felt as though I had lost everything.' 'It was like a piece being taken from me.' 'Something of me went with the West End.'

Similar reactions were described by Young and Wilmott (1957) when they studied families moved from the East End of London to a suburban housing estate and by Marris in a study of slum clearance in Lagos, where residents complained bitterly 'it seemed like being taken from happiness to misery', 'I fear it like death'. Marris suggests that, like bereavement, a change of home should be understood as a potential disruption of the meaning of life. Those for whom a move represents the realization of a social status and way of life with which they already identify will be able to work through the loss and re-create what they valued in their former neighbourhood. 'But,' he says:

> for some, it may be a profound disturbance from which they never recover. And such tragedies are, I believe, more likely, the more slum clearance is

From A. Norman (1980) *Rights and Risk*. London: Centre for Policy on Ageing. pp. 14–19.

used as an instrument of social change, not merely physical development; and the more it is directed against groups in society, whose non-conformity with the ruling values seems to stand in the way of progress. (Marris, 1974)

Old people who are moved into sheltered housing or residential care may or may not be moved from slum conditions, but the sense of loss must surely be equally great for them. Indeed it may be greater if, in the process, they have to sacrifice not only a home and neighbourhood but the greater part of the possessions of a lifetime. It must also be true that they are likely to work through the loss only if they make a positive identification with their new life. If they are being moved in conformity with ruling social values which are offended by letting them stay where they are, or are forced to go by the physical duress of having no viable alternative, they are still less likely to recover from the loss.

A good deal of research data, much of it American, supports such a conclusion, and it is clear that the loss of a home may be particularly serious for those who are mentally impaired, physically ill, or depressed and thus unable to make a positive effort to identify with the new life. Gutman and Herbert in 1976 quoted 13 studies which showed that the death rate of elderly persons was unusually high during the first year after 'relocation' and particularly during the first three months. This was so regardless of whether the movement was from the community into a mental institution, from one institution to another, from one ward to another within the same institution, or from old to new facilities. (The same researchers showed from their own study however, that this effect does not obtain when the community moves *en bloc* to a new building with improved facilities and every effort is made to prepare patients and relatives for the move well in advance, to keep friends together in their new quarters and to transfer staff as well as patients.)

M.A. Lieberman, in an important paper on relocation and social policy described four studies which he had made: 'one on healthy moving into affluent high-care, sophisticated institutions; others involving sick, highly debilitated human beings moving into circumstances that would delight a muckraker' (Lieberman, 1974). These 'have yielded roughly comparable findings. Namely, no matter what the condition of the individual, the nature of the environment or the degree of sophisticated preparation, relocation entails a higher than acceptable risk to the large majority of those being moved.' Given that relocation may sometimes be inevitable, Lieberman goes on to ask what steps can be taken to minimize the risk but cannot suggest a solution. He concludes that careful preparation and 'working through' of the transitional process and impending loss, important though it may be in relieving human misery, is not a powerful tool in minimizing relocation risk. 'The reason,' he says, is not poor practice but rather incorrect strategy. Relocation is a risk to the individual not because of the symbolic meaning that such transitions imply, but because it entails radical changes in the life space of an individual that require new learning for adaptive purposes. Over and over again, studies on relocation report findings that physical status, cognitive ability and certain other characteristics of personality are powerful predictors to the outcome of relocation.

In other words, those who need institutional support the *least* are those who are most likely to survive the move into it, and 'it is often the very people who require supportive services that can be shown to entail the greatest risk'. (He adds that this is another illustration of how the results of empirical research often fail to help with the nitty-gritty of policy issues.)

A study of fatal home accidents made by the Tavistock Institute of Human Relations on behalf of the Department of Prices and Consumer Protection also suggests that old people are not necessarily safer when they are 'in care'. The authors found that out of 133 fatal accidents studied in the '65 and over' age group (75 per cent caused by falls) 35 per cent were in institutional care, although only 4.8 per cent of this age group live in institutions. They comment: 'Even considering that residential institutions contain a higher proportion of the infirm, the difference in accidental deaths is high' (Poyner and Hughes, 1978).

It would seem to follow from all this, that if avoidance of 'risk' is indeed a prime objective, moving people out of their homes may not be the best way of achieving it, and that the more they appear to be at risk where they are, the worse will be their prognosis if they are moved. Yet this is a factor which is seldom taken into consideration when considering transfer into residential care, and still less is it taken into consideration when deciding on hospital admission.

Elderly people, like members of any other age group, are of course often admitted to hospital for surgery or investigation which could not be provided in their own home; and they may benefit greatly from such treatment. (For example, a study of 248 patients over 80 admitted as emergencies to acute surgical wards of the Reading hospitals in 1976 showed that the overall mortality rate was 21.8 per cent and it fell to 12.5 per cent if terminal disease was excluded. All but seven patients were discharged home: Salem et al., 1978.) However, there is another large group of elderly people who become patients not so much because their condition demands full-scale hospital treatment as because there is a crisis in their system of social support. The social crisis then has a medical label attached to it in order to make the admission acceptable to the hospital. For example, if an elderly person develops pneumonia and the spouse finds the anxiety of nursing at home too much to bear, an admission will probably be arranged, but the diagnosis is pneumonia, not 'anxiety in spouse'. Very often the admission may be occasioned by some incident or accident which proves to be the last straw on an already overstrained support system, or because there is no time to arrange for the domiciliary services required by a change in circumstances (such as the caring relative becoming sick). Or, if an elderly person presents at an Accident and Emergency department of a hospital after, say, a fall in the street, a harassed houseman may 'play safe' and keep the person in for 'investigation' just to make sure no damage has been done.

The problem is that it is much easier for an elderly person to become a hospital patient than to cease to be one. There are a number of reasons for this. The 'social space' in which the person has been living may close behind him on admission, so that he cannot get back. A family may heave a sigh of relief, having realized, perhaps for the first time, what a burden it has been carrying and say, 'He's not coming back here.' A landlord may take the opportunity to repossess his house, or the warden of a sheltered housing complex say, 'He needs too much nursing now, I can't cope.' Ironically, it is often the person who would appear to be most at risk, who lives alone in his own home, who is in least danger of having his social space close up on him.

It is also often the case that if a person has only just been coping with independent life, hospital admission breaks a tenuous level of confidence which can only be restored with time, care and skill. Elderly people who are suffering from some degree of dementia are specially at risk because the experience of admission to a totally strange and unfamiliar environment is likely to increase confusion and generate problems such as falling and incontinence which may not have been present before.

Another possibility is that hospital 'investigation' may show up undiagnosed diseases which a person has been living with for years, but which, once diagnosed, the hospital may feel compelled to treat. Observation after a fall may then become treatment for something quite different, so that the person is confirmed in his patient status. Moreover, if the person is being treated in an acute ward, the nursing staff may not have the time, interest or training to help the patient to retain independence and mobility, and even a few days of inactivity may produce disuse atrophy which involves not only loss of muscle power but also loss of the range of movement normally possessed by a joint. Simple skills required for daily living such as combing one's hair, fastening a button or rising from a chair may then be lost. (It has been shown that even the muscle disuse occurring during normal sleep leads to significant weakness on waking: Browne, 1978.) A period of treatment in an acute ward may therefore mean that an elderly person requires a prolonged period of rehabilitation in a geriatric ward before he can recover his skills sufficiently to manage at home again – and the longer the period in hospital, the more likely it is that the 'social space' at home will have closed up.

For all these reasons, hospital admission – which can undoubtedly be 'life saving' – may also be dangerous to elderly people, and the dangers need to be weighed against the advantages when deciding whether or not to admit someone to hospital.

## References

Browne, B. (1978) 'Inactivity in the elderly', *Health and Social Service Journal*, 88(4575), 10 January.

Gutman, G.M. and Herbert, C.P. (1976) 'Mortality rates among relocated extended care patients', *Journal of Gerontology*, 31(3): 352–7.

Lieberman, M.A. (1974) 'Symposium – long term care: research, policy and practice', *The Gerontologist*, 4(6).

Marris, P. (1974) *Loss and Change*. London: Institute of Community Studies/Routledge & Kegan Paul.

Poyner, B. and Hughes, M. (1978) *A Classification of Fatal Home Accidents*. (Report to the Department of Prices and Consumer Protection, 2T140). London: Tavistock Institute of Human Relations.

Salem, R. et al. (1978) 'Emergency geriatric surgical admission', *British Medical Journal*, 2: 416–7.

Young, M. and Willmott, P. (1957) *Family and Kinship in East London*. London: Routledge & Kegan Paul.

# 10

# The Physical World

*D. Willcocks, S. Peace and L. Kellaher*

Our understanding of the lives of both residents and staff in old
people's homes would be incomplete if it was not set in context. The
environment therefore becomes a crucial factor in our analysis and in
this chapter we focus on the impact of built form, on the lives of those
who use residential buildings, and on their relationship with the
wider community. [. . .]

## Internal spatial arrangements

It is common to describe the internal spatial arrangements of domestic
buildings in terms of public and private space (Rapoport, 1982;
Lawrence, 1982) and our detailed observations within four homes
confirmed the importance of these divisions within the residential
setting. Public space includes lounges, dining rooms, halls, and circulation spaces. Private spaces consist of bedrooms, bathrooms, and
WCs. It is true that in public spaces such as lounges, certain strategies
may be employed by residents to ensure a degree of privacy, and the
private spaces, such as bedrooms and bathrooms, can become relatively public. However, the public/private distinctions of space –
which follow traditional patterns and expectations of congregation
and segregation – did persist in most homes.

Although the public and private spatial distinction could be applied
to all residential homes, the distribution, and hence the integration of
such areas varied with the size, complexity and age of the building. An
examination of the amount and variety of space provided for each
resident shows that since the 1970s there has been a considerable
increase in the amount of private space provided, notably private
single bedrooms. But this has not been at the expense of public space,
which has also increased, though less dramatically. An example of an
integrated spatial arrangement can best be seen in the group living
model where bedroom and lounge-dining areas are intermixed,

From D. Willcocks, S. Peace and L. Kellaher (1987) *Private Lives in Public Places.*
London: Routledge & Kegan Paul. pp. 77–99 (abridged).

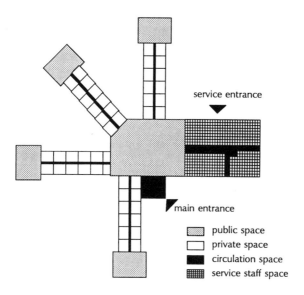

Figure 10.1 *Very integrated homes – where bedrooms, bathrooms, and WCs are sited close to lounges and dining areas.*

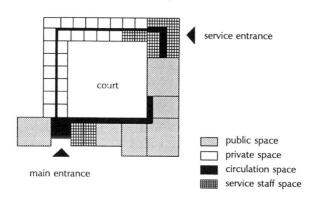

Figure 10.2 *Very separate homes – where clusters of lounges often adjacent to the dining room are some distance from the bedroom/bath block.*

whereas adapted property, with a modern extension accommodating a bedroom wing, may be said to be segregated in so far as the public and private spaces are quite separate (Figures 10.1 and 10.2). Several authors have commented on the importance of internal scale in facilitating resident behaviour. Lawton (1970) comments that activities of daily living are more easily maintained if toilets, bathrooms and dining facilities are situated close to sitting areas and Rosow has suggested that the proximity of residents' rooms is an

important determinant in friendship formation (1967). However, it can
be shown that the spatial proximity and functional centrality of areas
within the building are only one influence on social integration.
   [. . .]


## Privacy

The analogy of the domestic home as compared with residential care
reveals the different levels of privacy associated with each setting.
Given the experience of old people within their own homes, the
maintenance of privacy, as defined within our culture, may have an
important influence on resident well-being. We can define various
levels of privacy ranging from the complete separation of solitude to
the anonymity of being within a group and yet apart from it (Westin,
1967). While certain kinds of privacy obviously do not pertain within
domestic settings, in a residential home different modes of privacy
become more important, thus illustrating the dissimilarity of the two
environments.

   Within this context, solitude implies that the individual can be
separate from the group and unobserved by others. This entails seclusion within a personal space. Yet we have noted that only half of all
the residents in the hundred homes [in the study carried out by the
authors] had a bedroom of their own. The others shared, mainly with
one or two others, but in a few cases with as many as seven. Opportunities for solitude may, therefore, be limited and even those with a
room of their own may be prevented from experiencing privacy. Only
eight of the homes had bedrooms that were lockable, and in only two
were residents allowed to lock their rooms from the inside. We can
argue that space which is not defensible undermines the sense of
ownership which residents may wish to attach to their rooms; without
such control this private space becomes common territory.

   Within the broad concept of privacy, intimacy entails the needs of
people who are close, such as family or friends, to get together in
seclusion to talk, share activities, express their sexuality, or just be
together. These are important aspects of life which do not translate
well to institutional settings. The quality of visiting may be affected
by the kind of privacy available for such meetings. While nearly half
of the residents used their own rooms for such visits, many were
forced to use public spaces such as lounges and hallways. Thirty-eight
of the homes in the study had a visitors' room but in many cases these
rooms were under-used, being rather formal places which deterred
intimate conversation.

   In contrast to the desire to be with chosen others, the need to be
anonymous in a public setting represents a facet of personal privacy.
Within our own homes the living room or sitting room becomes public

space in that people from outside are admitted. However, it is not usually a place in which we expect to feel anonymous. Yet, in the lounge of an old people's home, anonymity may take on a new meaning. The sedentary and passive nature of residential life often provokes comment from practitioners, especially on the arrangement of chairs in lounges and the tendency for residents to occupy particular chairs. Unlike the resident's bedroom, the chair in the lounge may become defensible space, and it is common to see chairs adorned with blankets and cushions, defended by the owner's zimmer frame.

In most of the lounges in the hundred homes, chairs were positioned around the walls or in rows, rather than in arrangements thought to be conducive to social interaction. Whether chair arrangements should be changed in order to encourage interaction or whether residents prefer the present arrangement has been the subject of much debate (Lipman, 1967). In the present study residents and staff voiced differences: staff preferred the arrangement which appears less institutional but residents preferred chairs placed around the walls or in rows facing the television set. It can be argued that, at a purely practical level, the latter choice supports the need to have spacious access to and from lounges for elderly people who may need to use walking aids. However, it also has to be acknowledged that this arrangement allows residents to avoid prolonged social interaction and to withdraw to relative anonymity. There is, after all, no reason why residents – generally strangers to each other – should wish to engage in continuous interaction, especially when they may be sitting in the same seats for up to eight hours a day. If this period were not so long then interaction might be more acceptable. The 'backs to the wall' strategy may be construed as a retreat position, and the somewhat uninterested focusing upon the television as a further strategy for avoiding eye contact with other residents.

## Autonomy

The degree to which residents determine their own lifestyle within the residential home will vary with individual personality and as a result of the constraints placed upon people by the organizational style of the home. The physical environment may be thought of as secondary, although it is possible to identify situations where the physical environment either facilitates or hinders resident autonomy. Moreover, we can argue that an institutional environment which is resource-rich has the potential for enhancing resident autonomy through environmental control. In this respect the importance of having a single bedroom is brought into focus. While the single bedroom offers the resident the potential for privacy, it also offers the potential for an expression of self-identity in the form of personal territory or as a power base from which the resident may engage in some form of exchange relationship with staff. This relationship contains a number of factors, not least the expectations of residents and staff concerning the functions of care.

The concept of the bedsitting room was more generally understood by residents who had a single room rather than a shared room, and there was, not surprisingly, a significant association between residents who brought to the home items such as televisions, radios and furniture and their labelling of rooms as bedsitters, thus confirming the relationship between personalization and the more varied use of bedroom space. Personalization was most common in single rooms that were slightly larger than the average 10 square metres. Many single rooms revealed a remarkable design ingenuity in that the basic trappings of daily life were represented within a small space. At the same time the token nature of such efforts was obvious, given the restrictions posed by fitted furniture – most frequently a washbasin and a wardrobe.

Control of the immediate environment was also something to which residents attached considerable importance. [. . .] Over two-thirds of respondents signalled the importance of the following items: openable windows, easily opened doors, storage space, good sound insulation between rooms, and a power point in the bedroom. In 78 of the homes residents were said by staff to be able to open their bedroom windows. In 68 homes all rooms had at least one electric socket and in 64 homes residents could regulate the heater in their rooms. Yet in only a third of homes could residents control all three of these environmental features. In only half of the homes were residents provided with somewhere in their bedrooms to lock away small private possessions, a problem remarked upon by a third of the residents. Thus scope for personal control was very basic, and available to only a minority of residents.

While personal autonomy for residents within an institutional setting is constrained by the existing operational policy, the availability of certain physical resources may encourage, or at least underpin, a more independent lifestyle. Yet relatively few homes had facilities for residents to make a cup of tea or coffee, a shop within the home, or an activities room. All these amenities may enable some residents to maintain everyday domestic activities or encourage them to take up new hobbies.

## Negotiability

Within the context of negotiating the home environment, three themes are particularly important: rights of access, orientation, and ease of mobility. Each of these can significantly influence resident behaviour.

*Rights of access*

Within homes in the community, most household members have rights of access to all rooms in their house or flat. Such rights may of course be modified. For example, children may have limited access to their parents' bedroom or a front room may be under-utilized except when visitors call. These are modifications which develop through traditional custom and practice and they reflect a separation of public and private spaces in domestic settings; they do not reflect a separation of living and working spaces for two distinct groups within the same setting. Yet within the old people's home there are several areas to which residents do not have free access – for example service areas such as kitchens, laundries, boiler rooms, garages, as well as staff living-in accommodation, night duty rooms, and staff common rooms. Residents would not generally expect total access, given the traditions and explicit rules prevailing in institutional settings. However, such exclusions will distance residents from tasks which concern basic activities such as providing and preparing food, washing clothing, and arranging for heating. In an environment where a high percentage of residents are women, the separation from domestic activities is particularly problematic, and it is only in recent years that homes have given residents facilities for making tea or coffee when they wish, an amenity which is still not universal.

In some ways, rights of access within the residential homes are also defined by circulation spaces – routeways through the building. Circulation spaces have both connecting and separating functions: they enable people to move between places and they also mark the boundaries of spaces. While these spaces tend to have a public rather than a private character, this can change according to the kind of areas served by the route. In private spaces such as bedroom areas, circulation space should buffer as well as link the public spaces. It is also important that these circulation spaces maintain a semi-private character so as to support rather than erode the private areas. In some group-living design homes, where public and private areas are integrated, main circulation routes pass through private areas, thus reducing privacy but increasing rights to access. To counteract this problem, some architects have created a form of buffer by placing bedroom doors in recesses off the main corridors.

Staff have rights of access to all circulation routes as a consequence of their duty to care for and watch over residents. Residents, however, behaved as if there were a policy of restricted access. They were rarely to be found on routes other than those which linked the particular private and public spaces they were accustomed to use. Occasionally the fitter – and most typically male – residents used the main routes for exercise and for chatting.

*Orientation*

Familiarity with a building often means that it is comprehensible; we know what to expect from it in terms of limitations and possibilities. Yet in residential homes there has been a trend towards large and more complex buildings which may affect orientation. It has been suggested that ambiguity and complexity may be necessary if we are to be engaged by and participate in a particular environment (Rapoport and Kantor, 1967). On the other hand, it has also been noted that difficulty in forming a mental picture of an organization in spatial terms may lead to the individual's greater reliance upon those who work in the organization – in other words to greater dependency, if not total passivity (Canter and Canter, 1979). The large and complex building, instead of offering a variety of settings, may limit activity and reinforce feelings of disorientation and bewilderment not typical of smaller adapted homes. The use of appropriate signs to identify parts of the building was not common in the homes studied and systematically maintained colour coding was extremely rare, although toilets and resident bedrooms were often identified in some way.

*Ease of mobility*

Many residents suffer mobility problems and have to negotiate their environment using a walking aid or a wheelchair. Ease of mobility is therefore an important feature of resident autonomy and here the prosthetic nature of the physical environment becomes very important. At the very broad level of spatial arrangements, the degree of integration of public and private spaces is fundamental to mobility. Where sitting and dining areas are quite separate from bedroom areas, the old person needs considerable independent mobility to make use of both settings unaided. Long corridors linked by steps or ramps represented serious physical obstacles to frail, elderly residents, and provided a partial explanation for the concentrations of residents in public spaces during the daytime.

   The problem of the distance between facilities is highlighted in relation to the provision of WCs which must be in places accessible from both public and private spaces. Yet in large, traditionally organized homes they tend to serve one or other zone. The public and communal nature of residential life means that those in bedroom areas are under-utilized during the day; indeed they will not even be needed at night as residents habitually use commodes. The most successful solution to this problem was found either in group unit homes, where public and private spaces were adjacent, or in those few homes which had WCs distributed along wings between bedrooms but within easy reach of public areas. In this way the public/private boundary is maintained together with some privacy for residents.

Given that supervised bathing arrangements are usual in residential homes, neither the number of baths available nor the siting of bathrooms was seen as particularly problematic by staff except in some older adapted properties. Residents usually have a bath once a week, in some cases at a set time and day, and long trips to the bathroom can be speeded up in a wheelchair if necessary. However, the size of the bathroom and the location of the bath can become a problem and over a third of staff interviewed commented on limited bathroom space. Yet while centrally placed baths in standard-sized bathrooms were seen to lead to congestion, baths positioned against walls caused staff problems when lifting residents.

Nevertheless, distances between facilities can hinder negotiations for residents, as does the amount of space provided in enclosed areas. In many homes there was not enough space within WCs for those who used either wheelchairs or walking aids or those who needed assistance, and the space provided in dining rooms, especially in group living homes, could also be problematic for those with mobility problems. In some cases the least mobile residents had to be seated first as staff could not get wheelchairs between tables once the residents sat down. As a result, 41 officers in charge commented that the dining rooms were too small and one solution to the problem was the introduction of two mealtime sittings. Staff commented that the design of the building can directly affect behaviour, home routines, and consequently resident lifestyle:

'It becomes cramped with wheelchair users and this means that wheelchair residents have to be put in convenient places, they can't go anywhere they want.'

Ease of mobility within different parts of the building can obviously be assisted by the availability of prosthetic aids to daily living. Lifts, grab-bars, handrails and ramps can all make the environment more accessible to a frail or disabled older person, yet the availability of such devices varied widely. Four out of five homes had rails and handgrips in all WCs; only two of the sampled homes had no rails in any toilets. Yet, while 90 per cent of the homes had handrails along the corridors, nearly one in five had corridors that were interrupted by steps – a particular feature of older adapted properties and a definite hindrance to mobility. Twenty-nine homes had rooms that were difficult to reach or inaccessible for residents, either because of the distance to the room or because of steps or stairs in corridors. In a further eight, access to the grounds was difficult for residents unaided by staff due to steps and slopes or the need to negotiate heavy doors.

Eighty of the homes had lifts, two having more than one. Most lifts could accommodate wheelchairs but only 21 per cent could cope with a stretcher, a factor particularly worrying to staff. It is of major concern that the 1970s purpose-built homes are characterized by obstacles to mobility which are traditionally associated with older homes. Although problems associated with access to bedrooms, bathrooms and toilets show a marked diminution in new homes, crucial areas of mobility such as manoeuvrability through doorways and along corridors continue to create difficulties for physically frail residents.

**Safety**

The safety of residents in care is of paramount concern to the staff and to the local authority. This is demonstrated in the staff preoccupation with watching over residents. In terms of the physical environment, safety precautions manifest themselves most dramatically in relation to fire, and in all of the 100 homes an approved fire alarm system was provided, in accordance with the 1973 building note and the fire regulations (Home Office, 1983). Four out of five homes were fitted with smoke and heat detectors and in all homes fire doors were fitted along corridors, which were mainly open during the day and closed at night. Yet, in spite of these precautions, senior staff in only 55 homes felt that their system was adequate. Problems arose due to a lack of emergency lighting (with some staff having to resort to using torches), too few staff on duty at night, a shortage of smoke or heat detectors, and the likelihood of problems in evacuating residents from first and second floors.

Apart from fire precautions, resident safety is seen to depend on staff surveillance. However, as a mediator between resident and staff, personal alarm systems are widely used. In three-quarters of the homes, call systems were installed in both bathrooms and WCs, and in all but one home there were call systems in residents' bedrooms (Table 10.1).

The location of call systems in private areas of the home rather than in public areas suggests the patterns of surveillance common in the residential setting. Emphasis is placed on the congregation of residents in public areas during the day, which enables staff to keep a watching eye over residents, and at night on the provision of alternative call systems to cover for staff when few are on duty. Yet, even given the wide coverage of bedroom alarms, only 53 per cent of staff felt that the home had adequate emergency facilities in resident bedrooms. The main problems concerned resident access to the alarms in their bedrooms, the need for more flexible controls, and an easier system for locating calls once the alarm had been raised.

Daytime surveillance by staff is often facilitated by the existence of glass panels in doors and by the location of the main office within sight of the main entrance. During the night the use of lights enables staff to observe resident behaviour. With the exception of three homes, all bedroom corridors were lit at night, and in a third all or

Table 10.1   *Types of alarm systems*

|                                         | % of homes |
|-----------------------------------------|:----------:|
| Call system in bathroom and WC          | 75         |
| Call system in bathroom only            | 18         |
| Call system in WC only                  | 2          |
| Call system in bedrooms                 | 99         |
| Call system can be reached from all residents' beds in 81% of homes. | |

some resident bedrooms were lit by night-lights, with lights over the washbasin sometimes used where night-lights were not provided.

Very few homes enable residents to lock their bedroom doors. In all cases this practice was justified by staff as a safety precaution. In some homes locks were provided, but it was often reported that keys had been lost and that residents could not be trusted with keys. In contrast to bedrooms, most bathrooms and WCs could be locked from the inside and there were emergency unlocking arrangements to enable staff to assist a resident who needed help. It is interesting that this principle was not applied to bedrooms.

The importance placed on safety in residential homes relates to anxiety about risk-taking. This in itself stems from the responsibility vested in local authorities whereby they are accountable for the lives of individuals. For example, a dilemma arises with regard to the policy and practice concerning residents bringing to the home large items of furniture. In three-quarters of the homes, all or some resident bedrooms had fixed furniture, especially fitted wardrobes. This arrangement was explained as an attempt to eliminate the danger of residents pulling a heavy item of furniture down on top of themselves, or that some old people's furniture from home would be worm-infested and unsuitable, and finally that the local authority did not have anywhere to store excess furniture. These explanations serve to support practices which minimize risk-taking and expressions of individuality, and emphasize safety and block treatment.

## References

Canter, D. and Canter, S. (eds) (1979) *Designing for Therapeutic Environments: a Review of Research.* Chichester: John Wiley.

Home Office/Scottish Home and Health Department (1983) *Draft Guide to Fire Precautions in Existing Residential Care Premises.* London: Home Office.

Lawrence, R.J. (1982) 'Domestic space and society: a cross-cultural study', *Comparative Studies in Society and History*, 24(1): 104–30.

Lawton, M.P. (1970) 'Institutions for the aged: theory, content and methods for research', *The Gerontologist*, 10(3): 305–12.

Lipman, A. (1967) 'Chairs as territory', *New Society*, 9: 564–6.

Rapoport, A. (1982) *The Meaning of the Built Environment.* Beverly Hills, CA: Sage Publications.

Rapoport, A. and Kantor, R.E. (1967) 'Complexity and ambiguity in environmental design', *Journal of American Institute of Planners*, 23: 210–21.

Rosow, I. (1967) *Social Integration of the Aged*. New York: Free Press.

Westin, A. (1967) *Privacy and Freedom*. New York: Atheneum.

# 11

# Black Perspectives on Residential Care

*Black Perspectives Sub-Group*

The Wagner Report, like many such reports before it, failed to address the crucial issue of black people's rights to a 'positive choice'. As a result, the Wagner Development Group requested the Race Equality Unit (REU) to undertake a piece of work to examine residential care from a black perspective. The REU subsequently commissioned this work through the establishment of a Black Perspectives Group, which formed a sub-group of the Wagner Development Group. The Black Perspectives Sub-Group accordingly undertook a study, the results of which were published in full by NISW [the National Institute for Social Work] in 1992 as *A Home From Home*. The text which follows here summarizes the larger lines of the study, emphasizing the crucial issues – for both black and white people.

It is a truism that Social Services and related mainstream agencies have not adequately fulfilled their responsibilities in providing sensitive social care to black families and their communities. In general, the nature of services provided (or available) has either exacerbated the social problems experienced by black families with controlling and disempowering outcomes, or has failed to respond to their social needs; and the manner in which the services have been planned and resourced has left the black community at the periphery of the service provision at best, or outside the service agencies at worst.

For black communities, residential care has not only been unequal and inappropriate, but inaccessible and unavailable. On the one hand, those members of the black community who have received mainstream residential care have experienced prejudice and racism which has denied them their cultural reality, racial pride, self-dignity and black identity. On the other hand, myths and stereotypes of black families such as 'they look after their own', 'residential care is not part of their culture', have worked against the interests and welfare of their members in need of residential care.

In the past few years, the philosophy and quality of residential care has gone through critical evaluation out of which has emerged a push

First published in NISW (1993) *Residential Care: Positive Answers*. London: HMSO. pp. 68–85 (abridged).

for change not least as a consequence of the Wagner Report. There is now greater advocacy for transforming residential care from institutionalized services to personal services, where residents can live a life with choice, options, dignity and esteem, not forgetting a sense of belonging. This is based on a firm belief that residential care should not be a dumping resort or a poor option for users and that the standard of care must be maximized to enhance the quality of residential life. It cannot be stressed enough that this transformation must take account of the black experience, as no other experience has exposed the shortcomings of residential care so acutely and painfully.

There is considerable evidence which demonstrates not only that black people are not receiving the care to which they are entitled, but also that while being under-represented in the welfare provision of social work, they are over-represented in the controlling aspects of social work. Surveys have indicated that the view black people have of Social Services departments is that they fail to offer relevant services, and as a consequence are used as a last resort only.

At a policy and planning level, the situation provides little scope for optimism. The disproportionate number of black children and black persons with mental illness in residential care, and little or no presence of black elders, disabled and black persons with learning difficulties in residential care are not accidental. There is a direct connection between the over-representation of certain members of black communities in residential settings, and control and under-representation of other members of black communities. Any further debates on black people and residential care need to acknowledge this, understand it within the context of racist oppression and deal with it.

This scenario of lack of appropriate services, coupled with the experiences of black people and their families in accommodation geared to the needs of white people (and therefore by definition the exclusion of black people) has led to black people organizing and securing appropriate care in residential accommodation geared specifically to meet their needs. This care has predominantly taken the form of black-led voluntary and private organizations, although there are also some examples of provision in the statutory sector.

### The experience of black residential projects

The aims of the study carried out by the Black Perspectives Sub-Group were:

1  to explore projects which are established specifically to provide residential care to black people;

2  to identify and develop models of good practice in residential care
   for black communities from material thus obtained;
3  to highlight areas of work for further research and development.


The primary purpose was to identify ways and approaches that
would be effective and useful for moving forward in enabling residential care to be delivered in a manner which is relevant and
appropriate to black people, their families and communities. The
methodology employed to collate information reflected the conviction
that black projects provide examples of good practice, which is
informed by their experience of the provision of appropriate services
to black communities. The study explored the work of eight residential establishments. The projects which agreed to participate provide
a range of services:

    to children;
    to young mothers;
    to adolescents;
    to elderly people.


The findings of the study which follow are organized within the
context of practice and service issues, using headings for ease of
reference and not in any order of priority.

*Advantages of black leadership in providing residential and
personal care*

The emergence of black voluntary organizations providing residential
care has not been in a vacuum. While such residential provisions have
been the outcome of active responses to establish alternative services
in the absence of mainstream services, more importantly black-led
residential care has been rooted in the black history and tradition of
care. The philosophy of looking after the vulnerable members of
communities and taking care of family and community members is
right at the heart of black culture and the way of life. Black-led
residential care is a continuation of the caring tradition and manifestation of the caring philosophy. While the failure of (white) residential establishments in providing appropriate care to black people is
part of this scenario, it is not the entirety. Black people are not only
reacting to white failings, but are creative, skilful and able to identify
and meet their own needs, and it must be acknowledged that the
blockages of white control and racism have sought to prevent them
from doing so.

A clear philosophy underpinned most of the projects involved in the
study. This clarity encompassed an agreement of needs which is based

on the acknowledgement, understanding and experience of racism and
its effects. It is important to highlight here some differences between
the one establishment that was not black-led and the other projects.
In providing a service to both black and white residents, while they
had a clear philosophy, this did not integrate black people's experience of racism. The realization that there was a need for appropriate
care for black elders was precipitated by the admission of an Asian
Muslim elder to the home. This is in marked contrast to the black-led
homes in the study, which were based on an understanding of racism
as the starting point of service provision, as opposed to a process
which was underpinned by lack of services – one is a proactive
process and the other is reactive. In the latter case, the situation then
developed of the issues of racism having to be dealt with as an
afterthought, not as integral to the process of change. The process of
change focused not on the black experience, but on the white perception of the black experience which was founded on notions of
exotic culture and language. Staff therefore had to be convinced,
trained and cajoled into an understanding of racism and its effects,
whereas in black-led homes this was the starting point, and therefore
the understanding *ipso facto* existed. This fundamental philosophical
base was the keystone on which meeting the needs of black residents
was built and was reflected in the experiences of both children and
adults in black-led homes, where they did not have to convince carers
of the importance of their cultural traditions. In relation to children,
developing a sense of self-worth, being able to locate their place in the
community, and learning to cope with matters which affect them as
black children were identified as critical. This included the development of pride in who they were and a feeling of ease with themselves.
This facilitated their return to black families and the black
community with less disruption and a greater ability to deal with
the experience of care. This contrasts sharply with the experiences of
black children in white-led homes.

   A fundamental issue affecting practice here is the underlying
acknowledgement and acceptance the homes had that all black
children are part of the black community. This aspect guided all
decisions and actions. The marked difference here is the debate that
white workers engage in when attempting to decide where the child
belongs, and therefore they develop practice which is based on
underestimating or misunderstanding the need for belonging and
cultural and racial identity.

   This philosophy applied to all black children, including those with
one parent who was white. For these children, in particular, it
provided the necessary baseline for helping them to work through
problems relating to identity confusion, problems related to negative
feelings about being black and poor self-images, and also in helping
them to develop the strengths to deal with racism in a society which

would always view them as black. The value of this philosophical base is that in valuing the black heritage of these children, their white heritage and parentage was not negated. It is extremely difficult within a report like this to encapsulate the importance of the values that are intrinsic to such a philosophy and this particular aspect of the study has left us without doubt that care for all black children can never meet their needs, unless it incorporates care by black adults.

Elders found reassurance and comfort in being with others from a similar background. The common bond existed of originating from Africa or the Indian subcontinent, but with considerable cultural and life experience difference between islands in the Caribbean or differences between Gujarati and Punjabi Asian people. These differences were not a source of conflict and provided a reason for finding out about each other, sharing information, learning and establishing commonalities, without the negative effects of racism. It gave elders a sense of being valued and wanted in a society which is generally hostile to them. Matters of racism and cultural traditions were taken as read, and allowed people to progress with other issues, without these becoming the only focus of attention. Essentially the approach and philosophy of black-led homes can be described as holistic, an approach which not only recognizes and seeks to care for the whole person, responding to body, mind and spirit, but also places that individual within the context of their family, and their community.

Another major aspect of black leadership in homes is the 'community approach'. This recognizes and understands the needs of the community, and adopts a flexible approach to the needs of both the community and the individual as they arise. The reverse could be said to be true of white-led organizations, which establish 'rules' (in the form of assessment procedures, etc.) and expect individuals and communities to fit into their regulations, not vice versa. Such an approach is not only an indication of their flexibility, but also of their creativity and ability to develop services and respond to a range of needs despite the constraints of tight budgets, and the restrictions of the local authority.

A community approach incorporating these characteristics should not be confused with 'disorganization', or 'unprofessionalism', labels which are often attached to black-led projects. Structures and systems clearly exist and work in such projects, but these do not function to restrict initiative, rather to accommodate it. The shared experience of both staff and users ensures an environment where trust and confidence can be established. For example, experiences of past or current racism do not have to be explained in 'rational', i.e. unemotional terms, but can be shared or explored in an environment which is empathic and rational, rather than judgmental or collusive. Anger can be freely displayed, without requiring justification or explanation.

At a broader level, there appeared to be more expression of feeling than is experienced in white-led children's homes. An example is the expression of anger, which was regarded as positive and healthy whether by staff or residents. The size of establishment clearly has an effect on the service offered. Black projects tend to be smaller: this is not by accident, but by design. Local authority service users have encountered a number of difficulties which are a result of being housed in large, in flexible institutions. Black projects have sought to avoid these obstacles.

Cultural identity, encompassing different values, traditions, linguistic, artistic and religious attributes is nonetheless very important in providing appropriate care for people; but what the study revealed is that this is achieved not by having 'Bob Marley' pictures on the wall or curry on the menu, but through a holistic approach which is evident in the feel and smell of the establishment, and the sense of belonging and peace which is created by black people's presence. Indeed, to the Sub-Group, the physical environment of the home, e.g. books, ornaments, etc., seemed of less importance than they had expected. They found that in their experience of white-led homes, racial and cultural identity, although expressed visually in some places, was, in effect, used to divert attention from the fundamental issue of racism that creates the very conditions in which the culture of some groups is devalued. It also led to an over-reliance on cultural explanations to explain human behaviour or problems. This is the very backbone of multiculturalism, the shibboleth of a patronizing liberalism that encourages one to acknowledge cultures of so-called ethnic minorities whilst leaving intact the racism of the dominant white majority. Black staff within the project establishments understood this issue, and central to their experiences was therefore an understanding of what identity means and the knowledge that for black people, this does not separate out from being black. This is in marked contrast to white workers who grapple unsuccessfully with the concept and conclude that for a child or elderly person being black is an 'additional need' to be met, rather than the context in which their needs should be met. Such muddled thinking leads to muddled practice, and black people in need of care suffer as a consequence.

*Practical care*

The components which contribute towards appropriate care for black people should not be viewed in isolation from each other, but as part of a whole process of care.

Language was viewed as a major issue in terms of the spoken language (i.e. English, Gujarati) and also the use of language, and the language environment of the organization. It was found to be essential that workers and residents were able to relate orally, both in terms of worker to resident, and also resident to resident. Language is not only about the actual spoken word, but also about the meaning attributed to the use of particular words within a cultural and experiential framework. The commonality of understanding in relation to these goes some way towards ensuring that people feel valued. The issue of language is viewed by the Sub-Group as an essential feature of good care which provides a common bond between staff and residents, and for elders in particular has the effect of lessening isolation and increasing feelings of importance. Even for children whose language was English, the Sub-Group found 'Black English' and patois served a similar function. Language is more than communication: crucial though 'good' communication is in providing 'good' care, it is also about freedom of expression, release of emotions, cultural identity and shared values. The language environment within a home or day centre should fulfil the resident's right to be understood without a constant battle to be understood, or without having to justify the need/importance of this to white workers. The study highlighted the fact that where the language environment is appropriate, stress and anxiety levels are considerably reduced.

In one home providing care for people from several linguistic backgrounds, the issue of a resident speaking a language which staff were unable to understand arose. In this case, access to a 24-hour interpreter was seen as vital, alongside regular sessions, both for the user and their family. Similarly, the translation of written material is important. Where people are not literate even in their own language it is still important that information is translated: it demonstrates respect and accords dignity, and most people can find someone who can read to them.

Access to and use of natural medicine such as herbalism was regarded particularly by elders as being important to their sense of well-being. Some of the homes in the study were open to exploring the possibility of alternative medicine, and often tips for 'cures' were picked up by staff through contact with members of the community. The greatest source of knowledge was the elders themselves, who had a wealth of tradition and expertise around health care. This is very different from the experience of elderly people in white-led homes where the only experts are the GPs and residents are not expected to contribute to their own health care. The value of having workers who can not only be receptive to the possibility of using traditional medicines but will also actively seek and utilize the wisdom of other black people is very clear. One Asian woman, during an interview, turned to a member of staff to remind him that he must remember to liquidize her kerala. He reassured her that he had not forgotten and understood that this was not merely an eating fad, but that the liquid from this vegetable was a natural method through which she controlled her diabetes.

There was also an understanding by most of the staff that black people are particularly affected by certain health conditions, e.g. thalassaemia, sickle cell anaemia, diabetes and high blood pressure and that the home environment needs to be a place in which stress and anxiety are reduced, thereby contributing to the prevention and treatment of these conditions. Residents also seemed well aware of this and home was viewed as a kind of haven where one would not experience the stress of racism that occurs outside.

With young people, staff assumed an educative role and, in some homes, organized sessions on sickle cell and other health-related issues.

Regular meetings of residents are a mechanism for ensuring the integral involvement of residents in decisions taken in the establishments. It is important that meetings are 'free-flowing', not merely a forum for endorsing decisions already made by management of the home.

Food was viewed by all homes as a crucial factor in creating an atmosphere of comfort and belonging: 'No one turns up their noses at the smell of my food.' The range of different foods provided by the establishments which the Sub-Group visited was surprising. Each establishment provided a variety which gave residents real choice in their individual food preferences. In some homes, particularly those catering for younger people, they were encouraged to cook their own food. This not only develops survival skills, but also contributes to a sense of control over an important aspect of life. Children were invited to widen their experience by trying food which they might not have experienced. Elders on the other hand were able to share their culinary expertise with staff by teaching them about the preparation of food. This provided an important role for elders, and in one establishment they had been involved in the recruitment of the cooks and were then helping to train them. As one man said, 'at first the food wasn't so good, but we've been teaching them and it is getting better, although it's not like my mother's cooking'. The elders took a real pride in their knowledge of cooking, and felt respected in that their views were sought and contributed to improving the quality of care for everyone. Knowing who is preparing the food is as important as having the right type of food.

Food is not just about 'eating' at meal times but is a source for engaging in social relationships. Residents conveyed the importance of not feeling 'odd' or being an object of curiosity because they were eating their 'own' food.

The involvement of family was viewed as crucial, not only in terms of assisting staff to make the 'right' decisions, but also in creating an atmosphere which made them feel welcome. Elders had a strong sense of mutual caring, in relation not only to other residents, but also to workers and their families. Some elders had a strong feeling that they had been let down by their families, and therefore in many cases had to adjust psychologically not only to not returning 'home', but also to the inevitability that they would not live the remaining years of their lives with their families.

The elders have nevertheless coped with their changing circumstances and expectations, and are still able to be positive about their families and themselves. Some had strong links with their families, whilst some did not. In some cases the mutual feeling of rejection formed a common bond between the elders. In white homes the feeling of rejection is usually not reduced but often increased to 'being dumped'.

In most cases, the families of staff members at these homes were also in some way involved in the running of the home.

A shared faith and the practice of religion was supported and encouraged. A strong sense of spirituality prevailed in some homes, with joint worship, and a sharing of spiritual experience, e.g. through singing.

*Staffing*

The study demonstrated clearly that the type of care provided depends very much on the type of management and staff that are employed. Staffing also has a bearing on the impression that the community has of the home. The importance of appropriate staffing cannot be over-emphasized.

The under-resourcing of the homes in the study resulted in limited formal staff development and training. The release of staff has cost implications in terms of cover for the home when the staff are away on training. This situation led to the restriction of opportunities for staff in seeking professional training and qualifications. However, it also meant that managers were innovative and creative in setting up training programmes and sharing skills and expertise through networks. The use of independent black trainers and consultants has developed to provide in-house training but this is limited to a few projects. Where available, such training provides a wider perspective and ensures that workers are informed of changes in legislation, the development of practice, as well as generating support networks and forums for workers to experiment and be challenged in.

Evidence from the projects suggests that whereas key worker and counsellor systems occur in children's establishments, this is not the case in those for elders. The principle of key workers is important, but is not the only system which can be employed. It cannot be disputed that clear care plans are good practice and should extend to all residents, regardless of which 'client group' they are perceived as belonging to.

Care plans should be drawn up with residents and if appropriate their families or friends. They provide an opportunity for people to say what help they need in caring for themselves and to negotiate how this help should be given. The process allows residents to share with staff the issues that are important to them and is a means by which they can maintain some control over their own lives. Within the study, several projects used care plans. These did not have race and culture as aspects to be considered but as central to the care of the person; so that the questions became (for example) not whether a child's contact with a grandma in Jamaica was important, but how that contact should be maintained. This example demonstrates the way in which a black perspective is vital to the care of black children. Many white-led homes focus on attachment and separation work with children in a way that negates the value of relationships they may have. It is commonly assumed that a child cannot be 'attached' to a parent or grandparent who lives a long way away and whom the child has not seen for a long time. However, black staff had a different understanding based on the knowledge that because of immigration controls, colonization, etc., black people have developed the capacity to maintain relationships over vast distances in time and miles, and consequently worked with the child in maintaining the relationships that were important to the child. Similarly in placing children in alternative families, white workers have often based their practice on the belief that a child won't settle or become attached unless they have been psychologically 'separated' from former carers. A black perspective on this issue as highlighted by the study is one that promotes the concept of shared care and the view that attachments need not be mutually exclusive. It is interesting that this concept has now been taken on and is a fundamental aspect of the Children Act 1989. The key worker system is also valuable since it provides residents with a sense of continuity. However, this should not occur in isolation from interaction with other staff, as the effects of staff sickness and annual leave have to be taken account of, and planned for accordingly.

Whatever system is used within the home, it is vital that the care provided ensures that each resident has an appropriate worker with particular responsibility for meeting their needs.

The reliance of the projects on a community approach embodies the principles and practice of multidisciplinary working and flexible, participative management styles.

It is an approach that was demonstrated by the utilization of

- youth workers for outside activities;
- teachers and social workers as night staff; and
- outside workers to establish carers' support groups.

The involvement of teachers in projects is based on the belief that education is crucial to the survival of black people. Local authority schools have a history of rejecting black young people through labelling them and dismissing their potential in various ways. Teachers in some projects have been involved in additional teaching, to facilitate the re-entry of children into mainstream schools. Our experience generally of children in care is that workers have low expectations of them educationally. Black workers were not willing to accept this view of the children in their care, believing that it contributes to low self-esteem and as such cannot be a feature of genuine care.

The relationship of staff with residents was perceived as fundamentally different to that which is experienced within a local authority setting. One way in which this was reflected was in the roles that workers undertake having a 'fluidity' as opposed to the 'rigidity' often experienced. Flexible use of staff enhanced the services available to residents, and also enabled the staff to further the development of their skills. The ethos of the staff/residents relationship was based on respect for the person, not on their job or job title. This approach leads to a less hierarchical atmosphere, which was preferred by residents and staff. The resident/staff relationship also mirrors the experience of the community: for example there is respect for elders. Elders in the residential establishments regarded the staff 'like their children', but also recognized the boundaries of the relationship. Similarly, staff in children's homes have a sense of parental responsibility for the young people in their care. The belief of staff that 'yes, I do expect a lot from you', as opposed to having low or no expectations, led to a situation in which young people were able to develop their potential. The parental role of staff was over and above the usual more limited role of residential social workers. One of the features of black-led homes is that unlike their white counterparts, black workers are more likely to live within the community of the home. As a consequence, their relationship with the young people extends beyond the walls of the home. It was quite unusual, in fact expected and valued, that workers off duty and seeing young people out on the streets would still be 'caring' for them, reprimanding them for misbehaviour, etc. Black staff often expressed the view that to allow young people too much freedom under the auspices of 'trust' and 'independence' was a liberal approach they could not afford. As black adults they were aware of the criminalization of black young people, plus the dangers of drugs, harassment, etc., and had a responsibility to support and protect them out of the home. This approach was expected and welcomed by young people's families. Elders did not view themselves as passive recipients of care, but as having an active role in the development of services to them, and ensuring a good quality of life for each other, as well as the workers and their families. [. . .]

## A focus of good practice?

In sharing their experiences and knowledge, the eight projects highlighted a broad spectrum of issues which have clear implications for
local authorities, funding bodies and residential establishments alike.
The most fundamental of the issues highlighted is the philosophy
which underpins the work of black-led organizations. A philosophy
developed from black histories, cultural experiences and resistance to
racism/oppression. A philosophy based on a view of life and the world
which acknowledges the wholeness of the being and does not com-
partmentalize their behaviour, experiences, needs, expectations,
cultures into neat and separate boxes.

We believe there is much to learn from the experiences of black
organizations and we hope local authorities and other organizations
will begin to value their experiences and expertise. The starting point
must surely be in white organizations examining the ethos and culture
of their own organization. Do they provide services and practice that
devalue black people and consistently fail to see them, their experiences and their cultures in any contextual framework? Perhaps this
will result in a more critical analysis of the way in which white
individuals and institutions operate with black individuals and
organizations. We believe that development of positive partnerships
with black voluntary organizations, as part of legislative requirements, would be one way of developing models of good practice based
on the experience of black projects.

If local authorities and other organizations are to provide a more
equitable service to all the communities, then services to black communities must of necessity be high on their agenda. To this end,
agencies should support and encourage the development of more
black-led residential establishments, and begin to incorporate some of
the philosophies and models identified by black professionals, communities and organizations into the establishment of 'good practice'.

*Recommendations*

Residential homes should:

1  have clear aims and objectives, outlining who they are providing a
   service to and what that service is; the service must reflect the
   needs of black residents;
2  have a black perspective fully integrated into all policies and
   practices;
3  ensure that the recruitment of staff reflects the community reality
   and the needs of the residents;
4  ensure that the staff have an understanding of the realities and
   needs of black residents;

5  develop links with and support black organizations and individuals within the community;
6  develop processes of supervision of staff which incorporate
   exploration of race and cultural dimensions;
7  meet all the physical needs of the residents; this includes health,
   skin care, food and language;
8  ensure that they are able to communicate with residents and their
   families in a means and language which they feel comfortable
   with;
9  ensure that care builds on the positive strengths of black people;
10  respect residents' practices of faith, and make the necessary
   arrangements for them to fulfil these;
11  develop relationships with the local community which will enrich
   the lives of residents.

Local authorities and funding bodies *must*:

12  ensure that assessment procedure and processes incorporate the
   black reality;
13  make available to residents and potential residents information
   necessary to enable them to make personal choices;
14  establish and maintain fruitful partnership relationships with
   black projects;
15  ensure that black projects are supported, not only in terms of
   financial concerns, but also other broader resource issues, e.g.
   training;
16  review their terms and conditions of funding to guard against the
   abuse of black projects.

### Brief bibliography

Ahmad, A. (1988) *Social Services for Black People: Service or Lip Service?* London: REU.
Hughes, R.D. (1986) *Social Services for Ethnic Minorities: Policy and Practice in the North West.* London: DHSS/SSI.
Jones, A. (1991) *Report of the Black Communities Care Project.* London: NISW.
Jones, A., Phillips, M. and Maynard, C. (1992) *A Home from Home.* London: NISW.

**Black Perspectives Sub-Group:**
**Adele Jones**
   National Institute for Social Work
**Charles Maynard**
   Bradford Social Services
**Marcia Richards**
   Race Equality Unit
**Daphne Statham**
   Chairman

# 12

# The Shifting Concept of Community

*Marjorie Mayo*

The concept of 'community' is notorious for its shiftiness. Beside the term 'community', the myths and ambiguities inherent in some of the notions surrounding 'the mixed economy of welfare' could be considered to be relative models of clarity. There is a case to answer as to whether 'community' should actually continue to be used at all.

This chapter explores some of the ambiguities and contradictory uses of the term. Community has been used in different ways over time. And it has been used within the context of alternative sociological approaches and competing political orientations. These fundamental differences are key, it will be argued. It is not just that the term community has been used ambiguously; it has been contested, fought over, and appropriated for different uses and interests to justify different politics, policies and practices. [. . .]

## Historical approaches to 'community'

In his critical collection, *Keywords*, Raymond Williams (1976) included an entry on the keyword 'community', which provides a useful starting point from which to disentangle the history of the term's conflicting uses. Williams pointed out that community has been in the English language since the fourteenth century. Originally it was used to refer to the common people, as opposed to those of rank, or to a state or organized society. Subsequently (by the sixteenth century) the term was used to refer to 'the quality of having something in common' and to 'a sense of common identity and characteristics'. Community also came to be used to refer to a particular quality of relationship, as well as to a distinction between community and civil society on the one hand and the state on the other, and between 'more direct, more total and therefore more significant relationships of community and the more formal, more abstract and more instrumental relationships of state, or of society in its modern sense', as developed in the work of Toennies

From Marjorie Mayo (1994) *Communities and Caring: The Mixed Economy of Welfare*. London: Macmillan. pp. 48–56 (abridged).

(1957). From the nineteenth century, then, the term was used to contrast communities and localities with larger, more complex industrial societies.

Williams pointed to further uses, including the notion of community in relation to alternative, often Utopian ways of group living. And he included the use of community in the term community politics,

> which is distinct not only from national politics but from formal local politics and normally involves various kinds of direct action and direct local organisation, 'working directly with people', as which it is distinct from 'service to the community', which has an older sense of voluntary work supplementary to official provision or paid service. (Williams, 1976: 65)

Williams concluded that there is a common thread in these different uses, in that community tends to be used as a 'warmly persuasive word' whether this is to describe an existing set of relationships or an alternative set of relationships. Unlike all other terms of social organization, he argues, 'it seems never to be used unfavourably, and never to be given any positive opposing or distinguishing term' (ibid.: 65–6). This stakes out a useful agenda for reviewing the use of the term 'community'. The final point, however, about the predominance of warm and favourable connotations turns out to be more problematic than Williams seems to have recognized.

William's approach in *Keywords* has provided a starting point for further historical analysis. Eileen and Stephen Yeo's survey of the use of community picks out three different and competing aspects and meanings. They start from the sixteenth-century usage of community as 'holding something in common, a feeling of common identity and, most positively of all, a quality of mutual caring in human relations' (Yeo and Yeo, 1988: 231), the type of community envisaged, for instance by the Diggers in the seventeenth century and by socialists such as Robert Owen and William Morris in the nineteenth century. This community of mutual caring – a community 'made by people for themselves' (ibid.: 231), community as a 'vision of a fully liberated humanity living in supportive social relations' (ibid.: 232) – is contrasted with two alternative approaches: community as service and community as the state.

Community as service, it was argued, was developed in the nineteenth century as a middle-class ideal of service to the poor, in place of working-class mutuality and community. University settlements, for example, provided vehicles for middle-class philanthropy in 'suitable centres of a strong community life' (ibid.: 239). This middle-class approach to community, the Yeos argue, 'with its stress on service within formal organisations tended to restrict working class women and to displace their communities' (ibid.: 241). And it tended to be invoked 'in and against situations of working-class militancy' (ibid.: 242).

Following on from this, they argue, 'community as the state' refers to a usage which sets out 'the community' and community interests as interpreted by the state, in opposition to independent working-class action. They suggest that the term has been increasingly hijacked for this type of more coercive use during the twentieth century. In 1925 Stanley Baldwin when commenting on the miners, said: 'If the will to strike should overcome the will to peace temporarily . . . let me say that no minority in a free country has ever yet coerced a whole community. The community will always protect itself' (ibid.: 247). The use of community may be found more recently of course, and once again in relation to the miners, who were defined in terms of the community's 'enemy within' in the strike of 1984–5 (Samuel et al., 1985).

## Sociological approaches to 'community'

Sociological approaches to the concept of community provide another way into the contradictory and conflicting usages of the word. Bulmer's 1987 study *The Social Basis of Community Care*, unpacks some of the most frequently used bowdlerized versions of sociological ideas and studies. Community, as Bulmer illustrates, can be defined in terms of people who live in a common geographical area. Or it can be defined in terms of common interests, interests which may be as diverse as 'ethnic origin, religion, politics, occupation, leisure pursuits or sexual propensity, as in the Jewish community . . . the occupational community of the police' or the 'gay community' (Willmott, 1984: 5). 'The two types of community are not mutually exclusive – quite small areas may have different interest communities within them – but they tend to point in rather different directions' (ibid.). As Bulmer points out, such diverse uses can cover a very wide range of meanings. As he went on to demonstrate, in an article back in 1955 Hillery found 94 sociological definitions, and all that they had in common was that they dealt with people. Similarly Bulmer quoted Halsey's conclusion that the term has so many meanings as to be meaningless (Bulmer, 1987: 28). Such a wide-ranging description describes everything and therefore nothing.

So does it help, to unpack the term further, to investigate community's relationship with different sociological approaches in more analytical terms in order to analyse the nature of social relations and social change more generally?

In classic sociological usage, Toennies's terms of *Gemeinschaft* and *Gesellschaft*, approximately translated as 'community' and 'association', relate to a particular sociological approach to the interpretation of social change. According to this approach, earlier stages of social development tended to be characterized by social relationships that were small-scale and personal; community ties based upon the family and traditional community ties, Toennies argued. In contrast, industrialized, urban societies tended to be characterized by 'individualism, contractualism and the rational pursuit of interest' in an abstract, impersonal city (although Toennies was also concerned with the possibility of reintroducing traditional personal ties within modern society) (Toennies, 1957: 42). The disintegration of primary groups, the decline of 'community' and the development of more impersonal social relations in complex, urban, industrial societies have featured in the work of a number of the founding fathers of sociology.

As Bell explained, 'Behind such theories – whether of the left or the right – lay a 'romantic notion of the past that sees society as having once been made up of small "organic" communities that were shattered by industrialism and modern life, and replaced by an "atomistic" society which is unable to provide the basic gratifications and call forth the loyalties that the older communities knew' (Bell, 1956: 77). Community is seen in these terms as idealized, a lost world which may or may not be recoverable; a nostalgic approach which has nevertheless had considerable influence in sociological debates. This has also been the starting point for a range of empirical studies that have set out to explore how far this 'lost community' relates to the reality of particular communities. Such an approach has interest in its own right. And it is clearly highly relevant in policy terms for community care to know to what extent community ties still persist, or could at least be revived, to provide informal caring (whether or not such a revival of traditional neighbourhoods would be desirable, in any case, marked as such neighbourhoods were by insecurity and constraints, as well as by solidarity and mutual support).

The empirical evidence for the community-lost theory does not, Bulmer argues, turn out to be overwhelming. People in cities tend to draw upon the same sources of support as people in rural areas: kin, neighbours and friends. This seems to have been found in both British and US studies. On the basis of such studies, Bulmer (1987) concluded that there was little empirical evidence for the 'community-lost' thesis that urban residents lacked sources of support in comparison with rural residents.

Conversely, however, the alternative thesis of 'community saved' is not clearly documented either. Studies such as Young and Willmott in Britain (Young and Willmott, 1957) and Gans in the USA (Gans, 1962) have identified the continuing existence of communities of urban 'villages' with strong social ties within particular neighbourhoods. But Bulmer argues that it is essential to consider the total picture of these residents' social networks. Typically the locality was an important source of networks in these studies, but so too were wider, external networks. Focusing on the neighbourhood provided only part of the total picture.

As an alternative then, Bulmer considers the value of Wellman's term 'community liberated', an approach which takes account of this wider framework of networks where ties of kin, work and residence are not necessarily combined. This approach 'frees the concept of community from its purely local roots and allows for informal ties in terms of social networks' (Wellman, 1979). This takes the concept of community back to some combination of community in terms of locality, and community in terms of shared interests, but with the major focus on the networks and ties of individuals and their families. [. . .]

Marxists have emphasized the importance of unpacking the term and disentangling the different implications for different social classes. Harvey, for instance, argues that: 'Different classes construct their sense of territory and community in radically different ways' (1989: 265).

> Low income populations, usually lacking the means to overcome and hence command space, find themselves for the most part trapped in space . . . . In this space, the community can be positive, in terms of mutual aid and defence, but conversely, for the poor, the community can be limiting, and can lead to mutual predation, with tight but often highly conflictual interpersonal social bonding in both private and public spaces. (ibid.: 267)

These negative aspects of community for those on low income are increasing, Harvey argues, with the process of impoverishment, more generally, and with the spread of informalization (by which he is referring to the increasing spread of the informal economy as a means of survival in poor areas, together with the increasing casualization of formal employment in the wake of economic restructuring). This leads to increasing racial tension (and black and ethnic minority communities are, in any case, disproportionately at risk here). Restructuring has increased the incidence of poverty and unemployment in US cities, he argues, while neo-conservative policies have undercut the flow of public services, 'and hence the life support mechanisms for the mass of the unemployed and the poor . . . . The balance between competition, mutual predation and mutual aid has consequently shifted within low income populations' (ibid.). In the USA, he argues, as in Europe, there has been a dramatic rise in, for instance, drug trafficking and prostitution, as well as in legal forms of the informal economy.

Conversely the term community has very different connotations for the affluent. For them, Harvey argues, the construction of community relates to the preservation of privilege: community organizations are formed, for instance, in order to maintain the 'tone' of the community, to maintain property values and to keep 'undesirables' out. The affluent are more mobile, with wider choices altogether, and they have greater access to power and can therefore influence the use of wider resources; a point which has of course been noted widely, and not just by Marxists.

For Harvey, however, there are positives as well as negatives in the 'postmodern' city. He sees a role for campaigns for community control, to be waged as part of wider struggles for decentralized socialist solutions. 'True empowerment,' he argues, 'must be won by struggle from below and not given out of largesse from above', and community struggles have a role, alongside class struggles, in this scenario (ibid.).

At this point it might be useful to pause briefly and draw attention to some of the differing ways in which the term 'empowerment' is used. Here Harvey is using this term within the context of the wider changes that will be required if the powerless in society are to gain power. The term empowerment is often used far more loosely however, almost as if empowerment were a technique that individuals or communities could acquire in order to gain power. Logically such an approach would imply that power in society is there for the taking; you just need to learn how to do it, to be more assertive or whatever.

If power were, in reality, equally accessible to all, in a truly pluralist, democratic society such a view would reasonably follow. But alternatively, if power is conceived in terms of its relationships with other interests in society, such as major economic interests, as Marxists for instance would argue, then power is not simply there for the taking, because the powerful have vested interests in defending their power. According to this type of analysis empowerment is a key concept, but this is in the more specific and limited terms of enabling people and organizations to use most effectively the power that they do have, whether to press for immediate improvements and/or to press for longer-term goals of social change (the sense in which Harvey is using the term).

In addition to his focus on class relations, Harvey also considers the implications of polarization and impoverishment for women in the community. Poverty has been feminized, and women have been particularly vulnerable to the processes of restructuring and informalization, although they have also devised mechanisms for survival within this informal economy, including homeworking and informal childcare. Women have been particularly trapped within these low-income communities, although community organizations have also played a key role in their survival.

This ambivalence about the community, for women, has been considered from a number of perspectives. Bulmer, for instance, considers ways in which community can be oppressive for women. In particular community care, as a number of authors have pointed out, typically implies care by women (Finch and Groves, 1983; Ungerson, 1987; Baldwin and Twigg, 1991). Caring responsibilities, whether for children or for elderly or handicapped relatives, are an important enough issue in their own right. And caring responsibilities effectively bind women to particular localities and limit their search for work, their opportunities for education and training, their social and leisure activities and their scope for wider political involvement. The community can be a prison as well as a source of mutual aid and collective solidarity.

## References

Baldwin, S. and Twigg, J. (1991) 'Women and community care', in M. Maclean and D. Groves (eds), *Women's Issues in Social Policy*. London: Routledge.

Bell, D. (1956) 'The theory of mass society', *Commentary*, July.

Bulmer, M. (1987) *The Social Basis of Community Care*. London: Allen & Unwin.

Finch, J. and Groves, D. (eds) (1983) *A Labour of Love: Women, Work and Caring*. London: Routledge & Kegan Paul.

Gans, H. (1962) *The Urban Villagers*. New York: Free Press.

Harvey, D. (1989) *The Urban Experience*. Oxford: Basil Blackwell.

Samuel, R. et al. (eds) (1985) *The Enemy Within: Pit Villages and the Miners' Strike of 1984–5*. London: Routledge & Kegan Paul.

Toennies, F. (1957) *Community and Society*. Lansing, MI: Michigan State University Press.

Ungerson, C. (1987) *Policy is Personal: Sex, Gender and Informal Care*. London: Tavistock.

Wellman, B. (1979) 'The community question: the intimate networks of East Yorker', *American Journal of Sociology*, 84(5): 1201–31.

Williams, R. (1976) *Keywords*. London: Croom Helm.

Willmott, P. (1984) *Community in Social Policy*. London: Policy Studies Institute.

Yeo, E. and Yeo, S. (1988) 'On the uses of community', in S. Yeo (ed.), *New Views of Co-operation*. London: Routledge.

Young, M. and Willmott, P. (1957) *Family and Kinship in East London*. London: Routledge & Kegan Paul.

# SECTION 3

# MODELS OF CARE: CHALLENGE AND CHANGE

This section contains a deliberately large and diverse set of readings. What unites them is a struggle to find ways of giving care that do not always assume that the expert knows best and that respond more effectively to the different needs of service users. The success of medicine has provided something of a strait-jacket for thinking about what professional care is and how it should be delivered in health and social care settings. In many instances workers are not the all-knowing experts and clients not the straightforwardly dependent and compliant creatures that the doctor/patient relationship of old has seemed to imply.

The first two readings, deriving from health care settings, are strongly critical of the status quo. Pinder carried out a series of interviews, repeated over time with 10 Parkinson's Disease sufferers. This leads her to call for more respect for the day-to-day challenges that this chronic disease brings and 'a more participatory model of information-sharing and decision-making'. Doyal's wide-ranging review demonstrates the value of an approach that regards childbirth as normal until proved pathological, and shows how highly technical procedures in medicine have been effectively questioned by feminist research.

Innovation and change are the themes of the next few readings. Killick is a writer and an outsider to the care professions. Working on life histories in a care setting for residents with dementia, he shows how practices can be challenged and suggestions can be made as to individualized care for people who seem to have lost their individuality. Bornat's chapter charts the changes in thinking about the value of life experience in social care settings which have prompted such innovations. Duffy and McCarthy demonstrate how, in a residential setting for adolescent girls, the routine weekly house meeting was transformed so that, over time, the girls themselves were taking responsibility, suggesting solutions to problems and helping each other to develop. The adjustments that staff have made to enable this to occur are also clearly documented. Fisk is a health visitor involved with the Teamcare Valleys (TCV) initiative in South Wales. She describes moving from a one-to-one model of tackling individual problems to a community-oriented approach which aims 'to enable people to increase control over, and to improve, their health'. She gives a vivid account of the need for health visitors to become facilitators and to be prepared to set aside their status as 'experts'.

It is not by chance that it is people with physical, mental and learning disabilities, people from ethnic minorities, feminists and others, who have often led the way in questioning health and social care – searching for ways these services might free them from rather than tie them more tightly into the inequalities and oppression they experience. Morris does this in a particularly powerful and thought-provoking way. She delivers an eloquent plea, informed and illustrated by interviews with disabled women, for forms of help that enable them to create homes, rear children, and engage in intimate and caring relationships with others. She makes clear that statutory services can often do the opposite of what they intend – locking women into dependency on a carer, paid or unpaid. Her solution is paid assistance under the control of the service user herself, and some of the advantages of this emerge vividly from the extract reprinted here. In part, Morris was driven to this work by her dissatisfaction with early research on caring led by feminists who focused on white, middle-class and able-bodied women and adopted the carers' point of view to the detriment of that of the cared-for (see Introduction, p. 3). All voices need to be heard and although carers have come on to the policy agenda in recent years with legislation to give them support and recognition, Bibbings's article (Chapter 20) shows how far there is still to go.

Shah carried out research into services for children with disabilities in Asian families. Her contribution provides telling examples of the ways in which the needs of black and ethnic minority service users can be overlooked or distorted by stereotyping and by the institutional racism embedded in the structures of organizations. It is important to acknowledge, as she does, good as well as bad practice in this field and also to assess the contribution of agencies such as CCETSW (the Central Council for Education and Training in Social Work) in their efforts to promote debate and to develop training materials. Davies's article, drawing from a rather different tradition of feminism than some of the work criticized above, sees the very idea of professionalism itself as stemming from an old-fashioned notion of masculinity. She holds out hope for a future in which there are fewer unilateral decisions on the part of the expert and more involvement of all parties in decisions as to the kinds of health and social care that we need.

How, then, at the level of service planning, would we ensure that diverse voices are heard, that services respond to need and do not unwittingly make people more dependent than they need to be? Hearing user voices, involving the local community, responding to a consumer voice are all phrases much in evidence in present policy documents in health and social care. The section ends with a statement suggesting eight principles through which user empowerment might be more fully achieved. Barnes and Walker are deeply critical of the model of empowerment which underpins the NHS and Community Care Act of 1990, and their list of eight principles renders what is often an ambiguous concept both practical and usable.

Celia Davies and Martin Robb

# 13

# Striking Balances: Living with Parkinson's Disease

*Ruth Pinder*

Like other chronic illnesses which are of unknown aetiology, progressive and incurable, the trajectory of PD in any individual is uncertain and unpredictable. Its manifestations vary considerably from person to person. The classic triad of symptoms – tremor, rigidity and slowness of movement – is supplemented by a host of others which may affect some patients but not others. These range from chronic fatigue, early morning immobility, 'mumbly' if not incomprehensible speech, stooping gait, freezing or start/hesitation episodes, to mask-like facial immobility, all of which may be thoroughly disconcerting socially.

Superimposed on these symptoms – and often difficult to separate – are problems arising from the side-effects of the medication. Whereas the drugs mask some of the illness symptoms some of the time, they can produce other symptoms, such as mood and memory disturbances, involuntary movements, end-of-dose deterioration, and various forms of fluctuations, most dramatically the 'on/off' syndrome, where a patient changes from mobility to total immobility, often many times a day and with startling rapidity. In its extreme form this is known as 'yo-yoing'. Levodopa does not halt the underlying progression of the illness itself and tends ultimately to lose its efficacy. To add to the confusion, some symptoms are both illness- and drug-related and, as the illness progresses, these become increasingly difficult to disentangle. More importantly, *subjects* often have difficulty distinguishing them. For the purposes of analysis I have, therefore, treated them together. Patients must contend with multiple layers of uncertainty and unpredictability.

Even though he saw himself as being only mildly disabled, uncertainty as to just what he could usefully accomplish had led Mr C into a kind of mental paralysis where avoidance of all activities was his temporary mode of adaptation. As he commented:

Originally published in Robert Anderson and Michael Bury (eds) (1988) *Living with Chronic Illness*. London: Unwin Hyman. pp. 67–88 (abridged).

You see when I retired I had this plan of campaign . . . I wanted to continue flying which I can't any longer . . . I had visions of joining an organization like the Citizens' Advice Bureau, doing something useful which would occupy my time . . . . But I mean I'd have to write notes over the phone, I'd have to speak to people. I get this — like a frog in my throat occasionally – and they'd either take you for an idiot or something wrong with you and your advice wouldn't be accepted as sensible, or you'd have to explain what the matter was and I wouldn't want to. But that was going to be secondary to my main hobby which was flying. The difficulty now is to think of something which I could do which is going to replace that. And also, of course, the will to do it which is difficult . . . I haven't been able to start something else, you see.

It cannot, of course, be assumed that balances are always neatly struck. One of the most handicapping features about such a chronic illness is the precarious nature of the trade-offs which are made and the frequency with which one is caught off balance. Periods of equilibrium are interspersed with periods of intense *dis*equilibrium while new balancing plateaux are being negotiated – possibly one reason for the discrepancy between Mr C's perception of his sense of disability and handicap.

## Covering

As with any potentially discrediting condition, questions of visibility and unpredictability constantly have to be juggled with decisions about whether or not to tell, a factor which affected other subjects [in the study carried out by the author] in various life areas. Covering tactics designed to reject the social significance of disability are generally employed, but the risk of inadvertent disclosure and the incurring of disbelief, or even accusations of malingering, are always present.

Mrs F, however, felt sufficiently stable to be able to calculate within fairly fine limits what she was able to accomplish. With experience she has learned about the pattern of symptoms, their likely duration and intensity, and their implications for sustaining work and social demands – for the moment. As she explained:

I arrange things at the office, appointments, when I know I'm going to be in an 'on' situation, which is why I put Thursday night for the interview because I don't work Friday mornings. If there are any repercussions it doesn't matter.

Nevertheless, she, too, is well aware of the ways she can still be 'caught out'. Foot spasms, or as she describes it 'curly toes episodes' occur periodically and may last anything from 10 minutes to an hour, stretching her covering strategies to the limit. She describes one such episode at work:

It happened once when I was taking a property on and I didn't know what to do, because he didn't know and I was trying to carry on a conversation and trying to control it from the inside. I can't talk and control it at the same time. You need to be very careful not to have too long a day and take an outside appointment at the end of the day. It's at the end of the day when it happens.

Strict timetabling is crucial to her work management. It is, however, a price she readily pays for enabling her to lead a reasonably normal and satisfying work-life. Covering is facilitated by the gatekeeping tactics of her secretary who is 'in the know'. [. . .]

## Balancing between spouses

Balancing essentially involves other people, particularly patients' immediate families. Any differences in the definition of the illness trajectory *between* spouses may lead to serious difficulties. Although Mr Y defined himself as 'mildly disabled', this was not an interpretation accepted by his wife. Their lives were subject to intense disequilibrium as Mrs Y oscillated back and forth, from minute to minute, hour to hour and day to day over the question of whether to put her husband in a home, trading off the fears of her own loneliness against her perceived inability to manage him.

Differences in definitions also occurred between other spouses [. . .]. However, it seemed these could be contained within the supportiveness of their respective relationships. For Mrs Y, the perception of her husband's trajectory was not purely a physiologically objective fact. She was also weighing up definitions of her own deteriorating health against her perceived ability to manage her husband's frequent falls. A high price had been paid in terms of social isolation. As Mrs Y said:

> Friends, the don't *come* here very often. They phone me and tell me this and tell me that. But they don't actually *visit* here any more. They don't know how to behave towards him, I suppose.

It was a painful contrast to the rich social life enjoyed by the couple prior to the onset of Mr Y's illness. However, it was compounded by additional loneliness experienced within the confines of their marriage. Mr Y was virtually incapable of speech. With the greatest difficulty he said: 'I have decided not to let the loneliness bother me.'

Social isolation is perhaps one of the more distressing features of chronic illness. It is often both self-imposed – as in the case of Mrs P who withdrew altogether when her face 'froze' and speech was impossible, such was the felt stigma of her impairment – as well as being imposed from outside. Mrs U, like Mrs Y, felt the handicapping effects of illness as the unaffected spouse. As she commented, 'Well, we're both disabled, aren't we . . . I can't do what I'd like to do. I can't just go swanning off, can I? I'm tied up. My first priority is him.'

Others, however, found ways of circumventing this. Mr I, for instance, had a wide circle of friends who were not deterred if they inadvertently caught him in an 'off'. And Miss N, bereft of speech after brain surgery in the late 1960s, had nevertheless managed to carry on in spite of many years of loneliness and the inability to find a marriage partner. Her courage in 'getting things out of life' was attested to both by the nurse who called and her gentleman friend with whom she had formed a new relationship – and a new equilibrium – in life. She wrote:

> I've got a lot to be thankful for, but there I had it so young and without having the [brain] operation, who can tell what would have happened. . . . But I was a fighter and I was determined it should not win. . . . And I feel that life is sweet, or so they say.

## Over time

The need to accommodate to the increasing severity of symptoms often involves a radical restructuring of life. Some of the themes indicated so far are illustrated in more advanced form by Mr U. Additional considerations also have to be balanced. Mobile for only two hours in the morning, he is dependent on others for help the remainder of the day. The inability to reciprocate was initially felt to be particularly galling but accommodation has been made to this over time. As he commented (not without difficulty): 'I've got used to it now. Having to ask people to come and help you. And *waiting* for 'em to come and help . . . . You've got nothing to give in place of it though.' Time is a factor which increasingly dominates lifestyle. All normal activities, such as having a bath or socializing with the other residents, have to be squeezed into that two hours before his symptoms return.

Temporal considerations are even more complicated when periods of symptom relief are themselves unpredictable. Mr I's life was characterized by unpredictable and often violent 'yo-yoing'. Arriving one morning to talk I found him glued in frozen immobility in his chair. Enjoined by his wife to tell him a story, it was like watching a butterfly emerge from its chrysalis as he retrieved his speech, loosened up, flexed his muscles, and came to life before my eyes. Within an hour he was conversing animatedly and then performed his 'party trick', running up and down the stairs to his flat. An hour later, darkness descended again and he was reduced to total dependence on his wife. He described this as 'the Lazarus effect':

> I cram into the periods when I'm flexible all the things I would have liked to have done the rest of the day. It doesn't always work that way though. One day I may be nine-tenths of the day free, although that's very rare, and another much less. There's nothing I can do about it.

Life was structured round these precious intervals during which energies were stretched towards restoring some semblance of normality.

## Resources for coping

Implicit so far in what has been said is the use of self-help measures as a strategy. More explicitly, they are also a resource. Mrs Q, for example, practises physiotherapy exercises by marching down the corridor to empty her rubbish. 'There's a fear of taking those little steps I see some people doing. I do think it helps if you march along,' she said. Although the total unpredictability of Mr I's swings made attempts to plan life impossible, he took part in yoga classes when he could. As he put it, 'It's a bit less of lack of control really.'

Although seemingly small and insignificant, such attempts indicate the struggle to regain some purchase on the arbitrariness of the illness. To a greater or lesser extent, similar tactics were engaged in by most subjects in the group [interviewed by the author].

Information about the implications of PD is a crucial resource. To know the implications, as far as they can be known, is also to be 'in control' of the illness, and is, I suggest, part of the broader attempt to restore that sense of taken-for-grantedness enjoyed by others. Subjects, however, can only balance what they understand.

The role of doctors as a source of information was seen as problematic. Subjects rarely felt the implications of PD were discussed with them by their doctors. It must be stressed that the exact prognosis cannot be predicted early on. It is often only after a period of time that a likely pattern can be discerned. Yet certain *general* features of PD *can* be explained. Such bits and pieces as were assembled by patients were often the result of reading. Membership of the Parkinson's Disease Society was an important supplementary source of information. At different stages of their illness careers, therefore, patients had variable amounts of information with which to weigh their ability to carry on.

The complexity of the issue is well illustrated by Mrs P who discussed her changing needs for information:

> I would like to discuss a lot of things with him [Dr X]. . . . Well the symptoms really. I've never had the opportunity to discuss the symptoms. And what to expect. I'd like to ask him. It's hard, isn't it? The whole thing really. I'd like to discuss how other people cope with the illness on a fuller scale.

The amount of information held profoundly affects the considerations which are taken into account. In the earlier stages of her illness Mrs P was ignorant of the side-effects of drugs. She continued:

He told me nothing at all. It would have been a help if I'd known because after each appointment I thought it was part of the illness, the side-effects. I used to spend so much time in bookshops trying to find out. If I'd known that I'd have sorted something out.

The relief Mrs F felt when she did finally acquire and assimilate the information she was searching for demonstrates its central importance:

I found it much easier to come to terms with everything when I knew exactly what was happening, in laymen's terms . . . because I'd read the books I was better able to explain my situation. I could describe it in more accurate terms.

The need for patients to feel in some sort of control over what is going on, yet confronted with a profession apparently reluctant fully to share the information necessary suggests that an inappropriate model for dealing with a chronic condition is being applied (Barnard, 1985). A similar ambiguity will be seen to surround the question of developing expertise in managing the daily drug routine. [. . .]

## The drug regimen

This section will explore some of the group's efforts to balance the additional uncertainties, unpredictabilities and intrusiveness posed by the administration of the drug regimen. Clinically a balance is being sought between minimizing the symptoms of the illness consistent with incurring the lowest possible incidence of side-effects. It is a balance which, as the illness progresses, needs constant renegotiation. Subjects' recourse to lay knowledge, additional timetabling and scheduling strategies, and the development of a degree of expertise in managing the regimen illustrate the complexity of this additional balancing exercise.

Lack of information again appears to be an important consideration. The rationale of drug treatment and the decreasing efficacy of the drugs over time rarely appeared to be adequately explained to patients. Mr C expressed this most forcibly but his remarks were by no means untypical of those made by subjects diagnosed less recently than he.

I mean there doesn't seem to me even the remotest rationale as yet for the treatment. . . . You wonder why one drug is picked rather than the other. I think it just depends which specialist you go to. I mean why use Madopar instead of Sinemet? There must *be* a difference. But no specialist I've met is prepared to say 'Well, I would choose Sinemet for this patient and Madopar for that patient.' And give me a concrete reason for doing so.

Not surprisingly some subjects were often bewildered and confused. Mrs J, for instance, was obliged to rely on familiar recipes of knowledge gained over long experience with her husband's migraine medication to try and explain the apparent lack of efficacy of his current Levodopa regime:

> The basic problem is that a doctor will re-prescribe. And you had these migraine tablets for 20 years constantly churned out and the same thing's happening for Parkinson's. . . . It's what I've been saying, isn't there anything else they can do now this is levelling off a bit? I mean if you go for any other complaint and it doesn't seem any better or worse you'd want to say 'Well, let's try this, let's try that.'

In the ensuing vacuum Mr J had evolved a strategy of his own, that of adjusting his drug schedule according to how he feels.

> It's something I've done off my own bat. I believe my body tells me what is required. I say to myself 'I'm getting a bit of the shakes, I need so-and-so.' I'm usually right.

To a limited extent he felt 'in charge', but this was a precarious equilibrium as his wife strongly disapproved, wanting him to stick to the 'rules'.

Although Mr J and Mr C generally felt the current drug regime was not entirely helpful and its clinical administration haphazard, it did not constitute an intrusive element in their lives.

### Invasion

For Mrs P, however, the regime management quite dominated her life space and additional strategies were employed to manage it, namely strict timetabling and scheduling of all other activities around the regime. Her medication had recently been altered so she was faced with the problems of balancing all over again. She explained:

> Nothing could interfere with the taking of pills. They structure my life. Pill-taking, if you like, has ruled my life. . . . For example this morning [when she slept through the alarm] my first thought was 'I've got to get those tablets down me before you come'. . . . I've got to take medicines at different times *to enable me to do things*. It's not a case of 'take one tablet twice a day'. (emphasis added)

Talks with her were punctuated by pauses to consult the clock, calculate to the nearest five minutes the timing of her next dosage and decide what topics we could accomplish in the intervening time. Although defining herself as only moderately disabled and handicapped, the intrusiveness of the regime was the price she was prepared to pay to achieve some of the things she wanted and to sustain some semblance of a normal lifestyle.

The devastating effects of *mistiming* the pill regime were painfully illustrated in one of the first talks I had with Mr I early in the project. In his interest in the conversation, he had missed his 11 a.m. pill and I was insufficiently aware at the time of the necessity of checking people's schedules before embarking on talks. When I left him half an hour later, I found him virtually collapsed outside the door, an image of himself he had rigorously controlled for my benefit. One of the few strategies left open to him, as he explained later, was that of 'putting on a show', no matter what the cost was to him afterwards. Again the struggle to normalize social relationships is a powerful one, even if room for manoeuvre is minimal. [. . .]

*Patient expertise*

The fragility with which Mr R defined his position highlights a facet of PD which often characterizes chronic as opposed to acute illness careers: the necessity of developing a degree of expertise in handling both the illness and the drug therapy. However, the transition from patients' early expectations of medical control over their regime to a recognition that some control of drug balancing lies in their hands often comes as a shock. This was vividly expressed by Mr R: 'I wish the specialist would take me by the neck and say "Look, here's a regime, now go away and *stick* to it"', rather than being 'given permission' to adjust his dosage.

Mrs F, however, enjoyed relying on her own expertise. She was able to look back on her own period of disequilibrium when she had been dried out and experienced to the full the extent to which her illness had progressed, with some detachment. Now, with the approval of her doctors, she makes her own small adjustments according to the demands of the day:

> What they are nice about, they say in their letter 'This lady is intelligent, she knows what she's doing, will adjust her own dose.' So they just put one of the doses on the bottle, but I don't necessarily follow that.

The dependence of doctors on patients' *own* evaluations of what is going on in their bodies is perhaps one of the more equivocal considerations involved in managing the drug regime. As with other older patients, few subjects had been socialized into expecting to share with their doctors in any decision-making process. Patients such as Mr R were ill-prepared for such a role. It was felt that doctors were rarely explicit in guiding subjects towards a *modus vivendi* where their own daily knowledge and experience would be the linchpin in future illness and drug management.

Thus handling the additional demands of a drug regime, with its own almost independent career, only serves to accentuate the unpredictability, uncertainty and intrusiveness which already have to be contended with in managing symptoms. Additional strategies have to be adopted in weighing up how best to manage a therapeutic regime which is in itself problematic.

## Discussion and implications

[. . .] The struggle appears to be one of carrying on as normally as possible in an attempt, I suggest, to recapture some of that 'taken-for-grantedness' enjoyed by others.

Whereas many of the above features are common to other chronic illnesses – and indeed other life situations which represent loss and threat – some aspects are condition-specific. The use of a replacement therapy brings additional complications, uncertainties and unpredictabilities. The regime is not a constant. Periodically it has to be juggled and readjusted as the illness progresses, and ultimately it tends to cease to be effective. This calls for the adoption and refinement of very particular coping strategies by patients, chief of which are strict timetabling and scheduling of activities around the regime. [. . .]

The need for patients to develop some expertise, both in handling the daily demands of living with PD and coping with the exigencies of the drug regime, requires the development of policies more appropriate to the management of long-term illness. Patients need to be helped and guided towards what seems to some an unfamiliar role. Doctors, in effect, must act as facilitators in this process if they are to be of help and relevance to the chronically ill.

This demands new patterns of interaction based on a more truly participatory model of information-sharing and decision-making. The paradox of expecting patients to acquire some expertise but without sufficient information to do so has been demonstrated. This means a much closer appreciation of the way *patients* define their priorities and needs, and a respect for *their* – perhaps competing – preferences.

Two practical considerations suggest themselves. One is for the current emphasis in medical training on an interventionist approach to be shifted towards one geared to an understanding and supportive role. The second is the use by the medical profession and other health carers of the Parkinson's Disease Society as an educative and enabling resource.

## Reference

Barnard, D. (1985) 'Unsung questions of medical ethics', *Social Science and Medicine*, 21: 243–9.

# 14

# The New Obstetrics: Science or Social Control?

*Lesley Doyal*

For pregnant women living in the rich countries, risks [of the kind experienced by women in poorer countries] are now a thing of the past. Very few die in childbirth or suffer long-term problems as a result of pregnancy. The importance of these developments for women's health and well-being cannot be overestimated. However they do not mean that all maternity services are now as effective as they might be. Nor are all mothers satisfied with the care they receive. Indeed many have argued that recent developments in 'high-tech' obstetrics may be meeting doctors' needs more effectively than they meet those of their patients.

**New technologies for old skills**

Over the past hundred years or so the place of birth, the participants and the techniques employed have all changed in ways that have profoundly affected women (Arney, 1985; Garcia et al., 1990; Oakley, 1984). In most of the developed countries births have now been removed from the home. Ninety-eight per cent of British women currently deliver their babies in hospital, despite the lack of compelling evidence that this is safer than a home birth (Campbell and Macfarlane, 1990). The only exception to this pattern is the Netherlands, where about a third of deliveries still take place at home. As births have been institutionalized, the hospitals themselves have also grown larger, sometimes creating an inflexible and depersonalized environment for women in labour.

Most women now give birth in the presence of people whom they do not know. One study found that women in labour in a Canadian hospital faced an average of 6.4 unfamiliar professionals (Keirse et al., 1989: 807). Another noted that a low-risk mother in a British teaching

From Lesley Doyal (1995) *What Makes Women Sick: Gender and the Political Economy of Health.* London: Macmillan. pp. 133–8.

hospital saw 16 people in six hours, yet was often alone at crucial moments (Chard and Richards, 1977).

Assessing women's response to such situations is difficult, since they will have very different experiences and expectations. Many feel relieved to have their babies safely delivered, are grateful for whatever care they have received and are reluctant to complain. However others report feeling uncared for, and research in a number of countries has shown that they often lack both the emotional support and the factual information they would like (Kitzinger, 1978; Oakley, 1979; Reid and Garcia, 1989). In one British study the average time women spent with a doctor on ante-natal visits was 3.9 minutes (Oakley, 1984: 229). Similar experiences have been reported by women in Australia:

> The medical care which I received at the clinic was adequate. However waiting times of up to three hours, a different doctor each time and being invariably told 'not to worry' in reply to many of my questions, and a three-minute consultation did little to make me feel I was being 'cared for' in any way. (Health Department, Victoria, 1990: 28).

There is a wealth of evidence to show the importance of social and psychological support in enhancing the well-being of mothers and babies, yet these are often given very low priority (Elbourne et al., 1989).

Childbirth is increasingly defined as 'doctors' business' and as a result most pregnancies are treated as pathological unless proved otherwise. Most women begin their labour in a healthy condition and want medical care on hand in case it might be needed. Most doctors, on the other hand, have been trained to see labouring mothers as 'at risk' patients, whose 'normality' can only be proved after the event. This leads many to intervene in straightforward labours when it may be unnecessary and possibly even damaging. While some women will be prepared to accept whatever treatment is offered, others will be reluctant and it is this unwillingness to accede to medical control that lies at the heart of many women's dissatisfaction with their experience of contemporary childbirth. Again, an Australian mother expressed the feeling reported by many others:

> The doctor seemed to be working to an unspoken timetable. If I hadn't delivered in a certain time, he was going in there to bring the baby out, whether it was necessary or not. I thought, 'what the heck, I may as well give up, let him do the lot'. (Health Department, Victoria, 1990: 35)

Mothers in many countries have voiced their disquiet about the inflexibility of hospital routines as well as the demeaning nature of much medicalized childbirth. The rituals of shaving of pubic hair for instance, or giving an enema at the onset of labour, can cause considerable discomfort, yet there is no evidence that they are effective in achieving a more successful outcome. Indeed enemas can actually be hazardous as documented cases of rectal irritation, colitis, gangrene and anaphylactic shock have demonstrated (Garforth and Garcia, 1989: 823–4).

Similarly, there are no data to show that routine episiotomies do anything to improve either delivery or post-partum recovery (Chalmers et al., 1989). Sheila Kitzinger has described such procedures as 'genital mutilation' and they are certainly the commonest cause of perineal damage (Kitzinger,1989: 107). An episiotomy can be painful, leaves a wound that requires suturing and forms a scar. It remains the most frequently performed surgical operation in the United States and in several European countries, yet many women do not even realize it is being done to them and certainly do not give their active consent (Banta and Thacker, 1982; World Health Organization, 1986).

These concerns about modern obstetrics have intensified with the growth of what has been called 'active management of labour'. During the 1960s and 1970s the science of pregnancy developed dramatically (Schwartz, 1990). Obstetricians were no longer reliant on rudimentary empirical techniques and a 'wait and see' approach. Instead they were able to utilize a whole array of new technologies that facilitated the electronic surveillance of women in labour and encouraged early intervention at any sign of apparent abnormality. For obstetricians these developments have meant an enhancement of their professional status and a bolstering of their scientific respectability. They have also been able to lay claim to a new patient – the foetus – who had hitherto been hidden from view and largely untouchable. However, the implications for women and their babies remain a matter for debate.

The new reproductive technologies have attracted a great deal of attention and a large amount of resources. Yet we still know very little about their effectiveness since few clinical trials preceded their introduction (Chalmers, 1989). Their impact on women's psychological experiences of childbearing and on the emotional relationship between mother and baby have received even less attention. As a result many of those on whom they are used have been made into unwitting 'pioneers' on the road to medicalized birth (Rapp, 1987). As the routine use of these new technologies increases, there is growing concern that women are not consenting to them in any active way – or sometimes in any way at all (Faden, 1991; Whitbeck, 1991).

## Managing labour

The new interventionism in obstetrics began with the development of a range of technologies for monitoring the foetus *in utero*. These include biochemical tests such as amniocentesis to identify genetic abnormalities, ultrasound imaging to give a visual impression, and electronic monitoring to assess various aspects of physiological functioning. In most countries the growing use of these surveillance techniques has been accompanied by an increased rate of other interventions in labour – more induced births and Caesarean sections in particular. They have also led to a growing desire on the part of many doctors to 'manage' the unborn baby, sometimes at the expense of the mother. Thus it is doctors who are increasingly active in labour while women take it lying down, too often becoming the passive recipient of medical ministrations.

Significantly, doctors often initiate labour itself through inducing contractions by artificial means. Most commonly a hormonal drip is used either to start the uterus contracting or to speed it up if the process is judged to be too slow. While there are clearly circumstances in which such techniques can be valuable, their use cannot always be justified in terms of immediate clinical need. In the United Kingdom inductions rose rapidly in the late 1960s and early 1970s, reaching a high of 40 per cent of all births. Numbers levelled off in the mid-1970s, but by 1978 about a third of all labours were still being started by artificial means (Macfarlane and Mugford, 1984: 162). The World Health Organization recently recommended that the induction of labour should be reserved for specific medical indications and that no geographical region should have rates of induced labour over 10 per cent (World Health Organization, 1985).

These techniques are no longer confined to sophisticated hospitals. There have recently been alarming reports of a growth in their use on women giving birth at home without medical back-up. Fifteen per cent of mothers interviewed in the North Indian village had been given an injection of synthetic oxytocin if labour did not proceed as expected. As the authors of the study comment,

> The popularity of these injections could hardly be more ironic. Male practitioners display no inhibition about administering them, relying simply on the dai's assessment of cervical dilatation and the baby's presentation. The injection of a standard dose of oxytocin (rather than a steadily monitored intravenous drip) results in acute discomfort from the almost instantly amplified pains. Moreover there are risks of rupturing the uterus, damaging the cervix or causing severe foetal distress or after-pains. (Jeffery et al., 1989: 112)

In developed countries, most induced labours also involve continuous electronic foetal monitoring (EFM) of the baby through electrodes attached either inside or outside the mother's body. In the United States EFM is now used in at least 50 per cent of all births, though randomized controlled trials have failed to demonstrate that it benefits either mother or child (Grant, 1989; Simkin, 1986). On the contrary, a 'managed' labour of this kind may involve a significant loss of autonomy for the mother, causing both physical and psychological distress: 'I felt my labour had been taken over by strangers and machines . . . any fragile confidence I may have had in my body's ability to handle birth had vanished. I was frightened and despairing' (Health Department, Victoria, 1990: 100).

While some women will find the presence of technology reassuring, others resent the inevitable restrictions on their freedom. Many find that medical attention is focused not on their own judgements or feelings but on the messages coming from the machines. Thus the new technologies have frequently led to a deterioration in personal care, with women left to labour under the less than tender gaze of a bank of machines.

> I was put on a drip which was switched off at frequent intervals to 'get some action here'. After four or five hours I was told that my baby was distressed and I was only two centimetres dilated. I believe this was because I was induced when my cervix wasn't ready.
>
> They were helpful and sympathetic but they could not allay my feeling that the baby's distress and the Caesarean section could have been avoided if I'd been left alone. (Phillips and Rakusen, 1989: 391)

As well as the experiential problems associated with induction there is also a clinical literature connecting it with increased rates of premature labour, foetal distress, jaundice and maternal infections (Chard and Richards, 1977). Both induction and EFM appear to have contributed to the recent increase in other forms of active intervention, particularly Caesarean section. Between 1968 and 1983 the proportion of babies born by Caesarean section rose by 250 per cent in England and Wales, by 300 per cent in the Netherlands, and by 380 per cent in the United States (Grant, 1989: 1185). Increases have also been noted in some third world countries, especially in Latin America (Janowitz et al., 1982). Attempts to reduce the rate of operative deliveries have met with considerable resistance from doctors (Ruzek, 1991; Stafford, 1990). By 1986 about a quarter of all North American babies were being delivered by surgical means, and some commentators have suggested that this figure could reach 40 per cent by the year 2000 (Placek et al., 1988: 562).

# References

Arney, W.R. (1985) *Power and the Profession of Obstetrics*. Chicago: University of Chicago Press.

Banta, D. and Thacker, S. (1982) 'The risks and benefits of episiotomy: a review', *Birth*, 9(1): 25–30.

Campbell, R. and Macfarlane, A. (1990) 'Recent debate on the place of birth', in J. Garcia, R. Kilpatrick and M. Richards (eds), *The Politics of Maternity Care: Services for Childbearing Women in Twentieth Century Britain*. Oxford: Clarendon Press.

Chalmers, I. (1989) 'Evaluating the effects of care during pregnancy and childbirth', in I. Chalmers, M. Enkin and M. Keirse (eds), *Effective Care in Pregnancy and Childbirth*, Vol. 2. Oxford: Clarendon Press.

Chalmers, I., Garcia, J. and Post, S. (1989) 'Hospital policies for labour and delivery', in I. Chalmers, M. Enkin and M. Keirse (eds), *Effective Care in Pregnancy and Childbirth*, Vol. 2. Oxford: Clarendon Press.

Chard, T. and Richards, M. (1977) *Benefits and Hazards of the New Obstetrics*. London: Heinemann.

Elbourne, D., Oakley, A. and Chalmers, I. (1989) 'Social and psychological support during pregnancy', in I. Chalmers, M. Enkin and M. Keirse (eds), *Effective Care in Pregnancy and Childbirth*, Vol. 2. Oxford: Clarendon Press.

Faden, R. (1991) 'Autonomy, choice and the new reproductive technologies: the role of informed consent in prenatal genetic diagnosis', in J. Rodin and A. Collins (eds), *Women and New Reproductive Technologies: Medical, Psychosocial, Legal and Ethical Dilemmas*. Hillsdale, NJ: Lawrence Erlbaum Associates.

Garcia, J., Kilpatrick, R. and Richards, M. (1990) *The Politics of Maternity Care: Services for Childbearing Women in Twentieth Century Britain*. Oxford: Clarendon Press.

Garforth, S. and Garcia, J. (1989) 'Hospital admission practices', in I. Chalmers, M. Enkin and M. Keirse (eds), *Effective Care in Pregnancy and Childbirth*, Vol. 2. Oxford: Clarendon Press.

Grant, A. (1989) 'Monitoring the fetus during labour', in I. Chalmers, M. Enkin and M. Keirse (eds) *Effective Care in Pregnancy and Childbirth*, Vol. 2. Oxford: Clarendon Press.

Health Department, Victoria (1990) *Having a Baby in Victoria: Final Report of the Ministerial Review of Birthing Services in Victoria*. Melbourne: Health Department.

Janowitz, B., Nakamura, M., Lins, F., Brown, M. and Clopton, D. (1982) 'Caesarean section in Brazil', *Social Science and Medicine*, 16(1): 19–25.

Jeffery, P., Jeffery, R. and Lyon, A. (1989) *Labour Pains and Labour Power: Women and Childbearing in India*. London: Zed Press.

Keirse, M., Enkin, M. and Lumley, J. (1989) 'Social and professional support during childbirth', in I. Chalmers, M. Enkin and M. Keirse (eds), *Effective Care in Pregnancy and Childbirth*, Vol. 2. Oxford: Clarendon Press.

Kitzinger, S. (1978) *Women as Mothers*. London: Fontana.

Kitzinger, S. (1989) 'Childbirth and society', in I. Chalmers, M. Enkin and M. Keirse (eds), *Effective Care in Pregnancy and Childbirth*, Vol. 1. Oxford: Clarendon Press.

Macfarlane, A. and Mugford, M. (1984) *Birth Counts: Statistics of Pregnancy and Childbirth*. London: HMSO.

Oakley, A. (1979) *Becoming a Mother*. Oxford: Martin Robertson.

Oakley, A. (1984) *The Captured Womb: a History of the Medical Care of Pregnant Women*. Oxford, Basil Blackwell.

Phillips, A. and Rakusen, J. (1989) *The New Our Bodies Our Selves: a Health Book by and for Women*. Harmondsworth: Penguin.

Placek, P., Taffel, S. and Moien, M. (1988) '1986: C-sections rise; VBAC's inch upward', *American Journal of Public Health*, 78: 562–3.

Rapp, R. (1987) 'Moral pioneers: women, men and fetuses on a frontier of reproductive technology', *Women and Health*, 13(1–2): 101–16.

Reid, M. and Garcia, J. (1989) 'Women's views of care during pregnancy and childbirth', in I. Chalmers, M. Enkin and M. Keirse (eds), *Effective Care in Pregnancy and Childbirth*, Oxford: Clarendon Press.

Ruzek, S. (1991) 'Women's reproductive rights: the impact of technology', in J.Rodin and A. Collins (eds), *Women and the New Reproductive Technologies: Medical, Psychosocial, Legal and Ethical Dilemmas*. Hillsdale, NJ: Lawrence Erlbaum Associates.

Schwartz, E. (1990) 'The engineering of childbirth: a new obstetric programme as reflected in British obstetric textbooks 1960–1980', in J. Garcia, R. Kilpatrick and M. Richards (eds), *The Politics of Maternity Care: Services for Childbearing Women in Twentieth Century Britain*. Oxford: Clarendon Press.

Simkin, P. (1986) 'Is anyone listening? Lack of clinical impact of randomised controlled trials of electronic fetal monitoring', *Birth*, 13: 219–22.

Stafford, R. (1990) 'Alternative strategies for controlling rising Caesarian rates', *Journal of the American Medical Association*, 263(5): 683–7.

Whitbeck, C. (1991) 'Ethical issues raised by the new medical technologies', in J. Rodin and A. Collins (eds), *Women and New Reproductive Technologies: Medical, Psychosocial, Legal and Ethical Dilemmas*. Hillsdale NJ: Lawrence Erlbaum Associates.

World Health Organization (1985) 'Appropriate technology for birth', *Lancet*, 2: 436–7.

World Health Organization (1986) *Having a Baby in Europe*. Copenhagen: WHO Regional Office for Europe.

# 15

# Listening and Life-History Work

*John Killick*

For the past three years I have worked in nursing homes as a Writer in Residence with people with dementia. My aim has been to form relationships and to write down the words of residents as a contribution to care planning. I must stress that my approach is that of a writer and not of a mental health trained professional, and so my personal observations and interpretations offered here should be read with that in mind. Nevertheless I believe that the 'outsider' does have something to offer in this situation – an unprejudiced view, and the time to concentrate upon communication as a significant element in the care process.

Most care in institutional settings, regrettably, appears to be reactive in nature, concerned to resolve problems as they present themselves in an empirical manner. This is crisis management, but what happens when there is no crisis? Too often everyone relaxes into a status quo that is routinely unstimulating. When challenged as to why there is such a low level of activity staff will probably say something like 'The resident is comfortable, clean, tidy, warm, well-nourished. What more is there for us to do? He/she just wants to sit in a chair and not participate in anything.'

The proactive care I wish to advocate involves helping the person with dementia to function so that they are more fulfilled. And the main characteristics of such an approach are that, firstly, it should be individualized, secondly that it should be based upon a person's current abilities rather than deficits, and thirdly that it should function at all times and in all situations.

In many nursing homes there are times set aside for activities, and organizers are appointed for the purpose of providing such stimulation. Extremely valuable though such sessions can be, they are only a partial contribution to proactive care. They tend to be of a group nature, so as to involve as many residents as possible, and so they rarely reflect individual characteristics or take account of individual preferences. And they are of limited duration, and are preceded and succeeded by long wastes of unstructured time. What is needed to complement these is one-to-one sessions where the residents are given the opportunity to unburden themselves, and also a regime where all staff are positively encouraged to listen carefully at all times to what the individuals in their care have to say and to write these observations down. In that way a picture of the past lives of residents is built up, as well as valuable insights being cast upon their state of mind in the present.

This view of life-history work as something all-embracing to which all staff contribute is one which is gaining ground. Amongst its positives are the following:

1  We are helping individuals to remember, a very important process for those who are experiencing the loss of that faculty which gives them a sense of perspective on their lives.
2  We are inevitably involving relatives, who can often supply vital pieces of information – in some cases even the clues which will enable us to complete the jigsaw. Relatives often feel helpless in the face of the disease and this provides them with an opportunity to make a contribution.
3  We are reminding ourselves that those in our charge have led full and interesting lives and it enables us to see them as complete human beings.
4  Lastly, it will make our work as enablers more fulfilling. Life-history compiling with people with dementia will of necessity prove difficult, painstaking, and often painful, but it will be enriched by bringing us closer to our colleagues, because it can only be carried out effectively as part of a team.

I believe it is important that life histories should contain as much as possible of the individual's own words. Before the dementia struck they were the ultimate authorities on themselves; some of that will remain, and even when they present us with their lives in fragmented form there is much to be learned about their present perceptions; their hopes and fears, from what they say and the way that they say it.

There follow three accounts by individuals of their lives, followed by my suggestions of some of the ways in which they might be used to influence the design of the care offered to them. All the writing has been done by myself, either at the time or subsequently from a tape recording. My own contributions to the conversations have been edited out. Although I sometimes prompt with a question, generally speaking I intervene as little as possible, offering support and showing interest. I try *not* to set an agenda: my role is to befriend and then give space to the person to say as much or as little as they like on whatever topics they choose. Although there are many differences between the accounts, I believe all three to be full of human interest and value, if interpreted with insight and empathy. All the names of places and people have been changed to safeguard anonymity.

### Albert Edwards

Do I mind whether you write down what I say? I was under the impression that it was your job to do that. So what are you moaning about?

Conway? Oh you do know where I was born! Right on the seafront near the old General Hospital. How many children in the family? Five. Well that might be on the narrow side. Seven actually. Neither all boys nor all girls but a mixture of the two kinds. Do you want a stab at my placing? I was the penultimate one. Mind, over that time there was a marriage which altered things a bit. In those days that was quite common.

My father had his own business. Coach-building. Most of our life we worked in a garage and he was repairing horsedrawn vehicles. I can't comment on the skill of it. What you'd get now is private bus hire. He would hire and sell, a bit of each. We lived in the house attached to the garage. The horses were kept in stables. Not only that, there was a smithy attached. In those days we didn't mend so many punctures, we shoed horses.

I passed my fair share to end up where I did. It was general subjects. You tell me one that wasn't covered. I did studies bordering on chemistry. It was chemistry, though it wasn't called that. Everything was in my curriculum.

When I left school I could drive the horses. I could do my bit in all the trades. And, of course, in those days garage was coming into its own. It was gradual. I can't remember the first car, because I wasn't in the business at that time.

[*to another resident*] Have you ever tried not interrupting people? It would thrill you to the bone!

I should mention that I had no trouble in persuading the girl-friend that we should become a pair. But I don't say that romance was accomplished.

[*to another resident*] Are you addressing me? Well I'm having a conversation here. Come over if you want to speak with me. I'll talk to anyone as long as they take the trouble to observe the priorities.

Later I became a house-builder. Coach-building and house-building are really nothing alike, but I moved from one to the other. You can't really compare them at all. Built my own home? Now you've hit the nail right on the cross with that question. That achievement came quite a bit afterwards, I believe.

If they were playing true to form the fish would still be swimming in my fish pond. Two were possibly gold-coloured. The others were anything from black to white. I don't know why they call them goldfish.

Answer me this now: Tea, why has it got to be at three o'clock precisely?

Now the tea-making got mixed up with the building. No, the tea-making was the mainstay of the building. If that was not the case you might as well pack up. The building work was secondary. Of course, if the lady of the house didn't make one you didn't get one. My tribe would never go in and make their own. If I think of it, tomorrow I'll show you a letter from one of my clients, a very nice lady. I put a bungalow on the side of her house.

Funnily enough, I was never a drinker. If it came to a choice between alcohol and tea the decision was clear.

And then there was the golfing. You can't frequent a golf course in a pub. The object of the game is to hit the ball as fast as you can, direction immaterial. The force is the object. There were four of us played together, and three had a hole in one. I've never owned a set of clubs in my life. And I've never owned a trolley. Maybe that's why I always carried aluminium clubs. Playing Gleneagles by moonlight? – That's one of the stories that may have been exaggerated. I enjoyed my golf. I wasn't the best. The other three were.

Shall I tell you something I don't want too broadcast – I'm here on a golfing holiday, and they haven't even got a course!

I have two sons, and there's a girl knocking about somewhere.

Tell me, if you were breaking your neck for a cup of tea, who amongst all these people would you approach?

I'm wondering how much my eldest son was involved in my return to North Wales. I believe I may have been in hospital before I was here. I can't tell you how much Wales has changed.

[*A care assistant arrives with tea.*] Do you remember eight seconds ago how you smiled at me? You've got teas made for life! But in this place you have to beg for it.

I'm on tablets continuously. I think I've taken six every morning for years. To find out if they do any good I'd have to stop taking them for months and that's a bit of a risk.

[*to the same care assistant*] In this place all the cups of tea end halfway up. If I get tea in a saucer anyone can have it. If a girl is cheerful I don't care how she makes a cup of tea – so long as it's like this one!

In the past I've enjoyed my living. So I do today . . . but I've got to go very careful now. The consequences is why I've got to be careful.

The best way to improve this place is . . . bigger cups! I don't know whether that's my view of tea or golf!

I never saw quite so many people in one place with feet trouble; I only notice this because I'm forced into it. And there's a devil of a sight more ladies interesting than there are men.

About this place, I can't say I don't like anything, because there isn't anything I dislike. Since I've been here I've acquired two lockers. Whether that's a good or a bad thing is a difficult question to answer. The problem is: I'm more used to playing with gentlemen

than ladies. Another time I sit down and think: where the devil's the
money coming from to pay for all this?

Do you have to go? Please don't. I'm enjoying this conversation.

What I want to know is: what am I doing here, and for how long? I
don't know where my sons live now. I don't want it to be Conway. I
want it to be Kendal because that's my home.

I'll add the swear-words after I've read the piece you've written.
Leave plenty ,of blank pages.

[*to another care assistant*] Is there any limit to when I get the top
half of this cup of tea?

### Commentary

The first issue raised by this piece, and the easiest to resolve, is
Albert's perception of the limitations of his freedom of action, which
has become concentrated on the provision of cups of tea.

Secondly, there is the sharpness of Albert's tongue exercised on
staff and other residents. Is it a characteristic of his conversational
style, or a symptom of his illness, or has it been developed as a
reaction to being in an institution? This is a matter which merits
further investigation.

Thirdly, there is his declared interest in golf and conversation
(particularly male). Opportunities should be found, if possible, for him
to indulge in both.

Lastly, there is his demand to know why he is there and for how
long – both perfectly reasonable requests. If it is judged that he is able
to cope with the facts then surely staff are morally obliged to present
them to him?

### Jessie Jamieson

I'm Jessie from Jedborough. There's some beautiful people in it.
Like me. I've always looked after myself.

I was a schoolteacher. I was 18 years old at the time. I can't see
you doing it. You can keep the weather in order there. Just across
the road. The war broke out and we all had to do our own bit. Our
Sunday School was lovely, writing letters and that. So we made our
almanac.

We've all had children. I had six: James, Jane, Audrey, Alice,
Alan, Heather. Then we came to the farmhouse. There's little places
for you to come and sit. Down there there's so many teachers. And if
you come up there's lots of schoolchildren. You don't know what
there is at Jedborough.

My family name was Allan. My father was a shepherd. I had a
sister called Jemima. I had a brother became a cobbler.

The children would say 'Can I go with you, Aunt Jessie?' And I'd say 'Yes, if you're good bairns.'

My parents were very strict. But when I got older, I told them what to do.

I've had some good times and some bad times, but I do love children. But they're all lazy and scruffy today.

We had to walk there and back. Mother said, 'When you go show that you're there to walk.'

It was powerful and strong, what they were giving us.

I know what you did: you pinched out of character.

They're better now, things. You used to ask the teacher if you could have a bag of chips for sixpence. When I started teaching, I got 12 shillings. You earned it.

'If you're going in the street, remember your manners!'

I still have my school teaching clothes yet. Mortarboard. We went down this morning at a quarter to six. I taught all subjects. Some of my pupils were very good. But others said 'We'll come another day.' Some of them are still living here now.

This place is for juicy apples and plums. It's beautiful here. Our children think the world of it. Every Sunday morning I go to the chapel.

We're having stuff that's pinched for our lunch today.

You men are too lazy to work. We women – we're ironing and doing all sorts all the time.

Sea sand's all right. It's dear, but you get good value.

This is all that we've knitted around me. But they pay us well.

I never liked all this writing. I never liked school but we had to do as we were told.

It's harder work for the teacher than for the kiddies.

I can't get about much. But we have everything at home. Daddy has a big garden there.

I've travelled – Melstone, Tweedham. I'm just having a few days' leave.

She wears no fancy clothes. I wear shepherd's clothes. She's a lassie from Lancashire. And you need to get your hair cut!

Jedborian I am. And I like boats.

Spending my time? I never earn any, with four little girls and two little boys. I love bairns.

My dad said 'An' you can stop that an' all. You'll not be bringin' fellers to this hoose!'

## Commentary

A number of pieces of information (that she was a schoolteacher, the size of her family) are vouchsafed here.

Her personality traits shine through clearly – forthrightness, organizing ability, warmth, wit. She is attached to place, family, profession.

Her conversation is fragmented. Coherent patterns of facts and ideas can be assembled by piecing items together afterwards.

The caustic references to men suggest that she prefers the company of other women.

Her organizing ability might be harnessed to mutual advantage. Perhaps she could be encouraged to assist with a domestic routine or recreational activity?

## Jane Arnell

I did notice you before, I've been here for quite a while. I have become very merciless or mercenary. I can never think of the word. Anyway the person goes wandering off. I've become like that and it worries me. [*cries*]

Walking is so difficult. I take about an hour to go down to the lav. I never thought that this would come to me. I'm becoming . . . I don't know what. [Of my tape recorder] That's your philharmonic, isn't it? Or am I getting that way?

I'm fostering, I've become more . . . well, put it this way, nothing would stop me talking if I could find something to talk about.

People haven't time to talk to me now because it takes such a long time. I've never been an over-volulous person. I'm feeling I'm getting more silent. I feel that no one wants to bother with me any more. [*cries*]

My mind, my whole sphere of life, is full. I was very fond of my life. It seems that I'm leaving it more and more. Oh dear, it isn't fair when your heart wants to remember! [*cries*]

I often wonder why people bother with people like us. I could have reeled it off for what you are doing. It's a life story. It's the bibliography of the person you are writing about. It's me.

There's one thing about this world – they're very good to them, bringing them to the table. This is a mental home, you know. Most of the people here need looking after. And if I were truthful, I would say that includes me.

I've always had dogs. And puppies as well. They'll always tack into me. I prefer large dogs, but I don't mind what kind. I had up to two or three at a time. Black Labradors I had for 15 years. I like every dog that will take to me. I have a photograph of Sal, my golden retriever.

I was a keen gardener, but I didn't like getting my hands dirty. My brothers only minded it.

I'm tammering, stammering again. I've freed myself, but next week I'm having my conversation through breath.

He's a new gentleman. He's like a set of sentences: 'How do you settle? What do you do?'

Yesterday morning we thought she must have mistaken me for someone else. She goes around and around. I think she's a little confused. Everybody knows her. She's a menace in a nice way.

I'm suffering from the same person. It is a sufferer. I don't like to hurt her. And I don't like to say anything. I haven't got the tongue for it.

I've known her since when. But even still I don't know her intimately. But she never insists on stressing me. It's very difficult to say no to people. . . .

This lady who cries understands my voice. Some time during every conversation she goes into a grizzle.

When that chap leaps up, I have to be careful.

That man, he's riding in a nice setting.

There are 30 people here, and they were settling in. . . . That was last week. Funny how people wanting to know you . . . and it's very difficult.

*Commentary*

In this piece we see the beginnings of loss of speech, which shows itself in tailed-off sentences and mistaken uses of words.

Jane is very distressed, cries often, and knows the reason why (see the paragraph beginning 'My mind, my whole sphere of life . . .'). Indeed, she shows great self-knowledge (see the paragraph beginning 'There's one thing about this world . . .') which must be a burden.

She feels neglected, and more time must be found for listening to her and reassuring her that she is valued as a person.

At the same time she shows intense interest in her fellow residents, and this can be harnessed by helping her to make relationships and giving her opportunities to take part in social activities.

Finally, she loves dogs, and ways can surely be found of ensuring that she sees one regularly.

As a writer for Westminster Health Care, my task is in a sense completed when I have word-processed a particular piece of writing. But, of course, this is only the end of a stage of the process. I may return to the nursing home and present the piece to the resident personally. It may be appropriate to share it with relatives (sometimes relatives request that I work with their loved one, and keenly discuss the text with me afterwards). Certainly copies will be presented to the home manager and head of unit, who in turn will share the insights gained with staff. It may be decided that another conversation, or a series of conversations, with the resident would prove valuable.

But every piece of writing can have practical outcomes. In the case of Albert Edwards, for example, for whom frequent cups of tea assume such importance, the provision of a Teasmade in his bedroom solved this problem at a stroke. The resolution of other issues can take longer and involve a concerted staff effort. Answering Albert's questions about his presence on the unit involved conversations with his relatives and some sensitive conversations with Albert over a period of time.

Confusion and the resultant isolation felt by the individual, as expressed most poignantly here by Jane Arnell, is the most widespread characteristic revealed by my work, and this is where the atmosphere of a unit can contribute much. An environment which is relaxed and compassionate can encourage someone like Jane to participate more. The very act of self-expression is itself a means of staving off despair, and if she is helped to talk more and develop relationships she may well be a happier, more rooted individual.

# 16

# Approaches to Reminiscence

*Joanna Bornat*

This chapter begins with a quotation from Dobroff (1984), who is remembering the impact of a particular piece of writing – 'The life review: an interpretation of reminiscence in the aged', by Butler (1963), a US psycho-geriatrician. I quote from Dobroff's article at some length because of its importance on a number of counts. Though it was written in the mid-1980s and describes experiences on the other side of the Atlantic, it neatly and dramatically illustrates some key themes relating to reminiscence work in Britain which I will be developing in this chapter.

> Perhaps tape recorders and word-processing machines are to the spoken word what the phonograph is to music: they make it possible for us to preserve the voices of our mothers and fathers telling us the history of their times. Technology expands the possibilities, and interest rises with the dawning recognition of the possibilities. In the field of aging, interest began with the publication in 1963 of a seminal paper by Dr Robert Butler. . . . It is not often that one paper has so important and immediate an effect. I was then a very junior social worker on the staff of a home for the aged. I remember well being taught by our consulting psychiatrists and the senior social work staff about the tendency of our residents to talk about childhood in the shtetls of East Europe or arrival at Ellis Island or early years on the Lower East Side of New York. At best, this tendency was seen as an understandable, although not entirely healthy preoccupation with happier times, understandable because these old and infirm people walked daily in the shadow of death. At worst 'living in the past' was viewed as pathology – regression to the dependency of the child, denial of the passage of time and the reality of the present, or evidence of organic impairment of the intellect.
> It was even said that remembrance of things past could cause or deepen depression among our residents, and God forgive us, we were to divert the old from reminiscing through activities like bingo and arts and crafts.
> And then the Butler paper came out and was read and talked about and our world changed. The Life Review became not only a normal activity; it was seen as a therapeutic tool. . . . In a profound sense, Butler's writings liberated both the old and the nurses, doctors and social workers; the old were free to remember, to regret, to look reflectively at the past and try to understand it. And we were free to listen and to treat rememberers and

First published in I. Norman and S. Redfern (eds) (1996) *Mental Health Care for Elderly People*. Edinburgh: Churchill Livingstone. pp. 393–417 (abridged).

remembrances with the respect they deserved, instead of trivializing them by diversion to a bingo game. (Dobroff, 1984: xvii–xviii)

Talking to long-experienced staff members in health and social care it is often possible to hear a similar watershed experience being described. There was a time, 15 or 20 years or more ago now, when reminiscence or reminiscence work as it has commonly come to be known was not regarded as an acceptable activity. Older staff will remember, like Rose Dobroff, that they were expected to discourage or distract the older people in their care from talking about the past. Some found it very difficult to stick to this prohibition. They knew that many older people, like people from any age group, enjoy talking about the past. They also knew that they themselves enjoyed listening to stories and accounts of past times which were irretrievably lost. One such person was Susan Hale, a psychiatric social worker who, in 1960, wrote how she had become 'quick to spy out possible openings, a given away testimonial or framed photograph on the wall, a presentation clock, a pair of clogs or a case of tropical butterflies, and one sits on tenterhooks manoeuvring to get the conversation round to them' (Hale, 1960: 153).

Of course those older workers also remember people whose memories were painful and upsetting. Looking back now it seems cruel to expect that pain and guilt should have to be silently endured in isolation. Again Rose Dobroff recalls how sharing those feelings could help to relieve painful memories. Speaking of a man who blamed himself for the deaths of his wife and daughter in the Holocaust because however hard he worked in the 1920s, he had not been able to save enough money to pay for their fares from Poland to New York, she observes: 'How could anyone understand his pain and try to find an anodyne for it if his story remained private, isolated from the history of the pogroms of the late 1800s and the immigrants' experiences, including their failures, in the New World?' (Dobroff, 1984: xix).

The memories of older workers are witness to a profound change in thinking about the part which the past plays in the lives of older people. Elsewhere I have called this a 'social transformation' (Bornat, 1989: 16) because the changes in attitude and in practice were sweeping and dramatic and involved a broad swathe of people caring and working with older people. [. . .]

I have laid much emphasis on the impact of one person's contribution to a change in thinking about reminiscence. It is certainly the case that Butler's paper in 1963, with its focus on life review as a 'naturally occurring, universal mental process characterised by the progressive return to consciousness of past experiences, and, particularly, the resurgence of unresolved conflicts' (1963: 66) did much to assert a key role for remembering in a re-evaluation of relationships between psychological processes and old age. Butler's suggestion that life review is a normal part of human mental activity, but with particular significance at later stages in life, helped to initiate debates and research which increasingly looked at old age in more positive and sympathetic terms. The idea that older people faced a certain inescapable existential issue – death, loss, finitude – was increasingly seen by some psychologists as generating particular mental strategies.

Erik Erikson's theory that individuals pass through a series of developmental stages of psychosocial development was particularly important in debates which highlighted the contribution of life review to later life: 'Part of the old-age process of reviewing the sense of oneself across the life-cycle involves a coming to terms with perceived mistakes, failures and omissions – with chances missed and opportunities not taken' (Erikson et al., 1986: 141).

Many of the early studies in the 1960s and 1970s sought to validate Butler's theory that life review is a necessary part of successful ageing. McMahon and Rhudick's (1964) study of veterans of the Spanish–American war, for example, found a group of men who were well adjusted psychologically and who were actively engaged in reminiscence. Lewis (1971), again studying a group of older men, found that reminiscence provided a possible support against threats to present views of self. Kiernat (1979) studied a group of nursing home residents who were mainly women and found that behaviour changed favourably during an opportunity to engage in life review. Lewis and Butler (1974), reporting on life review work with individuals and groups, suggested that life review helps older people to establish meaning in their lives.

Haight, in reviews of the literature (1991, 1992; Haight and Hendrix 1995), suggests that nurses were amongst the first to report on positive research findings in relation to life review in clinical settings. In some cases, nurses pointed to the way in which life review enhanced group processes (Burnside, 1978), while Ebersole (1976) and Safier (1976) suggested that life review offered itself as a means to promote self-understanding, to reinforce coping mechanisms and to organize thoughts, feelings and experience more meaningfully. [. . .]

The fact that studies might conflict or be inconclusive has been noted by a number of observers. Thornton and Brotchie (1987), in an often-quoted critical evaluation of the empirical literature, drew three rather damning conclusions: that the role of reminiscence cannot be seen, contrary to Butler's proposition, as specifically functional to the lives of older people; that reminiscence cannot be shown to have any therapeutic value beyond use as a diversionary activity; and that there is no clear evidence as to the function of reminiscence in terms of personal or social adjustment. [. . .]

Partly in response to an awareness of conflicting and, in some cases, negative findings, some researchers have sought clarification through classifications of reminiscence activity. In an early paper, Coleman

(1974) put forward the suggestion that there might be three different types:

- simple reminiscence, in which recall of the past provides a source of strength and esteem in the present
- informative reminiscence, where recall of the past is used as a way to pass on knowledge
- life review, which involves 'analysing memories of one's life to integrate a proper image of oneself in the face of death'. (Coleman, 1974: 283)

[. . .]

One of the main problems which researchers have faced is the observation and measurement of reminiscence as an activity. Most researchers have kept to a strictly experimental design in which a group of people, usually captive as residents in a home or visitors to a day centre, or volunteers invited to a laboratory setting, are subjected to some kind of stimulus to reminiscence. Measurements of, for example, mood, depression, cognition, self-esteem, ego integrity, have then been made before and after the introduction of the stimulus. The problem with this type of research is that it cannot match the natural surroundings in which people live their lives, nor can it allow for changes over time.

Some researchers have divided groups of subjects into age groups to see if the role played by reminiscence changes as people age. Here again there are difficulties. There is the effect of cohort. Elder (1982) in his study of people who lived through the Depression in Oakland, California, suggested that particular historical events and experiences stay with an age group, giving it particular characteristics. In England, Victor (1987) suggests, in a study of take-up of welfare benefits, that older people's evaluation of their standard of living tends to be related to their experience early in life, rather than prevailing standards today. And of course, between the ages of 60 and 90 there may be more than one cohort experience.

Another problem arises from the fact that before-and-after studies, and even observation studies in naturalistic settings, tend only to cover a short period of time. Few studies have been able to show what part reminiscence plays over a number of years.

Finally there is the issue of subjectivity and experience. Most of the experimentally designed projects have tended to focus on older people as objects of research; few have been drawn into the process or have been invited to reflect on their own feelings as part of the research.

All these limitations suggested a need for a longitudinal study which might provide insights into the part played by reminiscence as people age. Coleman's (1986) study of 27 women and 23 men living in sheltered accommodation in the London borough of Camden, whom he visited and talked to over a period of 15 years, more than met this

Table 16.1   *Coleman's types of attitudes to reminiscence and related
morale*

| Reminiscers | Value memories of past (n = 21) | High morale |
|---|---|---|
| | Troubled by memories of past (n = 8) | Low morale |
| Non-reminiscers: | See no point in reminiscing (n = 15) | High morale |
| | Have to avoid because of contrast between past and present (n = 6) | Low morale |

*Source*: Coleman, 1986: 37

need. His account is richly illustrated by the reminiscences of the
people he talked to; however, its greatest strength lies in the theory
which he developed from the accounts he heard. While earlier researchers had focused on the process, he focused on the people, drawing
the conclusion that reminiscence was not, as Butler and Erikson had
claimed, always an acceptable or welcome experience. Analysing his
data enabled him to draw up a typology (Table 16.1).

Coleman's work was important for its recognition that reminiscence
can be a painful and unwelcome mental activity. Nurses, community
workers, social care staff and others are aware of this and, in training
sessions, frequently seek guidance. Acknowledging the existence of
painful memories and of avoidance of the past has become a focal
point for preparation for reminiscence work. However, his work is
also important for the emphasis it places on the present. And here we
come back again to disengagement theory. Fifteen of the people
Coleman studied saw no point in reminiscing. As he put it 'not reminiscing can be purposeful because there are better things to do'
(Coleman, 1986: 37). [. . .]

I introduce these debates and discussions at this stage as part of the
scene setting for reminiscence work. Enthusiastic reminiscence work
has brought about many positive experiences for older people and
those involved in their support and care. However, we need to be
aware of the fact that the processes we engage in may be complex, and
may bring about results we may not have anticipated. An awareness
of the interaction of the many factors which lead to the generation of
recall and memory is a necessary accompaniment of sensitive and
appropriate approaches to reminiscence work. [. . .]

## References

Bornat, J. (1989) 'Oral history as a social movement: reminiscence and older people',
*Oral History*, 17(2): 16–24.
Burnside, I. (1978) *Working with the Elderly: Group Processes and Techniques.* North
Scituate, MA: Duxbury Press.
Butler, R.N. (1963) 'The life review: an interpretation of reminiscence in the aged',
*Psychiatry*, 26: 65–76.
Coleman, P.G. (1974) 'Measuring reminiscence characteristics from conversation as

adaptive features of old age', *International Journal of Aging and Human Development*, 5: 281–94.

Coleman, P.G. (1986) *Ageing and Reminiscence Processes: Social and Clinical Implications*. Chichester: Wiley.

Dobroff, R. (1984) 'Introduction: a time for reclaiming the past', *Journal of Gerontological Social Work*, 7(1/2): xvii–xviii.

Ebersole, P. (1976) 'Problems of group reminiscing with the institutionalized aged', *Journal of Gerontological Nursing*, 2(6): 23–7.

Elder, G.H. (1982) 'Historical experience in the later years', in T.K. Hareven and K.J. Adams (eds), *Ageing and Life Course Transitions: an Interdisciplinary Perspective*. London: Tavistock.

Erikson, E.H., Erikson J.M. and Kivnick, H.O. (1986) *Vital Involvement in Old Age: the Experience of Old Age in Our Time*. New York: Norton.

Haight, B.K. (1991) 'Reminiscing: the state of the art as a basis for practice', *International Journal of Aging and Human Development*, 33(1): 1–32.

Haight, B.K. (1992) 'The structured life-review process: a community approach to the aging client', in G.M.M. Jones and B.M.L. Miesen (eds), *Care-giving in Dementia: Research and Applications*. London: Tavistock.

Haight, B.K. and Hendrix, S. (1995) 'An integrated review of reminiscence', in B.K. Haight and J.D. Webster *The Art and Science of Reminiscing: Theory, Research, Methods and Applications*. Washington: Taylor & Francis.

Hale, S. (1960) 'The horse buses stopped north of the Rye', *Case Conference*, 7(6): 153–5.

Kiernat, J.M. (1979) 'The use of life review activity with confused nursing home residents', *American Journal of Occupational Therapy*, 33: 306–10.

Lewis, C.N. (1971) 'Reminiscing and self-concept in old age', *Journal of Gerontology*, 26: 240–3.

Lewis, M.I. and Butler, R.N. (1974) 'Life review therapy: putting memories to work in individual and group psychotherapy', *Geriatrics*, 29: 165–9.

McMahon, A.W. and Rhudick P.J. (1964) 'Reminiscing: adaptational significance in the aged', *Archives of General Psychiatry*, 10: 292–8.

Safier, G. (1976) 'Oral life history with the elderly', *Journal of Gerontological Nursing*, 2(5): 17–23.

Thornton, S. and Brotchie, J. (1987) 'Reminiscence: a critical review of the empirical literature', *British Journal of Clinical Psychology*, 26: 93–111.

Victor, C. (1987) *Old Age in a Modern Society*. London: Croom Helm.

# 17

# From Group Meeting to Therapeutic Group

*Bernadette Duffy and Brian McCarthy*

In residential care, much of one's life is spent in group settings. There is a danger that the potential of group experiences can be taken for granted, and as a result valuable opportunities for achieving goals important to clients may be lost. This article reviews the conversion of a routine house meeting in a hostel for teenage girls to a therapeutic group with more emphasis on personal growth and relationships. The aims and development of the group are outlined with comment on the implications for staff–client and staff team relationships. Some theoretical aspects of work with adolescent groups are considered and the need identified to use a model of group behaviour which not only analyses the interactions and atmosphere of group sessions, but also relates to the system of interactions in the agency as a whole.

## Context

There are groups that have identified treatment goals and can be described clearly as group therapy. There are other groups which 'offer experiences which are not intended to be therapy but which may often be therapeutic' (Aveline and Dryden, 1988: 2–4). It is to the latter category that the work described in this article belongs.

Most residential agencies have regular meetings which have the function of organizing living arrangements and duties, reviewing recent events, sharing information, and dealing with disciplinary issues. Such meetings have a value in their own right and serve the purpose of achieving organizational aims. It is the authors' contention however that those meetings often have the potential for a more developed use as a key element in the life of the agency. This is much more clearly the case in those organizations which are explicitly described and developed as therapeutic communities; here the therapeutic group can be seen as a central therapeutic force.

In the case of group homes and hostels, sensitive decisions and planning are required to make better use of group meetings while at

Originally published in *Groupwork*, 6(2), 1993: 152–61.

the same time not converting a residential centre into a treatment centre. This article traces the development of a house meeting in a residential hostel for adolescent girls from the stage where it was simply a functional meeting in the weekly cycle of events to the point where it had become an important forum for the expression of feelings and conflicts and had a significant role in the lives of both staff and clients.

The setting is a residential hostel for adolescent girls, some of whom have lived rough; some have come directly as a result of intolerable circumstances at home, others have been referred by social workers. About 12 girls live in the hostel at any one time. Problems of depression, moodiness, anxiety, excessive use of alcohol, solvents or drugs are common, and behaviour can be aggressive with occasional outbursts of violence. The principles and methods of work are closely related to reality therapy as outlined by Glasser (1965), with particular emphasis on the taking of personal responsibility, the challenging of unrealistic behaviour and the development of commitment to relationships. A house meeting was held regularly; it was short, mainly administrative and tended to be squeezed in between dinnertime and favourite television programmes.

**Aims**

The idea of working with the group meeting in a different way was stimulated by a few factors. Social education groups had been held in the hostel for some time with the purpose of social skills training and discussion of personal problems. This programme had made use of role-play, drama and relaxation exercises, as well as structured discussion. However, the sessions were usually run by an outsider and attendance was voluntary. There was agreement that a more intensive group meeting was required, involving all members of the hostel, clients and staff, with one outsider in attendance. Thus the idea developed of using the existing structure, i.e. the weekly house meeting, but with new aims and methods.

The new style of meeting was planned to encourage clients to verbalize conflicts. They had a tendency to resort very easily to shouting and violence. To go through the process of talking conflicts and problems through would constitute important learning for them.

Difficulties with staff should be aired. Staff were often construed as authority figures and could be associated with the sources of much anger and resentment. The emphasis in discussion would be to encourage alternative perceptions.

Through the pressure of the group, unrealistic behaviour could be challenged. In line with reality therapy principles, there would be analysis of current behaviour with encouragement for clients to take responsibility for their own actions and consequences. In this way, the group might become a forum for reality testing. They might test their opinions and views of themselves and others. They were never slow to offer such opinions; to give opinions constructively and with some sensitivity could have useful application in many of their relationships.

The review of the preceding week and planning of the week ahead should play a part, but unlike previous meetings they should be used to make sense of the past and facilitate thinking beyond the present moment, something that many adolescents are uninterested in. One could make use of role-play, drama and relaxation exercises etc. as before, but more as required by the situation than as part of a programme. Above all the clients should in time have a sense of the group meeting being 'their' time, with a sense of participation and a sense of safety and security.

Clearly some of these aims could be in conflict at times, and in these circumstances the priorities of particular situations would have to take precedence.

## Development of the group

The early meetings centred on allowing the culture to change. This required staff to become less directive and resulted in discomfort and questioning by the clients. These meetings tended to highlight the staff–client, us and them division. The more staff stood back, the more clients claimed their new-found role and used it to accuse, attack and indicate injustice. 'I was blamed in the wrong', 'punished in the wrong'; was a regular cry. A period of testing the limits occurred: how far a staff member should be pushed; how much bad language could be used. This created a difficult dilemma for staff. To open the possibility of the group becoming 'theirs' in any significant way requires a certain *laissez-faire* attitude; to move clients towards taking personal responsibility requires some direction; to encourage people to be sensitive to each other requires that staff make observations and give feedback.

In this instance, the dilemma was resolved by different staff members taking on different roles, as agreed at staff meetings. This stage of the group can of course be a period of defensiveness and ambiguity for a team who are not familiar with each other.

The content of the early meetings tended to focus on domestic issues – mealtimes, duties, who did and did not do their share; issues of discipline, especially house rules, now that there was a new forum to question them. These domestic debates could quickly move to more serious or significant issues or provide the possibility of dealing with issues of power.

*Ann:* I don't know if this has anything to do with the meeting, but I am not cooking dinner again. All I get are insults from certain people.

*Mary:* If you are hinting at me would you say it to my face.

*Ann:* Don't you start me – it's not the first time you did it. You are always insulting others as well. If you don't like the dinners you don't have to eat them . . . or else cook them yourself if you are so smart and see if you like being insulted.

*Mary:* How can I cook dinner if I am at work all day. I would not give your dinner to my dogs.

*Staff:* Would somebody like to tell us what is going on.

*Mary:* It's not fair me working all day and then having to come home and eat that! I hate mince.

*Staff:* We don't have mince every day, Mary.

*Mary:* Yes, well I wish I knew when we were having it so that I could buy my own dinner.

*Theresa:* Well how are we meant to know what's for dinner? We don't know until the house-parents give us the meat just before we cook it.

*Ann:* Maybe it's a menu you want!

*Mary:* Well it wouldn't be a bad idea!

This resulted in a decision to organize menus themselves and was an early indication to clients that discussion could resolve issues.

An important development occurred after six weeks. Because some of the meetings had become unwieldy with everybody shouting together, an idea emerged that a chairperson was required; further, that the chairperson should be one of the girls. This role of chairperson came to assume importance; it rotated and in time the person in the role was accorded considerable respect. A book for meetings, where people would enter an issue they wished to discuss, happened as a result of further discussions.

The emergence of a chairperson, the 'minutes' notebook, and rules about listening and talking one at a time, marked a move to a new phase of the group. The range of issues discussed grew wider and showed greater depth of feeling and thought. Given the chance and the time to talk, some individuals began to verbalize their aggression especially in relation to fights with other house members and in relation to drinking and 'sniffing' (which was very popular at this time). On one occasion a client described having arrived back at the hostel drunk, as a result of which she had been 'grounded' for a week. The discussion of this incident led to the conclusion that they would prefer to be refused entry, to have to survive the night, rather than 'get grief from the staff'. This issue of being drunk or high, and the related one of making decisions and taking responsibility, came up at nearly every meeting. At least the group was leading to realistic discussion of the problem and the fights and violence that might ensue.

A discussion on bad language led to some restrictions on its overuse in the group. The girls initiated a system of fines at one point which would operate during the week and was administered entirely by themselves. This did not last for very long, but was evidence of a type of initiative; it was the operation of peer pressure rather than a behaviour management programme.

The theme of authority, power and the role of staff continued to arise. On one occasion this led to the opinion that the house would be a very happy place to live in, if the staff were not there. They pointed out how 'the fight the other night finished as soon as you [staff] left the room!'

*Staff*: So you feel that by us paying attention to the fight, it goes on longer?
*Client*: Yes, nobody would want to give in to you, they can sort it out themselves.
*Staff*: OK, say the staff decide for the next week not to call you or ask you to do jobs, what would you say?
*Client*: You mean you would sit in the office all day?
*Staff*: We would be in the house, but we would not be telling you what to do or checking on you.

It was agreed to try this experiment. Things ran smoothly for three days; staff were then 'invited to come back on duty'.

There was some change in the membership of the group from time to time. A practice developed whereby a group member would have the responsibility of 'initiating' a new client both to hostel life in general and to the group in particular. This was accomplished with considerable maturity by most and where it was neglected, the group member was challenged and censured by the group.

With the group now working for about six months, it moved subtly into a third phase. This was most clearly marked by the commitment people felt to be present. To miss the group meeting was to miss two hours where 'anything might happen'. Thus, curiosity alone provided good reason to be there. In the course of one very volatile session, an individual's behaviour had become so unruly that she had to be asked to leave the room; she remained in the hallway, trying hard to listen and interjecting comments in a relevant and reasonable way (in contrast to earlier behaviour). The need to be there was strong.

The group meeting at this stage could be a barometer of the atmosphere and level of tension or excitement in the hostel as a whole. A meeting might begin with all 10 clients sitting bundled together on one couch, clearly and distinctly away from staff; other meetings began with very civilized, polite adolescents, spaced appropriately about, and ready to solve whatever problems might come their way. For staff prepared to listen and observe there was feedback, verbal and non-verbal, on all aspects of hostel life.

Discussion about the hostel itself was a recurrent theme; sometimes this would occur because of some particular complaint or bad feeling about the place. More often it arose from a need to discuss the image of the hostel or as a vehicle for trying to make sense of why they were actually living here at all.

*Mary*: Let's talk about this place.

*Staff*: Well would you like to tell us what you think of the hostel?

*Ann*: Don't ask me that question – I don't know anyway.

*Sonya*: I think it's gear – great crack – forget it, I didn't mean it, I said forget it – you turned on me straight away!

*Staff*: Why is it gear?

*Sonya*: Forget it – I said.

*Staff*: [*turning to others*] Why are you here?

*Nuala*: I have no place else to go.

*Staff*: So it's a house that you can sleep and eat in if you have no place to go?

*Nuala*: No, it's my home, it's all our home.

*Staff*: If I asked you to tell me about the hostel, just say I was never here before, what would you tell me?

*Sonya*: I'd tell you to mind your own . . . business.

*Kathleen*: Don't look at me like that. I don't want to talk about it – Right.

*Patricia*: I'll tell them the truth, you all annoy me. If you don't like it here, go home and let us alone.

*Sonya*: Don't start me, you big-mouth!

*Staff*: Do you like it here?

*Sonya*: Oh, here she goes again, always me . . . of course I like it here, I'm here, aren't I?

In this dialogue we can see the way in which a sense of victimization or an opportunity to insult can be integrated with any discussion; staff had to learn to notice but not necessarily react.

The issue of confidentiality took on a more serious meaning. Lengthy arguments occurred about clients respecting stories or information outside the hostel. This was interesting as it showed a developing sense of privacy and respect for their own affairs. With time, the level of confidentiality did improve, resulting in mature and often quite personal discussions of sexuality, marriage, pregnancy, personal hygiene, habits of excessive drinking, etc. It was during these interactions that some individuals became aware for the first time of their patterns of excessive drinking. Suggestions and advice from other group members were valuable and could carry more weight than staff comment.

### The role of staff members in the group

Staff members tended to avoid 'being Solomon' on matters of right and wrong and systematically tried to comment more on the group processes as appropriate. This had interesting effects. Some of the girls became more alert to the mood of the group. This would often lead to discussion of the reasons for particular tensions, angers or depressions. One such discussion led to an acknowledgement of the frequency of bad humour, aggressive outbursts and generally negative feelings. A practice developed of asking each member of the group to recount one pleasant event or feeling. This was an example of a practice which allowed staff to introduce exercises to identify and explore feelings, e.g. exercises from the Gestalt therapy literature (Perls et al., 1973). Opportunities like this would be used, where possible, to highlight the 'here and now' and to anchor their awareness in the present where they might compare each other's feelings and reactions.

There were times when they tired of observations being made about the group. One client commented: 'You're always saying things like that about the way we say things.' In its way, a very succinct description of group processes.

Another function of staff members was to be the group memory. It could be useful to remember a piece of dialogue or a sequence of events from an earlier meeting; this could be relevant to issues of taking responsibility or to the origins of a specific quarrel. Some people have a flair for retaining the storyline; it is a valuable asset, especially where there is not the time to listen to tape recordings of group meetings.

The confronting of inappropriate or unrealistic behaviour was accomplished frequently by the group itself; this was the preferred method of achieving the aim. There were inevitably occasions where it fell to a staff member to do this; to confront without becoming the ogre of authority was a delicate balance to hold. Again a solution was for members of staff to alternate this role, while others moved towards intermediary or supportive roles.

The atmosphere could change rapidly, one minute easygoing and trivial, next minute highly charged and serious; the beginning of a session inactive and lethargic, later active and creative. This demands of staff an ability to move with abrupt and often inexplicable shifts of mood. Awareness of one's own temperament, and more precisely, one's humour and level of flexibility on a given evening, is valuable.

There is no doubt that involvement in this group had implications for staff roles and behaviour. Some staff felt quite vulnerable at the early stages of the group, especially on evenings where the group seemed interested only in attacking members of staff. It can take time to develop the resilience needed to weather these storms with the small comfort that more civilized discussion would eventually emerge. The sense of 'clearing the air' did however usually outweigh the discomfort and this played a part in reducing barriers. Staff–client communication was thus enhanced both within and outside the group meetings. It was noticeable that staff roles often changed in the context of the group itself. A staff member who ordinarily tended to be strict could take on different roles within the group, e.g. being supportive, more open, devil's advocate. This was interesting in that it could help change stereotyped views clients might develop of staff. It also contributed to staff learning to expand their repertoire of possible roles.

The group meeting has continued to be a feature of life in the hostel. It is now run almost entirely by staff, which raises the issue of the use of an outsider as consultant. It is a matter of constant debate whether more can be gained from reflections on group meetings when an alternative perspective is available. While the value of consultation is appreciated, limitations on funding restrict the use of extra resources. It is generally felt however that the group meeting has proven itself and should continue to provide a forum for discussion and resolution of issues.

## Some theoretical considerations

Various theorists of group behaviour have considered the question of whether groups develop through recognizable stages towards maturity. Tuckman (1965) surveyed therapy groups, training groups and groups within laboratory settings; he delineated four developmental phases which he termed 'forming, storming, norming and performing'. Yalom (1975) posited a model whereby psychotherapy groups were seen to move from a phase of orientation through conflict and rebellion to a stage of cohesion and closeness and finally to issues concerned with termination. Spitz and Sadock (1973) described a pattern of change from an initial stage of guardedness and anxiety to the group moving through a period of group interaction with the growth of trust, to a period of disengagement, separation anxiety and positive feelings towards the leader.

Bennis and Shepard's model (1965: 415–57) suggests that power relations are important in the early stages and need to be explored and confronted before interpersonal issues can become part of the agenda. Reitz (1981) provides a model which is an amalgamation of some of these approaches; this view emphasizes the latter point that issues of power tend to precede the development of cohesiveness and the capacity to deal with interpersonal matters. This model provided a useful frame of reference to review sessions. The issues of power and authority, dependence and independence, did not however disappear. The developmental stage of the client group is of course relevant here, in so far as most teenagers would be concerned with these issues on a regular basis. A point did come when power issues were less salient; perhaps the period where the clients deemed the staff 'redundant' marked the change most dramatically. Certainly interpersonal issues were discussed more thereafter. This pattern fits the broad thrust of theoretical accounts of group development.

Inevitably the movement of group sessions was fuelled by adolescent energy or stagnated by adolescent lethargy. James Anthony described the regressive and progressive 'movements' of adolescent groups and the need to treat 'members as potentially mature adults, with the right to regress on some occasions. Too much should not be expected nor disappointment shown when the group fails to live up to expectations' (Anthony and Foulkes, 1957: 221).

These words are still relevant to such groups and highlight the demands made on staff adaptability and energy. Mapping the changing cultures of the group presented an interesting challenge. Just as Bion (1961) described the group culture changing from theocracy to playgroup in the case of adults, so the adolescent group could switch from street corner to household to courtroom. To capture the essence of that culture and feed it back to the group represents one of the important skills of the group leader. It was often after a group meeting that significant aspects of changes in atmosphere were appreciated; to feed this back to the group closer to the moment would be more valuable. Further development of this type of groupwork skill would be useful.

It is ultimately of most importance to relate the group events and atmosphere to the overall context of the hostel and to the lives of the individuals. A systems approach might better facilitate an analysis which can relate the micro-events of the group meeting to the macro-system of relationships and patterns of living in the hostel.

## Conclusion

This account of a specific set of group sessions is inevitably a brief survey of the many, complex interactions that occurred. If it makes one point, that there is potential for growth and development in the routine spheres of an organization's life, it will have served its purpose. In commenting on how people learn from groups, Smith (1980: 78) makes the point that learning occurs 'where two paradoxical messages impinge on the learner, the messages being identified as support and confrontation. Where this occurs, the learner is seen as able to take greater personal responsibility for actions and therefore able to sustain changes subsequent to the group.' Certainly both of these messages were there at various times in the group meetings; whether they occurred in adequate or appropriate form can only be assessed by relating future life experiences of the clients to these interventions.

## References

Anthony, E.J. and Foulkes, S.H. (1957) *Group Psychotherapy*. Harmondsworth: Penguin.
Aveline, M. and Dryden, W. (1988) *Group Therapy in Britain*. Milton Keynes: Open University Press.
Bennis, W.G. and Shepard, H.A. (1965) *Group Development: Human Relations*, Vol. 9.
Bion, W.R. (1961) *Experience in Groups*. London: Tavistock.

Glasser, W. (1965) *Reality Therapy: A New Approach to Psychiatry*. New York: Harper & Row.

Perls, F., Hefferline, R.F. and Goodman, P. (1973) *Gestalt Therapy*. Harmondsworth: Penguin.

Reitz, H.J. (1981) *Behaviour in Organizations*. Homewood, IL: R.D. Irwin.

Smith, P.B. (1980) *Group Processes and Personal Change*. London: Harper & Row.

Spitz, H. and Sadock, B.J. (1973) 'Small interactional groups in the psychiatric training of graduate nursing students', *Journal of Nursing Education*, 12: 6–13.

Tuckman, B.W. (1965) 'Developmental sequence in small groups', *Psychological Bulletin*, 63: 384–99.

Yalom, I.D. (1975) *The Theory and Practice of Group Psychotherapy*. New York: Basic Books.

# 18

# Housing Primary Health Care in the Community

*Lyn Fisk*

The past 10 years have seen a radical shift in emphasis in health care provision and in health visiting practice. The move has been toward a more consumer or client-led approach to health. Health visitors have been encouraged to examine new ways of addressing the health needs of communities and groups (Goodwin, 1988). The swing away from the individualistic approach towards the model of community-oriented health care has, in part, resulted from international pressure. In particular, the 1978 World Health Organization Conference on Primary Health Care challenged health workers to work in partnership with individuals and groups, to enable them to define their own health needs and to encourage self-reliance (WHO, 1978).

The aim of a community-oriented approach is to enable people to increase control over, and to improve, their health. Community-based work in this context does not focus on problems, it aims to promote skills, knowledge and confidence. The health worker becomes more of a facilitator, whose role is to validate, encourage and empower people to define and meet their own health needs (WHO, 1991). It has long been established that primary health care workers, working in groups in a participatory way and drawing upon experiential learning, are a powerful tool for change (Billingham, 1989).

## The Community Health House

Health visitors have in the past focused largely on work with individuals and families. More recently, they have been exploring different ways of working with groups and communities. The project that I undertook aimed to meet the wider health, social and personal needs of women living on an estate, through the provision of a drop-in centre. The project sought to test the effectiveness of a community

Originally published in R. Bryar and B. Bytheway (eds) (1996) *Changing Primary Health Care: The Teamcare Valleys Experience*. Oxford: Basil Blackwell. pp. 158–66.

development approach to health promotion with families (Fisk, 1992). It had the following objectives:

- to engage the community in discussion and planning with regard to issues with a bearing on health;
- to provide a place that would serve as a centre for health promotion activities;
- to enlist the support of various other agencies and professional workers;
- to establish a wide range of health promotion activities on a group basis;
- to evaluate the approach and develop it according to the results of the evaluation.

To compound the poor environment, the estate has many recognizable elements of poverty and disadvantage, including low average household income, a high proportion of single parents, weak social support systems, a high rate of social difficulties and few shopping, leisure or communal facilities. These factors tend to produce a sense of isolation and a feeling that change is difficult to achieve. People living there feel they have little control over their lives.

The estate is adjacent to a village community high on the edge of a valley. The area consists largely of council properties. Most families housed on the estate were placed there because they needed emergency accommodation; they were not there by choice. Among the residents there is little sense of commitment to the community. In October 1990 Ogwr Health Unit was granted the lease of a house on the estate for two years.

Throughout the year prior to the opening of the house, a small group of women from the estate worked hard to form a committee. It later took on the task of fundraising for equipment and of planning how the house could be used. It was hoped that the committee would eventually take on full ownership of the project. This committee drew up a constitution and became known formally as the Families Association. The committee met regularly on a monthly basis and eventually obtained charitable status.

It was recognized that, if mothers were to have a break from their children to be able to take part in any activities, a crèche was essential. The Families Association successfully obtained one year's funding for a nursery nurse from the Opportunity for Volunteering Scheme, and a further grant was received from the BBC Children in Need Appeal.

A series of activities were identified through discussion with the women using the house. Those that were instigated included:

- shared shopping for the preparation of a daily lunch;
- outside trips such as swimming;

- courses provided by various health professionals on topics such as first aid, talking about feelings, ante- and post-natal care, children's illnesses, nutrition, cooking, hobbies and crafts.

Social activities included strawberry picking, a barbecue, and outings, for example to a local animal centre, with the children. Jumble sales and running a handicraft stall acted as social events as well as fundraising ventures.

## The evaluation

As the above description shows, activities were initiated in the house in relation to the first four of the five objectives set for the project. The fifth, the evaluation of the approach, was more difficult to achieve. To develop the house I had been released for two and a half days per week from my general caseload, some of which a colleague had taken on. I had no time to develop tools to evaluate the initiative. With the support of my manager I applied and was appointed to TCV [Teamcare Valleys] as a short-term half-time clinical fellow for six months. My salary costs were paid by TCV and a bank health visitor appointed to my caseload while I combined work on the evaluation with work in the house.

Following many discussions, it was decided that the central purpose of the project would be to devise an assessment procedure which could be used with women before they attended the house and then again after a period of attendance. Clearly, a considerable range of process and outcome factors could have been evaluated. I decided to focus on the development of an assessment procedure that could be used as part of ongoing health visiting work with families attending the house.

The aims of the assessment procedure were to:

- determine the residents' beliefs and attitudes about their general health;
- determine the extent of their social contacts and their perception of social support;
- assess their level of self-esteem using the Battle Culture Free Self Esteem Inventory (Battle, 1988);
- formulate plans and strategies for intervention – in particular activities that were being offered in the house;
- gather baseline information with a view to repeating the assessment at a later date in order to evaluate the effects of taking part in activities at the house.

The procedure consisted of a semi-structured interview and the Battle Inventory. The interview comprised questions grouped in five sections:

- family structure and background;
- general attitudes and beliefs about health;
- social support;
- attitudes to parenting;
- attitudes to, and experience of, the Community Health House.

After the tools had been piloted, a purposive sample of 23 women was drawn from my caseload to participate in the main study. These were women who were not using the house but who, I considered, might benefit from attending. They each had at least two of the following features: single parent; isolated mother/family; child under five who might benefit from purposeful play; new to the area.

Notes were taken during the interviews which were also tape-recorded with the women's permission. The following discussion is based on some of the results of the assessment procedure and my experience of working in the house.

## The definition of health

Central to the whole project is the concept of health, how it is defined and what factors are perceived to affect it. Table 18.1 displays the frequency with which factors were selected by the women as having an adverse effect on health, and Table 18.2 the factors selected as promoting good health. It should be noted that lack of money, crime and violence feature prominently in Table 18.1. Behavioural factors such as smoking and alcohol are comparatively less important. The state of the area, stress and worry are also key factors.

Table 18.2 shows that the women considered factors concerned with emotional health and relationships to be the most important for well-being. These women, therefore, defined health as rooted in social and economic factors rather than personal behaviour and lifestyle.

These findings are in line with recent research studies that show that reference to socio-economic and environmental factors are more frequently associated with people in working-class groups and may well reflect their experience of adverse living conditions (Graham, 1984; Calnan, 1986; Coulter, 1987; Farrant and Russell, 1986; Davies, 1995). In the Milton Keynes Felt Needs project lack of money was perceived as having a detrimental affect on health (Liddiard, 1988). [. . .] Traditionally health services and health professionals have been concerned with the provision of curative and preventative services rather than with seeking to influence the wider social and economic determinants of health. Changes in the organization of the NHS in the 1990s may have reinforced the focused approach of health trusts. However, there is evidence that policy-makers are being encouraged to take a wider view of the determinants of health and to be more active in influencing the social conditions which affect the health of communities (Benzeval et al., 1995).

Table 18.1  *The factors which were selected as having a negative effect on health (Fisk, 1992: 45)*

| Factor | % |
| --- | --- |
| Crime and vandalism | 70 |
| Not enough money | 65 |
| State of the area | 61 |
| Stress and worry | 61 |
| Smoking | 52 |
| Lack of shops | 48 |
| Few facilities for the under-fives | 39 |
| State of your home | 39 |
| No paid work | 30 |
| Poor health service | 30 |
| What happened to you as a child | 30 |
| Noise | 30 |
| No leisure facilities | 26 |
| Alcohol | 26 |
| Pollution | 26 |
| Total (= 100%) | 23 |

Table 18.2  *The factors which were selected as promoting good health (Fisk, 1992: 44)*

| | % |
| --- | --- |
| Good friends and neighbours | 83 |
| State of your home | 61 |
| Family support | 52 |
| Enough money | 43 |
| Good health facilities | 43 |
| Your diet | 43 |
| How you were brought up | 39 |
| Transport | 39 |
| Good sexual relationships | 35 |
| Facilities for the under-fives | 35 |
| The area you live in | 30 |
| Taking exercise | 26 |
| Total (= 100%) | 23 |

That the public has a wide definition of health is a very positive attribute in any area where community development activities are being considered. The health visitor who has to mediate between the two views held by the community and the health trust, however, has certain difficulties. Women living in a poor estate know that an afternoon spent out in the fresh air picking strawberries will do more for their health than a home visit from the health visitor. But how can a manager justify investment in such an outing? How will it contribute to health gain targets?

*The users of the house*

The house itself was initially viewed with suspicion by the local community. Members of the Families Association were aware of the conditions of the lease of the house and of the financial support given by the health unit to the project. Some residents may have felt that the house – and therefore the project – was owned by the health unit or the council. However, by working flexible hours, I was able to become involved in many activities and, with this closer involvement, a better partnership was achieved between myself and local people.

An unexpected problem that occurred was that the women who were involved early in the project became very possessive of the house, and this tended to deter other women from using it. Those working in PHC [Primary Health Care] are always concerned about people who do not use a particular service that could be of benefit to them. Along with other professionals, I tried to support the users in developing skills themselves. Some attempt was made at encouraging the Newpin befriending system (Pound et al., 1985). This, however, would have required more skilled training for myself and for some of the mothers.

While the presence of the core group may have deterred some from using the house, low self-esteem among women on the estate might have been another factor limiting their participation. The Inventory was used as part of the assessment procedure to measure the self-esteem of women who were not using the house but who, in my opinion, could benefit. Over half of the 23 women interviewed had low or very low personal self-esteem scores. Eight had very low scores, indicating a poor sense of self-worth.

In the absence of good-quality support from family or friends, women with low self-esteem find it difficult to motivate themselves to meet others even though they may be in need of support. Women living in poverty have so many problems they tend to be unwilling to make friends and thereby risk taking on more problems – they recognize that friendship requires reciprocity.

The interview schedule used in the project showed that these women, despite having few friends, did have support from their families. Interviewees were asked how many times they had had contact with their family over the two weeks prior to the interview. For the majority there was contact occurring on a daily basis either by visiting, telephoning or having family to visit. Contact with friends was considerably less. Four respondents had no contact with friends and six said they had little contact.

How one perceives support is a key concept in enhancing self-esteem and a feeling of 'self worth' (Parry, 1988). A third of the interviewees were well supported. They felt that they belonged to a family they could rely on, who accepted and loved them as they were.

However, three said there was no one they felt they could rely on, and another 10 thought there was no such person in the local community. These were the women who potentially stood to benefit most from the health house.

*The multidisciplinary team*

From the outset I realized a multidisciplinary team of people would be essential to provide support and activities in the house. Numerous statutory and voluntary bodies were approached. Those that provided ongoing support throughout the two years included a community development worker, community education tutors, psychiatric nurse therapist and occupational therapist. Some individuals approached were supportive but unable to offer their time, including the local GP. Others, including Social Services and Women's Aid, participated initially but found the numbers attending their sessions did not warrant the time spent in the house. Those most involved worked within different organizations, each with particular aims and objectives and constraints. For example, the two adult education tutors were enthusiastic about working with the women, but funds had to be raised for them to undertake this work. Women attending the house organized numerous events to raise these funds.

As a team we found we were having to resolve many financial and other management problems to maintain our work at the house. We felt that these should have been dealt with by managers within our respective organizations. Further, while we met on a regular basis with a manager from the health community authority unit, we felt that the project required a steering committee with management expertise, drawn from all the organizations involved.

## Conclusion

In deprived estates where there is a high proportion of families with difficulties, there exists a need for well-organized support from a variety of sources. At present there is a tendency for social work to be fully occupied with personal crises and for GPs to focus narrowly on health problems. Health visitors alone cannot provide the preventive care that is needed.

There is a clear need for health visitors to reorient their approach to practice and to acknowledge the valuable resources that exist within the local community (Bryar and Fisk, 1994). They should draw upon and develop the expertise that residents acquire through force of circumstance. My experiences of working in the Community Health House suggest that health visitors working with the aim of community development should be prepared to set aside their status as 'experts'; to be flexible, honest and willing to share their knowledge and experience; and to be well informed about where other relevant information and expertise can be found.

This project illustrates some of the issues that need to be addressed if health visiting is to adopt this more participatory approach to work at the community level. Health visitors need to develop new skills and they need support in using these skills. Managers and health visitors need to explore new ways of recording outcomes of health visiting practice, moving away from counting contacts to measuring the quality of these contacts.

Health visiting has developed in an *ad hoc* manner over the past century. The new strategies for health, incorporating the targeting of activities, provide a new impetus to health promotion. The community development approach provides an opportunity to pursue a more people-centred, health-oriented strategy.

## References

Battle, J. (1988) *Culture Free Self Esteem Inventory.* Windsor: NFER Nelson.
Benzeval, M., Judge, K. and Whitehead, M. (eds) (1995) *Tackling Inequalities in Health. An Agenda for Action.* London: King's Fund Centre.
Billingham, K. (1989) '45 Cope Street: working in partnership with parents', *Health Visitor*, 62: 156–7.
Bryar, R. and Fisk, L. (1994) 'Setting up a community health house', *Health Visitor*, 67(6): 203–5.
Calnan, K. (1986) 'Maintaining health preventing illness: a comparison of the perceptions of women from different social classes', *Health Promotion*, 1(2): 167–77.
Coulter, A. (1987) 'Lifestyles and social class: implications for primary care', *Journal of the Royal College of General Practitioners*, 37: 533–6.
Davies, J. (1995) 'A study of family networks and relationships in community midwifery', in J. Reed and S. Procter (eds), *Practitioner Research in Health Care: The Inside Story.* London: Chapman & Hall. pp. 130–46.
Farrant, W. and Russell, J. (1986) *The Politics of Health Information.* Institute of Education, London University. Cited in: Liddiard (1988).
Fisk, L. (1992) *Bettws Community Health House: Investigation into a New Approach for Health Visiting.* (TCV Project Report). Cardiff: TCV, Welsh Office.
Goodwin, S. (1988) 'Whither health visiting?' Keynote speech, Health Visitors Association Conference, HVA, London.
Graham, H. (1984) *Women, Health and the Family.* Brighton: Harvester Wheatsheaf.
Liddiard, P. (1988) *Milton Keynes Felt Needs Project. A Preliminary Study of the Felt Health Needs of People Living in Relative Poverty on a Milton Keynes Housing Estate.* Milton Keynes: Department of Health and Social Welfare, the Open University.
Parry, G. (1988) 'Mobilising social support', in N.W. Fraser (ed.), *New Developments in Clinical Psychology*, Vol. 2. Chichester: British Psychological Society, John Wiley. pp. 83–104.
Pound, A., Mills, M. and Cox, T. (1985) 'A pilot evaluation of Newpin: a home visiting and befriending scheme in South London', summarized in the *Newsletter of the Association of Child Psychology and Psychiatry*, October: 13–15.
World Health Organization (1978) *The Alma Ata Declaration.* (Health for All, Series no. 1). Geneva: WHO.
World Health Organization (1991) *Community Involvement in Health Development: Challenging Health Services.* (Technical Report Series 809). Geneva: WHO.

# 19

# Creating a Space for Absent Voices: Disabled Women's Experience of Receiving Assistance with Daily Living Activities

*Jenny Morris*

## Silencing our voices

Feminist research during the 1980s stressed that the unpaid caring work which women carry out for children and for family members who are old and/or disabled is an important part of women's experience of oppression. This research was particularly addressed to the development, during the same decade, of government policies aimed at reducing the numbers of people in various forms of institutional care, increasing the opportunities for disabled and older people to live in (or remain living in) 'ordinary' homes in the community. These policies, which were finally implemented in the 1990 NHS and Community Care Act, were undoubtedly primarily motivated by the tenfold increase between 1978 and 1986 in the Social Security budget being spent on residential care for older people. While Social Services departments – as the main agency involved in implementing the 1990 Act – have been exhorted by government guidance to see living in the 'community', rather than residential care, as the preferred option for older and disabled people, feminist research has constantly reminded both policy-makers and Social Services practitioners that all too often it is women's unpaid work of looking after disabled and older family members which makes such an option possible.

During the 1980s, this unpaid work has become more recognized by policy-makers and by health and Social Services professionals – partly because it *has* to be recognized in order for community care to succeed as a policy. However, the identification of 'informal carers' as a social group was also firmly placed on the social policy agenda by the growth of the Carers' National Association and by the increasing body of research on the experience of 'caring'. The foundations for this research were laid down by a paper presented by Janet Finch and

Originally published in *Feminist Review*, 51 (Autumn 1995): 70–93 (abridged).

Dulcie Groves in 1979 which cut through 'the euphemistic language of 'community' and 'family' to argue that community care was essentially about the care provided by women; and it discussed the effects of caring on women's life chances in terms of equality of opportunities with men (Baldwin and Twigg, 1991: 118). There followed a decade of research and theorizing about 'care' and 'caring', dominated by a feminist agenda of challenging the economic dependence of women created by their role of unpaid carers within the family.

This agenda constructed older and disabled people as 'dependent people', focusing on 'the burden of care' which was imposed on women within the family. Such an agenda excluded the subjective experience of older and disabled people. As both Lois Keith (1992) and myself (1991: Chapter 6) have pointed out, feminist researchers on 'informal care' concentrated almost solely on the experience of those women they called 'carers', constructing an analysis which allowed no room for the subjective reality of those who are 'cared for'. This research therefore colluded with prejudicial social attitudes which are commonly held about older and disabled people – at the core of which is the failure to identify with such experiences.

Feminist research on community care identified the area as a 'women's issue' but generally failed to incorporate old or disabled women into the category of 'women'. One result of this has been the ability of some feminists to feel that a denial of a home and family life – i.e. consignment to residential care – are appropriate policy reactions to the needs associated with growing older or experiencing physical, sensory or intellectual impairment (see Morris, 1991: Chapter 6 and Morris, 1993: Chapter 3 for a detailed critique of feminist research on informal care). Dalley, for example, has argued that the 'bed-bound' young mother could develop an 'ungendered' role if she lived in a group house (Dalley, 1988: 122). And Finch claims that taking disabled people out of their own homes and providing the help they need in 'a range of residential facilities' is to be supported because it would de-emphasize 'family care as the central feature of community care'. She goes on to say that this

> might well receive the support of handicapped people [*sic*] themselves, for whom personal independence is a key goal. . . . Of course within such settings attention would need to be paid to enabling people to maintain links with people (relatives or friends) to whom they are emotionally close, that is, people who care 'about' them; but in my view, removing the compulsion to perform the labour of caring 'for' one's relatives is likely to facilitate rather than to obstruct that. (Finch, 1990: 55)

Such patronising, cavalier, *discriminatory* attitudes towards disabled people are only possible because feminists such as Finch and Dalley do not identify with our subjective reality. Our rights to have a home of our own, to live with those we love and who love us, our rights to have children and to bring them up in the way that non-disabled women take for granted, are not even considered in the debate about the sexual division of the labour of caring within heterosexual family households.

The denial of the opportunity to create a home, bear and rear children, to care generally for others, has particular implications for disabled women and this is discussed later in this chapter.

In the last few years the perspective on women's caring role which dominated feminist research in the 1980s has started to be re-examined in the light of a recognition that some groups of women experience a denial of the opportunity to care for children and other family members and that this may also be part of an experience of oppression. Hilary Graham, for example, has reassessed her earlier analysis of the concept of caring (Graham, 1983) and argues that, while the feminist research on caring in the 1980s was actually about white, middle-class women's experience, Black, working-class women are often denied the opportunity of caring for family members. 'Thus, rather than experienced in oppressive ways, caring for partners, children and older relatives can be experienced as a way of resisting racial and class oppression' (Graham, 1991: 69). Jan Walmsley, in looking at the lives of women with learning difficulties, argues that 'For some women who are denied the opportunity to be carers caring becomes a valued activity to be sought, rather than an oppressive burden to be shifted' (Walmsley, 1993: 131).

There has also been increasing criticism in recent years of the way that feminist research, purporting to be giving voice to women's experiences, has been from the point of view of non-disabled women (Keith, 1992; Morris, 1991). In *Pride Against Prejudice* (1991) I argued that a failure to consider the point of view of those who receive 'care' means that research and analysis on the experience of caring is very incomplete. Research which concerned this experience may well challenge the assumption that, within families, there is a straightforward division between those who are carers and those who are cared for.

> If we focused not just on the subjective experience of those identified as carers but also on the other party to the caring relationship we may find that in some situations the roles are blurred or shifting. We may also want to expand our definition of caring to encompass not just physical tasks but also the emotional part of caring for relationships. Research carried out by disabled feminists would therefore focus not so much on *carers* as on *caring*. (Morris, 1991: 167)

The present article is a partial attempt to take up my own challenge. While motivated by a feminist perspective it is also framed by the concerns of the disabled people's movement and, in particular, by the concept of independent living as it has been developed by that movement. I therefore now want to look at how the disability movement has challenged the concepts of 'care' and 'caring' by the re-examination of the meanings of 'dependence' and 'independence', before moving on to identify that this challenge raises particular issues for disabled women, issues which reveal significant limitations to the feminist research on caring.

## Challenging concepts of dependence and independence

The meanings of the words 'dependence' and 'independence' have been re-examined and redefined by many disabled individuals and disability organizations since the 1970s. There is a strong sense among such people of belonging to an international independent living movement which had its origins in Berkeley, California but which now has a presence in many other developed, and developing countries. This was reflected in the worldwide representation of disabled people at the international congress Independence 92.

Unfortunately, the term 'independent living' has, during the 1980s and early 1990s, sometimes been used by health or Social Services professionals to describe initiatives which they have developed in the context of community care policies. Focusing on professional assessments of functional ability and inability, these initiatives often bear little relationship to the principles and practice of the independent living movement. It is therefore important to set out clearly the philosophy and practice of that movement.

The philosophy of the independent living movement is based on four assumptions:

- that all human life is of value;
- that anyone, whatever their impairment, is capable of exerting choices;
- that people who are disabled by society's reaction to physical, intellectual and sensory impairment and to emotional distress have the right to assert control over their lives;
- that disabled people have the right fully to participate in society.

The concept of independent living is a broad one, embracing as it does the full range of human and civil rights. This means the right to have personal relationships, to be a parent, the right to equal access to education, training, employment and leisure activities and the right to participate in the life of the community. The movement is clear that its aims and aspirations are as relevant to those with intellectual impairments, to older people (including those with conditions such as Alzheimer's Disease), and to those who are survivors of the mental health system, as they are to the stereotype of the fit, young male paraplegic.

In developing the philosophy of independent living, disabled people have had to redefine the meaning of the word 'independent' (see

Oliver, 1991: 91). In Western industrial societies, this term has commonly been associated with the ability to do things for oneself, to be self-supporting, self-reliant. When physical impairment means that there are things that someone cannot do for themselves, daily living tasks which they need help with, the assumption is that this person is 'dependent'. And in Western culture to be dependent is to be subordinate, to be subject to the control of others. Much of the literature on community care refers to 'dependent people', most rehabilitation services focus on the 'independence' which is to be gained by maximizing physical mobility and physical ability to do daily living tasks. Those who cannot do things for themselves are assumed to be unable to control their lives.

In the context of the economic inequality which accompanies significant physical impairment in industrialized societies (and this is particularly the case for women), the need for personal assistance has been translated into a need for 'care' in the sense of a need to be looked after. Once personal assistance is seen as 'care' then the 'carer', whether a paid worker or an unpaid relative or friend, becomes the person in charge, the person in control. The disabled person is seen as being dependent on the carer, and incapable even of taking charge of the personal assistance s/he requires (see Mason, 1992: 80).

The independent living movement challenges all this. Simon Brisenden pointed out that disabled people experience

> an ideology of independence. It teaches us that unless we can do everything for ourselves we cannot take our place in society. We must be able to cook, wash, dress ourselves, make the bed, write, speak and so forth, before we can become proper people, before we are 'independent'. (Brisenden, 1989: 9)

Brisenden goes on to say that the independent living movement, in contrast, uses the word 'independent'

> in a practical and commonsense way to mean simply being able to achieve our goals. The point is that independent people have control over their lives, not that they perform every task themselves. Independence is not linked to the physical or intellectual capacity to care for oneself without assistance; independence is created by having assistance when and how one requires it. (ibid.)

Control over the assistance that is required to go about daily life is crucial, therefore, to the concept of independent living. It is this control which enables the expression of individuality and from this then flows the assertion of disabled people's human rights and their status as citizens. Control over personal assistance is necessary if those who need help with physical tasks are to achieve both human and civil rights, in other words not only the right to have control over basic daily living tasks (such as when to get up, go to bed, go to the toilet, when and what to eat) but also the right to have personal and sexual relationships, to seek employment, to engage in leisure and political activities. [. . .]

## The experience of statutory services

It was clear from the experience of those women interviewed that a reliance on services (provided by Social Services and health authorities) did not generally enable women to participate in personal relationships or engage in work or social activities outside their home in a way which they would choose.

There was a particularly common failure of statutory services to respond to the personal assistance needs that women had related to their roles as carers within their household. This has been encouraged by the tendency of home *help* services in recent years to turn themselves into home *care* services, focusing on personal care (see, for example, RADAR and Arthritis Care, 1991). This means that not only is it now more difficult to get help with housework but it is particularly difficult to get help with looking after children or anything else which is not deemed to be personal care (i.e. getting up, getting dressed, bathing, going to the toilet, eating).

Moira, for example, found that when her daughter was born her Social Services department said that their home carers would not be able to help her care for the baby. 'It wasn't in their job description and they suggested that my mother helped me.' This was an important motivation in her application for a cash grant from her Social Services department to enable her to employ her own helpers who make it possible for her to look after her daughter.

Jackie found that, when she became unable to do the kind of things which she normally did as part of her contribution to running the household, the only help she could get from the Social Services department was with personal care.

> The thing that they didn't recognize at all . . . they didn't accept that there were things that I did in the household [and that] therefore part of what the carers [from Social Services] should do should be the things that I would have done. Like the shopping, putting Dan's washing on and, I don't know, we worked out a great long list of domestic things that I normally did.

To women who see their role within their household as that of the homemaker and child-carer, the inability to get the help they need to continue this role is a particularly oppressive experience. Disabled women are commonly represented as passive recipients of care yet the role of caregiver is an important one to many of them.

Outside the home and family life, there are few roles open to disabled women. Only 31 per cent of disabled women of working age are in paid employment (OPCS, 1988). Statutory services add to the pressures on women to be confined within their own home by failing to offer any help with going outside the home, or even help to leave the home. For example, while Bina's Social Services department provides her with help within her home, they will not help her with getting in and out of her car. And Elizabeth, who relies on the Meals-on-Wheels service, found that, once she got a part-time job the service could not respond to her needs. 'I wanted them to bring it to my workplace, which is only just across the road, but they said it wasn't on their route.' Elizabeth's request for a service to be delivered to her workplace was not compatible with the assumption that Meals-on-Wheels deliver a service to people in their own homes.

Valerie summed up the experience many women had of statutory services when she said:

> I think the community care philosophy doesn't understand what independent living is. . . . They seem to think that community care is about someone being cosy and comfortable, being kept clean. To me that's a step back into the situation of residential care – living in the contained environment of your own home.

A further barrier to disabled women exerting control over their lives is that statutory services tend to be delivered in ways which make it difficult for disabled women to assert their own perceptions of what they need. Elizabeth described how her local authority family aides are 'very patronizing. . . . They're overbearing. . . . They want to give help in a custodial sense rather than facilitate. It's a big difference. When you're being custodial you're . . . well you're dictating aren't you, more or less, you're smothering a person's sense of independence'. She spoke eloquently of how the service providers' philosophy doesn't fit in with what she perceives her needs to be.

> For example, I had a confrontation with them when I returned from university last summer. I put it to them that when I got a job I would get more exhausted and I would want to have help in ways which I hadn't had before . . . like feeding. Because when I'm tired my athetoid movements [which mean that her body shakes] become more uncontrollable and obviously feeding myself becomes even more of an effort. So I just said, 'would you help me, say, on the day I had an interview and I wanted to conserve all my energy?' One of them said that was like regressing. They more or less implied that when I was at university and got support from Community Service Volunteers (CSVs) that I had become lazy. They were trying to make out that I was sort of trying to put one over.

Disabled women often try to assert their independence, in the sense of taking control over the help that they need to go about their daily lives, only to be confronted by the assumption commonly held by professionals and care workers that *they* have the right to define what is needed and how help should be given. This creates a real barrier to disabled women's participation in both personal relationships and the wider society generally. Particular difficulties are created by the common failure to recognize disabled women's caring role.

# References

Baldwin, S. and Twigg, J. (1991) 'Women and community care: reflections on a debate', in M. McClean and D.Groves (eds), *Women's Issues in Social Policy*. London: Routledge.

Brisenden, Simon (1989) 'A charter for personal care', *Progress*, 16, Disablement Income Group.

Dalley, Gillian (1988) *Ideologies of Caring: Rethinking Community and Collectivism*. Basingstoke: Macmillan.

Finch, Janet (1990) 'The politics of community care in Britain', in C. Ungerson (ed.), *Gender and Caring: Work and Welfare in Britain and Scandinavia*. Hemel Hempstead: Harvester Wheatsheaf.

Graham, Hilary (1983) 'Caring: a labour of love', in J. Finch and D. Groves (eds), *A Labour of Love: Women, Work and Caring*. London: Routledge & Kegan Paul.

Graham, Hilary (1991) 'The concept of caring in feminist research: the case of domestic service', *Sociology*, 25(1): 61–78.

Keith, Lois (1992) 'Who cares wins? Women, caring and disability', *Disability, Handicap and Society*, 7(2): 167–75.

Mason, Philip (1992) 'The representation of disabled people: a Hampshire Centre for Independent Living Discussion Paper', *Disability, Handicap and Society*, 7(1): 79–84.

Morris, Jenny (1991) *Pride Against Prejudice: Transforming Attitudes to Disability*. London: The Women's Press.

Morris, Jenny (1993) *Independent Lives? Community Care and Disabled People*. Basingstoke: Macmillan.

Oliver, Michael (1991) *The Politics of Disablement*, Basingstoke: Macmillan.

OPCS (1988) *OPCS Surveys of Disability in Great Britain: Report 2, The Financial Circumstances of Disabled Adults Living in Private Households*. London: HMSO.

RADAR and Arthritis Care (1991) *The Right to a Clean Home*, London: RADAR and Arthritis Care.

Walmsley, Jan (1993) 'Contradictions in caring: reciprocity and interdependence', *Disability, Handicap and Society*, 8(2): 129–42.

# 20

# Carers and Professionals – the Carer's Viewpoint

*Annie Bibbings*

I see so few people that if the world outside went away in the night, I would not notice it. (Husband caring for wife)

Although all carers have some needs in common, their circumstances can vary enormously. The reasons for this are the nature of the disability of the person cared for and the fact that 'informal caring' takes place within an existing relationship unlike other forms of care provided by nurses, doctors, etc. The person needing care may be a frail elderly mother, a physically disabled husband, a son who has learning difficulties or a friend experiencing mental illness. On the whole, carers are poorly prepared for the task they face. Whatever their circumstances, there are few carers who do not need some help.

This chapter looks at the difficulties experienced by carers, the assumptions and contradictions surrounding their role as both care providers and users, and the support they want from service providers. The chapter concludes by looking at some implications for inter-professional work in the context of working towards partnership in caring. [. . .]

## Needs of carers

It is not difficult to sit down with any group of people – service providers, social workers, district nurses, carers themselves – and quickly reach agreement about what should be done to help carers. Broadly, this will consist of: more recognition; providing better financial, practical and emotional support; improving access to information; increasing the opportunities to combine paid work and caring; and developing better awareness of the problems that carers face.

---

Originally published in A. Leathard (ed.), *Going Interprofessional*. London: Routledge. pp. 158–71 (abridged).

### More recognition – 'I'm a daughter, not a carer'

> Now my task is complete and she is at rest. I have no regrets. I would do it all over again for her. She never in words expressed her appreciation until a few days before her death when she said, 'You're a good daughter; no one but me knows what a good daughter you've been'. (Daughter recently caring for mother)

Many carers, particularly women, do not identify themselves as carers but see their role as a natural extension of family obligations. Carers' own expectations combined with the expectations of the cared-for person, other family members, peers and professionals can make it difficult for carers to feel that they have any control over whether they take on (or continue) the caring role or not.

Once a carer is able to identify herself as such and say 'I'm a daughter and a carer' this may often be the first step in recognizing that she too has needs and that it is quite legitimate to ask for help and support. It is therefore essential that proactive and energetic approaches are developed to help carers identify themselves early on in their caring role and before a crisis is reached.

The attitudes of and assumptions made by professionals can also make it difficult for carers to ask for help. Usually the presence of a carer in a household is the signal for service providers to breathe a sigh of relief and think that this is one problem they can ignore, 'Is there a daughter?' being one of the first questions to cross the lips of many a consultant, doctor or social worker when faced with the problem of needing to organize community care for a patient or client. The aim should be for carers and professionals to work towards partnership in caring, with the carer being seen as at least an equal partner and not just a passive recipient.

### More money

> I gave up my job at 60. I now have a reduced occupational pension because of early retirement – one-third of my salary. The hot water tank went and that cost £200. I lost an income of £9,000 a year. (Husband caring for wife)

The financial effects of providing care can be devastating. Extra heating, washing, special food and equipment, transport and substitute care all put a huge strain on household budgets. Additionally, many carers may have given up a paid job and therefore suffer not only the loss of income but also the loss of future promotion and pension income. State benefits are grossly inadequate and unavailable to most carers anyway. Invalid Care Allowance, the only specific benefit for carers, is so tied up with restrictions that of the 6.8 million carers, only about 170,000 actually receive this allowance.

### More practical help

> You've got to remember that if you have flu, you can't go to bed – so you just add depression to your physical problems. (A carer)

A major survey of nearly 3,000 carers carried out by the Carers National Association (1992), as part of its Listen to Carers campaign, showed that 65 per cent of carers said that caring had affected their health. The reasons for this are twofold: first, caring is hard work. It consists in many cases of a great deal of lifting and handling which is usually undertaken singlehandedly, and without any training. Many carers injure themselves in the course of their caring. Secondly, there are insufficient or inappropriate services to enable them to seek health care when they are injured or become ill. For example, a back injury cannot be rested. A hernia cannot be repaired if there is no one to take over the caring while the carer goes into hospital. Caring is often undertaken by the least fit members of the community.

*More emotional and moral support*

> I found that there was a complete assumption that, because I was the wife, I would take on the total care. I found this amazing and later realized how angry this assumption made me feel. I would have liked to have been *asked* and there to have been *some* discussion as to whether I could manage and what help and support would be available. There are times when I feel like nothing more than a housekeeper, cook, nurse, gardener, shopper and organizer. I often feel like a widow but without the freedom. Tiredness also plays a large part. In addition to all the practical problems, the fact that we no longer have a sexual relationship has an enormous impact and puts a great strain on our marriage. I feel it would be so helpful if my husband and I, jointly and separately, had someone to talk to who was experienced in spinal injury or perhaps in sexual counselling. The physical care that my husband received was outstanding but our emotional problems have been ignored and neglected. (Wife caring for husband with spinal injuries)

Although the physical burden can be heavy, many carers would say that their worst problems are of an emotional nature. Carers feel isolated. They may also feel angry, resentful and embarrassed by the tasks they have to perform; they often feel a sense of loss for the person for whom they are caring, and in addition they feel guilty for having these feelings in the first place. Having someone to talk to, whether a friend, relative or sympathetic professional, can be of immense help to carers as can opportunities to engage in social activities. Carers' support groups can play an invaluable role here in providing moral support, social contact and information.

The total subordination of one's own needs and preferences to those of another – together with the feeling of being out of control of one's own life – are major causes of depression in carers. This depression can make every day an eternity and in extreme cases can result in suicide or physical violence.

Old age abuse, or indeed abuse of a dependant of any age, is only one way in which some carers try to establish some control over a situation which is running away with them. Research carried out by

Homer and Gilleard (1990) shows that households particularly at risk are those that are socially or geographically isolated with a carer who is also suffering from significant illness and depression. Other significant risk factors are alcohol consumption by the carer, a poor pre-existing relationship with the cared-for person and a history of abuse over many years.

### More information

> I only recently found out about Attendance Allowance by accident after caring for my mother full time for over ten years. I had been ill and arrangements were being made for Mother to go away for two weeks so that I could have a break. An independent doctor arrived to make an assessment for a suitable place for her to go. He finished the assessment and asked, 'Of course, she is getting the Attendance Allowance.' Attendance Allowance, what's that? said I, whereupon I thought he was going to shoot up to the ceiling with annoyance. He told me to go to the local Social Security office for a form. I did not need telling twice! (Daughter caring for mother)

Carers need information about services available in their area, about the benefits to which they are entitled, about being a carer, about changes in legislation which will affect them and about the condition of the person for whom they are caring. The problem for carers is that over half of them are not in touch with any support service except their family practitioner. While much information does exist, these carers do not have access to it. GPs therefore form the only common link for these hidden carers and their surgeries are the place where such carers are most likely to go. A good GP can transform a carer's life simply by putting him or her in touch with support. However, all too often carers say of their GPs, 'He isn't interested in *me*' or 'She doesn't know anything.' It is hoped that this situation will improve as GPs are now obliged under the terms of their 1990 contract to give advice 'to enable patients to avail themselves of services provided by a local social services authority'.

In order to ensure that carers obtain the information they need, a 'saturation' policy is necessary. Carers' handbooks, factsheets, newsletters and information packs are useful but great care must be taken not to use professional jargon and also to provide multilingual leaflets where appropriate. Nor should information be confined to written material as many people are more likely to obtain their information by word of mouth or through the media. Carers' groups can be vital in passing on information and are particularly useful in persuading carers that a benefit or service might be available to them and indeed that they might even be entitled to it. It should be recognized that a major part of the job of all professionals must be to provide information to carers or at least to steer them to appropriate sources of help.

*More respite care*

> I have to prepare Dad for days before he goes into the local nursing home
> and he has tantrums when he comes back. He makes our life hell – so I ask
> myself, 'Is it worth it?' (A carer)

There is an urgent need for more or different respite care to give
carers both short but regular as well as longer breaks from caring.
There is a wide variety of need, so there must be a wide variety of
provision. The key requirements are the flexibility of the relief care
offered and its acceptability to both the carer and the cared-for
person. Some people want respite care provided in the home, some
want it provided in a residential setting, and some want a mixture of
both, including good day-care facilities. The high demand for home
care attendants and sitters reflects in part the unwillingness of some
frail elderly and disabled people to travel away from home. In
addition, carers and users are sometimes unhappy about the quality of
hospital and Social Services respite care provision which then puts
them off using the service a second time. Another form of respite care,
a lifeline to carers of children with special needs, is summer and
holiday play schemes. These can be vital if there are other children in
the family.

*More employment opportunities*

> It has been universally assumed that I can cope, that I will cope, that I will
> continue to cope. This includes the assumption that I can take time off work
> to take Mother to various medical appointments, to be present when
> various professional helpers wish to call. I have tried to explain my position
> at work and my own health problems. Ignored! (Daughter caring for
> mother)

Trying to combine paid work and care can cause immense difficulties
for carers in terms of stress, strain and loss of work opportunities. In a
survey of full-time carers undertaken by Opportunities for Women
(1990) 55 per cent of carers said that they had to give up their job
because of caring responsibilities, 5 per cent took early retirement, 16
per cent decided to work fewer hours, and 7 per cent were working
from home. The same survey interviewed a cross-section of people in
work and found that 17 per cent of employees had major caring
responsibilities for an adult or elderly person. Carers also reported
that they felt that their caring responsibilities affected their ability to
apply for promotion, seek a new job or relocate to a better job within
the same company. There are also considerable difficulties for carers
returning to work after they cease caring. 'I had to go straight from
the graveside to the Job Centre, only to be told I wasn't qualified
for anything and what had I really been doing for the last ten years.'
This is how one carer described the experience. Much could be done to

help carers combine caring with paid employment. This includes: reinstating the right to unemployment benefit after caring has ceased; increasing the amount that carers can earn before losing state benefits; setting up support schemes that will allow people to combine paid work and caring; setting up workplace carers' groups to provide advice and information to employees with caring responsibilities.

### Young carers

> The nine-year-old was no help, but the four-year-old was a great help. (From hospital case note)
> My one regret is that I have been robbed of my youth. The past five years have been traumatic; I have had to become an adult before my time. I often say I'm 19 going on 40. (Young carer)

Estimates based on survey work in Tameside and Sandwell (Page, 1988) suggest that nationwide there are well over 10,000 children acting as primary carers. Usually, they are from single-parent families in which a parent develops a disabling illness. There are also an unknown number of children living with an elderly relative, who are providing emotional or practical stability in a family that is experiencing mental distress. Older children are also often needed to help out with a disabled youngster.

Scarce resources and lack of information mean that there is little incentive for families to ask for help. In addition, the fear – real or perceived – that statutory intervention will result in the removal of parent or child (or both) into care is all-pervasive. The media view which paints these children as 'angels' or 'victims' reinforces the pressure felt by disabled parents when appropriate support is not available or is denied. Clearly, there is the problem for professionals of striking a balance between accepting the role of young people helping out with the care of a relative and advocating their rights as children – rights to leisure and uninterrupted education. Children should have the right not to be carers but when they *are* they must be consulted and their role valued. Research carried out by Bilsborrow (1992) shows an urgent need for services and further research into this area. The report, the first to focus on the quality of life for young carers, looks at the views of 11 youngsters aged between 9 and 21. They were caring for relatives with a variety of disabling conditions including arthritis, multiple sclerosis and tranquillizer addiction. Researchers also spoke to a variety of professional groups about their knowledge of the number of young carers in their area and their needs. Not surprisingly, the researchers found that most professionals knew little about young carers and focused attention on the relative being cared for. The problem was one of double invisibility: families were reluctant to ask for assistance because there were few support services available and families feared being labelled as 'problem families'. The Carers National Association young carers project wants to see local authorities:

- include young carers within the 'children in need' priorities for implementing the Children's Act 1989;
- set up a process for multidisciplinary collaboration and planning and delivery of services;
- take steps to combat the stigma felt by families who ask for services; and
- address the particular needs of different racial groups.

*More equality*

> When this project started not one family was claiming Invalid Care Allowance. No one had told them they were eligible. (Worker in a project for Asian parents of severely disabled children)

Carers face discrimination in many areas of their lives – from employment through to opportunities for leisure and recreation. Without sufficient private income carers have few meaningful choices as they have no automatic rights to services, training or an adequate income. The discretionary nature of service allocation means that decisions about 'who gets what' are often influenced by the attitude of a particular professional towards a particular carer or are based on unspoken assumptions.

Much also depends on the carers' attitudes, how good carers are at articulating their own needs and their skills in negotiating. Research (Charlesworth et al., 1984) indicates that issues of age, class, gender, race and cultural expectations all play a significant part in determining who is likely to receive services. Under-representation of black and ethnic minority carers receiving services suggests that they are a particularly vulnerable and disadvantaged group. Service providers need to be aware of the additional obstacles that such carers face. Time and resources must be spent on training staff in statutory and voluntary organizations to understand the various cultures and religions of their area; providing multilingual information and interpreting services; and undertaking outreach work with ethnic communities so that their views can be properly taken into account in community care planning [. . .]

## Conflict and contradictions

> If you are not confused about community care policies you are not thinking clearly! (Department of Health official)

The question remains that if the needs of carers are now generally better understood, why is it still so difficult for carers to obtain the help and support they need? Part of the answer is to be found in the conflicts and contradictions that exist in the way in which policy-makers, service providers and carers themselves see their respective roles.

### Conflict for the carer

Carers have the difficult job of trying to balance their own needs with the needs of the person they care for, often at a time when the relationship between them is at its most intense and fragile. Deep feelings of love and responsibility may be mixed with feelings of bereavement, resentment and anger. The huge amount of guilt that many carers feel can make it almost impossible for them to feel able to ask for help or indeed to accept it when it is offered.

### Conflict for the cared-for person

There is a natural desire in people to maintain their own inde-pendence and not be 'a burden' on others. This is combined with a strong British tradition of 'keep it in the family', 'we can manage' and, for some cared-for people, a strong message to their carer that 'only you can do it'. The result is that some frail, elderly and disabled people are unhappy about accepting help with daily living and per-sonal care tasks from anyone other than a close family member. On the other hand, some disabled people dislike the term 'carer' as they feel it perpetuates the idea that disability means dependency. They don't want to be 'looked after' by their relatives, but want the right to access to resources to enable them to appoint their own personal assistants or helpers. Thus, not only is there a wide range of views among people with disabilities themselves about who should be providing them with assistance, but there are often areas of conflict between the person needing care and the carer about choices and needs. Service providers need to recognize and address the complex-ities of this situation and attempt to mediate and balance the interests of both parties whenever possible.

### Conflict for professionals

Carers often praise the help that they receive from the caring pro-fessions but some also complain bitterly about 'being taken for granted' or not understood. Usually, this is not intentional. It is simply that the training of professionals has not taught them to recognize the needs of the carer. Another reason for ignoring carers is fear – fear which often stems from an awareness of a lack of resources. If carers' needs *are* identified, service providers often fear that they will be unable to meet them, leaving them feeling inadequate and guilty. This lack of resources is, of course, a reality and many mem-bers of the public seeking assistance for themselves or their relatives are likely to be caught in the care vacuum. As a consequence, many professionals see increasing the expectation of carers for more help as something to be avoided. The way that carers and professionals perceive each other can also give rise to conflict. Many carers express the view that they feel in awe of professionals and are intimidated by them. These perceptions may have more to do with what people in particular professions are expected to be like than with the actual people involved. Similarly, professionals may regard a carer as some kind of 'selfless angel' and this makes it hard for carers to confess their anxieties and fears in case they disillusion the professionals. Alternatively, professionals may regard a carer as someone who is too deeply involved in a mutually dependent relationship to be able to think rationally and in the best interest of the patient or client. By describing four models of caring – carers as a resource, as co-workers, as co-clients and superseded carers – Twigg and Aitken (1991) provide a helpful framework for understanding the ambiguous situation that carers occupy in relation to service providers.

Seeing carers as *resources* reflects the way that carers are perceived as 'free' community care providers or cheap labour. The aim, if services are provided at all, is to keep the carer caring but at minimal cost. Describing carers as *co-workers* is where service providers aim to work in close collaboration with carers and there is recognition of the importance of the carer's morale and support in the rehabilitation of the client. Carers as *co-clients* is where service providers see carers as having needs in their own right. The fourth model of the *superseded* carer usually applies to parents who have sons or daughters with special needs. Here the aim of services is to move the client away from support provided by family carers into 'independent living'.

### Conflict for policy-makers

The different ways in which carers are seen and defined makes it difficult for policy in relation to carers to be consistent and specific in terms of service provision, eligibility and allocation. A great deal of 'paper' recognition is given to carers and warm sentiments are expressed about the valuable job they do. However, there is still little real commitment in terms of resources to translate these good intentions into practical action. Conflicts also arise between different areas of government policies. For example, women are encouraged back into paid employment, while in reality many women carers are unable to take up paid employment as no affordable relief care is available.

### Conflict for society

Whatever the uncertainty about resources, it is clear that over the next decade, owing to demographic and medical advances, there is going to be an increase in the number of people living at home and needing care with a corresponding decline in the number of carers available. The impact of changes in marriage patterns – more divorce and remarriage and more single-parent families – is not yet clear but it seems likely that, in the long term, they could lead to a lessening of the moral imperatives and the close family obligations which give rise to caring. We may not feel the same love or duty to our ex in-laws or to our step-siblings as we do to closer family, and indeed may even lose touch with them completely. In addition, a single parent with children to care for as well as a job is unlikely to have the time to care for an elderly relative.

There are also fewer single women, who have in the past traditionally been those most likely to become carers. There are fewer children in most families, family members live further apart and the proportion of childless marriages is growing. More elderly people will therefore have no immediate kin to care for them. Lastly, since being a carer can isolate you from your community and from the rest of your family, it may mean that carers themselves are deprived of the opportunity to build up the kind of social networks which give rise to caring. Neither will they have much opportunity to build up any financial reserves. Who will care for them? The world is changing and, like it or not, professionals, carers and users are going to have to learn to understand each other and work together better.

## Working towards partnership in caring

[. . .]

Carers need opportunities to engage in debate with both service providers and with the politicians who control the resources for the services they need. To achieve this, consultation and participation with carers in community care planning should become an integral part of every element in the work of local and health authorities, family health service authorities, housing authorities, voluntary organizations and other bodies providing community services. Consultation should be shaped to suit the needs and culture of an area and encourage maximum participation from all members of the community. There can be no single, neat definition for consultation, but it should encompass a wide range of activities which together constitute the process of listening to carers.

It is vital that carers know about their right to ask for an assessment of their own needs and a confidential interview should always be offered. Honesty about what is on offer and what is not is essential too. Without a designated care manager, many carers are left with the impossible task of trying to co-ordinate their own care arrangements across a variety of occupational groups and organizations. When problems do occur (e.g. a home care assistant does not turn up or day centre hours are cut) carers and users are frequently told, 'It's not our problem – it's Social Services' responsibility' or 'We have to give priority to elderly people living alone.'

Carers, therefore, report that they spend a great deal of their energy and time trying to understand who is supposed to be responsible for doing what and in plugging the gaps in communication and co-ordination between professional groups.

The experience of the Carers National Association, which is a national charity for all carers, has shown that, in order to get better support and more choice for carers, it is essential for them to have a 'collective voice' at both local and national levels. As part of the Association's Listen to Carers campaign, carers were asked what they felt was the most important piece of advice that they could give other carers. Overwhelmingly, most respondents gave advice on the theme of making yourself heard and being recognized. Their comments included:

'Speak up, speak out and keep doing it.'
'Shout and keep shouting.'
'Keep shouting and don't be shy.'
'Ask and keep asking.'
'Shout and push – it's an uphill battle but I won eventually.'

Perhaps only by carers speaking up, and speaking out, will enough influence be brought to bear on policy-makers, service providers and professionals to ensure that carers have a better deal. But, like Oliver Twist, it cannot just be up to the disadvantaged and vulnerable to 'keep asking for more'! Professionals must become effective advocates and allies of carers too.

## References

Bilsborrow, S. (1992) *Young Carers on Merseyside*. London: Barnardos.

Carers National Association (1992) *Speak Up, Speak Out*. London: Carers National Association.

Charlesworth, A., Wilkin, D. and Durie, A. (1984) *Carers and Services: A Comparison of Men and Women Caring for Dependent Elderly People*. Manchester: Equal Opportunities Commission.

Homer, A. and Gilleard, C. (1990) 'Abuse of elderly people by their carers', *British Medical Journal*, 30: 1359–62.

Opportunities for Women (1990) *Carers at Work*. London: OFW.

Page, R.W. (1988) 'Report on the initial survey investigation, the number of young carers in Sandwell secondary schools', *Social Services Research*, 6: 31–6.

Twigg, J. and Aitken, K. (1991) *Evaluating Support to Informal Carers*. York: Social Policy Research Unit, University of York.

# 21

# 'He's our child and we shall always love him' – Mental Handicap: the Parents' Response

*Robina Shah*

It is Monday morning and there's a call from a desperate social worker seeking advice on a new referral.

> 'Hello, how can I help you?'
> 'Hi, I'm a social worker from x district and I'm wondering if you can help me. Yesterday I received a note from the duty officer about a referral concerning an Asian woman. It seems that she had a forced arranged marriage with a man from Lebanon, and is being evicted from her home – she has three children and is in an extremely distressed state of mind. I would be grateful if you could advise me on the languages she may speak and how I can best empathize with her about her marital situation.'

I asked,

> 'How do you know she doesn't speak English? And why do you think she's unhappy about her marriage?'
> 'Well, she's Asian and I thought that all Asian women were forced into marriage at an early age and then expected to have many children. Most of them can't speak English and have difficult relations with their parents – don't they?'

Such a dialogue is not unique and strongly exemplifies how perceptions about Asian people, and Asian women in particular, are formed on the basis of preconceived notions about Asian family life. In this particular case, as a result of misinformation and a dependence on stereotypes, the whole referral had been completely misinterpreted. Here, a simple request – for nursery places for her children, some support from Social Services while her Pakistani husband was away working in Lebanon, and advice on how she could obtain some council accommodation as her parents' house was a little overcrowded – had created a picture of a poor harassed Asian woman, threatened with eviction from her parents' home and experiencing marital problems with her husband. The fact (as was subsequently discovered) that she

From Robina Shah (1992) *The Silent Minority: Children with Disabilities in Asian Families*. London: National Children's Bureau. pp. 15–25 (abridged).

was born in Britain and could speak perfect English was given no substance at the time of referral. Equally, the fact that she had been happily married for six years and loved her husband bore no relevance.

Services to Asian people often demonstrate expectations among social workers and health workers which are neither congruent with, nor relevant to, the felt and actual needs of the Asian communities. This is most implicit where expectations are significantly different from one individual to another – especially in the area of mental handicap. Statutory agencies are ideal places either to improve or hinder positive imagery of minority ethnic groups. Of course, many of us have prejudices about something or other and stereotypes do exist, but they become most harmful when they are used as a yardstick to measure and complement irrationality – where social workers are led into errors and into needless problems through tendencies to prejudge people and situations.

The tendency to form judgements about others solely on the basis of racial, ethnic or religious identity lies at the heart of the processes to be examined in this chapter: prejudice/stereotypes and discrimination. First I shall offer definitions for both prejudice and discrimination. As will become apparent, the two are closely related yet are distinct in important ways. Secondly, I shall examine how these two processes are instrumental in inhibiting social workers from providing an appropriate and equal service to Asian clients with a disabled child, and how their understanding of the Asian community and disability is distorted by a lack of understanding about cultural and religious needs – where individuality falls prey to perceived group norms at the expense of the disabled client.

Prejudice/stereotypes and discrimination can also be classified as personal and cultural racism, which are enhanced by institutional racism. [. . .] Institutional racism is embedded within an infrastructure, resistant to change as a result of policies and practices installed and perpetuated by white professionals working within the organization. Institutional racism may be endorsed in any institution, whether it be social work, health, education or in the voluntary sector. [. . .]

It is hoped that the information presented in this discussion will be of benefit in two ways: first as a means by which one may understand the nature and causes of both prejudice/stereotypes and discrimination; and secondly, to counteract the negative impact of both on one's own feelings, beliefs and behaviour, not only towards the Asian community but towards the Black community in general.

### Prejudice, stereotypes and discrimination – potential bombs?

The terms prejudice and discrimination are often used synonymously in everyday speech. However, prejudice generally refers to negative attitudes of a special kind; in contrast, discrimination describes negative actions directed against the persons who are its objects – the victims of prejudice.

Prejudice is an attitude (wholly negative) towards the members of some specific group (racial, ethnic, religious and so on) that causes the persons holding it to assume other negatives solely on the basis of membership of that group. Since attitudes often operate as frameworks for organizing or recalling information, persons who are prejudiced tend to notice and only remember certain kinds of information about the groups they dislike – 'facts that are largely negative in nature'. When prejudice is defined it refers to the beliefs and expectations an individual holds about the members of a particular group. Often these beliefs and expectations form clusters of preconceived notions known as stereotypes. Unfortunately, once they are formed, stereotypes lead individuals to assume that all members of a racial, ethnic, religious or other group possess similar traits or act in the same manner. In short, stereotypes lead persons who hold them to ignore important differences between unique individuals. This can involve tendencies to act in negative ways towards the persons who are the objects of such attitudes and these, translated into overt actions, constitute discrimination.

Discrimination often takes open and direct forms, but it is frequently much more subtle in nature. That is, even highly prejudiced individuals seek to conceal their negative feelings, expressing them openly only in situations where they think they can safely 'get away' with harmful actions towards disliked groups. While many forms of subtle discrimination exist, two are deserving of specific attention in the context of this study:

- the withholding of aid from people who need it; and
- the performance of trivial or tokenistic actions.

Both of these are extremely important in determining and predicting the provision of services to Asian families who have a disabled child. For example, many social workers assume that Asian families do not require respite care services since this is already structured within the extended family system; thus, they may withhold aid from people who need it. Tokenism also occurs, that is the effort involved to promote better services is minimal, but enough to constitute a means of continued discrimination: 'Haven't I done enough for those people already – after all I use an interpreter on my visits.'

Throughout our lives we rely on our values, beliefs and norms of behaviour to assist us in analysing and preparing what we hope will be an adequate response to persons who are, in some way, perceived to be different from us. In terms of delivering a service this may result in a worker drawing upon a pool of stereotypes in order to administer help in an 'acceptable' way. This can create problems for both the provider and the user. During the course of [the research on which this chapter is based] it was found that stereotypes played an important role in confusing social workers about the needs of Asian parents, and more importantly about the attitude of these parents towards their handicapped children.

### 'Look behind the word Asian and see me'

Social workers have various expectations of how Asian parents view their mentally/physically handicapped child. In recent years efforts have been directed towards what many believe to be the single most significant barrier – that of attitudes. If attitudes can be changed, solutions to the specific problems confronting disabled children and their parents will fall into place as a matter of course. Associated with attitudes, the general level of knowledge among social workers is of decisive importance to the quantity and quality of the services they offer. Where ignorance and adherence to inappropriate beliefs prevail, there is low motivation to develop services and even sometimes a hostile attitude towards the Asian community in general. However, there are some practitioners in the caring services who work to a model of practice by challenging stereotypes, through consultation with members or workers from the community in which they are involved and by their own personal commitment.

By looking at various verbatim comments from social workers, a range of attitudes about Asian parents and disability can be demonstrated. It is important to note here that such attitudes clearly indicate the anxiety and frustration of dealing with a client group where the only information one can draw upon is based on stereotypes, assumptions and hearsay. In brief these stereotypes include assumptions such as the following:

- Asian parents reject their child immediately on finding out that he or she has a disability or disabilities.
- Asian parents encounter feelings of resentment from other members of their family.
- Asian parents feel stigmatized by the community.
- Asian parents see the birth of a disabled child as a punishment for sins or a test from God.
- Asian parents suffer feelings of inadequacy, especially the mother.
- Asian parents express embarrassment.
- Asian parents fail to see a necessity to prepare for the future welfare of the child, that is they feel God will protect him or her.
- The Asian male is the dominant figure of the household and all communications should be made through him.
- Parents show little interest in using toys to develop the child's abilities.

- Parents depend on the extended family to provide care to disabled children.
- Asian parents don't understand the necessity for genetic counselling – there are too many inter-family marriages.

Although there are some Asian parents who express and confirm the above stereotypes, these attitudes are not absolute or representative of all Asian parents. Such stereotypical attitudes are also frequently reported by White parents of children with disabilities. Therefore, for any service provider it is essential that individual needs are given priority and the importance of parents' views acknowledged. [. . .]

Disability, whether it is physical, mental, sensory or auditory, is not prejudiced in any way: it transcends all races, beliefs and cultures. It creates similarly profound emotional, practical and psychological experiences for all parents, whoever they are. Unfortunately, where Asian families are concerned, common sense about a valid generalization of attitudes towards disability is lost in the mists of ignorance and perceived cultural differences. Little or no attention is given to what is in fact a natural and universal response to having a child who is born with a disability or who, later on in childhood, is diagnosed as 'disabled'. Looking for differences where none exist or assuming homogeneity of feelings when differences need to be identified is a form of cultural racism.

Throughout this research, communication has been highlighted as the main barrier in preventing adequate assessments and the building up of relationships between social worker and parents. While for a few of the parents interviewed in this study language did pose some problems, the majority of parents had a good command of English and for some, English was their first language. In spite of this, communication problems persisted; cross-purposes increased and a general situation of misunderstanding between parent and social worker was encountered. However, the problem is often not generated by the parent: it derives frequently from the inability of the social worker to recognize meanings because of strong accents and bias. Where interpreters are used, social workers may be reluctant to depend on the accuracy of the information translated. It has often been said by professional interpreters that they are not used often enough by social workers and other professionals in cases where English is poor. This in itself may convey how personal racism often prevents the intervention of bilingual workers to assist in assessing Asian families' needs. [. . .]

Evidence also suggests that the assumption of Asian male dominance is not irrefutable. Many Asian women who were interviewed indicated that their husbands were the sole communicators with social agencies but that this did not imply that they were unaware of what had been discussed. All decisions were shared decisions, and both parents shared the caring and responsibility for their child. Where fathers were absent during some social workers' visits, this was usually a consequence of employment rather than a lack of interest or responsibility. It is important to remember here that where mothers are seen to be playing a quiet and passive role, it does not mean that they are illustrations of the stereotype of the subservient Asian woman. The mother is concerned about her child, shows an increased interest to communicate, but may decide not to for fear of being ridiculed because her standard of English is poor. In response to views concerning the extended family network and the assumed preference to refuse outside help, these are again the product of myth. Such a caricature is founded on a vision of the White British family, which stresses that it is open and non-patriarchal. It is clear that Asian parents do not utilize services to their fullest potential, but this is not necessarily because they have their own resources; rather, they may not want to be accused of being a burden on the state and taking more than their share. Similarly, they may be reluctant to sit down and explain the importance of their religious and cultural identity to social workers.

Counselling for Asian parents is also fraught with difficulties as they may be subject to victimization and cultural racism such as statements that 'first cousin marriages are always prone to producing a child with some disability, so why do these people do it?' The genetic risks of marriages between family members are frequently raised with regard to the Asian community. Inter-family marriages do not necessarily lead to an increased risk of inherited disease or disability. However, Asian families – like those from other racial backgrounds – *may* be at risk if there is already a family history of congenital disability or an inherited disease. In the past few years there has been general concern that *all* parents of whatever racial or cultural background should have access to information on the possible risks of genetically determined diseases. The option of genetic counselling should be available for those who wish it and should be provided sensitively by someone familiar with the views and values of the families concerned. The possibility of gene therapy being introduced within the next few years (which may make some disabilities and diseases treatable before birth) is likely to raise the public debate about how parents are told of possible risks and what advice they are given about further action. Open and honest discussion with people who are known to work in the community will be essential to avoid misconceptions and to ensure that any advice is relevant, non-judgmental and fully accurate.

Similarly, behavioural programmes for young children are based on White cultural behavioural patterns; there is no scope for integrating other cultures and this results in providing inappropriate skills for children from an Asian background. For example, teaching a child with a mental handicap to eat with a knife, fork and spoon can sometimes leave him and his parents completely at a loss, since most Asian children who eat Asian food do so with their hands and not with cutlery.

Social workers and psychologists might assume that the absence of toys in the living room suggests that toys are not seen as important by parents in assisting the development of their child's motor or sensory skills. It may be that the toys are kept upstairs or in another room, so it is always better to ask rather than to assume the worst. The social skill development and cognitive development of their disabled children are as important to Asian parents as to other parents; like all parents they realize the need to address the future welfare of their child, but they may find services to enable this to be estranged from their co-operation and understanding. Religious belief here is very strong: that God will provide for him/her is not questioned. However, at the same time, they realize that responsibility for the future of their child must be undertaken by them and they should therefore take the initiative in preparation for him or her – with or without the help of a social worker.

At this point, a number of social workers I interviewed have commented on how disabled Asians are prepared for marriage. In some cases, the girls have severe mental handicaps and are totally dependent on their carers and this may be considered on two levels. First, securing a marriage partner for their daughter will serve to relax and provide some comfort to parents who will be reassured that, after their death, someone will be looking after their daughter; secondly, it suggests that some parents are not fully aware of the degree of disability their daughter has and that the condition is incurable and will never be normal. The latter is probably due to poor parent counselling at the identification of disability, and ineffective health and social work intervention to educate parents about the prognosis for their child.

Lack of social contact between White and Asian parents has also been highlighted as a point of concern. Attitudes among Asian parents with a disabled child are probably no different from those of their White counterparts. Most of the big voluntary agencies which are said to assist parents who have a child with a disability display an under-representation of Asian people; these agencies find it difficult to develop appropriate strategies to welcome Asian families as members.

On the basis of such attitudes as those discussed, it is not surprising that Asian parents feel judged even before they have had their first visit from social workers or other practitioners in the health and social work settings. For this reason many Asian parents have a particular difficulty in seeking the assistance of Social Services because they feel that their cultural beliefs or religious needs will be ignored, misunderstood or ridiculed. Rather than face this type of situation, they prefer to withdraw from using statutory services. The emphasis is on individuality; they don't wish to be placed in the 'pool of generalizations'. And they would rather not be told that 'Mrs Dutt didn't wish her child to be taken into short-term care' – for them, Mrs Dutt does not speak for the whole Asian community.

Asian parents no longer accept the reasoning used to deprive them of their uniqueness – stereotypes which may categorize Asians and provide some social workers with an overall impression about Asians and their expectations regarding behaviour, may be used to render their social work task easier; but Asian parents will no longer allow it to justify their actions or to perpetuate further discriminatory practices against them. So 'Look behind the word *Asian* and see *me*.'

# 22

# The Cloak of Professionalism

*Celia Davies*

The image of professionalism as a cloak seems in many ways highly appropriate. A cloak is first of all a form of protection against the hostile elements. It is a large and rather unwieldy garment, and one that needs to be worn with some degree of panache. A cloak has an air of mystery about it, for it hides more than it reveals. It is not a garment that is at the height of fashion; indeed, in these days of serialized historical novels on television, it conjures up the image (rather conveniently it will turn out) of the nineteenth-century gentleman.

This cloak of professionalism has been judged differently by the arbiters of fashion through the years. Nurses, for the most part, have been among the admirers – reaching and trying to draw it about them. I suggest it is time to stop hankering for something that has become an anachronism and, furthermore, something of an illusion. There is a lot of padding under the impossibly broad shoulders from which the cloak of professionalism hangs.

I believe that all health professionals need a new garb. It is not enough to chop the cloak off halfway and give it a red lining. We need a new professionalism to fit the changed circumstances in which we find ourselves at the end of the twentieth century.

The doctors drew the cloak of professionalism around themselves well when the NHS came into being. Concessions to their concerns and places for them at the policy table were won in ways that proved serviceable for nearly 40 years. But by the end of the 1980s, even their cloak was tattered and torn. Economic stringency and New Right policies had seen to that. Professionals, not only in health but in education, social welfare, local government and more besides, were tarred with the same brush as the bureaucrats – as altogether too profligate with the resources of the state, needing to be subject to the tougher discipline of general management and the market. [. . .]

When I left the United Kingdom Central Council for Nursing, Midwifery and Health Visiting (UKCC) in 1987, having spent more

Compiled from two separate articles originally published in *Nursing Times*, 92(45), 6 November 1996, and 92(46), 13 November 1996.

than two years as a non-nurse working on Project 2000 (a government supported reform of nurse education) it was with a strong sense of the inhospitable terrain on which nurses struggled. Nurses' protests that they were a profession and should be treated as one seemed regularly to fall on deaf ears. This, I was convinced, had something to do with the fact that nursing was devalued because it was seen as women's work. The sheer numbers and the complexity of nursing, midwifery and health visiting made the project of regulation and educational development an unwieldy one. Would other occupational groups be lumped together in the same way – was it that they were all seen as 'just nurses really'? It was not until much later that I saw how these concerns about gender would enable me to look at the concept of a profession with new eyes.

There is a lot of talk about gender issues that frankly serves to trivialize and confuse. We can easily become locked in heavily emotionally charged debates about whether women and men are intrinsically different and caught up in feelings of anger or guilt. But there is no denying that the idea of intrinsic or innate differences is around. I have regularly found that students can unhesitatingly produce the familiar lists of stereotypes – men are active, independent, strong, confident and rational; women are passive, dependent, weak and unsure of themselves, and get emotional. The challenge is what to do with lists like this. I do not think it is helpful either to dismiss them out of hand, as manifestations of prejudice, or to spend precious academic time on studies of how far they fit real women and men. Instead, I maintain that we should see gender differences like this as a set of immensely powerful cultural ideas about the sexes – about the apparently essential nature of masculinity and femininity and about the ways these relate to each other.

These ideas may or may not be the ideas we live by, but they are culturally available to us all. They permeate our sense of identity, affect our day-to-day interactions and, most especially, are embedded in complex ways in the organizations that frame our lives. It is important to acknowledge that although these cultural codes of masculinity and femininity are defined in relation to each other, they are not complementary. It is masculinity that is the yardstick, the culturally privileged term. Qualities associated with femininity take on a negative tone, or appear to be somehow residual – the absence of something rather than the presence of something else.

Culturally, then, there is not a clear definition of the feminine at all, but there is a masculine notion of the self as strongly bounded, as separate from others, as an individual aiming ideally to make his own way in the world and to make a difference to that world.

Masculinity, in this sense, means being detached and calmly evaluating the options, being strictly in control of self and, indeed, of others. For if the world is populated by other masculine selves, each with its individual project, then there is little room for shared enthusiasms or co-operative activity. The logic of masculinity's project (not necessarily the project of individual men, please note) has to be to control relations with others in a world that is otherwise bleak in its competitiveness and individual striving.

If this sounds extreme, it is. Culturally understood masculinity and femininity, as I am discussing them here, represent a splitting of human qualities and a tidying away of those to do with warmth, spontaneity and recognition of interdependence by assigning them to the feminine – to the private sphere of home and family.

This brings me to the crucial next step, which is to see that it is a belief about individuals as masculine selves that is written into the public world of organizations and professions. Our organizations may not actually work according to this cultural idea of masculinity, but the ideal of the bounded masculine self still underlies them.

How then does the notion of profession reflect this masculine self that I have just described? Consider the appearance of the consultant on a hospital ward. He (and for the most part it is still he) makes a momentary appearance, quizzes those who have more continuous association with 'his' patient, gives an opinion, proposes or confirms a course of action and moves on. His demeanour is cool, calm and collected; his decisions appear to arise rationally from his evaluation of the evidence as marshalled before him. The work is organized according to his convenience. What he does takes on an active and decisive character; he has 'mastery' of relevant knowledge, he is in command. Others offer him deference and respect or, at the very least, rarely offer an overt challenge to his autonomy and authority.

Interestingly, it is the work of others that actually lets him behave in this way. His juniors, all in training grades, are important here, and so too of course are the nurses who prepare the patient and who mop up tears and fears. There is a real and unacknowledged sense in which the classic way of being professional – all-knowing, distant and detached – cannot be produced without the support of others; particularly, but not exclusively, nurses.

In one way, this is about the familiar notion of the nurses as handmaid to the doctor, but it is more than this. For to understand medicine's professionalism as an embodiment of masculinity in this way also entails an understanding of nursing as a necessary adjunct to professionalism, letting it take this particular form.

I have elsewhere encapsulated this in the idea of the 'fleeting encounter' (Davies, 1995). Aloofness and confidence can be sustained partly through the sheer brevity of the relationship. The doctor does not need to build relationships: he does not need to see or consider much of the work that others do. In a study of revised medical staffing structures in an obstetric unit where the post of registrar was removed and consultants spent more time on the labour ward, much of

Table 22.1  *Old and new concepts of professionalism*

| Old professionalism | New professionalism |
|---|---|
| *Mastery of knowledge* | *Reflective practice* |
| Unilateral decision process | Interdependent decision process |
| (patient as dependent) | (patient as empowered) |
| (colleagues as deferential) | (colleagues involved) |
| *Autonomy and self-management* | *Supported practice* |
| Individual accountability | Collective responsibility |
| *Detachment* | *Engagement* |
| Interchangeability of practitioners | Specificity of practitioners' strengths |

this pattern appeared to break down and the work of midwives and the junior doctors changed. Some doctors would not accept it and felt it downgraded them. As one said: 'My job is not to come in but to be consulted' (Kitzinger et al., 1993).

Where do we go from here? Is it possible to argue for a feminine interpretation of professionalism and professional behaviour? No. If masculinity is a one-sided accentuation of certain human properties, an emphasis that denies emotions, vulnerability and dependence on others, then the goal is not to build something new out of what is repressed, but to seek to transcend the polarization that gendered thought invites – to dislodge the culturally masculine ideal of professionalism and to envision something that is deliberately degendered.

We need to recognize the cloak of professionalism for the outdated and male-tailored garment that it is. Nineteenth-century ideas of what it was to be a responsible gentleman, to work hard to cultivate, not land but knowledge, and to apply it from a lofty and distant class position, need serious amendment in the society of today – not only because relations between the sexes have changed, but because relations between those who need health services and those who supply them have also been the subject of change. [. . .]

Professionalism still has much to do with nineteenth-century ideas about masculinity which stress the active, competitive person, instead of the more reflective, interdependent one. Rather than work with the legacy of this artificial polarizing of properties, we might do better to try to transcend it.

Table 22.1 sets out six characteristics, each of which tries to steer a path away from the gender-dichotomized thinking towards a new vision of what it is to be a professional. First, and most fundamentally, we need to look again at the characterization of the professional practitioner.

Old professionalism makes a lot of sense as the project of a masculine self – one set apart from, and in competition with, others; one seeking to expunge emotional commitments and forge a place in a competitive world.

Old professionalism involves the mastery of knowledge. In a competitive world, knowledge becomes a personal possession. All the verbs we use in relation to knowledge have a property connotation – knowledge is something we acquire, possess or hold. The struggle is to master, subdue and control – to create order, to reduce uncertainty. From this point of view it is not surprising that it is the specialist not the generalist who has higher status.

I would like to suggest that there is another approach to knowledge, one that sees it as confirmed in use, that values things other than the formal and abstract, copes with uncertainty, acknowledges the intuitive and accepts the importance of experience. The idea of reflective practice works towards this alternative concept – seeking knowledge as something that grows and develops from the fusion of expertise and experience and the formal and the intuitive (Walmsley, 1993).

Once knowledge has been reconceptualized in this way, surrounding social relations can be transformed. Old professionalism, for example, sees the decision process as essentially unilateral. After all, faced with the possessor of superior knowledge, the patient can only react with gratitude and colleagues can only defer.

This set of ideas has already been strongly challenged, for example by patient support groups, campaigners around particular forms of disability and disease, and by those in the women's health movement. Nurses too have sometimes taken on the role of patient advocate – user participation and empowerment is now a distinctly contemporary policy theme.

Closely linked with unilateral decisions are two further features. The classic professional, because of superior knowledge, will claim autonomy and self-management, arguing that practice cannot be regulated by those who are not versed in the requisite knowledge bases. Each professional must be self-regulating and peer review is the only appropriate form of monitoring. The corollary of this is that the professional bears a heavy weight of personal responsibility for decisions made.

Such a burden serves further to separate the professional from others, and indeed nurses often report that they will defer to the doctor because in the end the doctor carries the can. However, here too there is the beginning of a shift in emphasis with preceptorship and mentoring and also clinical supervision.

Individual responsibility for maintaining and developing standards gives way, for less rigidly bounded individuals, to an acceptance that care is a team phenomenon, and drawing out and enhancing the contributions of others, whatever their formal roles and titles, can be beneficial. This raises the challenge of how a collective can be held to account if boundaries between professions and between professionals and non-professionals remain as strong as they are today.

The shift from detachment to engagement, as described in the table, represents a careful selection of terms. The dangers of over-involvement and burnout in health work are beginning to be discussed: the notion has recently come into play of a 'meaningful distance', which acknowledges that there will be a committed and emotional response, but seeks to avoid over-identification on the one hand and under-involvement on the other. We need new terms to acknowledge, value and harness the commitment that health professionals often show instead of the detachment of the classic professional or the money motivation that advocates of market incentives seem to want to evoke.

Health professionals are not always the detached possessors of an equivalent knowledge. Factors such as age, class background, ethnicity and life experience can facilitate or hamper their professional practice. This suggests not only the 'therapeutic use of self' but also the 'therapeutic use of others' who may have much lower status in the care team. For example, in hospice care it is the care assistant who in some cases may have the most to offer the dying patient (James, 1992).

## A half-open door?

The ideas set out here are not entirely new. Others have been moving in similar directions. Two should be singled out. Margaret Stacey, drawing on her experience as a lay member of the General Medical Council, produced a swingeing critique of that body with a call for a 'new professionalism' in the shape of a rethinking of the agenda of regulations (Stacey, 1992). Richard Hugman's comparisons of nursing, the remedial therapies and social work and his plea for a 'democratic professionalism' also sought to empower users and professionals alike (Hugman, 1991).

Much has already changed – a number of activities that nurses are carrying out individually in their practice and collectively in statutory bodies and associations might well be said to be steps on the road to the kind of new professionalism that I describe.

What can we start to count as changes in the direction of new professionalism? It has been pointed out that old professionalism, in the shape of an uncritical adherence to the idea of a set of traits to which nursing aspires and in terms of which it energetically presents itself, is still widely prevalent in academic circles (Porter, 1995). Yet nurses do, with more or less success, embrace patient empowerment, seek to work in multidisciplinary teams, and sometimes challenge those above them on the ladder.

The promotion of continuing professional education is a form of a lifelong learning model that in part confronts the idea of complete and once-and-for-all mastery of knowledge that underpins the old model. The UKCC's recent position paper on clinical supervision has at its heart something too of a vision of practice (UKCC, 1996). Such points cry out not for confident pronouncements, but for discussion, dialogue and exchange.

Some final observations. First, old and new professionalism are likely to continue to coexist. Some of the ideas of new professionalism are much less enthusiastically endorsed than others – those looking for ways of including the less qualified in the division of labour, for example. Secondly, where nurses are sometimes tempted to see themselves as having a monopoly on altruism, caring and commitment, what they are doing is replacing the celebration of cultural masculinity in professions with an alternative celebration of femininity rather than, as I have advocated, transcending the two. Thirdly, alongside the attractions of new professionalism are fears of the deterioration of the status of nursing and of the quality of the care it can give. Recent reactions to the idea of a generic helper bear witness to that (*Nursing Times*, 1996).

My attempt to redefine professionalism has involved locating the origins and the distinctiveness of its model in a mid-nineteenth-century battle between gentry, professions and trade from which the doctors won a form of respect. This model, on reflection, is unsuitable material from which to fashion professionalism today. My hope is that having identified the legacies of old professionalism and the sources of their coherence, we may all be freed to envision something new. We live in a culture that has denied and repressed a whole series of important qualities by labelling them as feminine and inappropriate for governing our relations in the public world. That culture has created the feminine as 'other', erasing the qualities it stands for from a place in public discussion.

Those who continue to try to define the essence of nursing, who write about the art as well as the science of it, who try, as the RCN [Royal College of Nursing] did recently, to put into words the value of nursing, are all struggling against this masculinist world view (RCN, 1992). Perhaps it is time to challenge and confront it, to renew and revitalize the concept of profession that embraces us all.

## References

Davies, C. (1995) *Gender and the Professional Predicament in Nursing*. Buckingham: Open University Press.

Hugman, R. (1991) *Power in the Caring Professions*. London: Macmillan.

James, N. (1992) 'Care = organisation + physical labour + emotional labour', *Sociology of Health and Illness*, 14(4): 488–509.

Kitzinger, J., Green, J. and Coupland, V. (1993) 'Labour relations: midwives and doctors on the labour ward', in J. Walmsley, J. Reynolds, P. Shakespeare and R. Wolfe (eds), *Health, Welfare and Practice: Reflecting on Roles and Relationships*. London: Sage.

*Nursing Times* (1996) 'Pandora's box of tricks', editorial, *Nursing Times*, 92: 15.3.

Porter, S. (1995) *Nursing's Relationship with Medicine*. Aldershot: Avebury.

RCN (1992) *The Value of Nursing*. London: RCN.

Stacey, M. (1992) *Regulating British Medicine*. Chichester: Wiley.

UKCC (1996) *Position Statement on Clinical Supervision for Nursing and Health Visiting*. London: UKCC.

Walmsley, J. (1993) *Health, Welfare and Practice: Reflecting on Roles and Relationships*. London: Sage.

# 23

# Principles of Empowerment

*Marian Barnes and Alan Walker*

[What follows is] an elaboration of the key principles which we believe should underpin attempts to empower users of health and social care services. In setting out these principles, we make particular reference to the way in which they could underpin the development of practices capable of empowering frail older people. Nevertheless, we think these principles have broader application and suggest that they could be adopted by agencies wishing to develop strategies to empower all groups of service users.

## Empowerment should enable personal development as well as increasing influence over services

Initiatives to involve users of services have often been developed from within service systems by those who wish to obtain feedback as a preliminary to achieving service improvement. While there were examples of such initiatives during the 1980s (see Barnes, forthcoming: Barnes et al., 1990; Connelly, 1990), they were given added impetus by 'top-down' policy directives and guidance coming from the Department of Health in the wake of the 1990 Act. The focus of such initiatives, understandably, is on the potential benefits of user involvement to the service itself, rather than to the service user whose views are being sought. In this context, the methods of seeking involvement from people are not always designed to contribute to their personal empowerment. People may be selected to provide feedback as representatives of all users of a particular service (as in a market research survey), rather than themselves choosing to participate. Their views are depersonalized and the process of seeking those views is not intended to have any effect on those giving them. Motivation to participate is encouraged by reference to the potential longer-term benefits to be derived from the intended service improvements. In view of the time scale within which such improvements may

Originally published in *Policy and Politics*, 24(4), 1996: 375–93 (abridged).

be achieved, this requires a degree of altruism on the part of those giving their views. Input may be brief, with no guaranteed feedback about any outcomes that may be achieved.

Older people who make substantial use of services often do not have the time to wait for long-term service improvements. Promised service developments to be secured following the implementation of the next community care plan may well be too late to produce any benefit for people who simply may not live that long. An empowering approach intends to produce change in people as a result of the process of participation. The intrinsic benefits of participation mean that involvement is an end in itself as well as a means to securing service improvements. Identification with others in similar circumstances can reduce isolation and perceptions of being a lone voice, unlikely to be able to [exert] any influence. Empowerment can be achieved through the growth and development which comes from the experience of being able to develop and articulate views, and from the learning which takes place through doing this in partnership with others. Participation over time also enables feedback to be provided about any developments within the service system, and the opportunity to respond to such feedback. Sharing of knowledge, information and skills among those whose views are being sought leads to the development of skills, confidence and knowledge within individual participants, as well as providing a location within which personal support can be provided when needed (Thursz et al., 1995). Those who participate are changed by the experience, deriving a more immediate benefit and thus not solely dependent on somewhat uncertain service development outcomes for continued motivation to contribute (Barnes, 1995).

## Empowerment should aim to increase people's abilities to take control of their lives as a whole, not just increase their influence over services

One outcome of the principle outlined above is that the benefits of participation can extend beyond the particular context in which this is sought. The experience of having one's ideas and opinions valued in one context can be transferable. For example, developing confidence to speak up about the quality of domiciliary care services may also lead to increased confidence in questioning others who are claiming to offer services or advice. This could provide benefits in particular to older people living on their own who may be in danger of being exploited by unscrupulous financial advisers or salespeople.

People may also be persuaded that it is worth their while registering their views in other contexts. This could, for example, encourage an increase in participation in local, national and European elections.

Such an outcome implies an awareness of the obligations as well as the rights of empowerment. A sense of the possibilities of being heard is one of the prerequisites of a participative citizenship (Prior et al., 1995). Participation is not solely a means of securing improved individual outcomes, but of strengthening democratic processes in general and support for public services in particular. Increasing the strength of the voices of those for whom public health and social care services are an essential resource increases the likelihood that public spending priorities will support their provision. The power of older people as a constituency is potentially a considerable force in electoral terms. Whilst differences of class, race and gender mean that older people are unlikely to constitute a unified political force, their potential collective influence on decisions about issues such as the provision of continuing care is substantial (Walker, 1996a).

A widespread acceptance of community care as the most appropriate service option for people in need of care has wider implications than for the design and organization of services. The presence of older people, of disabled people or those with mental health problems or learning difficulties within the social space from which they have previously been excluded means that social and civic institutions will also have to undergo change (Barnes, forthcoming). Empowerment should be understood as enabling people to participate within those wider arenas, not solely as increasing their influence within welfare organizations.

## Empowerment of one person should not result in the exploitation of others: either family members or paid carers

Feminist critiques of community care have highlighted the privatization of care in ways which increase the burden placed on women providing care within families (e.g. Dalley, 1988). Discussions of initiatives to give a voice to users of services have pointed out the importance of recognizing the separate voices of family and other unpaid carers, from those of the people they care for (Barnes and Wistow, 1994a; Ellis, 1993; Grant, 1992). Services such as respite care have been developed explicitly with carers' needs in mind, and those charged with responsibilities for community care assessments were asked to take account of carers' needs and wishes as well as those of the person who may be regarded as the direct user of services. Subsequently, the 1995 Carers (Recognition and Services) Act gave legislative force to the recognition of carers' needs as distinct from those they care for.

Twigg (1989) has described a typology of ways in which statutory agencies relate to family carers: as resources, co-workers or clients.

As resources, carers are in danger of being exploited by statutory services who use their presence to justify not providing a service. Carers themselves are not entirely happy with being seen as 'clients', whilst the 'co-worker' model carries a danger that alliances between paid workers and family carers may further disempower direct users. Nolan, Keady and Grant (1995) have discussed the role of carers as experts in the provision of care, and Barnes (1996) has considered ways in which families might contribute to the empowerment of direct service users. Policies and practices which seek to empower older people and other users of welfare services should recognize the way in which action within the public sphere can generate conflict between direct users and family carers. Such policies should be based on a recognition of dynamics within the three-way relationship between direct users, family carers, and paid service providers.

Feminists have also pointed to the gendered nature of paid care in public services, in which senior management positions are dispro-portionately occupied by men and front-line, low-paid caring jobs are primarily occupied by women. Many of the initiatives to give users a greater say have come from those in management positions and there is a danger that front-line providers may find themselves squeezed or scapegoated as a result of an apparent alliance between managers and users. User empowerment should be accompanied by management and work practices which enable workers throughout the organizational hierarchy to exercise influence over their work, and which support opportunities for partnership between workers and users at all levels throughout the organization (Carpenter, 1994).

The concept of empowerment implies shifting the balance in exist-ing relationships already characterized by imbalances of power and influence. Such imbalances derive from structural as well as personal aspects of the relationship. Whilst service users correctly perceive themselves to occupy a position which provides them with little formal power in comparison with workers who can appeal to or hide behind other authorities in justifying their decisions, user empower-ment should seek to avoid adding another dimension to structural inequalities which place many women workers as well as carers in positions in which they have little room for exercising either dis-cretion or choice.

### Empowerment should not be viewed as a zero sum: a partnership model should provide benefits to both parties

We do not believe that shifting the balance of power tells the whole story. The implication that there is an absolute amount of power which can be shared out in different ways according to currently fashionable beliefs about the relative merits of producers or consumers suggests a narrow understanding of the nature of power. Our first principle, that power should be understood as personal development as well as an increase in influence, illustrates one aspect of this. Both individual and collective growth deriving from the experience of participating in decision-making demonstrates the way in which power may develop where it did not previously exist and where it is not at the expense of anyone else. Indeed, such growth may contribute to the personal and/or professional development of individuals occupying different positions within the producer–consumer relationship. Such development can derive from increased understanding of user needs and circumstances, resulting in more confident decision-making and more effective working. It can also derive from renewed or increased motivation to act. Trust is a vital ingredient in the establishment of relationships capable of empowering users while not disempowering workers (Barnes and Prior, 1996). Trust is necessary both at the individual level, that is, in the relationships between the service user and the direct service provider, and at the institutional level. A reciprocal relationship of trust has advantages for both users and producers of welfare services.

This is not to suggest that user empowerment does not imply any requirement on producers to give up some of the control which they currently exert. A useful example can be considered from work reported by Marsh and Fisher (1992). Social workers resisted attempts to develop partnership practice (even though they professed to hold partnership values) because they saw giving up control of problem definition as a process of de-skilling. They found it hard to shift their notion of professional expertise to one which focused on problem negotiation. A preparedness to loosen control and embrace users' own definitions and solutions requires different skills from those which professionals may have been taught. This can have implications for the practice of all those working in or associated with health and social care services. It is also an issue which researchers are facing as they are challenged to treat service users as participants in rather than subjects of the research process (Beresford, 1992; Barnes, 1992). New skills and new ways of working are required by a commitment to empowerment. This is not the same as de-skilling or disempowering those paid to work in services, but it does require a change in both professional attitude and practice.

## Empowerment must be reinforced at all levels within service systems

Many of the earliest initiatives to give users a say in relation to services were primarily concerned with involvement in service planning. The All Wales Strategy is one such example (McGrath, 1989), and the Birmingham Community Care Special Action Project also gave little attention to involvement in individual service decision-making in comparison with obtaining collective feedback from users and carers (Barnes and Wistow, 1994a). The 1990 NHS and Community Care Act contained a requirement for Social Services departments to consult with users and carers about their community care plans, but was less decisive when it came to requiring input to individual care planning. Health services were encouraged to become 'Champions of the People' in terms of consulting about priorities for health service development (NHSME, 1992), but it is still up to individual professionals whether they seek to engage their patients in decision-making about their health care. Arguably, the challenge to professional expertise coming from lay people, particularly those deemed not competent (Barnes and Wistow, 1994b), presents more of a barrier to empowerment within the 'doctor–patient' relationship than to the exercise of influence over service design.

If people are canvassed for their views about service development priorities during collective consultation exercises, but are then given no say over when the home help will call, nor any opportunity to discuss and agree priorities for the tasks she should undertake, the outcome will be frustration and cynicism rather than feelings of empowerment. If health authorities seek to involve local people in rationing decisions about health expenditure, but then provide neither the information nor the opportunity to exercise choice about the preferred location for the receipt of palliative care, then not only will people feel personally disempowered, but a potential opportunity for learning will have been lost.

The organizational levels and processes in which people who use services can be involved have been analysed in various ways (Barnes et al., 1990; Beresford and Croft, 1993). Underpinning such analyses is the principle that empowerment requires a change in the way in which those responsible for services undertake their responsibilities. It is not enough for purchasers and providers to receive feedback from users while retaining complete discretion over whether or not they make use of it. Empowerment implies participation in the process of decision-making which causes changes in the nature of the process itself. That in turn requires changes throughout the decision-making system: within the individual service providing and receiving relationship; in service planning and monitoring; in decision-making about resource allocation; and in staff appointments and training. As Parsloe and Stevenson (1993: 24) have pointed out, two factors must be acknowledged if empowerment is to occur: 'the complexity of the task and the need for the whole organisation to change'. In order to succeed, empowerment requires a 'facilitating environment' (Braye and Preston-Shoot, 1995: 120).

**Empowerment of those who use services does not remove
the responsibilities of those who produce them**

None of this implies that user empowerment can or should result in a
handing over of power, nor an abnegation of the responsibilities of
those paid to take difficult decisions or to utilize the knowledge and
skills in which they have been trained. People seek to use health and
social care services because they have needs which cannot be met
from within their own personal resources. They are seeking to benefit
from knowledge and expertise which professional training should
confer. Part of the frustration that is sometimes reported is with the
failure of those from whom users seek help to demonstrate the
knowledge or understanding they would expect.

Nor do many, perhaps the majority, seek to commit substantial
personal time and resources to engaging with the detail of administrative and managerial processes. Whilst younger people active
within user movements may welcome opportunities to engage directly
in service management, or to work in partnership with purchasers to
plan and evaluate services, frail older people who cannot leave the
house without assistance may justifiably feel that these are tasks to be
left to others. Such responsibilities should clearly rest with those paid
to do the work. It would also be unreasonable and unrealistic to
expect those whose frailty and isolation has led to their use of services
to act as representatives, seeking out and reflecting the views of
others in similar situations. We are not suggesting that there is no
possible role for directly elected representatives of older people or
other service users in decision-making about services. Our focus here
is on the empowerment of older people whose frailty often means that
a representative role is not practical. Collectivities of older people
could develop their own representatives, as have other groups [. . .]
but our argument at this point is that both politicians and officers in
welfare services have responsibilities to seek out the 'quiet voices'
which are too often not heard.

The principle we are advocating here is that empowerment should
not be seen as involving a handing over of power from those currently
exercising it to those previously occupying powerless positions. This
can be understood as another dimension of the principle which does
not define power as a zero sum resource to be moved from one place to
another. As we noted above, empowerment does imply the development of new types of skill and the preparedness to recognize and make
use of different types of knowledge which may not be considered
compatible with existing 'professional' knowledge. But disempowering professionals and managers is unlikely to lead automatically to
the empowerment of users, and the aim should be to develop
partnerships capable of drawing on the knowledge of users as well as
providers.

There is another dimension to this principle in practice. User involvement can provide a new source of interest for sometimes jaded and cynical professionals. It can simply be more interesting to meet with older people to hear their stories about their lives and their experiences of services than it is to attend yet another departmental management meeting. Whilst re-motivation is a potentially empowering outcome for paid staff involved in such exercises, it should not stop at that. There is an obligation on paid staff to do something with what they have learned from the people who use their services. It is their task to consider how users' experiences and ideas can be used to improve practice; the onus should not be on the users themselves always to translate their experiences into a format which is immediately usable by purchasers or providers.

## Empowerment is not an alternative to adequate resourcing of services

People who use services are usually acutely aware of the difficulties of managing on an insufficient budget. This is part of the reality of their daily lives and they do not expect health and social care services to have unlimited resources on which to draw. But they are also extremely frustrated at being invited to contribute their views about how services should be developed only to be closed down by being told that nothing is possible because of a lack of resources.

There are differences of view among those involved in user movements about the extent to which they want to become involved in decisions which are effectively concerned with resource rationing. But just as the managerial decentralization of services has been resisted where this has been seen to be a way of decentralizing decisions about making cuts in services, people will neither feel nor be empowered if their involvement is being sought within a context in which resources are being reduced. Identifying ways in which services might be made more sensitive to users' needs without substantial additional expenditure is one thing, but generating a short-term 'feel good' factor by inviting people to participate whilst failing to commit sufficient resources to finance adequate provision is a cynical exploitation of good will.

## Empowerment should be a collective as well as an individual process; without this people will become increasingly assertive in competition with each other

Consumerist models of user involvement view those who use services as individuals seeking to maximize their own need satisfaction without reference to others with similar needs, or to groups who might be making competing demands on services. The logical outcome of competitive forces is the tyranny of the majority in determining the priority given to different needs, or even the very survival of services which are least in demand and thus least economical to provide. Both factors mean that the consumerist approach would produce an outcome detrimental to those with quiet voices; those whose needs are complex and shared with few others; and those who can command little public support and sympathy.

The model we propose emphasizes, on the one hand, enabling users to identify their collective interests in order to empower people individually through their identification with others but also, on the other, the need to seek a collective position which enables the fair treatment of all. For example, a group of carers rejected the policy of targeting domiciliary care services on those whose needs were determined by service providers to meet the highest 'dependency' criteria because this would also involve removing the very limited service already received by others. They felt that it was not fair to deny someone one hour a week of service because removing this could be like removing the stone which formed the centre point of an arch – the remainder would be in danger of falling in without that support. Further discussions with other carers' groups revealed the way in which perverse incentives can operate to encourage people to accept more services than they would choose to receive because asking for less could place them in too low a category to receive any help at all.

Whilst not all citizens are active users of health and social care services it has been argued that the social rights of citizenship entitle all to receive the welfare resources of which they stand in need (Plant, 1992). Hence, all citizens can be considered to have an interest in services and to be entitled to have their voices heard in relation to them. We argued above that the concept of empowerment needs to be understood as extending beyond the boundaries of individual services and we also contend that it should extend beyond those who are currently using those services. The support of citizens who, as voters and taxpayers, have a say in decisions concerning policies and resources can contribute to creating a context in which welfare is understood as a benefit and not a cost to society. Such a context provides a much more secure environment in which to seek to empower those currently in need of support than one in which welfare is seen as something only to be afforded in times of plenty.

This has a particular significance in the context of decisions about the responsibilities of one generation to another (Walker, 1996b). Older people who have seen the introduction of the welfare state are understandably disgusted that the services they have paid for through their taxes and national insurance are being denied to them. Public debate about the collective benefits and responsibilities of welfare can strengthen an increasingly fragile intergenerational contract.

Thus, our final principle is that empowerment should not only be sought in the collective organization of service users, but in the collective involvement of citizens in decision-making about services generally.

## References

Barnes, M. (1992) 'Introducing new stakeholders: user and researcher interests in evaluative research', *Policy and Politics*, 21(1): 47–58.

Barnes, M. (1995) 'Evaluating user and carer involvement in community care', in J. Waterson and M. Bernard (eds), *Working Together: User and Carer Involvement in Community Care*. Evaluation Research Unit, University of Keele.

Barnes, M. (1996) 'Families and empowerment', in P. Ramcharan and G. Grant (eds), *Empowerment in Everyday Life: Learning Disability*. London: Jessica Kingsley.

Barnes, M. (forthcoming) *Care, Communities and Citizens*. Harlow: Addison Wesley Longman.

Barnes, M. and Prior, D. (1996) 'From private choice to public trust: a new social basis for welfare', *Public Money and Management*, 16.

Barnes, M. and Wistow, G. (1994a) 'Developing a strategy for user involvement', *Health and Social Care in the Community*, 2(2): 347–56.

Barnes, M. and Wistow, G. (1994b) 'Learning to hear voices: listening to users of mental health services', *Journal of Mental Health*, 3(4): 525–40.

Barnes, M., Prior, D. and Thomas, N. (1990) 'Social services', in N. Deakin and A. Wright (eds), *Consuming Public Services*. London: Routledge.

Beresford, P. (1992) 'Researching user involvement: a collaborative or colonising enterprise?', in M. Barnes and G. Wistow (eds), *Researching User Involvement*. Leeds: Nuffield Institute for Health, University of Leeds.

Beresford, P. and Croft, S. (1993) *Citizen Involvement: a Practical Guide for Change*. Basingstoke: Macmillan.

Braye, S. and Preston-Shoot, M. (1995) *Empowering Practice in Social Care*. Milton Keynes: Open University Press.

Carpenter, M. (1994) *Normality is Hard Work. Trade Unions and the Politics of Community Care*. London: Lawrence & Wishart.

Connelly, N. (1990) *Raising Voices: Social Services Departments and People with Disabilities*. London: Policy Studies Institute.

Dalley, G. (1988) *Ideologies of Caring*. London: Macmillan.

Ellis, K. (1993) *Squaring the Circle: User and Carer Participation in Needs Assessment*. York: Joseph Rowntree Foundation.

Grant, G. (1992) 'Researching user and carer involvement in mental handicap services', in M. Barnes and G. Wistow (eds), *Researching User Involvement*. Leeds: Nuffield Institute for Health, University of Leeds.

Marsh, P. and Fisher, M. (1992) *Good Intentions: Developing Partnership in Social Services*. York: Joseph Rowntree Foundation.

McGrath, M. (1989) 'Consumer participation in service planning: the all-Wales strategy experience', *Journal of Social Policy*, 18(1): 67–89.

National Health Service Management Executive (NHSME) (1992) *Local Voices. The Views of Local People in Purchasing for Health*. London: DoH.

Nolan, M., Keady, J. and Grant, G. (1995) 'Developing a typology of family care: implications for nurses and other service providers', *Journal of Advanced Nursing*, 21: 256–65.

Parsloe, P. and Stevenson, O. (1993) 'A powerhouse for change', *Community Care*, 18 February (24–5).

Plant, R. (1992) 'Citizenship, rights and welfare', in A. Coote (ed.), *The Welfare of Citizens*. London: Rivers Oram Press.

Prior, D., Stewart, J. and Walsh, K. (1995) *Citizenship: Rights, Community and Participation*. London: Pitman Press.

Thursz, D., Nusberg, C. and Prather, J. (eds) (1995) *Empowering Older People: an International Approach*. London: Cassell.

Twigg, J. (1989) 'Models of carers: how do social care agencies conceptualise their relationship with informal carers?', *Journal of Social Policy*, 18(1): 53–66.

Walker, A. (1996a) 'Political participation and representation of older people in Europe', in A. Capell et al. (eds), *Political Participation and Representation of Elderly People in Europe*. Bonn: Federal Ministry for Family Affairs, Senior Citizens, Women and Youth.

Walker, A. (ed.) (1996b) *The New Generational Contract: Intergenerational Relations, Old Age and Welfare*. London: UCL Press.

# SECTION 4
# WHEN CARE GOES WRONG

These chapters are longer than those in other sections of the book. They explore sensitive issues of abuse in a number of contexts. First we have an article by Wardhaugh and Wilding, first published in 1993, which sets out a number of explanations as to why and how care goes wrong in institutional and to some extent all care settings. It draws on material from an official inquiry into what became known as the Pindown scandal in Staffordshire children's homes but also cross-references this to conditions explored several decades earlier in hospitals for people with learning disabilities and residential care for older people. It highlights the need to look beyond individuals to the characteristics of the wider system – to societal attitudes, the isolation of institutions and individuals, the way staff are organized and (un)supported, the levels of resourcing, and the way the very tasks of care come to be defined. Although some of the features of care systems have changed, for example through the introduction of contracts and care management, these changes have often left in place those features identified here which contribute most to the 'corruption of care'.

Lee-Treweek, for example, explores issues of personal space and hierarchy in her paper on 'bedroom abuse'. She discusses the way in which the work, and the workspace, is differentially allotted to low- and high-status staff. The work of auxiliaries is defined in such a way that they are encouraged to treat people as objects to be processed in preparation for their display in more public spaces. Auxiliaries are left in sole occupation and control of the 'private' space of the bedroom, within which they are able to decide the rules and maintain 'hidden control' over residents.

Like Russian dolls these two papers convey the interlocking forces which isolate and insulate institutional care: first, the establishment itself may become isolated behind walls – geographically, socially and from professional discourse and debate. And then, within the already cut-off establishment, low-status staff are confined behind closed bedroom doors, with their unacknowledged tasks of tending and soaking up aggression or confusion. Where Wardhaugh and Wilding speak of the disparity between stated policy aspirations and under-resourced practice, Lee-Treweek demonstrates the ineffectiveness of 'soft' management within the home itself. Where idealism fails to address reality it is merely locked out of the places where these things *are* dealt with, and used as the script to put on a show for visitors, dignitaries and, we may assume, regulators. The hard core of the work remains untouched behind high walls *and* closed doors and if any meaningful attempts are to be made to limit mistreatment it is here, in the bedroom as well as the time-out room, that they must focus.

Lee-Treweek notes how 'normality' is banished in these spaces: for example, greetings are jettisoned when auxiliaries enter or leave someone's room and physical tasks are carried out in the absence of any social interchange. Lawler takes up these issues in the context of the training and acculturation of nurses. She looks at how workers can be helped to develop strategies that acknowledge rather than deny the awkwardness of providing care which inevitably crosses personal boundaries and social taboos. Rather than addressing the work as if it is merely a variant of an ordinary social relationship, this article seeks to establish the nursing task as significantly outside the rules and conventions of normal social intercourse and hence needing its own specific conventions.

Lawler documents the complexity of the work when its emotional content is not pushed aside but integrated into the ethos of professionalism. Whereas in Lee-Treweek's bedrooms 'emotional work had to be repressed and physical work prioritized', Lawler describes how becoming 'socialized as a nurse ... means taking on a new way of looking at the body', one which recognizes the 'extent to which nursing and illness are disruptive of social order and normal rules'. It is ironic that the increasingly outmoded production-line model which separates manual from other workers should persist in human services when it has outlived its usefulness in industry. It is only when the abnormality and complexity of the relationships involved in care are acknowledged that they can be influenced, managed and regulated by the inculcation of appropriate *emotional* skills and rules.

The family is also to some extent an 'institution', and the next chapter moves from this exploration of what can go wrong from within the care relationship to examine the role of social workers, health and other professionals in scrutinizing personal relationships and deciding when individuals within families, communities and neighbourhoods are at sufficient risk for public authorities to intervene. Here they take the outsider's role looking in on an otherwise private setting and deciding at what point any intervention is justified. The excerpt reproduced here, taken from a government review of recent research into child protection by the Dartington team, identifies the process a worker must work through to assess particular cases, understanding the need to make a sensitive evaluation of the threshold at which such an intervention is warranted, and to balance the inevitable intrusion such involvement brings with an appreciation of those cases in which the child or adult is at risk of significant harm.

The last chapter, by Biggs, examines the construction of elder abuse but this time against the ideological backdrop of a particular policy initiative – the increased reliance on informal carers to deliver care to older people. The chapter asks whether the discourse of abuse has become salient as a rationale for partial 'surveillance' of these carers. As Olive Stevenson wrote in a recent monograph on the lessons which can be transferred from child protection to the abuse of older people, there is 'a high degree of moral confusion about the status of adult relationships' (1996: 23). Society is less clear about the 'normal' obligations which should hold sway in adult caring relationships, and changes in family forms and networks further complicate this picture.

Although these readings deal with abuse in very different contexts, against the backdrop of public provision, family relationships and wider policies, they each address issues of power, isolation and inequality. Reading them together drives home the point that wherever people are not valued or accorded full human rights, they run the risk of being abused and neglected, whether they are *at* home or *in* a 'home'. They may be isolated as individuals or as a group; they may be abused by people who know them or by those who are paid to be with them and trusted to work in their best interests. Taken together, the chapters provide a strong argument for community-wide approaches to the prevention of and response to abuse wherever it takes place. Abuse can never be ruled out, but 'lowering the odds' (ARC/NAPSAC, 1993) has to be high on the agenda of society as a whole, and of the care services in particular.

Hilary Brown

## References

ARC/NAPSAC (1993) *It Could Never Happen Here: the Prevention and Treatment of Sexual Abuse of Adults with Learning Disabilities in Residential Settings*. Chesterfield: ARC/NAPSAC.

Stevenson, O. (1996) *Elder Protection in the Community: What Can We Learn from Child Protection*. London: Age Concern Institute of Gerontology.

# 24

# Towards an Explanation of the Corruption of Care

*Julia Wardhaugh and Paul Wilding*

In recent years, there has been a rapidly developing interest in the issue of quality in public services. [. . .]

The important question for students of social policy and for policy-makers is, how do institutions, organizations and staff, supposedly committed to an ethic of care and respect for others, become 'corrupted' and abuse their power and their clients?

The corruption which occurs is of various kinds. [. . .] It is important to distinguish between the kind of corruption which takes place in pursuit of acceptable policy goals and the kind of corruption which is quite unrelated to the aims of policy.

Pindown would be an example of the first category because, though judged 'intrinsically unethical, unprofessional and unacceptable' (Levy and Kahan, 1991: 167) in the subsequent inquiry, it was aimed at securing generally desired change in behaviour. On the other hand, violence towards long-stay hospital patients is quite unrelated to any official policy objectives and would be defended by no one. Corruption, therefore, can be of various kinds. The essential element, however, is that it constitutes an active betrayal of the basic values on which the organization is supposedly based. It is much more than a passive neglect of the principles of good practice. It amounts to active abuse of a position of responsibility and of a client's fundamental human right. [. . .]

The early hospital inquiries (see Martin, 1984) all began from the 'bad apple' assumption – that the scandal they were investigating was explicit in terms of the corrupting influence of particular individuals. [. . .] They were soon forced by what they found to look at the organization in which the corruption had taken place. In this, of course, they were following Goffman, who saw the corruption of institutional care as produced by the very nature of institutions (Goffman, 1961). Once corruption is seen as, in some sense, the product of particular

Originally published in *Critical Social Policy*, 37 (Summer 1993): 4–31 (abridged).

kinds of social systems, then the way is cleared for a social analysis of the problem.

Our aim in this paper is to construct a preliminary, provocative analysis of the problem. We do this by propounding eight elements in systems of organization which we see as playing a part in the corruption of care. [. . .]

Our eight propositions start from a general assumption [. . .] that the focus of an enquiry into violence should be not on the motives for violence but on the conditions in which the usual moral inhibitions against violence become weakened (Kelman, 1973: 38). [. . .]

### Proposition 1: The corruption of care depends on the neutralization of normal moral concerns

For people to be abused in long-stay hospitals, elderly people's homes or in children's homes, they have to come to be regarded as beyond the normal bounds of moral behaviour which govern relations between person and person or carer and client. They have to come to be seen as less than fully human. 'The workhouse paupers,' said Robert Roberts of his Salford childhood, 'hardly registered as human beings at all' (Roberts, 1973: 21). That is a necessary stage on the road to the corruption of care.

How does this come about? Ritualized admission procedures to institutions aim, of course, to humiliate. Stripped of identity, ritually bathed, dressed in institutional clothing, people become less than the people they were. Living in an institution also depersonalizes as it institutionalizes. In *The Last Refuge*, Townsend wrote of the gradual process of depersonalization which overtook elderly people in residential care (Townsend, 1962: 328–9).

Zygmunt Bauman has wrestled with the question of how the Holocaust could have happened. How could a situation have been created in which five million Jews were put to death?[1] His answer is that the Jews had to be placed beyond the bounds of moral obligation. Responsibility, he argues, depends on proximity. Therefore, the Jews had to be excluded from normal social life, depersonalized and dehumanized, before deportation and extermination could begin. They had to be

> transformed in practice into exemplars of a category, a stereotype – into the abstract concept of the metaphysical Jew – until, that is, they had ceased to be those 'others' to whom moral responsibility normally extends, and lost the protection which such natural morality offers. (Bauman, 1989: 189)

Exclusion led to depersonalization and a moral invisibility which were the necessary prelude to the organization of the 'final solution'. That was made possible by the very nature of modern bureaucratic forms of organization.

Bureaucracy seeks to adjust human actions to an ideal of rationality. What is involved, above all, in this, is what Bauman calls 'the silencing of moral considerations' (Bauman, 1990: 132). The task of the members of the organization is reduced to that of obeying or refusing to obey a command. Action is removed from the sphere of moral issues. In the bureaucratic organization, the wider consequences of the work of a single bureaucrat are not necessarily visible to the actor. Moral issues become matters of organization or technique. People become simple 'specimens of a category' (Bauman, 1990: 136).

Such neutralization of moral concerns may be expressed in terms of racism and cultural stereotyping. Black writers have commented on the adoption by some white social and residential care workers of a 'pathological' framework in their dealings with clients (Ahmad, 1990; Barn, 1990). Black clients may be related to more in terms of cultural stereotypes – 'Asian families tend to look after their own', 'West Indian families believe in firm discipline' – than in terms of their individual needs and experiences. In particular, a long history of white racism, encompassing slavery, colonialism and imperialism, serves to devalue the black child in care, or the black elder in a long-stay hospital (Ahmad et al., 1986).

Our argument is that the corruption of care depends on the neutralization of what Hannah Arendt calls 'the animal pity' (Bauman, 1988: 486) which she believes all normal people feel in the presence of the physical suffering of other people. That neutralization takes place via the processes of depersonalization and dehumanization which depend on the creation of moral distance. It is of the essence of some forms of organization to create this neutralization by depriving their clients of their basic humanity. Our concern now is to consider the mechanics of this process of neutralization. [. . .]

Let us examine [. . .] the extent to which pindown can be conceived of as a regime conforming to Goffman's analysis of the key processes by which institutions curtail an inmate's sense of self: will-breaking ceremonies; leaving off and taking on; humiliation; mortification; confession; and interpersonal contamination.

'Peter' was one of the first children's home residents to be placed on pindown, in 1983. He had a history of glue sniffing, truancy and stealing, and was placed on pindown in response to his having absconded from care. Along with two other boys, he

> had to take a cold shower and do some 'keep fit' exercises. Later they were moved into another room and slept on mattresses on the floor with no other bedding. . . . The log book recorded that they were to have 'no privileges'. The following morning the boys were required to do 'bunny hops' round a concrete square outside the building in their underwear for about twenty minutes. Peter described what happened: 'We were bunny hopping around and (a residential worker) had a stick . . . and he was saying move over and he was whipping us, he is mad, but I was laughing, so I was getting it and he was taking it worse because I was laughing'. (Levy and Kahan, 1991: 114–15)

Thus, many of the elements of pindown as a will-breaking ceremony were evident from the earliest days of the practice: as time passed, these elements were refined and perfected, becoming routinized as an essential feature of the institution. For example, the cold shower to which Peter and his peers were subjected became established as a routine stripping, bathing and donning of nightclothes on first entering pindown, accompanied by twice-daily baths while on the regime, along with the wearing of nightclothes or shorts (often inadequate for the un- or underheated conditions of the pindown room). This resonates with Goffman's observation that 'The admission procedure can be characterised as a leaving off and a taking on, with the mid point marked by physical nakedness' (Goffman, 1961: 27).

The leaving off of personal clothes serves, at a physical level, to induce discomfort, humiliation and embarrassment and, at a psychological level, to represent a loss of identity and feelings of self-respect. In terms of gender, this humiliation was likely to have been particularly acute for young women, given the social construction of the female body and, in particular, the sexualization of women's experiences as a means of social control (Griffin, 1985; Lees, 1986). Power imbalances between staff and residents were accentuated by gender inequalities: for example, male workers were known to have supervised the undressing of young women in their 'care'. [. . .]

Similarly, routine deprivation of bedclothes, food and drink, free access to bathroom, access to educational or recreational materials, represents loss of personal identity: the definition of such materials or actions as 'privileges' rather than as part of the ordinary routine of life constitutes a process of humiliation. [. . .]

Perhaps one of the most severe mortifications for any individual is involuntary isolation, confinement away from everyday social exchanges. For the adolescent, whose personal and social development is heavily reliant on peer group interactions, this form of deprivation is particularly harsh. [. . .] One person interviewed reported being required to copy out names and addresses contained in the telephone directory, beginning at 'A'. [. . .] Young people on pindown were frequently required to make a written record of where they thought they had gone wrong in the past. [. . .]

However, such young people were not allowed to overtly hate 'the people who've put you there': conversely, they were required, if not to love their gaolers, at least to enter into relationships with them. A central, and very public, setting for this relationship was the 'review' meeting, which [. . .] along with the rest of the pindown regime, was conducted within a therapeutic (or pseudo-therapeutic) framework, although there is little evidence that such meetings were of any positive benefit to *any* of the participants, let alone the child in question. [. . .] One boy, for example, was the subject of more than 50 review meetings during a five-year period: there is little or no record of any therapeutic benefits which may have resulted from this procedure.

Pindown appeared to be based on ideas drawn from the 'psy' sciences, in particular drawing inspiration from therapeutic regimes used in other institutions:

> it appears to include elements of the 'time out' system of stimulus reduction in behaviour therapy, the 'seclusion' of difficult patients in hospital, and the 'anamnestic' approach to offenders used in secure therapeutic communities, where offenders are encouraged to describe in detail their offences.

However, pindown

> managed to combine the dangerous aspects of almost all the groups of therapies they have drawn on without including any of the safeguards in any of them. (Dr David Foreman, quoted in Levy and Kahan, 1991: 124–5)

The foregoing analysis of pindown as a system provides ample evidence of 'calculated methods, techniques, "sciences"', and within that system there was considerable scope to exercise 'leniencies' (the giving or withholding of 'privileges'), 'petty cruelties' (the more or less arbitrary withholding of heat, clothing or food, or psychological and emotional cruelties, such as manipulating family conflicts as a means of control), and 'acts of cunning' (e.g. deliberate play-acting by staff during review meetings) (Foucault, 1977). All was intended to degrade and depersonalize those subjected to the regime and so neutralize ordinary moral concerns for the children and young people involved.

### Proposition 2: The corruption of care is closely connected with the balance of power and powerlessness in organizations

Most of those who have been victims of the corruption of care have suffered from powerlessness. Weakness and vulnerability are essential characteristics of long-stay patients in mental handicap hospitals or geriatric hospitals, or of children in care.[2] They have little power or influence, little knowledge of how the organization works, little awareness of how to assert their rights or how to call to account those on whom they often depend for the basic elements of living.

In addition to the powerlessness inherent in the position of being accommodated in such institutions, some residents are further disempowered on the grounds of gender or ethnicity. For example, black children in care may suffer particular disadvantages or incivilities as a result of racism or cultural stereotyping on the part of white workers (Ahmad et al., 1986; Johnson, 1991). [. . .]

Those responsible for these and other very vulnerable groups have almost absolute power over them. That is a potentially corrupting situation. If power corrupts, so too does powerlessness. While staff have near-absolute power over many clients, they are in many other respects powerless. They are taken for granted by the organization, seldom regarded as its heroes, given little support, not consulted about the organization of their work. There is considerable evidence (e.g. Raynes et al., 1979: 158–9) that for high-quality residential care, staff involvement in decision-making is crucial. Tizard found the same to be true in residential nurseries (Tizard, 1975). Involvement can increase commitment, can create a sense of personal worth in staff and of the worthwhileness of the job being done.

We must not make the simple leap from the association of staff involvement with high-quality care to equating non-involvement with the corruption of care, but the association sounds a credible one. Clearly, there is no simple causal connection but there seems to be an association between staff powerlessness and the corruption of care. We saw in Proposition 1 that a necessary precondition to the corruption of care is the depriving of clients of the status of full moral beings. If the staff's status as full moral beings is damaged by powerlessness, they may well cease to behave in a fully moral fashion. The crucial issue may be that staff are simultaneously powerless and powerful and that this creates a dangerous ambivalence.

In relation to pindown, it is evident that staff had considerable powers over the young people in their care. They had considerable degrees of control over the physical movements of their charges – confining them to a single room, giving or withholding permission to visit the bathroom, allowing or denying the 'privilege' of attending school – and there is also evidence of the considerable emotional influence they were able to exert. [. . .]

The dynamics of power and powerlessness between staff and residents was complicated by gender inequalities. The main architects and instigators of pindown were male (although at least one female senior social worker was involved in formulating the system), while the lowest-status care workers were primarily female. The possible permutations of power relationships were many, and ranged from the high degree of control exercised by senior male workers over female residents, to the more ambivalent power available to lower-status female care workers in relation to male residents. At one extreme of this power–powerlessness continuum lie those situations in which male workers deliberately employed techniques to humiliate young women, in public settings. Levy and Kahan report that: 'we heard that children often attended [family meetings] in their night clothes and girls who were wearing short night dresses felt very embarrassed and humiliated' (Levy and Kahan, 1991: 121). Such humiliation was, we would argue, specific to their positions as young women vulnerable to abuses of adult male power. [. . .]

Such evidence of staff's manipulation and abuse of the powers available to them may, however, be set against their self-perception as victims of emotional and physical abuse by their charges.

You can't see the marks now, but that's where he [a resident] hit her [another staff member] the other week. He's only 12 but as you can see he's big and strong. This kind of thing happens all the time.

The kids here, you just give them everything, but they give nothing back. They're ungrateful little bastards, excuse my language, but that's what they are. I really mean that. (Residential care worker, fieldnotes 1989)

In the family centre in question, these remarks were made within the context of a changeover of team leadership, rapid staff turnover, high levels of staff dissatisfaction and alienation, and deteriorating staff–resident relationships.

Paradoxically, these very conditions which made residential care staff feel vulnerable and powerless at the same time contributed to a climate within which abuses of power could easily take place. Inadequate supervision, lack of proper inspections, little accountability, absence of advocates for children in care: all of these factors allowed care staff to arrogate power to themselves. Children in care, at least equally subject to a sense of powerlessness and vulnerability, had no such scope for the exercise of power, and no legitimate outlet for their frustrations.

### Proposition 3: Particular pressures and particular kinds of work are associated with the corruption of care

Certain kinds of people seem to be particularly at risk from the corruption of care in human services – mentally handicapped people in long-stay hospitals, elderly people and children in residential care. What are the links between these groups and corrupted care?

They are all groups for whom – to put it euphemistically – society has little regard. They lack value and worth in the eyes of society. They are easily stereotyped, and this affects the resources made available for their care. Policy is built up of fine words but the reality of what is provided for these groups denies their truth. The work is wrapped round with high-sounding terms such as care, reform, rehabilitation, but the resources and facilities made available convey to staff the low value which society puts upon their work and upon their clients. Official aspirations and standards are therefore deprived of legitimacy.

This predisposition towards the corruption of care may be exacerbated by the over-representation of particularly disadvantaged groups within these already-devalued categories of clients. There has been much debate concerning the possible over-representation of black children in care. [. . .] Perhaps more importantly, white residential care workers may perceive that black children are in care in disproportionate numbers, thus serving to confirm their beliefs about the 'pathological' black family (Ahmad, 1990). [. . .]

In contrast to the over-representation of black children in care, there is some evidence that black elders are *under*-represented in receiving at least some of the social services, and that the services that they do receive may be inappropriate to their social and cultural needs. [. . .]

Where work is difficult, and resources are short, the emphasis is on survival, on getting by. That creates a dangerous situation for at least two reasons. First, Ryan and Thomas point out how it leads to all the emphasis being on control, on order, on an institutional rather than on an individual approach (Ryan and Thomas, 1987: 49). This is both the product of the depersonalization of patients which pressure causes and a cause of further depersonalization.

The Committee of Inquiry into Farleigh Hospital pointed out that North Ward took the most difficult male cases in the whole hospital group. Forty patients were crowded into one large room. There was a lack of equipment and a shortage of staff. The situation led to what was described by the committee as the staff's 'probably unnecessarily robust . . . handling of the patients' (HMSO, 1971: para. 123). Violence became contagious (para. 163). The slide from stress on control, inevitable in some situations of pressure, into violence towards patients is all too easy to comprehend.

The second way in which difficult work is potentially dangerous is that few questions will be asked by management about what exactly is being done so long as the lid is successfully kept on the system. Some kinds of work – for example caring for profoundly mentally handicapped people or for very disruptive children – put staff under enormous pressure. In different ways, members of neither group are perceived as being fully persons. Staff experience them as trying patience and reason to, and beyond, the limit. These pressures are exacerbated by lack of resources and the way the moral legitimacy of the work is undermined by the gap which separates the rhetoric of policy from the sharp reality of practice.

There is also the almost universal fact of social service provision that those staff with the most difficult jobs are the least trained, least supported and lowest paid. In many caring and controlling situations, staff are therefore simply out of their depth. [. . .]

## Proposition 4: Management failure underlies the corruption of care

[. . .] The corruption of care inevitably suggests a failure of management. What is striking is the totality of management failure which has been revealed by a range of inquiries. It was a comprehensive failure across most of the responsibilities which belonged to management at every level.

Managers failed to set clear aims and objectives. An organization without the direction and framework which clear aims and objectives provide is at risk. Secondary aims take over. Care and rehabilitation are replaced by the goals of order and control. The smooth running of the institution, rather than the individual patient, becomes the key concern. In this situation, it is easy for the staff and the organization to slide into corruption.

Clear aims and objectives provide an impetus and a framework for desirable patterns of practice. They can assert the basic humanity and rights of service users and reinforce ideas of good practice. Without such declarations of intent, too much depends on the attitudes and judgements of fallible individuals.

Clear aims and objectives are also important for they are a prerequisite of effective monitoring and evaluation. Without them, individual staff cannot engage in that self-evaluation which is a basic element in professional work. Equally, management cannot know what is being achieved. Nor is it in a position to call to account staff when their roles and tasks are undefined.

Managers also failed in that they allowed staff to become professionally isolated – Martin describes this as their most conspicuous failure (Martin, 1984: 87). They showed no understanding of the pressures on ward-level staff and their need for respite and the stimulus of new ideas or for job satisfaction. Managers failed, too, in their response to complaints. When complaints were made, management failed to investigate them, or simply rejected them out of hand. Martin talks of 'a remarkable resistance to internal complaints' (ibid.: 86).

What is remarkable is that every level of management seems to have been guilty. Middle and senior management were equally contemptuous of complaints and dilatory in pursuing them. So were hospital management committees, regional hospital boards and the Department of Health and Social Security. As Crossman's memoirs reveal, the Department knew about the unsatisfactory conditions at Ely Hospital long before the Howe Inquiry (Crossman, 1977: 411).

It is not only in relation to hospitals that management failures are striking. One of the features of the Beck case was the failure of Leicestershire Social Services Department to take any action against Beck in spite of countless complaints by children, a dozen formal complaints by staff and children at the Beeches home and four references to the police (*Guardian*, 30 November 1991).

Why did management fail so strikingly to provide leadership, supervision or control? It is possible to suggest a number of explanations. The enclosed world of the staff of many of the long-stay hospitals [. . .] clearly inhibited middle managers from exercising effective supervision or responding to complaints. If they fell out with their subordinates, then their social world collapsed. A second reason was that in some instances the pressures were so great that managers simply turned a blind eye to what went on so long as order was maintained and the institution continued to function in an outwardly acceptable fashion. Thirdly, middle managers were stranded in the middle ground without clear leadership and objectives from above. That is no excuse for their failing to respond to manifest abuse, but it helps to explain the atmosphere in which abuse could be ignored.

A fourth factor was the classic one of clinical and professional autonomy and lay reluctance to assert its management responsibilities. The Normansfield Inquiry vigorously asserted the right of a health authority to lay down standards and warned the members not to be confused 'still less stopped in their tracks by the use of such terms as "clinical responsibility"' (HMSO, 1978: 407). But such beliefs did inhibit management – or usefully justified inaction.

Fifthly, there was uncertainty in the Department of Health and Social Security about its role in relation to all the other bodies which shared responsibility. The tradition of the old Ministry of Health, still strong in the DHSS (now, of course, split into two separate departments), was one of *laissez-faire* in relation to health and local authorities. It legitimized an approach which those unfamiliar with departmental ways might have interpreted as an abdication of responsibility.

Finally, there was the failure of lay management. Underlying the very concept is the idea of ordinary people laying down standards in line with societal norms. Such a view fails to grasp the complexity of large organizations, the difficulty of establishing precisely what goes on inside them, and the timidity of most lay people when dealing with professionals trailing clouds of professional arrogance and expertise. Lay management has been exposed by the corruption of care as a dangerous fiction.

Management failure is, as Martin points out (1984: 87) both something to be explained and an explanation of how things come to go wrong in the hospitals. [. . .] Goffman points to the conflicting interests which may contribute to such a corruption:

> The obligation of the staff to maintain certain humane standards of treatment for inmates presents problems in itself, but a further set of characteristic problems is found in the constant conflict between humane standards on the one hand and institutional efficiency on the other. (Goffman, 1961: 76)

while the Levy Report identified as a factor the managerial tendency to opt for the easy way out of this conflict:

> Evidence from both county council and staff witnesses suggested that so long as there was no trouble, a blind eye was turned to some practices. (Levy and Kahan, 1991: 154)

The Levy Report concluded that the residential childcare service in Norwest was inward-looking, deficient in support and training of staff, and lacking any positive sense of direction. Team leaders of children's homes and family centres were isolated, 'grappled alone with problems', and were discouraged from aspiring to high standards of care (Levy and Kahan, 1991: 153). In such circumstances, it was highly likely that 'institutional efficiency' would take precedence over 'humane standards'.

There is strong evidence that this insistence on the pre-eminence of institutional efficiency originated at a senior managerial level, with middle managers reporting that there existed an ethos whereby any raising of concerns over standards or other 'care' issues tended to be regarded as evidence of individual inefficiency or lack of managerial ability. [. . .]

This notion of 'producing the goods' is central to our under-standing, not only of the pressures on team leaders to manage their institutions efficiently but also of the linkage between senior managerial attitudes and priorities and the creation of a context within which pindown was able to evolve and be maintained over a period of six years. [. . .]

Pindown existed more or less in a policy vacuum: it was able to develop and flourish precisely because of the absence of any viable alternative. [. . .] Operating within a context of serious underfunding of the service, lack of training, status or rewards for residential care staff, little or no encouragement of conscientious or forward-thinking management, frequent reorganizations of the service, the conditions were right for the primary aims of care to be neglected, and the subsidiary aims of order and control to take precedence – and for management relief when the situation was contained by those below them.

Pindown, we would argue, had as its primary aim the control and management of recalcitrant children. It was a measure of the extent of managerial failure, not only that this was allowed to take place, but that it was able to continue while the façade of a therapeutic regime was maintained. The presentation of a disciplinary and punitive system as caring or therapeutic is itself an example of the corruption of care.

**Proposition 5: The corruption of care is more likely in enclosed, inward-looking organizations**

'Isolated', 'enclosed', 'inward-looking' are words which appear again and again in the reports of the inquiries into the long-stay hospitals. Mary Dendy Hospital was cited by Martin as a powerful example of the danger of professional isolation (Martin, 1984: 41). At Winterton,

group loyalty was taking 'a dangerously inward-looking and protective character' (ibid.: 44). At Church Hill House Hospital, the
prosecuting counsel at the inquiry spoke of 'a closed society where no
one was to break ranks' in the ward. At Brookwood, there was 'an
ominous form of group loyalty' (ibid.: 50). The inquiry at Farleigh
reported that 'the standards by which the hospital was judged were its
own internal standards' (HMSO, 1971: para. 42). At Whittingham,
promotions were mainly internal (HMSO, 1972: para. 109).

What are the links between enclosed, tightly knit organizations,
inward-looking cultures and the corruption of care? There are at least
four.

First, such an organization can easily stifle criticism and complaints. Those who initiated the complaints which led eventually to
the hospital inquiries were almost always 'outsiders' – students, new
or junior staff, for example. It was easy for a tight-knit body to
suppress complaints – as happened at Whittingham (HMSO, 1972:
paras 21, 25–28) or at St. Augustine's (Martin, 1984: 33) or Farleigh,
where students and junior staff were laughed at by ward staff when
the complained of the ill-treatment of patients (HMSO, 1971: para.
121).

Secondly, there is the enormous difficulty of insider criticism.
Martin talks of 'the ingrained sense of staff solidarity' (Martin, 1984:
109). Ranks, he says, could close with formidable force – and they
could close on anyone who challenged group norms – and the norm
was group solidarity even if it did not necessarily approve of the ill-
treatment of patients. Raising awkward questions, or challenging
norms or behaviour, meant isolation at work and outside because the
worlds of work and leisure were essentially the same. In the enclosed
organization, group norms are powerful and the costs of challenging
them are often too great.

Thirdly, in the professionally isolated organization, there are no
new ideas, there is no renewal and strengthening of expectations and
possibilities. The organization comes to judge itself by its own
internal standards. There is no empowering, externally reinforced
concept of good and proper practice. The best elements of professionalism wither and perish for lack of nourishment.

Finally, the enclosed organization develops and maintains a pattern
of practice which is routinized and conservative. It expects little of
staff or of clients. Its aspirations are low – control, order and the
absence of trouble. Such a pattern of institution-oriented care can
easily tip over into corruption. The gap is dangerously small. Where
aspirations and expectations are higher, the slide is more noticeable
to all involved and so more difficult. [. . .]

Within such enclosed worlds, few were prepared to dissent, and
those who did so tended to be 'outsiders', non-participants in the local
(occupational) culture. For example, one juvenile justice worker,

newly appointed from another county, expressed his concern both at pindown itself, and its toleration by Social Services managers.

> [Pindown] is totally illegal, you know. The kids could complain if they wanted to. The procedures are very strict for juveniles in care. I think they are insane. If it got out! But presumably [a senior manager] and all the rest know about it. (Juvenile justice worker, fieldnotes, March 1989)

Senior and middle management did indeed know about it, but failed to intervene, largely on the grounds that the regime was successful in managing and containing troublesome youngsters. Their managerial world was sufficiently inward-looking to prove resistant to any challenges from the outside, just as the children's homes themselves were sufficiently enclosed to enable the practice of pindown to continue undisturbed for a period of six years. The system finally came to public attention thanks to the efforts of a local councillor and a local solicitor, who challenged the use of pindown in the courts, in council meetings and in the public arena. [. . .]

## Proposition 6: The absence of clear lines and mechanisms of accountability plays an important part in the corruption of care

One of the characteristics of the organizations and institutions which we describe as corrupt is that they are not clearly accountable to anyone. Users of the service lack the status, or the capacity, to assert themselves. Their families and friends lack the knowledge or the position to play a part. The local community is unorganized and usually uninvolved – and, as regards many long-stay hospitals, nonexistent. The enclosed nature of institutions and organizations means that there are few links to the outside world.

Management, as we have seen, often neglects its responsibility to know what goes on, to set appropriate standards and to insist on staff accountability. Front-line staff are frequently simply left to get on with things. Dr Knappe, the deputy medical superintendent at Farleigh, admitted to the inquiry that he did not know how the patients on North Ward spent their day. He had not enquired about this as he considered it a nursing issue (HMSO, 1971: para. 82). He saw himself as in no way accountable for conditions there. Unfortunately, no one else was really accountable either.

The danger of a lack of management and external accountability is plain. Everything depends on the quality, commitment and values of the front-line staff. That is fundamentally unsatisfactory. There need to be mechanisms for making staff effectively accountable. There must be checks and counters to the enormous powers they wield over very vulnerable people and the pressures they face. Society must accept, and assert, its own accountability for what happens to those in positions of such dependency.

Without mechanisms of effective accountability to management, front-line staff are, in effect, unsupervised. Without mechanisms of effective external accountability, the organization comes to judge itself by its own internal standards – which is dangerous in practice and unsatisfactory in principle. [. . .]

Senior and middle managers responsible for the 'pindown' institutions could be said to be culpable on one or other of the following two counts: either they were aware of the pindown system and failed to take steps to deal with it, or else they were ignorant of the system and thus guilty of a major lack of supervision of the institutions and staff under their control.

## Proposition 7: Particular models of work and organization are conducive to the corruption of care

Our argument is that certain approaches to work and organization [. . .] can play a part in creating the context in which such corruption takes place. We suggest five connections.

In the eyes of the world, professionalism stands for high standards of work. At its best that is clearly true, but, equally, some aspects of professionalism, as traditionally understood, can play a part in the corruption of care. In some of the hospital scandals, narrow clinical models of professional responsibility led doctors to ignore grossly unsatisfactory physical conditions which became a factor contributing to the corruption of care. Again, mistaken notions of professional autonomy contributed to management's failure to set standards and hold professionals to account for their achievement. Another factor was management's faith in the self-sustaining power of the professional ethic, however taxing the work involved – which led to the failure to provide staff with the support they so often needed.

Secondly, hierarchical structures make complaint from below very difficult. Organizational structures, in part, explain how difficult it was for complaints about patient ill-treatment to gain a hearing. Hierarchy also means that those whose responsibility it is to set standards and objectives are a long way distant from where the action really is. Distance deprives their views of legitimacy for front-line staff because 'they' do not really know what conditions are really like. Given the lack of legitimacy granted to the views of managers, secondary aims and goals take over.

Thirdly, size is a factor in that it contributes to the patterns of institution-oriented care which can tip over into corruption. Size leads to regimentation and batch living which contribute to depersonalization and can slip into corruption.

A fourth problematic element in the organization of human service work is the concentration of the most difficult cases. Most of the hospital scandals related to particular wards, often the 'back wards' where the most difficult and handicapped patients were concentrated. [. . .]

Meacher argued against the segregation of confused elderly people on the grounds that it encouraged infantilizing procedures and that such patients were less likely to have visitors (quoted in HMSO, 1978: 273). Treating mentally handicapped people or those who are mentally confused as children is one way in which staff have traditionally come to terms and coped with their condition. Nevertheless, it is potentially dangerous. Children lack the rights of adults and, till recently at least, a modest degree of violence in dealing with them was regarded as reasonable and appropriate. That could easily lead to more general violence. Visitors, too, are important as a way of combating enclosedness and opening the institution to wider accountability.

Finally, we need to recall Bauman's arguments about bureaucratic forms of organization and the direct links which he argues exist between bureaucracy and 'the silencing of moral considerations' and between bureaucracy and the loss of individuality and personhood on which moral behaviour depends (Bauman, 1990: 132). There is no deterministic relationship between particular models of work and organization and the corruption of care, but clearly there are links. [. . .]

## Proposition 8: The nature of certain client groups encourages the corruption of care

The groups where there is most evidence of the corruption of care, people experiencing mental handicap, people who are classified as 'frail' elderly and children, share certain common characteristics. Our argument is that these contribute to the corruption of care. Most of them are seen as less than fully sentient beings because of their age, and disabilities. Once defined as less than fully persons, the way is clear to forms of behaviour and treatment which would be unacceptable with those not so stigmatized.

As we saw earlier, defining mentally handicapped people as children opens the way to certain patterns of potentially risky treatment. One way in which some of the perpetrators of violence in the long-stay hospitals justified or defended their behaviour was with the argument that 'they don't understand'. The same argument was used to justify not improving physical conditions in wards. Those conditions made the lives of staff more unpleasant than they need have been and conveyed to them a message about the valuation society placed on the groups for which they were caring.

Given the way in which society provides for them and the resources made available for their care, certain groups are obviously more difficult and trying for staff. They tax the patience of staff. They may create permanent anxiety about the possibility of violence. They offer staff few rewards in the sense of positive achievements. Low expectations feed a philosophy of containment and control which, in turn, can lead to boredom among clients and a spiral of violence.

A third link between the corruption of care and the nature of certain client groups is the lack of interest society shows in their care – in terms of resources, support for staff, training and so on. A lack of society's interest is evident in low material standards which legitimize low standards of care and behaviour by staff.

Finally, the relatives of certain groups may not be much involved in their care. They may visit infrequently because they have lost touch and because of the stigma of having relatives in these groups. So they can provide no effective commentary on standards of care or influence for change. Their expectations, too, are low.

It is indisputable that the care of any special needs client group can be a difficult occupation, and that working with particular groups can be especially stressful – we think here of children and teenagers, mentally handicapped people and frail elderly people. It is not insignificant that pindown developed at a time when the residential childcare institutions were dealing with older teenagers rather than younger children, many of them from difficult and disruptive backgrounds, some with a history of offending, and few with a prospect of successful foster placement. When high staff turnover, low staff morale, a service frequently in 'crisis' are added to this picture, it becomes clear that staff could expect few rewards from their task of caring for these youngsters. [. . .]

At the same time as we recognize the pressures on staff which cause such feelings of frustration, we must identify the particular processes by which client groups are perceived as not just causing feelings of irritation, hostility and animosity, but also become defined as 'the Other'. Just as 'A man in a political prison must be traitorous; a man in prison must be a lawbreaker; a man in a mental hospital must be sick' (Goffman, 1961: 81), so a child in residential care must be difficult, troublesome and disruptive? The point is not so much whether these young people engaged in troublesome behaviour – which they undoubtedly did at times – but that *all* of their actions were interpreted in the light of their presence in the institution, that is, as troublesome. [. . .] This interpretation, that everything a child in care does is symptomatic of their essential troublesomeness, can be extended beyond behaviours under their direct control to include physical or psychological states of health. Thus:

She ... *claims* to have asthma ... need to clarify if she does suffer or if it is attention seeking. (Levy and Kahan, 1991: 59; emphasis added)

## Conclusion

The corruption of care is a fact and a problem. [. . .] Obviously, it is important to try to understand how it is that care becomes corrupted. Our approach has been to set out eight general propositions about the corruption of care developed from an examination of relevant literature and to test them out as explanations. [. . .] They are not all relevant in all situations but they are certainly helpful in pinpointing circumstances in which care systems are at risk.

## Notes

1  Bauman's focus is on the Jewish victims of the Holocaust. In addition to five million Jews, there were a further two million victims including gypsies, homosexuals and mentally handicapped people. They were also categorized as less than fully human.
2  We use the term mentally handicapped rather than the more contemporary designation 'people with learning difficulties' because that was the term in current use at the time of the various hospital inquiries on which we draw.

## References

Ahmad, B. (1990) *Black Perspectives in Social Work*. Birmingham: Venture Press.
Ahmad, S. et al. (1986) *Social Work with Black Children and their Families*. London: BAAF.
Barn, R. (1990) 'Black children in local authority care: admission patterns', *New Community*, 16(2).
Bauman, Z. (1988) 'Sociology after the Holocaust', *British Journal of Sociology*, 39(4).
Bauman, Z. (1989) *Modernity and the Holocaust*. Cambridge: Polity.
Bauman, Z. (1990) *Thinking Sociologically*. Oxford: Basil Blackwell.
Crossman, R.H.S. (1977) *The Diaries of a Cabinet Minister*, Vol. 3. London: Hamish Hamilton and Jonathan Cape.
Foucault, M. (1977) *Discipline and Punish*. London: Allen Lane.
Goffman, E. (1961) *Asylums*. New York: Anchor Books.
Griffin, C. (1985) *Typical Girls?* London: Routledge & Kegan Paul.
HMSO (1971) *Report of the Farleigh Hospital Committee of Enquiry*. Cmnd. 4557. London: HMSO.
HMSO (1972) *Report of the Committee of Inquiry into Whittingham Hospital*. Cmnd. 4861. London: HMSO.
HMSO (1978) *Report of the Committee of Inquiry into Normansfield Hospital*. Cmnd. 7397. London: HMSO.
Johnson, M.R.D. (1991) 'Race, social work and child care', in P. Carter et al. *Social Work and Social Welfare Yearbook 3*. Milton Keynes: Open University Press.
Kelman, H. (1973) 'Violence without moral restraint: reflections on the dehumanisation of victims and victimisers', *Journal of Social Issues*, 29.
Lees, S. (1986) *Losing Out: Sexuality and Adolescent Girls*. London: Hutchinson.

Levy, A. and Kahan, B. (1991) *The Pindown Experience and the Protection of Children: the Report of the Staffordshire Child Care Inquiry 1990.* Staffordshire County Council.

Martin, J.P. (1984) *Hospitals in Trouble.* Oxford: Basil Blackwell.

Raynes, N. et al. (1979) *Organizational Structure and the Care of the Mentally Retarded.* London: Croom Helm.

Roberts, R. (1973) *The Classic Slum.* Harmondsworth: Penguin.

Ryan, J. and Thomas, F. (1987) *The Politics of Mental Handicap.* London: Free Association Books.

Tizard, B. (1975) 'Varieties of residential nursery experience', in J. Tizard et al, *Varieties of Residential Experience.* London: Routledge & Kegan Paul.

Townsend, P. (1962) *The Last Refuge.* London: Routledge & Kegan Paul.

# 25

# Bedroom Abuse: the Hidden Work in a Nursing Home

*Geraldine Lee-Treweek*

In Western society the bedroom has been constructed as a place of privacy. It has a unique symbolism for the individual in terms of personal choice. Even if other parts of the domestic home are open to public view the bedroom usually is not. (See Willcocks et al., 1987: 4–6; Goffman, 1959: 124.) Yet in forms of institutionalized care this is problematic, as these rooms are also workplaces for staff. The way that homes are organized leaves those with the least training to undertake the physical care work. This work is often bedroom-based work. It is physically hard and dirty. Also it is hidden.

The physical work behind the scenes is not seen, yet it is essential if the patient is to be presentable to others. In Goffman's (1959: 126) terms the preparatory work of the bedroom is backstage 'technical work' and is often undertaken by low-status workers whose product is then presented by higher-status workers. In the case of the nursing home the patient that the auxiliary washes, dresses and organizes is placed in the lounge where nursing staff then present the sanitized patient to visitors. [. . .]

This paper argues that in many homes the bedroom world is ordered and arranged by the nursing auxiliary [. . .] the aim of their work being the creation of the acceptable patient for public view. In this world mistreatment and punishing behaviours become acceptable, mistreatment being part of the daily grind of getting through the work – of organizing people in conveyor-belt fashion to time and chore constraints. Punishment, apart from being a more deliberate and personal form of cruelty, involved getting back at the job and taking it out on the objects of care. Both also appeared to create a subdued patient who was then easier to order. Lastly, I discuss how mistreatment and being hard towards patients had become part of the auxiliaries' subculture and had been elevated beyond simple necessity to being an essential attribute of the good worker. [. . .]

Originally published in *Generations Review*, 4(1), March 1994: 2–4 (abridged).

## The home and bedrooms

Cedar Court was one such home, sited on the outskirts of a major town in the south west of England (the name has been changed to preserve anonymity). On arrival I was immediately struck by the isolation from the general community by a large garden surrounded by trees and a long gravel drive. The exterior of the building was modern and anonymous, unlike a domestic home. [. . .] Heavy glass swing doors at the front of the building gave the appearance of a hospital entrance. Inside, the home was carpeted from bedrooms to lounge with a 'seconds flawed' carpet and the walls and ceilings were all painted magnolia. To the visitor the buzzers, smells of disinfectant, uniforms, trolleys and wheelchairs gave an impression of hospitalization and a medical order. Yet, although trained staff dominated public areas, the majority of staff were untrained auxiliary workers who worked mainly in the more private areas of the home. [. . .]

## The bedroom job

The bedroom was the main site of work for the auxiliaries and most of the patients' time in the home was spent there. Morning work was virtually all bedroom work and was officially begun by the auxiliaries entering patients' rooms on the tea round. This was a point of the day at which cups of tea were served and bottoms were washed. It was customary to present the patients to the new shift intact, clean and quiet in their rooms for 8 a.m. Presenting well-ordered bodies seemed to symbolize the job properly done. The next shift spent all the morning in the bedrooms, washing and dressing patients. The workers spent most of the morning getting patients ready, then taking them down to the lounge. By lunchtime they were all down, but straight after lunch it was time to put them back to bed for a nap and later get them up again.

In the evenings work again revolved around the bedrooms as staff got patients ready for bed. By the time the night shift came on, all patients were in bed. In this way the auxiliaries' work could be said to revolve around the bedroom. And it was in this private world that they were able to decide the rules and had total hidden control.

## The aim and nature of the work

The aim of work in the bedrooms was generally the creation of patients who could be presented into the lounge area: 'the lounge standard patient'. Those who were 'displayed' in the lounge were those who fitted the home's construction of the ordered patient – the physically and mentally ordered patient, dressed tidily, unsmelly and clean. The patient with whom the auxiliary worked in the bedroom was, by comparison, highly disorderly. Some states only existed in the bedroom areas: violent outbursts, confusion outbursts involving noise; shouting, spitting and other anti-social behaviour, such as continual rapping on tables or banging sticks on floors, and also very persistent and distressing crying and sobbing. Acute sickness was also visible only in the bedroom; but in these cases the trained staff took charge. All patients who exhibited these behaviours in the lounge were immediately physically confined to the bedrooms by the auxiliaries.

## Depersonalization and mistreatment – part of the job

Mistreatment appeared a fairly everyday strategy to get through the work. It involved depersonalization – ignoring the individual's spatial rights, ignoring the patient's words, or even their presence – to save time. Workers' felt resistance to the individual's emotional needs was central to time-saving. Emotional work had to be repressed and physical labour prioritized. Patients who demanded too much emotional time and refused the role of 'object' were negatively labelled as 'whiners' and were avoided. The more that patients demanded, the more resistance was employed to prevent their emotional needs from being fulfilled.

Auxiliaries often ignored the presence of patients, preferring to talk about them in the third person, and saying insensitive things. [. . .]

At night treating patients as objects was virtually the sole form of interaction observed. But for workers this was a time-saving device, as illustrated by the rituals of rounds.

> The same ritual is observed in each room entered: the auxiliaries go alone or in pairs, the toilet light is switched on, a jug is collected from the toilet, the patients' bed sheets are pulled back exposing them to the air, their night clothes are pulled up to allow the leg bag to be emptied. They might need to be rolled over to allow access. The urine is then thrown down the toilet which is flushed, the jug is washed, the sheets are pulled back over each patient and the auxiliary exits. If two auxiliaries are in the same room on the round they very often chat over the patients while they deal with them. Should a patient stir or open their eyes during this ritual they are told to go back to sleep. Any patient awake at night is considered an inconvenience to this two-hourly ritual. Many patients lie motionless with their eyes open and staring blankly as this ritual is performed. (fieldwork notes: nights)

Personal space and presence was also disregarded in the format of entrances and exits into rooms. Auxiliaries would often enter a room with little regard for the convention of traditional greetings. Brief introductions were often followed by invasive procedures to find out whether the patient was soiled, such as pulling sheets back, rolling patients over to look at their bottoms, and then giving some brief explanation of what the auxiliaries were doing.

The exit out of the room also tended to be unmarked by the usual rituals. Once a work chore was done the shutting of the door seemed to suffice as the end of the interaction. [. . .]

These acts of mistreatment involved the staff ignoring patients and not involving them in care. But other forms did involve the patient. Making jokes at the patient's expense was seen as 'having some fun with the patients' and workers argued that it involved patients in some way with the work. For example, patients who could not walk properly were told to 'race' down the corridor, and jokes would be made about Nigel Mansell, etc. Patients who were crying in pain would be told to buck up and smile. Mimicry was also common, with staff copying the words of confused residents. Most patients either could not hear, see or understand jokes that the workers made at their expense, while others became distressed at them. But 'joking' appeared to help auxiliaries get through the work; it broke up the stress and gave them some sort of control.

Mistreatment involved a wide range of behaviours all of which served to create compliancy in patients. Mistreatment served to give workers more control over the objects they had to process, within strict temporal constraints around the space of the home. They were partially a product of constraints on the job and also appeared to stem from ignorance about how to work with confused people and elevation within the subculture of the role of restraint and containment as part of the job.

## Punishment

Auxiliary staff believed that physical abuse towards patients was unacceptable, and many gave accounts of whistle-blowing on violent colleagues in the past. However, there was no notion of mental or emotional cruelty. Telling people off, ignoring them and 'teaching them a lesson' in ways other than physical violence were seen as acceptable. When working with nursing staff the auxiliary took the role of the verbally punitive partner. It was her role also to deal with the patient who behaved badly in the lounge, to make it clear that certain behaviours were not acceptable. [. . .]

Use of call buzzers was particularly disliked and one of the ways a patient could be punished was for their buzzing to be ignored. Due to immobility of patients, ignoring buzzing induced a powerlessness they could do little about. [. . .] Active stratagems were used to deal with other less capable 'buzzers'. [. . .]

Other 'harsh' night remedies included pulling the bed out from the wall, thus leaving the patient unable to reach the buzzer. Some 'naughty', persistent buzzers had begun to confound this punishment by calling to other patients to get them to use their buzzers for them. On one occasion a patient who was talking to another in the four-bedder was put in a chair, taken downstairs to the lounge and sat in a corner on her own until she 'seemed quiet'. Communication and group resistance from patients were not tolerated.

Day punishments went on mainly in the form of telling people off, teasing them or even denying their realities. More lucid patients were punished mainly through avoidance; their buzzers would be ignored and they would be left until last. 'Confused 'patients were generally treated with a much more confrontational form of punishment. For example, they were called names: 'dying duck', 'moaning Minnie' or told they were 'pathetic', 'stupid' or 'being childish'. With these patients fear tactics, such as using a threatening tone of voice or physically being noisy in the surrounding environment, ramming the metal sides of hospital beds down violently, were observed daily. Punishment and control strategies such as these seemed a way to get back at the job.

### The hard culture

Auxiliary work in nursing homes is hard work: low paid, low status, dirty, physically backbreaking and tiring. However, far from complaining about the conditions of their work the nursing auxiliaries appeared to have elevated the notion of personal hardship within their subculture. Personal hardship and hard behaviour towards patients seemed central to auxiliaries' understanding of what they were supposed to do. They spoke about others, such as residential home workers, and trained staff, as too 'soft'. A strong emphasis was placed upon coping and getting on with the work, even avoiding the use of hoist and aids, despite the frequency of serious back problems.

Violence from patients was experienced on a daily basis. Verbal and physical violence were common: swearing, biting, kicking, hitting (with the hand, stick or frame) usually occurred when patients were having personal care chores done. The physical violence was usually exhibited by those considered to be suffering from forms of confusion. Physical abuse was seen as funny – the basis for staffroom stories and myth-making; part of the job. Auxiliaries often invited me to watch certain chores that illustrated this type of violence. For example, one auxiliary invited me to observe a patient who was always aggressive in the evenings, referring to the chore as 'fun'.

The violent behaviour of patients was discussed at the end of shifts. The auxiliaries would recount patients' aggressive acts and compare bruises with pride. In situations where a trained staff member was present and a patient exhibited violent behaviour it was the auxiliary who physically positioned herself to take the brunt of it, restraining the individual and ticking them off for their behaviour. Taking and containing aggression was being 'hard', which itself was part of the role of being an auxiliary.

Within this subculture of personal hardship and the elevation of containment and ordering aspects of the job, it is unsurprising that acts of mistreatment and punishment were pervasive and unquestioned. [. . .]

## Conclusions

[. . .] In Cedar Court, bedroom work was auxiliaries' work and in some ways they had colonized the space as a workplace, with the patients having little control over these areas. The physical state of the patient was the only indicator of the job being done. Physical care was attained at Cedar Court through practices of daily mistreatment. Through these the individual could be ordered around the routine quicker, and they did appear to effect a state of compliance in most patients. Both punishment and mistreatment rapidly helped to create 'the lounge standard patient', which indicated that care was being carried out. Within this hidden bedroom world non-physical abuse was very difficult for trained staff, visitors or others to perceive. For example, it appeared that the trained staff who worked in fairly close proximity, but rarely in the bedrooms, were not aware of the existence of such abuse. The hard culture which had developed amongst auxiliaries positively sanctioned non-physical abuse as part of the work. Thus abuses could be carried out in front of other auxiliaries without being commented upon.

In Cedar Court the principal aim of the auxiliary was the ordering of the patient in the private world of the bedroom, and care was judged by the state of the patient's body. In this context non-physical mistreatment of the patient becomes routinized and difficult to detect. Research on institutional abuse needs to uncover both the hidden nature of care tasks and the meanings of such work to staff, to understand abuse more fully.

## References

Goffman, E. (1959) *The Presentation of Self in Everyday Life.* Harmondsworth: Penguin.
Willcocks, D., Peace, S. and Kellaher, L. (1987) *Private Lives in Public Places.* London: Tavistock.

# 26

# Body Care and Learning To Do for Others

*Jocelyn Lawler*

Nursing care requires access to every part of the body which is potentially touchable. However, in Western cultural traditions, certain parts of the body are more (socially) accessible and more readily touched than other parts. We are culturally 'non-touching' and this is especially so for the British. As nurses learn how to perform their work, therefore, they must overcome their own sociocultural backgrounds and adjust to a particular professional subculture and its established methods that permits handling other people's bodies. They must also confront the symbolism of certain parts of the body, in particular parts which have sexual significance, and they must find ways to manage social interaction during those times when they break taken-for-granted rules about the body.

The people whose experiences are discussed in this study [. . .] found some of their first experiences of working with other people's bodies to be socially awkward. Coming as they did from a non-touching cultural background, many of the nurses I talked with found that they were, among other things, acutely embarrassed in having to perform body care for others.

Those who had the least difficulty touching and handling the bodies of patients came from backgrounds with a relatively relaxed attitude to the body and exposure (but they were few in number) or had friends or family who were nurses. Most of the interviewees described a style of family life and upbringing where body functions were dealt with in a 'civilized' manner (see Elias, 1978). The sensitive bodily functions were carried out in private and they were not discussed. The body was almost always kept covered, consistent with the established cultural patterns of their families, and this socialization was acknowledged as a difficulty for a beginning nurse, as one nurse explained.

> *I*: I can remember the first man I had to wash. That was traumatic. . . . I was
> timid. I was embarrassed, I guess. The women weren't quite so bad, I
> mean that was a shock but a different sort of shock to the men.
> *R*: Why are the men worse?

From Jocelyn Lawler (1991) *Behind the Screens: Nursing, Somology and the Pattern of the Body*. Melbourne: Churchill. pp. 117–33 (abridged).

*I:* 'I had never seen men naked and – even though I had brothers – three
brothers. I mean you were just very modest, I guess, when you were at
home.

*R:* So you came from a family who kept things covered up?

*I:* Oh yes.

*R:* Did they talk about bodily functions?

*I:* No, see they were very English in that respect. They were something that
you didn't talk about. Nothing like that was.

*R:* So when people went to the loo?

*I:* It was behind a closed door and that was it.

*R:* Did that make it very difficult for you as a nurse to then have to do for
others what was [taboo], in your family life?

*I:* Taboo. Yes, I guess so, yes.

[. . .] There are other factors, however, that influence these experiences, and they have their origins in the way the body is constructed
in our culture. In particular the relationship of maleness and male
power to genitalia and sexuality had a powerful effect on some of the
female interviewees. The power invested in the male body is a theme
which recurs throughout this study. [. . .]

## First experience of body care for others

While much has been written to educate nurses, [. . .] nurses are
poorly prepared, educationally, for the breaking of social norms
which many nursing acts necessarily involve. What they learn of these
things they learn through experience.

> We are taught the proper way to carry out a bed bath, but not how to deal
> with the breaking of the social taboos when we wash a patient's body. Most
> nurses remember the fear they felt when doing their first bed bath. As a
> young female you work with a patient (who might well be male), behind
> drawn curtains and are expected to strip and wash his whole body. I
> remember feeling shamed and confused; my hands felt stiff, cold, awkward
> and useless. A bed bath can be embarrassing for the patient at the best of
> times – but far worse when the nurse herself [*sic*] is embarrassed. (Berry,
> 1986: 56)

Berry's experience is mirrored by that of the people interviewed for
this study. They talked of feeling terror, embarrassment and timidity
when they first had to confront other people's nakedness, and at
having to undress people, particularly men.

Normal male–female relationships in society are disrupted in nursing, especially when a beginning female nurse encounters her first
male patient. She has not yet learned the interpersonal skills that will
later make her work manageable. While male nurses experience some
feelings of embarrassment when they encounter female patients for
the first time, the data reported here suggest their discomfort is not as
acute. It is possible, however, that my data reflect what men were

willing to tell a woman about their sense of discomfort and also what women are prepared to discuss with another woman (see Warren, 1988).

For many, sponging a patient for the first time was highly significant, and they have retained vivid memories of that occasion. They acknowledge it as a major milestone – a time when the reality of nursing confronts them. After the first sponge, however, doing body care for others seems to become much easier. [. . .]

I asked each of the interviewees if they could remember the first time they had to 'do for someone else what that person would normally do for themselves'. Almost without exception they related stories of the first time they had to sponge a patient. [. . .]

*The naked male body*

In many of the accounts I heard from female nurses there was an early sense of profound embarrassment, lack of social competence and sometimes fear associated with men and having to deal with male bodies, particularly when the genitalia are exposed. It is an aspect of nursing practice which is often surrounded by social awkwardness and uncertainty. The following accounts indicate the early discomfort and fear of having to deal with the naked male:

> Yes. I can [remember my first experience with body care]. We went to . . . this *long* pavilion ward, a *men's* ward. [I] begged not to go to a men's ward first. [. . .] Anyway, went there, and was terrified through the whole procedure. . . . Just was terrified. . . . I remember it really clearly. . . . Women did not worry me. Men worried me a lot.

> I copped Male Ward. And I had to go to the corner [bed] – a boy about 18 he was. And he had a plaster on his leg, and so I gave him the dish and told him to wash himself, and he wasn't going to take his underpants off, and I wasn't about to take them off either! [*Laughter*] I can remember that as plain as day! [. . .] And I think that he was embarrassed and so was I. . . . I had seen men before, but we'd been reared, you know, you don't look at men. And that to me was just a problem. I was too embarrassed. . . . I still remember it as clear as day.

> I can remember the very first day on the ward . . . *begging* that they let me do a female one [sponge] first because I couldn't bear the thought of pulling down a pair of man's trousers. At that stage I don't think it ever occurred to me that my father had genitals. I was that protected from the male anatomy.

The first sponge is often the very first clinical act which beginning nurses perform where the body is completely exposed, and where they touch socially proscribed parts of the body. As the accounts illustrate, the male genitalia are especially problematic and many were very reluctant to touch those areas, as one would expect in a society where the male sex organs are invested with such meaning and kept covered, and where body contact in the genital areas is almost exclusively reserved for sexual contexts. In the absence of learned skills to manage these situations, the beginning nurse feels socially awkward and embarrassed.

Some interviewees remember their first experiences as occasions where they first saw suffering, disfigurement and death. And like the naked body, one does not normally encounter these things extensively in one's daily life, nor are they necessarily discussed in detail, and even within hospitals there is a limit to what the public sees, or is allowed to see or know. [. . .]

> In the very early stages . . . they took us over to the hospital – it was one of those old Nightingale wards. . . . It was a male medical ward and there was a guy in a bed near the office and he was obviously on his last legs. Now I had had nothing to do with death except seeing my grandmother who was . . . very unwell but she wasn't unconscious, she was a bit delirious. This guy in the bed was, you know, vomiting blood, and the whole ward was like a zoo, and I walked in with one of my mates and I thought 'my God, what have I got myself in for?' . . . and we had this guy who was in a single room, you know, he was Cheyne-Stoking and he died [Cheyne-Stokes Breathing is a type of breathing seen in some serious nervous conditions]. When he died we looked at each other and said 'God what are we gonna do now? He's dead'. . . . We thought he was dead. We weren't real sure. We weren't real sure. We kept saying to each other 'Is he [dead]? Is he?' Well, we were sort of hysterical with laughter for a while because we thought 'yeah, well he is dead 'cause that dreadful noise had stopped', but then we got sort of sad because we hadn't witnessed anything like this before. . . .

Other nurses remembered their first experiences because, as beginners, they were disorganized, they lacked skill and they encountered scenes for which they were completely unprepared. As a consequence they felt inadequate. It is important for nursing students to feel a sense of competence in their actions (Davis, 1968) and without it they feel unable to adequately convey a sense of being in control – a sense that is needed in order to promote a particular context in which to perform highly intimate care for patients. The following two accounts, given by nurses who are now very experienced and skilled at their practice, illustrate their felt lack of competence – a lack which meant they had not yet developed the occupationally specific methods that they could later use to manage such situations. Speed is often used by nurses as a method by which difficult things are managed, particularly those things which are potentially embarrassing. The first account was given by a male registered nurse, now in his thirties and skilled at care for acutely ill and intensive care patients.

> I can remember we went to the ward, and . . . I can remember lining up with all the bits and pieces, the bowl and stuff and thinking to myself 'I haven't got a bloody clue what I'm doing here'. We'd done it on models and dummies and that in the school but never actually done it on a person and I looked at the man I was about to sponge. I can remember him, he was a big man, fat man, and he'd had a cholecystectomy. He had an I.G. tube and he had a drain in and a drip and I thought 'Where will I start with all this – how will I get the pyjamas off?' – that sort of stuff. I was slow. I know it took me 55

minutes . . . and even then I forgot to do things like clean his teeth and do all that sort of thing. I was so intent on getting him washed. It was awful. . . . I knew to wash him, and I knew what I had to do as far as washing and drying and all that sort of thing, but not having any idea of the organization – and being slow. And it was hard because he knew that we were new.

I have often had that woman's situation in my mind since. You know, it's something I have not lost through the years, was going into a bathroom and seeing this elderly lady in a bath and seeing her arm and leg floating on top and she was weeping and couldn't express anything, and I later discovered she'd had a stroke and she was aphasic. She had been a doctor, and you know how stroke people cry, and she just cried and cried, and couldn't express herself and it was sort of a trauma to me that I have never really lost. I can remember her, and I think that's a terrible thing –for a woman like that to come to that state and – I mean she couldn't move anything, her leg and arm were floating on top and the nurses were trying to bath her in a bath, and she was just crying and drooling and couldn't speak. . . . It was 'Whatever do I do, whatever do I say?'

## Learning 'basic' nursing

When these nurses were taught how to do body care for others, it was in a particular manner – a manner that incorporated an emphasis on routine and procedure which involved no unnecessary exposure of the patient's body and which followed the recipe book approach characteristic of the texts. Additionally, the patient's embarrassment was to be considered, and nurses were also taught to maintain 'privacy' – a term which has a particular meaning where body care in nursing is concerned. Privacy has to do not only with avoiding unnecessary exposure, but it is also a notion about the vulnerability of patients. Instructions on clinical procedures emphasize privacy as a central consideration, along with the adherence to routine. [. . .]

### The emphasis on procedure

The accounts I heard in this study confirmed that nursing procedures, as they are described in texts, as step-wise and relatively stereotyped affairs, are indeed what nurses are taught as students. I asked those I interviewed how they had been taught to perform body care, especially sponging, which is the most central and comprehensive act of body care.

> I: They [the teachers] were very strict, very 'thorough' – the word is.
> R: But what did they teach you about how you might socially manage things like other people's nakedness, and embarrassment, and modesty?
> I: I don't think they ever prepared you for that.
> R: So they taught you how to do the procedure. . . .
> I: Physically do it, yeah. By the book! It was a procedure.

Yes, I can remember exactly what they [the nurse teachers] told us. Things they were more worried about were putting the sheets and the blankets in the right place and the towel in the right place and they never mentioned anything about how you should cope with the person, or the person coped with you. That was never, ever mentioned.

Others remembered being taught about a procedure which incorporated the notion of privacy, and how one might achieve this during the procedure. Privacy in this sense means not overexposing the patient, and it also means ensuring a visual privacy such that others cannot see the patient's nakedness. In effect, it is dealing with the body in a privatized and 'civilized' way, but it is also somological – the nurse must 'do for' the body while simultaneously recognizing personhood. The procedure, though, was dominant in their early formal education.

> We were always taught to screen the patient and we were always taught about privacy – privacy as in 'from the rest of the ward' – to screen the patient and make sure we were in this little closed-off area. We were taught nothing about embarrassment as far as the patient was concerned with the nurse. We were always taught to keep the patient warm which presumably meant you kept them covered, but then in the middle of summer you didn't need to be covered to be warm. We were always taught to keep them covered and taught to sponge by moving the sheet up and down various parts of the body – that sort of thing . . . . Exposing one bit at a time, but then at the same time we had to expose other bits, but nothing was ever talked about as far as patients' embarrassment or nurses' embarrassment. We were taught about privacy but it was privacy as in screening the patient from everyone else in the ward. . . . There was nothing about privacy between the nurse and the patient. It was always just there. . . .

[. . .]

## Learning to control emotions

Much of what nurses' (women's) work entails, represents what Hochschild (1983) has termed 'emotional labour' – a commodification of feelings to suit the public (paid) arena. [. . .] Nurses are heavily involved in emotional labour because, as well as learning physically and procedurally how to wash another person in bed, there is an expectation that students will learn to control their emotions. Such emotional control is part of the nurse's 'professional' approach, that is learning how to do body care and perform other nursing functions in a manner typical of the occupation.

Many aspects of nursing have changed since it embraced the concept of individualized patient care. One such change is the recognition that some emotions are normal, if not desirable, and that it is probably not healthy for nurses (or anyone else for that matter) to suppress them. Historically, however, one characteristic of a 'good' nurse, was the ability to hide emotional reactions and to cultivate an air of detachment – a sort of professional distance from one's work. Many of the nurses I interviewed remember being expected to learn such emotional control and to learn it as they developed their nursing skills, and as they coped with a daily working life that was often difficult and disturbing.

One British nurse, who is now in her fifties, described what she had been taught as a student nurse.

> I don't think we had very much at all on relating to people as individuals. . . .
> You have to remember I'm British and the British stiff upper lip. . . . I think
> it was just that it was not done. It was not done for the nurse to show
> emotion . . . it was to do with being professional and it upset the relatives. . . .
> I think it had to do with being a professional person . . . [and] we learnt it
> because I think if you showed any emotion you couldn't cope as a nurse you
> weren't made of the right stuff [*laughter*]. You weren't suitable if you
> showed emotion. . . . We certainly didn't look sad, I mean, you were not
> allowed to look sad or grieve, but neither were you allowed to giggle around
> the place. You had to comport yourself – with dignity. . . . No frivolity, not
> at all.

With experience and more generalized social change, many nurses re-evaluate those early influences, particularly as they affect the ways in which they help patients come to terms with illness experience and the lived body. The ability to control emotion is often used by experienced and expert nurses as one method to help patients through illness experience. [. . .]

Other nurses, who are much younger than the British nurse whose experience is related above and who trained in Australia, relate similar experiences to those of their British colleague. The occupational ethos of emotional control remains relatively pervasive.

> You were never allowed to [show emotion] – and you were never allowed to
> cry. You were only allowed to cry if the Charge Sister let you cry [*laughter*].
> You weren't allowed to cry if someone died or was really sick, you just felt
> that you had to give a little bit more to the patient – and you weren't
> allowed to laugh either if you could see the funny side of things. . . . You had
> to appear what they termed 'professional', which was very cold and caught
> up.

> We weren't taught about . . . emotions . . . and you weren't taught . . . that
> it's normal to feel disgust or things like that, which it is, isn't it. You know,
> you have a job to do and you do it, but no, not enough emotion or feeling
> was put into it.

> [I was] always told not to get involved and become attached to the patient
> or – it's hard not to get involved, I mean you do get involved. . . . I think it
> gets passed down, you know when you're looking after a really sick patient
> [other nurses say to you] 'you shouldn't get involved, you know' and so it
> goes on.

[. . .]

Emotional control, as an ideal aspect of professional practice, is now being seriously evaluated in the research literature. Benner and Wrubel (1988), for example, claim that it is impossible for nurses to care about what happens to patients and to help them during illness experience unless some degree of involvement occurs. Many of the nurses in my study would agree because they have recognized that emotional detachment does not work and that in some cases they have had to unlearn what had previously been taught to them. [. . .]

> I think probably we were taught that [emotional control] to start, but I think I've learnt over the years that that isn't always appropriate to the occasion, that there are times when I think . . . that as a person I have the right to let that other person know that they are embarrassing me . . . or that I feel uncomfortable in a situation. . . . I think that's improved. I think once upon a time you weren't expected to be emotional about anything. We weren't expected to feel emotion if a patient we cared about or cared for died. . . . Now I think it's quite acceptable for the staff to be just as emotional about the situation as the family is. I think that's good. I think it's important that we let the people we're caring about know – that we really do care . . . you can't do that if you remain detached. Looking back I think that in our early training – that we were sort of expected to be a bit remote, you know [we were told] 'don't be silly, Nurse. Pull yourself together'.

[. . .]

### Lack of affect as a clinical strategy

Nurses were expected to be controlled – to show no emotion. Many of them interpreted this to mean that they were to be emotionless, but lack of affect is in itself a response – a way of dealing with what would otherwise be a social mistake, a deviant act, an affront, an insult, a source of embarrassment. To show no affective change, for example, at another person's naked body is a way of conferring a very different meaning on nakedness from the usual effect of running naked across the field at a sports event. [. . .]

Lack of effect is a means by which nurses construct context, so in that sense it serves to assist in the management of otherwise potentially embarrassing situations. The problem for nurses, however, is that lack of affect can become *the* standardized and expected emotional response, in which case it excludes the possibility of sharing difficult moments for patients in a way which allows the nurse to 'make contact' with the patient existentially (see Benner and Wrubel, 1988: Chapter 1).

In many ways nurses operate in a social vacuum because they are often naive or ill-informed (at best) about the work they are expected to do and how they can behave, and little, if anything, in their lives prepares them for what they are required to do for others as basic nursing (body) care. Much of what nurses do is not public to protect patients' 'privacy', and it takes time and experience to feel comfortable in the role of nurse, doing things for other people. Talking with patients about some things is also difficult because there is a problem

with language. Not only is it not always socially appropriate, or
acceptable, to discuss what nurses do, there is a real difficulty in
choosing appropriate words or simply having conversation about
various things to do with the body. This [. . .] is richly indicative of
'the problem of the body' and privatized body functions and it
highlights the silence of the body in discourse generally.

## The problem of language

I asked the interviewees what they found most difficult to do when
they first began nursing, and while many found the physical and
procedural aspects of caring for other people's bodies awkward, there
was a very real problem with language and conversation. Nurses were
taught always to explain what they were going to do to patients,
because patients are often unaware of what could happen during a
certain procedure. [. . .]

Explanation, however, is not straightforward because some people
are not relaxed about discussing some body functions or body parts;
and the choice of words is far from straightforward. The two accounts
below illustrate some of the general aspects of this problem. I had
asked the interviewees if they found it difficult to know what to say to
people when they were doing nursing care.

> Embarrassing. Didn't know what to look at, what to say, because at those
> times I was quite shy and I can remember it was an old lady . . . with a
> fracture and . . . we had to . . . sponge and we had to do the whole works not
> knowing what to say or what to touch when you got to those bits . . .
> because it's something you don't ask. . . . We didn't know if that person
> would be offended by what we said. If you said 'your boobs' would she be
> offended by that. Being older she would probably be a bit strict.

> We were never taught how to deal with that [the language difficulty]. I
> mean, to ask a patient if they wanted to wash, for example, 'Would you like
> to wash between your legs?' or if you were being jovial you'd hear people
> say 'I'll wash down as far as possible and you wash "possible"'. And all this
> sort of thing – how do you ask someone if they'd like to wash between their
> legs. . . . The language is *always* a problem.

One of the major problems of language in nursing care is that there
are no widely accepted standards for the names of body parts and
functions. If, for instance, nurses call various body parts by their
anatomical names, there is a fair chance the patient will not understand, and if they use language that is in common usage, the choice is
by no means simple; furthermore, there are some things which people
do not readily discuss. [. . .]

> I think . . . [some] patients, when we ask them if they've had their bowels
> open, they tend to say 'yes' routinely because they don't know what we're
> talking about. That happens on a regular basis because they're not real sure
> what we're talking about. . . . People tend to call having your bowels open a

lot of stupid things. . . . I think it's classed as dirty. Whereas it shouldn't be. It's only your own body, but I think they're taught from a young age [that it's dirty].

With the civilizing process (Elias, 1978), body functions concerned with excretion have become highly privatized, at least by some social groups, particularly those of higher social status. [. . .]

> Oh yes. I think it's definitely class related. Joe Bloggs off the river bank is easy to talk to. They shit, they fart, they piss. You can communicate. It's the people with a middle-class presentation who don't have the vocabulary to match.

In summary, learning to be a nurse involves facing the reality of the place of the body in our society. [. . .] Becoming socialized as a nurse, however, means taking on a new way of looking at the body and learning to 'do for'. It requires unlearning ways of viewing the body. Such unlearning is necessitated by 'the problem of the body' and by the extent to which nursing and illness are disruptive of social order and normal rules do not always apply. [. . .] There is also no professional jargon that can be used to describe body functions which would make it possible to sanitize things people regard as dirty. [. . .] In the absence of discourse and socially acceptable language, some nursing functions are located outside socially condoned and accepted practices – they are dealt with by their absence and the silence which surrounds them.

## References

Benner, P. and Wrubel, J. (1988) *The Primacy of Caring*. Menlo Park, CA: Addison Wesley.

Berry, A. (1986) 'Knowledge at one's fingertips', *Nursing Times*, 3 December: 56–7.

Davis, F. (1968) 'Professional socialization as subjective experience: the process of doctrinal conversion among student nurses', in H.S. Becker, B. Geer, D. Riesman and R.S. Weiss (eds), *Institutions and the Person*. Chicago: Aldine.

Elias, N. (1978) *The Civilizing Process: the History of Manners*. Translated by E. Jephcott. New York: Urizen Books.

Hochschild, A.R. (1983) *The Managed Heart: Commercialization of Human Feeling*. Berkeley, CA: University of California Press.

Warren, C.A.B. (1988) *Gender Issues in Field Research, Qualitative Research Methods*, Vol. 9. Newbury Park, CA: Sage.

# 27

# Child Protection: Messages from Research

*Dartington Social Research Unit*

## The problems of definition

There are almost as many definitions of child abuse as there are books on the subject. The following are selected to illustrate some indication of the difficulties of reaching agreement.

The *Oxford English Dictionary* defines child abuse: as 'maltreatment of a child, especially by beating, sexual interference or neglect'.

The legal definition of child abuse is set down by the Children Act 1989. The primary justification for the state to initiate proceedings seeking compulsory powers is actual or likely harm to the child, where harm includes both ill-treatment (which includes sexual abuse and non-physical ill-treatment such as emotional abuse) and the impairment of health or development, health meaning physical or mental health, and development meaning physical, intellectual, emotional, social or behavioural development.

Physical abuse: 'Physical abuse implies physically harmful action directed against a child; it is usually defined by any inflicted injury such as bruises, burns, head injuries, fractures, abdominal injuries, or poisoning' (Kempe et al., 1962).

Sexual abuse: 'Sexual abuse is defined as the involvement of dependent, developmentally immature children and adolescents in sexual activities that they do not fully comprehend and to which they are unable to give informed consent or that violate the social taboos of family roles' (Schechter and Roberge, 1976).

Any discussion of child abuse and child protection services will benefit from agreements about definition. Unfortunately, there is no absolute definition of abuse. If, from a list of behaviours, ticks could be put against those which are abusive and crosses against those which are not, the task of practitioners and researchers would be made easier. In this list, hitting children might be ticked, indicating that such behaviour is abusive. But some might argue that in certain contexts it is good for children to be hit and, as at least 90 per cent of children have

From (1995) *Studies in Child Protection: Messages from Research*. London: HMSO. pp. 11–24 (abridged).

this experience at some time, the behaviour could be said to be 'normal'. The tick might be replaced by a cross or, at best, by a question mark.

There are many definitions of abuse in the legal and scientific literature. Most describe abusive *incidents*, especially beating, sexual interference and neglect of children. But policy-makers, researchers and practitioners are likely to consider the *context* in which such incidents occur before they will define them as abusive, a perspective that has been defined as phenomenological. [. . .] A weakness of this approach, however, is one of tautology: behaviour becomes abusive as soon as practitioners describe it as such. The researchers have helped with definitions of abuse by providing evidence on what normally happens in families and what are the long-term *outcomes* of different parenting styles. Such information, in combination with data on other harmful experiences, leads to a perspective on child abuse (as opposed to a definition of child abuse) which emphasizes the needs of children and the context in which maltreatment occurs.

Whatever approach is employed, it is important to reflect on what is considered abusive to children because this will determine whether, when and how to intervene. If professionals are certain that they are faced with a severe incident, in which there are no mitigating circumstances and which, left unchecked, will lead to significant harm, they have a duty to protect the child. In some situations, the authority of the court will be required, for example when an emergency protection order is needed. In other circumstances, it may be concluded that no abuse has occurred and that no action to protect the child or support the family is necessary. But most cases that come to the notice of agencies involved in child protection fall between these extremes. They very often concern children in need of support from outside the family as well as protection. Deciding whether child abuse has occurred in these – the most common – cases is difficult and forms the beginning of this discussion.

The first question is, what happens ordinarily in families?

**Normal behaviour within families**

Although maltreatment can occur in a variety of settings, the evidence on normal behaviour within families is important in defining what is abnormal or abusive. But even this approach has its difficulties. For example, what might be thought of as 'normal' in one generation is often 'abnormal' in another and what might be thought of as 'normal' in one social context can be 'abnormal' in another. Sending eight-year-olds to boarding school has been acceptable to many generations of parents in certain social classes but is considered neglectful by others. In addition, behaviour which is thought to be 'normal' because it is exhibited by the majority of parents is not necessarily 'optimal'. Most parents resort on occasions to hitting their children but many accept that it is not an effective or enduring means of control.

Nonetheless, by examining what typically happens in families, some light can be shed on the way a society decides what is abnormal. Both behaviour within families towards children – what some have described as parenting styles – and society's perspectives on what is good or bad for children change over time. No doubt, the one influences the other. Certainly the Victorian affection for the maxim 'spare the rod and spoil the child' was reflected in childrearing practices of the day, just as current attitudes towards young people are manifest in legislation and guidance.

So what are normal patterns of parenting behaviour? Most parents hit their sons and daughters, even babies in nappies. The Newsons' survey in the 1960s found that 95 per cent of parents hit their children and that 80 per cent of them thought it was right to do so (Newson and Newson, 1969). When they repeated the survey in the 1990s these proportions had fallen; four-fifths (81 per cent) of parents now hit their children but half thought they should not (Newson and Newson, 1989). Marjorie Smith and colleagues at the Thomas Coram Research Unit also found that most of the 403 children they surveyed had been hit (Smith et al., forthcoming). The overall rate was 91 per cent and three-quarters of children under the age of one had been so disciplined.

In an earlier study at the Institute of Child Health, Smith and Grocke (1995) looked at patterns of sexual behaviour within English homes. Their findings expose the gap between popular images of family life and what is actually occurring. Child protection professionals used to dealing with extremes of human behaviour tend to overestimate the levels of problem behaviour and sometimes misinterpret what is perfectly normal. To illustrate the gap between image and reality, consider the following list of behaviours and situations and try to estimate what proportion occurred within the families studied. (It might be helpful to know that the researchers focused on a random sample of children aged between four and sixteen who had not been abused.)

Parents report the child definitely or probably as having:

(a)   touched mother's breasts;
(b)   touched father's genitalia;
(c)   drawn genitalia;
(d)   been seen masturbating;
(e)   seen 'simulated' sexual intercourse on films or TV;
(f)   seen pornographic material;
(g)   seen horror movies;
(h)   bathed with parents.

These results are given below*. They encourage reflection on how abuse is defined and what behaviours are potentially abusive. Overtly sexualized behaviour, such as excessive masturbation, sexual curiosity or touching genitals, is sometimes thought of as an indicator of abuse. However, the Institute of Child Heath study (Smith et al., 1995) shows that such behaviours frequently occur in moderation in the homes of 'normal' English families and that they are not *in themselves* sufficient to suggest abuse. More important is the context in which the behaviour occurs: where it takes place; who else is present; what parents think about it; and the age of the child.

The difficulties of interpretation can be illustrated with the example of nakedness within families – a reasonably good indicator of parenting style. As the preceding exercise shows, it is not unusual for children to see their parents naked. But Smith and Grocke also found that the behaviour declined with age, for instance bathing with parents reduced considerably after the child's fifth birthday and did not occur post-puberty. Family type was also shown to be important; nakedness was more likely to occur in households which included both biological parents and among professional classes. The reduction in nakedness in the family is usually a natural process; parents start to cover themselves up when the children get embarrassed and bathing together becomes impractical as children get older and bigger. Again, understanding the context helps with an understanding of what is abusive. A parent walking naked before his or her children is not being abusive but if the same behaviour was occurring against the child's wishes, some maltreatment might be said to be taking place.

Does a combination of sexual behaviours indicate possible abuse? Probably not, since there is a natural association between different actions. A child who bathes with a parent is more likely to touch the parent's genitalia. Neither of these behaviours singly or in combination is a reliable sign of maltreatment. There was a small but significant group in the Institute of Child Health sample who had seen a sexually explicit video or who had witnessed sexual intercourse and, as a result, were likely to have greater sexual knowledge than their peers. In the context of an investigation this might give rise to suspicions of sexual abuse. Such a loss of innocence could be undesirable, but it would be presumptuous to call it abusive.

While it is relatively easy to chart patterns of punishment in families, these too prove inadequate indicators of abuse. Indeed, the Thomas Coram team observed that while factors previously found to be associated with physical maltreatment – such as mother's young age or children born in close sequence – were mild predictors of frequent or severe punishment, other factors more indicative of daily

* (a) 63% (b) 12% (c) 35% (d) 67% (e) 31% (f) 9% (g) 30% (h) 77%

life stress were stronger (Smith et al., forthcoming). Parents hit their children when they could not cope with minor difficulties, such as the child's own behaviour or disputes between siblings. Any practitioner knows that a lot can be done to improve the situation of these families – for example by providing general support to raise parents' irritation threshold and specific advice such as how to handle sibling aggression. Punishment can be abusive but it should not be the only focus of child protection interventions. Equally important is support for children and families in need.

## Thresholds for intervention

It should be clear from this evidence that child abuse is not an absolute concept. Most behaviour has to be seen in context before it can be thought of as maltreatment. With the exception of some sexual abuse, it should also be clear that maltreatment is seldom an event, a single incident that requires action to protect the child.

[. . .] Many of the researchers stressed that instances of child sexual abuse did not always conform to general findings about child protection. The following points which set out ways in which sexual maltreatment differs from other types of abuse therefore need to be borne in mind.

It is found that, in most contexts, single instances of maltreatment seldom warrant much concern on the part of professionals. It is the chronicity and severity of maltreatment that influence a willingness to intervene. This is not always true of child sexual abuse, as a relatively minor, one-off event can sometimes be damaging to children and may require a strong response from protection agencies.

Generally, it is difficult to define child abuse and there are no absolute criteria on which to rely. However, compared to physical maltreatment or neglect, the thresholds which define when sexual abuse has occurred are relatively clear. There is also more parental agreement over when a sexual act can be said to be abusive.

All the researchers agreed that while a behaviour in one context will be defined as maltreatment, the same behaviour in another context would not. This rule is less easy to apply in cases of sexual abuse. Much child protection work is principally concerned with problems within the family (although child maltreatment in other contexts, for example bullying in school, is a major worry to parents). In cases of child sexual abuse, outside perpetrators and maltreatment by 'known others' like neighbours or distant relatives is more likely to feature in professional inquiries. [. . .]

Some forms of parenting styles and ways of bringing up children are abusive – or at least potentially abusive. Maltreatment viewed in this way is unlikely to be just physical abuse or emotional abuse. Types of abuse overlap so that a child who has been physically maltreated will almost certainly have suffered emotionally, and sexual abuse may involve physical force or threat of punishment.

The association between types of abuse is illustrated in Farmer and Owen's study (1995). They found that the existence of secondary concerns was a factor significantly related to the placement of a child's name on the protection register. In one-third of cases where the main concern was *neglect*, there were also concerns about *physical abuse*. In one-fifth of cases where the main concern was *physical abuse*, there were also concerns about *neglect*. In one-quarter of cases where the main concern was *sexual abuse*, there were also concerns about *neglect*. In one-sixth of cases where the main concern was *sexual abuse* there were also concerns about *physical abuse*. In one-quarter of cases where the main concern was *physical abuse*, there were also concerns about *emotional* abuse.

If the focus is to be on events in context and the combination of types of maltreatment that can occur, how do professionals judge that a child is being abused? Some plurality will be necessary as no single definition of abuse is likely to satisfy all the different parties – the policy-maker deciding where to place scarce resources, the public worrying about how best to bring up children, the social scientist trying to estimate how much abuse exists and the professional making difficult judgements about child safety.

This complex situation is clarified by introducing the idea of a continuum of abuse. Several research teams concluded that abuse was better understood if the focus of concern was on behaviour which children ordinarily encountered but which in certain circumstances could be defined as maltreatment. Once this step has been taken, questions for researchers and practitioners tend to be about chronicity and severity of behaviours, such as how much shouting at children can be said to be harmful. This perspective is certainly an antidote to the idea introduced at the beginning where specific behaviour is defined as either acceptable or unacceptable. Gil's finding that physical abuse was often discipline gone too far is a good illustration of the continuum model (Gil, 1970). The studies by Marjorie Smith of normal family life found that most incidents that cause concern can be understood in this way but there are important exceptions (Smith et al., forthcoming). Dropping a baby onto a bed, for example, rests between gentle play at one end of a continuum and extreme frenzy at the other; pulling out finger nails can only be described as abusive.

Professionals see parenting behaviour on a continuum but they have the additional duty to decide whether to intervene and, if so, how. To do this they must draw a threshold; this involves deciding both the point beyond which a behaviour (or parenting style) can be considered maltreatment and the point beyond which it becomes necessary for the state to take action. Most of the researchers found

the idea of a threshold to be the best way of understanding gatekeeping at different stages in the child protection process.

Thresholds determine the key 'when' questions facing professionals:
when to define something as abusive, when to intervene, when to
confront or raise the issue with parents, when to call a protection
conference and when to remove a child.

Several thresholds exist. Some are clear and unequivocal but others
depend on context and cultural values. The placing of the threshold is
influenced by moral and legal questions, pragmatic concerns and,
recently, outcome evidence and the concerns of parents and children.
There are pressures for stronger gatekeeping, such as when parents
feel that their rights have been ignored by high-handed professionals,
and for opening the door further, for example to include bullying and
racial attacks. Once acceptable definitions of abuse have been
reached, the threshold for concern is clear; the Children Act 1989 and
*Working Together* specify that *all* reports and suspicions of child
abuse must be taken seriously and assessed. [. . .]

Hence, decisions about what is abusive are closely tied to decisions
about whether the state should intervene. [. . .] Viewed in this way it
can be seen how, even when parenting styles remain the same over
time, the amount of abuse uncovered by child protection agencies may
increase or decrease depending on the drawing of the threshold.

A look at changes over the last century would suggest that the
threshold beyond which child abuse is considered to occur is gradu-
ally being lowered. This is happening for a variety of reasons,
including an emphasis on the rights of children as individuals, ease of
disclosures, the influence of feminist social theories about victimization and public expectation that the state should intervene in the
privacy of family life. Society continually reconstructs definitions of
maltreatment which sanction intervention; in 1871 the concern was
abuse by adoptive parents; in 1885 it was teenage prostitution; in 1908
incest; then, later, neglect, physical abuse, sexual and emotional
abuse. The state remains selective in its concerns and there is a
difference between behaviour known to be harmful to children and
behaviour which attracts the attention of child protection practitioners. For example, professionals' interest in school bullying is
perhaps not as great as parents and children would wish it to be and
domestic violence is only just beginning to achieve salience as a cause
of concern. Jane Gibbons helpfully summarizes the situation when she
says that 'as a phenomenon, child maltreatment is more like porno-
graphy than whooping cough. It is a socially constructed phenomenon
which reflects values and opinions of a particular culture at a
particular time' (Gibbons et al., 1995a; see also Gibbons et al., 1995b).

If this perspective on child abuse holds, what are the influences on
the thresholds which separate non-intervention from intervention?
Nearly all the research teams provided evidence on this issue and four

dimensions were found to be important. Initially, there is a moral aspect, fundamental to any legislation. Over time, moral concerns change and policy-makers add, subtract and amend categories of abuse; witness the inclusion of sexual abuse and the dropping of grave concern as a separate category from *Working Together* in 1991.

Professionals, in addition to observing procedural rules, also make a number of pragmatic judgements related to whether interventions will help. [. . .] Ideally, professionals assess the severity and duration of the suspected abuse; they consider the child's reaction and his or her perceptions; they look at the parents' attitude and willingness to co-operate; and they sometimes think about the effects upon the child's development. Ideally, they look for any protective factors for the child, something that will make his or her life more viable. Professionals also have to weigh up the effects of the intervention on the child's long-term well-being.

The research teams also drew attention to important dimensions sometimes missing from assessments. Although procedures are constantly developing, child protection professionals remain tardy in using evidence about the effects of a behaviour or parenting style on outcomes for the child. Deborah Ghate and Liz Spencer (1995) in their feasibility study of the prevalence of sexual abuse found it unhelpful to refer to 'cases of abuse' without understanding the long-term effects. Does hitting a child once do any emotional damage? Can children who have been sexually abused make a recovery? This perspective defines a behaviour or way of upbringing as abusive only when it is debilitating for the child. It makes a distinction between abusive action – what carers do – and harm – the impact on the child. [. . .]

Thus there are several influences upon the drawing of the threshold for defining abuse and sanctioning appropriate action. At the time the research was conducted, the most important of these influences were: *moral/legal* questions and the *pragmatic* concerns of professionals. The researchers also concluded that *outcome* evidence and *parent/ child* concerns should play a greater role in professional decisions about what is and what is not abusive. [. . .]

## What is bad for children?

[. . .] In assessing the long-term effects of different parenting styles, the severity and endurance of particular incidents can be important. In a warm, supportive environment, children who have been hit once or twice seldom suffer long-term negative effects. Similarly, while a short period of neglect or emotional abuse is likely to cause children unhappiness and some harm, an important part of the professional task will be to understand the wider family context. With the exception of many child sexual abuse investigations, most professionals find themselves judging the severity and chronicity of experiences against the backdrop of other happenings in the child's life. [. . .]

Long-term difficulty for children is caused in several, sometimes unexpected ways. Waterhouse et al, (1993) for example, in cases of physical abuse found under-control to be as much a problem as over-control in the families she studied. Parents under pressure seldom had much time for their children and were apt to lash out in a range at the frustrations of everyday interaction. Waterhouse also emphasized the damaging effects of long-term family violence and that children regularly seeing their mother beaten can suffer as much as if they themselves had been frequently and severely hit. In contrast, in cases of marital breakdown, the conflict is rarely perceived as abusive to children even though it causes much unhappiness and may cause long-term emotional harm.

Although they differ in the detail of their results, those researchers that looked at the issue agree that long-term problems occur when the *parenting style* fails to compensate for the inevitable deficiencies that become manifest in the course of the 20 years or so it takes to bring up a child. During this period, occasional neglect, unnecessary or severe punishment or some form of family discord can be expected. It is a question of balance in the interactions with the child. If parenting is entirely negative, it will be damaging; if negative events are interspersed with positive experiences, outcomes may be better. In a warm supportive home, it may be better for a parent to get very cross with an errant child and later apologize than to do nothing at all. However, in families *low on warmth and high on criticism*, negative incidents accumulate as if to remind a child that he or she is unloved.

This pattern of low warmth, high criticism has been noted by several researchers. Thoburn and colleagues (1995) describe this context as one of 'emotional neglect', others prefer 'emotional maltreatment'. [. . .] Whatever expression is used, all of the researchers are trying to capture those contexts which are potentially harmful and generally inauspicious for children and which also place them at a higher risk of experiencing specifically abusive events, such as physical harm or even sexual maltreatment.

In these families, although parents behave badly or are unavailable to their children, they seldom – if ever – commit acts of deliberate cruelty. However, punishment, physical neglect and, very occasionally, sexual abuse are probably more likely to occur to children in low-warmth, high-criticism situations. There are chains of cause and effect in these families which can sometimes explain parents' maladaptive behaviour. An alcoholic father may drive a family into poverty, making a mother's task extremely difficult, or a violent partner might force the rest of the family to flee to poor or overcrowded housing. Alternatively, some emotional neglect might be explained by a mother's depression. However, it is important to emphasize that households under pressure – including many distorted, reconstituted and poor families – are frequently warm and loving places in which to bring up children.

Putting to one side the severe cases, for those children who suffer from a short period of emotional neglect, the child protection process may not be the best way of meeting their needs. If, however, the family problems endure, some external support will be required, otherwise the health and development of the child will be significantly impaired. These are clearly children 'in need' as defined by the Children Act 1989. In some cases, the severity of individual incidents, the long duration of poor parenting styles or the denial of abuse will result in the child suffering significant harm and stronger protection strategies will be required from the child protection process. There are, in addition, a small proportion of cases in which the abuse is extreme and cannot be explained by contextual factors; swift action to protect and possibly remove the child will be necessary.

As the following sections reveal, the research shows that many of the services provided by childcare agencies – including those offered with the intent of protecting the child – alleviate the pressures on the family, reduce emotional neglect by parents and so diminish the likelihood of long-term impairment or even significant harm. These services can increase the warmth and lower the criticism experienced by the child. Unfortunately, beneficial effects are often reduced because of a preoccupation with abusive events rather than with the processes that underlie them.

The Children Act 1989 defines 'children in need' in this way:

For the purposes of this Part (of the Act) a child shall be taken to be in need if,

a) he is unlikely to achieve or maintain, or to have the opportunity of achieving or maintaining, a reasonable standard of health or development without the provision for him of services by a local authority under this Part;
b) his health or development is likely to be significantly impaired, or further impaired, without the provision for him of such services; or
c) he is disabled.

'Development' means physical, intellectual, emotional, social or behavioural development; 'health' means physical or mental health. (From Sections 17(10) and (11) of the Children Act 1989)

## Causes of abuse

None of the studies was designed to discover the causes of abuse although some touched on factors associated with severe or enduring punishment and with emotional neglect. Many teams commented on the quality of parents' marriages; their mental health; possible drug misuse; parents' own experiences of abuse; their age, education and religion at the time the children were born and their living conditions. However, this evidence has little to say about the causes of abuse because scrutiny falls almost exclusively upon those children who come to the notice of child protection agencies. They tend to be working class and poor; little is known about middle-class parents who mistreat their offspring or about children abused outside the home.

Browne and Saqi's (1987) account of the various theories put forward since the Second World War illustrates the relationship between definitions and perceived causes of abuse. They identify five different models which explain why children are maltreated. Among them are:

- *psychopathic*: Fifty years ago child abuse was thought to be a rare event and North American researchers emphasized organic illness suffered by known perpetrators.
- *social or environmental*: As abuse came to be recognized as more widespread, it was clear that not all abusers had psychiatric difficulties. Problems of housing, unemployment and other social stressors came to be seen as important triggers of abusive behaviour.
- *special victim*: A handful of studies have emphasized the special problems facing some parents, such as those bringing up children with learning difficulties or disabilities.
- *psychosocial*: More recent research has demonstrated how certain social and psychological factors interact to predispose some people to violent behaviour.
- *integrated model*: Today, it is broadly accepted that a combination of social, psychological, economic and environmental factors play a part in the abuse or neglect of children. [. . .] Families overwhelmed and depressed by social problems form the greatest proportion of those assessed and supported by child protection agencies. Not included in this group is a small proportion with very different characteristics, such as those in which a parent has serious psychiatric problems or a predisposition to family violence.

## The problems of definition: summary points

- Child abuse is difficult to define but clear parameters for intervention are necessary if professionals are to act with confidence to protect vulnerable children.
- Thresholds which legitimize action on the part of child protection agencies appear as the most important components of any definition of child abuse.

- The research evidence suggests that authoritative knowledge about what is known to be bad for children should play a greater part in drawing these thresholds.
- A large number of children in need live in contexts in which their health and development are neglected. For these children it is the corrosiveness of long-term emotional, physical and occasionally sexual maltreatment that causes psychological impairment or even significant harm.
- Instances of child sexual abuse may not conform to general findings about child protection. For example, minor single incidents can damage children and thresholds and criminal statutes tend to be clearer than is found when dealing with physical abuse.

## References

Browne, K. and Saqi, S. (1987) 'Parent–child interaction in abusing families and its possible causes and consequences', in P. Maher (ed.), *Child Abuse: The Educational Perspective*. Oxford: Basil Blackwell. pp. 77–104

Farmer, E. and Owen, M. (1995) *Child Protection Practice: Private Risks and Public Remedies – Decision Making, Intervention and Outcome in Child Protection Work*. London: HMSO.

Ghate, D. and Spencer, L. (1995) *The Prevalence of Child Sexual Abuse in Britain: A Feasibility Study for a Large Scale National Survey of the General Population*. London: HMSO.

Gibbons, J., Gallagher, B., Bell, C. and Gordon, D. (1995a) *Development After Physical Abuse in Early Childhood: A follow-Up Study of Children on Protection Registers*. London: HMSO.

Gibbons, J., Conroy, S. and Bell, C. (1995b) *Operating the Child Protection System: A Study of Child Protection Practices in English Local Authorities*. London: HMSO.

Gil, D. (1970) *Violence Against Children*. Cambridge, MA: Harvard University Press.

Kempe, C., Silverman, F., Steele, B., Droegmueller, W. and Silver, H. (1962) 'The battered child syndrome', *Journal of the American Medical Association*. 181: 4–11.

Newson, J. and Newson, E. (1969) *Patterns of Infant Care*. Harmondsworth: Penguin.

Newson, J. and Newson, E. (1989) *The Extent of Parental Physical Punishment in the UK*. APPROACH.

Schechter, M. and Roberge, L. (1976) 'Sexual exploitation', in R. Helfer and C. Kempe (eds), *Child Abuse and Neglect*. Cambridge, MA: Ballinger. pp. 127–42.

Smith, M. and Grocke, M. (1995) *Normal Family Sexuality and Sexual Knowledge in Children*. London: Royal College of Psychiatrists/Gorkill Press.

Smith, M., Bee, P., Heverin, A. and Nobes, G. (forthcoming) 'Parental control within the family: the nature and extent of parental violence to children'. Papers from Thomas Coram Research Unit, tel. 0171–612–6957.

Thoburn, J., Lewis, A. and Shemmings, D. (1995) *Paternalism or Partnership? Family Involvement in the Child Protection Process*. London: HMSO.

Trickett, P. and Kuczyinski, L. (1986) 'Children's misbehaviours and parental discipline: strategies in abusive and non-abusive families', *Developmental Psychology*, 22: 115–23.

Waterhouse, L., Pitcairn, T., McGhee, J., Secker, J. and Sullivan, C. (1993) 'Evaluating parenting in child physical abuse', in L. Waterhouse, *Child Abuse and Child Abusers*. London: Jessica Kingsley.

# 28

# Elder Abuse and the Policing of Community Care

*Simon Biggs*

## The observation of elder abuse

Few social gerontologists could have failed to notice the growth in literature on elder abuse that has taken place in the UK since 1992. [. . .] Some commentators have suspected an 'ageing enterprise' at work. [. . .] This phrase, first coined by Carol Estes (1979), draws attention to the manipulation of newly recognized social problems affecting older people and the possibility of their being hijacked by professional agendas of various sorts. Her work raises questions about the genesis of issues, especially where policy seems to have relied exclusively on professional/political discourse. The sudden growth of interest in a problem first identified in the mid-1970s deserves some explanation, some sense of the historical context in which it is being problematized, and how our understanding of it is being shaped.

## Three strange features of existing policy

There are three features of this area that have, in my view, received inadequate attention. In combination they suggest some provocative questions about abuse as it is currently being conceived.

First, the Department of Health Guidelines, the campaign and the formation of the new pressure group Action on Elder Abuse all took place in the same year as the operationalization of the 1990 NHS and Community Care Act. This Act, it will be recalled, had amongst its guiding principles the notion of a residual state, which included care management being used to support informal care, now seen as the principal component in any care initiated by the community.

Second, as the full title of the DHSS Guidelines indicates (*No Longer Afraid: The Safeguard of Older People in Domestic Settings*) abuse has been positioned as a domestic phenomenon. [. . .] Whilst

---

Originally published in *Generations Review*, 6(2), June 1996: 2–4 (abridged).

institutional abuse is perhaps the area with the longest track record of maltreatment of older people (Glendenning, 1993), government policy has been consistent in seeing this sector's problems within a 'quality' rather than an 'abuse' framework. Community and specifically informal care seem, by contrast, to have become the focus of anxiety over abuse itself.

Thirdly, I am drawn back to an earlier observation that the history of policy in this area is one in which abuse has been simultaneously recognized and ignored (Biggs et al., 1995). For example the expansion of local authority policies on abuse (Action on Elder Abuse, 1995) has given considerable impetus to awareness of abuse in informal care, whilst relying almost exclusively on care management technology. It is indicated in the report that the employment of such technology relies heavily on assessment and monitoring in preference to intervention. We are thus observing, but doing little. [. . .]

## Elder abuse and informal care

To explore this conjunction explicitly: the problem of elder abuse has reached professional and policy salience at a time when the relationship between formal and informal care is being significantly restructured and can be thought of as being both contested and in a state of flux. The direction of this restructuring has been a tacit shifting of responsibility, both financial and in terms of direct caregiving, into the private sphere. There has been little policy concern about the ability or willingness of informal carers to care. Rather, a climate of obligation has been fostered, supported by a wider 'back to basics' political campaign contemporary to the implementation period, that draws on supposed traditional family values. [. . .]

Whether there ever was a time when an army of selfless and dutiful sons and daughters looked after their elderly parents is, of course, open to question (see Phillipson, 1996, for a recent review of family care). Further, current caring arrangements would appear to be much more a matter of negotiation within the context of complex family structures and affiliations. Whilst filial attachment plays a part in caring, it cannot be explained or encouraged by a simple call on obligation (Finch, 1995). The norms and values associated with intergenerational relations in later life are not as clear as for other life phases and, if anything, travel in the opposite direction to those that would underwrite filial care for the oldest generation (Finch and Mason, 1993). If obligation is to work as a policy strategy it would require considerable support itself.

The question of a blanket obligation to care becomes more problematic still once it is set beside key indicators of domestic abuse. Rather than the popular notion (and one reflected in *No Longer*

*Afraid* . . .) of abuse resulting from situational stress, itself induced by the demands of the cared-for, it would seem that the three clearest indicators refer to carer characteristics. These indicators are a history of mental illness, substance misuse and emotional or financial dependency on the part of the carer (Pillemer and Wolf, 1986). Each of these factors poses serious questions about a policy position that underplays the diversity existing in the 'carer' population. What this position does do is to confuse informal caring with a small minority of damaged or desperate people who should never be carers in the first place. It simultaneously makes every carer a possible abuser and serves as a warning to elders in receipt of care that they should not become too demanding. Obligation plus situational stress thereby supplies a justification for the policing of informal care as a whole.

### The policing of informal care

[. . .] It is in this context that an emphasis on monitoring, plus an unwillingness to explore appropriate interventions, begin to take on some form of coherence. *No Longer Afraid* . . . and its accompanying letter to directors of Social Services make the link between care management and a solution to abuse explicit. Yet this is a technology designed for quite different purposes. In the British context, care management has evolved into a means of administering and monitoring routine packages of care and is unsuited to the negotiation of complex emotional and relational problems. However, a regularity of visiting, the collation of information from others, an encouragement to support but not intervene directly, makes it an appropriate tool for surveillance purposes.

I have argued elsewhere that existing social policy on elder abuse has served to locate it as a problem of the domestic environment, and one that essentially takes place between dependent individuals and their individual carers (Biggs, forthcoming). This positioning obscures the possible social causes of abuse. It also masks abuse in collective settings. This is something that has become a familiar accompaniment to market models of welfare. The link between attempts to shift the focus of care away from the state and on to private citizens, and the need to ensure that those private individuals conform to newly emerging, if not to say engineered, patterns of care, has been less open to discussion.

[. . .] A new balance, at least in terms of policy, is being encouraged in relations between formal and informal care, in conditions where the norms associated with such caring are indistinct. These new expectations may [. . .] take time to be seen as natural and normal, and in the interim conformity will need to be monitored. The surveillance of care opens the possibility of an increasingly paranoid world in which care is to be managed. There are noble carers and there are wicked carers. There are professionals who observe and who might be called to the rescue (if only they were given increased legal powers). Be grateful, ye burdens, on succeeding generations, for the care you get; things could be much worse. In the meantime we will watch.


## Concluding comments

While at the time of implementation many applauded the 1990 Act in the belief that it recognized the importance of informal caring, its fiscal objective has always been to reduce the overall costs of public welfare. As Foucault (1979) has pointed out, the granting of a little freedom can easily protect the powerful as greater freedoms are taken away. In such situations, technologies of care that offer 'support' also act to maintain a state of unfreedom.

Increased interest in elder abuse has been limited in policy terms to domestic settings, has occurred at a time when the balance between formal and informal care is in flux and the status of care management is unsure. In these historical circumstances it is not unreasonable to ask why a technology of surveillance has eclipsed the possibility of developing services that directly address the complex and painful nature of abusive situations and that might inspire hope of resolution. This scenario gives new meaning and increased status to care management with older people, justifies adult services in a period of retrenchment, and suits a moral crusade on behalf of a residualizing government. It does little, however, to find lasting solutions, ease the negotiation of complex and often long-standing relationships that are in trouble, and give alternative specialist support to caring contexts that are beyond repair.

The strong hypothesis that emerges from this discussion is that elder abuse might become a sword hanging over every informal caring relationship and that the supportive management of that care carries with it the threat of surveillance. This is not to deny the very real needs of older people who are trapped in abusive situations. However, the current state of affairs offers little by way of repair to either elders or their carers. [. . .]

The argument pursued above also suggests a mindfulness that increased interest in elder abuse does not provoke the growth of a policy giant which, whilst espousing the protection of a minority, is used to police the majority. Elder protection is a field that lends itself to easy moralism. However, for effective progress to be made, movement towards conceiving appropriate and sophisticated services (which do not currently exist) must be made in harness with an awareness of wider issues affecting the lives of older people.

# References

Action on Elder Abuse (1995) *Action on Elder Abuse.* London, Age Concern.

Biggs, S. (forthcoming) 'A family concern: elder abuse in British social policy', *Critical Social Policy.*

Biggs, S., Phillipson, C. and Kingston, P. (1995) *Elder Abuse in Perspective.* Buckingham: Open University Press.

Department of Health (1993) *No Longer Afraid.* London: HMSO.

Estes, C. (1979) *The Aging Enterprise.* San Francisco: Jossey-Bass.

Finch, J. (1995) 'Responsibilities, obligations and commitments', in I. Allen and E. Perkins (eds), *The Future of Family Care for Older People.* London: HMSO.

Finch, J. and Mason, J. (1993) *Negotiating Family Responsibilities.* London: Routledge.

Foucault, M. (1979) *The History of Sexuality.* Harmondsworth: Penguin.

Glendenning, F. (1993) 'What is elder abuse and neglect?' in P. Decalmer and F. Glendenning (eds), *The Mistreatment of Elderly People.* London: Sage.

Phillipson, C. (1996) *Social Networks and Social Support in Old Age.* Keele: Keele University Press.

Pillemer, K. and Wolf, R. (1986) *Elder Abuse: Conflict in the Family.* Massachusetts: Auburn House.

# SECTION 5

# CONTEXTS OF CARE: POLICIES AND POLITICS

Severe financial pressures, combined with the New Right philosophy of the Conservative governments of the 1980s and 1990s produced dramatic changes in the policy context of all public services, including health and social care services, in the UK. The task of Social Services departments and health authorities, until then sole providers of a range of statutory services, became that of arranging for service provision through a mix of voluntary, private and state agencies. A purchaser/provider split was put in place whereby statutory agencies spell out local need and commission services by encouraging potential providers to compete for contracts. Service users, care providers and the public as a whole have had to adjust to an unfamiliar idea that putting public services in a competitive marketplace will generate both greater efficiency and greater choice.

Two White Papers in 1989 heralded these changes and were then embodied in the NHS and Community Care Act of 1990. *Caring for People* required local authorities to assess need, develop community care plans and encourage private and voluntary providers to create a mixed economy of care in which Social Services expenditure would reduce. *Working for People* created an 'internal market' in the NHS with, for example, GP fundholders buying services for patients and self-governing trusts competing for contracts. The history and the detail of these changes can be gleaned from other sources. What the readings in this section do is to give a range of insights into the significance of today's policy climate – from the point of view of the users, of workers in health and social care, of policy analysts and of those with political positions both to the left and the right of the new regime.

People will bring their own legacies of previous thought to major changes like these. For many of those over the age of 50, the 'cradle to grave' provisions of Britain's welfare state, and the NHS in particular, have been a matter of pride, and something to be supported rather than put in the spotlight of the kind of criticism they might invoke in other areas of their lives. In Chapter 29, Baldock and Ungerson provide a timely reminder that despite the rhetoric of greater consumer choice, many will find it hard to come to terms with an idea of a mixed economy of care and to make decisions as to whether they wish their services to come from the state, the private or voluntary sector. There are at least three other ways in which service users in the community may see themselves other than as consumers. Care management arrangements need to adapt to people rather than vice versa. Twigg's contribution is a short excerpt from a much longer article, containing an important discussion of the meaning of care given at home and the relations of power and dependency that this involves. In the extract reprinted here, she suggests that care previously defined as 'medical' is increasingly shifting to 'social'. One consequence, when care is defined as social, is less agreement that it should be paid for from a public rather than a private purse, and where provision does remain public, the tussle between health and Social Services as to who picks up the tab will almost inevitably, it seems, deflect attention from goals of ensuring a full range of relevant services to a local population.

Moving from thinking about users to thinking about providers in the new care regime, Annandale's research with hospital nurses provides a particularly vivid picture of the way in which new consumerist expectations on the part of service users can produce a sense of threat and defensive practice on the part of providers. She argues that today's nurses are experiencing a 'risk culture', in part because rising and sometimes unrealistic expectations are encouraged by the 'new NHS'. Another consequence of the new regime is revealed by Hadley and Clough. Their book *Care in Chaos* contains a set of profoundly pessimistic frontline accounts from service providers of the health and social care arrangements following the 1990 Act. Included here is the case of a social worker providing a service for people with learning disabilities. We cannot know at this stage how representative this account might be of services across the country as a whole, but the themes in this extract appear with some regularity in the writings of social workers who feel themselves de-skilled by the new regime.

The excerpt from the work of Linda Jones starts to show what a full evaluation would involve. She rightly points out that it is too soon for a full assessment of the consequences of the 1990 changes. Her detailed grasp of health care organization, however, gives a reader a sense of the complexity of the changes and the range of results, intended and unintended, that are emerging. Lack of accountability is the factor she particularly singles out. Since she wrote, some of the further restructurings that she hints at have come to pass, and a series of White Papers and consultative documents suggest that yet more change – to general practice and to Social Services, for example – could soon be under way.

What direction of change do we really want? The final two contributions provide a sharp contrast, judging the 1990 changes in the one case as a 'reform too far' and in the other as not at all far enough.

David Marsland is that rare breed, a right-wing sociologist. For him, the health and social care changes of the Conservative governments were only a start. He wants to see a thorough dismantling of the welfare state – in his view it has created dependency and brought expectations for care services which, far from addressing vulnerability, have served to extend it. For a contrast to this, we turn again to the authors of *Care in Chaos*. They would sweep away the market principles that are embodied in the 1990 legislation. They do not recommend a complete return to the previous regime, but a debate that recognizes the inevitability of dependency and creates a new consensus on how to approach care through a mix of public policy and mutual help. Two opposing principles for a good society – self reliance and mutuality – emerge starkly from this contrast. Probably neither can lead policy on its own. If we are to have a new debate, more people and more diverse people need to enter it to enrich our understanding of what is involved in health and social care and how it can best be provided. More people need to be asking the key policy question, 'In what combinations should the state be providing care for us, be enabling us to care for ourselves or be helping to foster some kind of community of mutual help?' After all, one thing that is certain is that we all need health and social care services at some time in our lives.

Celia Davies

# 29

# Becoming Consumers of Community Care: Households within the Mixed Economy of Welfare

*John Baldock and Clare Ungerson*

> Habits of the heart; notions, opinions and ideas that shape mental habits; the sum of moral and intellectual dispositions of people in society: not only ideas and opinions but habitual practices with respect to such things as religion, political participation and economic life. (Alexis de Tocqueville)

In a recent and very influential study of the culture and character of American life, a group of sociologists has built upon this idea [the idea that people have moral and intellectual dispositions which translate into habitual practices] to construct a typology of 'habits of the heart' (Bellah 1988: 37). Here we attempt to use the same approach to capture the variety of behaviour in the care market.

Figure 29.1 'Habits of the heart' describes the distinctions we wish to draw. It positions people along two axes. The horizontal axis describes the degree to which the stroke survivors and their carers [in our sample] expected their care to be provided from their own resources or from some kind of collective provision; it distinguishes an individualistic from a collectivist view of welfare. The vertical axis measures people's views of how active they would need to be in order to obtain services; it is a measure of participation. Thus, the figure presents a model that distinguishes four types of disposition towards the provision of care at the beginning of our study: consumerism, welfarism, privatism and clientalism. What we are presenting are 'ideal types' of care consumers. Rarely were any of our sample solely of one category or another. The function of ideal types is to represent the theoretical range of individual examples. No particular individuals or households corresponded exactly to one or another of the categories; in fact most cases demonstrated elements of each. We shall characterize the qualities of each category by constructing cases that typify them but which are no more than composites of cases we found in our sample.

From John Baldock and Clare Ungerson (1994) *Becoming Consumers of Community Care: Households within the Mixed Economy of Welfare.* York: Joseph Rowntree Foundation. pp. 49–54 (abridged).

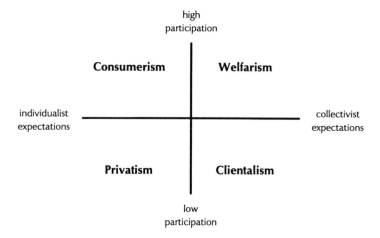

participation

**Consumerism**                    **Welfarism**

individualist                                               collectivist
expectations                                               expectations

**Privatism**                    **Clientalism**

low
participation

Figure 29.1   *'Habits of the heart': models of participation in the care market*

## Consumerism

At its extreme this is a view that expects nothing from the state and intends to arrange care by actively buying it in the market or providing it out of household and family resources. There were relatively few examples of this view in our sample. Such people were not ignorant of public provision but were sceptical about whether it would suit them. They might doubt its quality but more often they found it inconvenient and time-consuming to use. For example, they objected to the inflexibility of the day hospital or, at the other extreme, the uncertainty about who would come and when in the case of public domiciliary services.

Clearly this is a view which is easier to hold if one has enough money to pay for what one wants but it was not a position limited only to the better off in our sample. People in this category are used to the control and autonomy that being a customer brings and do not like the uncertainty about who is in charge that using voluntary or public services may bring. Thus we found some people with low incomes who would always prefer a private, for-payment arrangement where possible. For example, one elderly couple, both of whom were disabled, appeared to have over the years established very reliable relations with a local taxi driver, a local jobbing builder, a nearby grocer and a butcher (both of whom would deliver) and a number of neighbours who would do odd tasks for payment. For quite small amounts of money this couple appeared to be able to obtain very prompt and flexible attention which they could control. Their instincts were always to use their own initiative. They did not wish to be indebted to anyone and they regarded the increasingly occasional visits of social workers or community nurses as almost purely social events. It must be added that these two people were immensely charming, even jolly; their 'business relationships' had a large non-commercial component.

## Privatism

People who fell largely into this category did the least well in terms of support. Many sociologists have commented on the growth of what has been termed 'privatism' in British life.[1] It is associated with owner-occupation and thus, in retirement, quite often with moving to a new home in an unknown neighbourhood. Attention is 'devoted overwhelmingly to home and family based life rather than to sociability of a more widely-based kind' (Goldthorpe, 1969: 103). Privatism has also been closely associated with the growth of mass consumerism. 'Ordinary people now demand ever-increasing amounts of consumer goods which they place and use in their own homes. The result is that external and community facilities become marginal to their way of life' (Saunders, 1990: 277). This is a rather passive form of consumerism where most of the work is done by the producers and retailers and requires little initiative from consumers other than the act of purchase itself.

Such a privatized existence may work well when people are fit and well and the things they want are the products of mass consumerism. When they become ill and dependent and require products and services that are not available 'off the shelf' they have much more difficulty. In our sample these people had tended to refuse help when it was initially offered at the point of discharge. In some cases they very determinedly would not accept an assessment or any care management. They strongly valued their autonomy and would say things like 'we've never depended on other people. We've always looked after ourselves.' At home, as the months went by, we found them increasingly puzzled, embittered and, in some cases, frightened. Few of the skills and attitudes they had accumulated during their fit years seemed to serve them well now. What they needed was not advertised nor available in the ready way of the consumer goods they were used to buying. Neither were they accustomed to the ways of the voluntary and community-based support system.

Some found their few unavoidable encounters with neighbours or voluntary help very difficult. For example one carer-wife whose husband had always done the driving found the process of negotiating her way round the local parish lift scheme quite excruciating. She felt her privacy invaded, and she was having to beg and to justify her private choices. In seeking to take advantage of a private and market-based approach to home care, policy-makers do not seem to have appreciated how impersonal and passive much of more conventional 'participation' in the market is.

## Welfarism

This is a set of attitudes and an approach that is associated with such ideas as citizenship and welfare rights. These are people who believe in the welfare state and their right to use it. This implies the active pursuit of one's entitlements. People in this group tend to be educated, articulate and may well have worked in the public sector.

The clearest example in our sample was a retired physiotherapist married to an ex-headmaster. She was impressively effective in obtaining the best of what was available in the public and voluntary sector. By the end of the six months she was attending the day hospital three times weekly but only for so long as was required to receive the physiotherapy she wanted. She had used an NHS domiciliary dentist and an NHS chiropodist who also visited her at home. She attended the stroke club but had refused an offer from a private domiciliary agency because she 'didn't like their money-making approach'. This stroke survivor's most outstanding, but very rare, characteristic was the way she had very explicitly participated in the assessment made by her case manager. They had reached a clear agreement on what she needed, what she might need in the future and how she would go about contacting the social worker when necessary. However, much as this whole approach was in tune with a citizenship-based conception of welfare, it was equally obvious that if more than a very few people operated in this way the public sector would rapidly be overwhelmed.

## Clientalism

This was a common approach amongst our elderly and often low-income sample. It is the 'traditional' way of using the welfare state; passive, accepting, patient and grateful. These people, unlike the privatists, did not refuse or question what was offered. They are accustomed to using what the welfare state offers, adjusting to its rigidities and accepting its omissions. It is a stance that works well where one's needs are high and manifestly so, such as where the stroke survivor was bed- or chair-bound. One does best if one does not get better; indeed more services will tend to appear the longer one is known to the services and the less well one does. However, this approach also brings with it the classic and well-known disadvantages of public provision. It is inflexible and time-consuming. Those services one does receive (day hospital, home care) are rigid in what they can provide and when.

At the same time the public provision leaves gaps. There were things it could not do; for example, put one to bed late. One wheelchair-bound stroke survivor preferred not to go to bed before about 11 p.m. because otherwise her very frail husband would have to help her to the toilet during the night. Although a care assistant came each evening largely to help the woman to bed that is not in fact what happened. In other cases the classic inflexibility of public services was not a matter of timing but rather a bureaucratic inability to deal with a quite simple problem: for instance, removing a carpet that made it impossible for an elderly woman to use her walking frame or, in another case, providing a much-promised bed-board that might have allowed the client to sleep and so greatly improved the quality of life of an elderly couple who still shared a double bed.

It was amongst those in our sample who most nearly fitted this category that we found the puzzling denial of having been assessed, even of having a care manager where we now know one was very much involved. In its most extreme form, the passivity of this stance seems to hide from people even the organizing and planning that is being done for them. They find the ways of the welfare system and its staff unpredictable and do not attempt to understand or change them.

### Conclusion

The 1992 Conservative Party election manifesto emphasized ' a society in which government doesn't try to take responsibility away from people' and which gives 'the power to choose – to say for yourself what you want' (Conservative Central Office, 1992). This is a theme which has been pursued in many policy documents and in important legislation such as the National Health Service and Community Care Act 1990 which prescribes more explicit roles for the family and voluntary and private services in the provision of welfare. The argument is that these policies fit more closely with the preferences and habits of the British people.

We have *not* found this to be a false assumption but rather that the issues involved are far more complicated than has been allowed for. In the case of care in the community, we have discovered that the emergence of a satisfactory mixed economy of care will require not that people behave according to the established 'grain' of everyday life but that many of them make considerable adaptations. Most people are indeed capable of making such adaptations but the changes involved are not simple ones to do with obtaining information or receiving assistance with the organization of care. Both of those were offered in abundance to our sample but often fell on deaf ears and provided a rather poor return on effort.

What has been misunderstood is that effective participation by needy people in the mixed economy of care requires that they change values and assumptions that are quite fundamental to how they have lived their daily lives hitherto. We have called these 'habits of the heart' in order to emphasize how deeply embedded they are in people's existence. [. . .]

Movement across the 'map of care' requires that people learn new 'scripts' which describe and legitimize the choices they must make. If assessment and care management are to work, indeed if their existence is even to be grasped by some service consumers, then they must understand and contribute to this process of rescripting.

Two very practical lessons follow:

- Assessment is often unlikely to be understood and participated in by consumers in the early stages of their new dependency. Assessment must either become a more staggered, drawn-out and continuous process or it must be updated at specific intervals.
- The content of assessment and care management must move beyond questions of information and organization. In many cases, it will need to address directly the need that dependency brings to construct a new 'script' for life in terms of daily routines and the values that inform them. People find it difficult to choose their own community care; they need help to learn how to do so.

## Note

1  For a summary see Saunders (1990: 275–82).

## References

Anderson, R. (1992) *The Aftermath of Stroke: the Experience of Patients and their Families.* Cambridge: Cambridge University Press.

Bellah, R. (1988) *Habits of the Heart: Middle America Observed.* London: Hutchinson Education.

Blaxter, M. (1976) *The Meaning of Disability.* London: Heinemann.

Conservative Central Office (1992) *The Best Future for Britain.* London: Conservative Central Office.

Goldthorpe, J.H. (1969) *The Affluent Worker in the Class Structure.* London: Cambridge University Press.

Morris, J. (1993) *Independent Lives: Community Care and Disabled People.* Basingstoke: Macmillan.

Parker, G. (1993) *With this Body: Care and Disability in Marriage.* Buckingham: Open University Press.

Saunders, P. (1990) *A Nation of Home Owners.* London: Unwin Hyman.

Shearer, A. (1981) *Disability, Whose Handicap?* Oxford: Blackwell.

# 30

# The Medical/Social Boundary

*Julia Twigg*

## The medical/social boundary

The boundary between the medical and the social is a shifting one, constructed in complex ways that reflect both institutional and ideological factors.

### Institutional factors

Across modern welfare systems the boundary of medical and social care is an area of tension, where it falls a product of different institutional histories and different underlying philosophies of welfare (Esping-Andersen, 1990; Pierson, 1991). The boundary is not defined in a single, simple way but constructed by a series of overlapping distinctions in which payment, nature of care and locus of responsibility reinforce and interact with each other in complex ways, and that themselves change through time. Long-term care falls across the boundary of medical and social, indeed the fact that the health care needs so identified are long term and chronic is important in their construction as semi-social. The rising proportion of older people in the population and growing anxieties among policy-makers and politicians as to the future funding of their support has resulted in pressure to redefine the nature of the care of these groups and to shift its locus out of the medical and into the social sector. As we shall see, this recasting of chronic need as in some sense social in character is closely related to the question of payment.

As cost pressures have borne down on the NHS there has been a tendency for the institution to retreat to the medical heartlands of acute hospital care. Within the institutional culture, this represents 'real medicine', the territory whose status is high and unambiguous, as opposed to the grey areas of long-term and community-based care whose status is low and whose legitimacy as part of medicine less certain. High-tech intervention, orientation to cure, clear locus

Originally published in *Journal of Social Policy*, 26(2), 1997: 211–32 (abridged).

within the hospital, all characterize this medical heartland. The boundary between the medical and the social thus overlaps significantly with the boundary within health care itself between high-status medicine and what is seen simply as 'care'. Chronic conditions where there is little prospect of cure and few opportunities for medical intervention are relegated to the territory of care. As medicine retreats in its institutional basis, so these areas of long-term care are exposed as marginal, capable to some degree of being reconstituted as social care.

The retreat of medicine from the area of long-term care is not simply a negative one but results also from countervailing forces asserting the importance of the social. Concern with the over-medicalization of life problems arises out of the critiques of modern medicine made by Illich and others from the 1960s and 1970s (Illich, 1975; Doyal with Pennell, 1979). In recent years these arguments have been advanced particularly strongly by the disability lobby who reject the dominance of the medical model both in terms of the definition of disability and the model of care (Morris, 1991; Oliver, 1990). Similar ideas underwrite the emphasis on normalization within learning disability, with its desire to throw off medical dominance and assert instead the primacy of ordinary life (Ryan and Thomas, 1987). In relation to older people the issue has been less ideologically driven, but the influence of these ideas has still been felt and underwrites current debates as to where the boundary of medical and social care should lie.

The medical/social boundary needs to be understood in terms of public versus private responsibilities. Across welfare systems, medical care is recognized as having a special legitimacy. There is a wide acceptance that it is something that should be available to the individual free from direct concern over cost. In many systems this translates directly into the provision of medical care free at the point of use. The assumption is not a universal one and medical care in the US offers an example of a much more clearly commodified system. Even here, however, there are elements of recognition that medical care is not simply a consumption good. The special status of medical care lies in contrast to that of social care, where the legitimacy of public provision is weaker. Social care is part of social life, and as such it represents something that you are primarily expected to pay for yourself. Welfare states differ in the degree to which they regard social care as a private as opposed to collective responsibility: and that boundary is differently drawn in, for example, Sweden as opposed to Germany or the United States (Lesemann and Martin, 1993; Glendinning and McLaughlin, 1993; Evers, 1994). All systems, however, retain some sense of social care as an area of personal responsibility.

It is this traditional assumption that underlies the current – though still unacknowledged – attempt by the government in the UK, though also in other countries, to move the costs of long-term care away from the publicly funded sector of health care and into the arena of social care, which is increasingly seen as one where the individual must expect to fund him or herself. The broad distinction between free health care and self-funded or means-tested social care has become increasingly sharp in Britain as local authorities have moved towards charging for the principal services of community care – home, day and respite care – previously provided free or on a varying but nearly always non-commercial basis. The division between health and social care is increasingly a division between care that is free to the individual and that which has to be funded from his or her own purse.

The sharpening of the boundary between medical and social care at a national level has been reinforced by developments at the front line of provision (Wistow et al., 1994; Butcher, 1995; Lewis and Glennerster, 1996). One of the consequences of the purchaser/provider split in the UK is that patterns of payment and responsibility have become more transparent. Exactly who does what is increasingly defined not by institutional structures but directly in flows of money. [. . .]

## Touching

The empirical literature on touch has largely been concerned with rules regarding who may touch whom. Different parts of the body may be touched by different persons, and this reflects distinctions in relation to sexual and social intimacy (Jourard, 1966). But touch is also associated with hierarchy and the expression of authority, with the powerful touching the less so, superiors touching inferiors. Touch is thus a vector of status, authority and dominance. There are gender differences in the reception of touch, with women more likely than men to be touched (Jourard and Rubin, 1968). This appears partly to reflect their inferior position within patriarchy (Henley, 1973), but may also reflect a greater emphasis on tactility in the upbringing and culture of women. There is some evidence that while women evaluate touch by a service provider positively, men do not (Sussman and Rosenfeld, 1978; Whitcher and Fisher, 1979). Whitcher and Fischer suggest that this is because men interpret touch as a sign of inferiority and dependence which they have been socialized to reject.

Apart from this social-psychological literature, there has been little detailed treatment of the subject of touch. What there is, however, is a pervasive view in the literature that modern Western society is peculiarly non-tactile (Synnott, 1993). Contrasts are drawn with non-Western societies and with the historical past, both of which are perceived to be more tactile in character. Touch is thus drawn into the debates about modernity, with the decline of touching linked to the theme of the growing impersonality of modern society. Within a

Weberian perspective, the retreat from the tactile represents a bodily version of the established themes of rationalization and disenchantment.

Although it is hard to evaluate these claims adequately, there is some evidence to support the idea that there was more social touching in the past. In general, touch appears to have become narrower in its scope and more confined to sexual relations. Part of the difficulty in evaluating such claims lies in the fact that the literature itself reflects cultural shifts and preoccupations. Much of it dates from the 1970s, and its celebration of touch, of the bodily and the emotional as opposed to the cerebral and rational, is part of the periodic upsurge of neo-romanticist ideas, which in this period took the form of the counter-culture and its wider cultural manifestations (Roszack, 1969; Campbell, 1987).

The literature on touch has in general had little to say about the situation of older people. The bulk of this work is either about babies, stressing the importance of touch for thriving, or younger people (Montagu, 1986). This is despite the fact that there are reasons to think that the old are among the most deprived in terms of touch. Many older people have no close living relations who can be a focus for touching. The modern eroticization of touch may affect them in particular, as partners die and there are few opportunities to establish new touching relations. At a service level there is also evidence of an absence of touch, with nurses more reluctant to touch older compared with younger patients (McCorkle and Hollenbach, 1984; Aguilera, 1967).

The meaning of touch is also affected by its relation with employment. Touching work is, in general, lowly work. Within the care field there is a clear pattern whereby the more senior the profession or the grade of staff, the less likely the practitioner is to be directly involved in touching the patient. We can see this in the past in relation to the elite London physicians who did not actually handle the bodies of their patients. They might observe and diagnose, but did not condescend to touch; this was left to nurses or lower-status practitioners (Heath, 1986). Touch threatens care professionals with the status of the body servant. Part, though only part, of the low status of bone-setters and osteopaths lay in the fact that they touched and manipulated the bodies of their patients. There is a recurring pattern in professionalization whereby as an employment group establishes its body of theory and its status, so it retreats from manual labour and direct physical contact with the client. This tendency can be observed even in nursing where direct hands-on contact has always been a central part of the work. Dunlop criticizes a dematerializing tendency in recent nursing literature in which the body becomes etherealized as the focus of concern moves from the physiological level to the – academically more promising – psychosocial. She notes how this has gone hand in hand with a progressive devaluation of physical care, which is increasingly delegated to lower orders in the nursing hierarchy (Dunlop, 1986). The recent history of bathing in the community illustrates this, with the shift to skill mix in which tasks like bathing are relegated to unqualified staff (Lightfoot et al., 1992).

The association of touch with lowly status is in contrast to the earlier account in terms of hierarchy and the expression of power. The tension is however resolvable once we recognize that in work with clients and patients both meanings are present: the service provider is dominant through touch, but also reduced in status by virtue of it. Here we can begin to see some of the social ambiguities that mark this field.

Lastly we turn to the question of payment and the position of touch in a commercial setting. Touch, because of its associations with closeness and relatedness, is generally seen as something apart from the commercial, for-purchase world of the economy. Individuals do buy forms of personal attention like hairdressing or beauty treatments that involve touching, but this is rarely an overt aspect of provision (though critics of the non-tactile nature of modern society argue that it underlies their appeal). The direct purchase of touching services, because of the elements of intimacy and relatedness inherent in touch, tends to be, if not taboo, at least located on the edges of the socially respectable, as the ambiguous position of massage illustrates. The one area of touch where purchase is openly accepted is in relation to alternative therapies, one of whose strongest unifying themes is the direct use of touch in both diagnosis and treatment (this is in contrast to the a-tactile character of dominant allopathic medicine). In such cases the legitimacy of touch is in terms of medicine, or at least therapeutic intervention.

In relation to social care, however, the context is more problematic. Part of the difficulty that social care agencies have with the provision of bathing and other aspects of personal care arises from the absence of any commercial model of provision. To a significant degree, the community care needs that have traditionally been recognized and met by social care agencies are those that have had a prior existence within the formal economy. Certain needs, for example for meals or laundry, have proved relatively unproblematic to define and meet because there has been a pre-existing model for their public, social production. Housework has proved less easy to externalize as it cannot be taken out of the domestic sphere as meals and laundry can, but there is a long-established history of waged domestic labour (Gregson and Lowe, 1994) that underpins its provision in the public sector also. Personal care, of which bathing is an element, is however different. It has not traditionally been subject to this sort of commercial production; and that is one of the reasons why agencies have found its provision more ambiguous. The definition of personal care is that which an adult would normally expect to do for him or herself. It thus precisely delineates the aspects of daily life that are not externalized or commodified but that remain personal to the individual. There is no pre-existing commercial model of provision upon which social care agencies can draw; and the only available model, as we have seen, is a medical one.

# References

Aguilera, D.C. (1967) 'Relationship between physical contact and verbal interaction between nurses and patients', *Journal of Psychiatric Nursing*, 5: 21.

Butcher, T. (1995) *Delivering Welfare: The Governance of the Social Services in the 1990s*. Buckingham: Open University Press.

Campbell, C. (1987) *The Romantic Ethic and the Spirit of Capitalism*. Oxford: Basil Blackwell.

Doyal, L. with Pennell, I. (1979) *The Political Economy of Health*. London: Pluto.

Dunlop, M. (1986) 'Is a science of caring possible?' *Journal of Advanced Nursing*, 11: 661–70.

Esping-Andersen, G. (1990) *The Three Worlds of Welfare Capitalism*. Cambridge: Polity Press.

Evers, A. (1994) 'Payments for care: a small but significant part of a wider debate', in A. Evers, M. Pijl and C. Ungerson (eds), *Payments for Care: A Comparative Overview*. Aldershot: Avebury.

Glendinning, C. and McLaughlin, E. (1993) *Paying for Care*. London: HMSO.

Gregson, N. and Lowe, M. (1994) *Servicing the Middle Classes: Class, Gender and Waged Domestic Labour in Contemporary Britain*. London: Routledge.

Heath, C. (1986) *Body Movement and Speech in Medical Intervention*. Cambridge: Cambridge University Press.

Henley, N.M. (1973) 'The politics of touch', in P. Brown (ed.), *Radical Psychology*. London: Tavistock.

Illich, I. (1975) *Medical Nemesis*. London: Calder & Boyars.

Jourard, S.M. (1966) 'An exploratory study of body accessibility', *British Journal of Social and Clinical Psychology*, 5: 221–31.

Jourard, S.M. and Rubin, J.E. (1968) 'Self-disclosure and touching: a study of two modes of interpersonal encounter and their inter-relation', *Journal of Humanistic Psychology*, 8(1): 39–48.

Lesemann, F. and Martin, C. (eds) (1993) *Home-based Care, the Elderly, the Family and the Welfare State: An International Comparison*. Ottawa: University of Ottawa Press.

Lewis, J. and Glennerster, H. (1996) *Implementing the New Community Care*. Buckingham: Open University Press.

Lightfoot, J., Baldwin, S. and Wright, K. (1992) *Nursing by Numbers? Setting Staffing Levels for District Nursing and Health Visiting Services*. York: Social Policy Research Unit.

McCorkle, R. and Hollenbach, M. (1984) 'Touch and the acutely ill', in C.C. Brown (ed.), *The Many Facets of Touch*. New Brunswick, NJ: Johnson & Johnson.

Montagu, A. (1986) *Touching: The Human Significance of Skin*, 3rd edition. New York: Harper & Row. First published 1971.

Morris, J. (1991) *Pride against Prejudice: Transforming Attitudes to Disability*. London: The Women's Press.

Oliver, M. (1990) *The Politics of Disablement*. London: Macmillan.

Pierson, C. (1991) *Beyond the Welfare State? The New Political Economy of Welfare*. Cambridge: Polity Press.

Roszack, T. (1969) *The Making of the Counter Culture.* New York: Doubleday.
Ryan, J. and Thomas, F. (1987) *The Politics of Mental Handicap.* London: Free Association.
Sussman, N.M. and Rosenfeld, H.M. (1978) 'Touch, justification and sex: influences on the aversiveness of spatial violations', *Journal of Social Psychology,* 106: 214–25.
Synnott, A. (1993) *The Body Social: Symbolism, Self and Society.* London: Routledge.
Whitcher, J.S. and Fisher, J.D. (1979) 'Multidimensional reaction to therapeutic touch in a hospital setting', *Journal of Personality and Social Psychology,* 37(1): 87–96.
Wistow, G., Knapp, M., Hardy, B. and Allen, C. (1994) *Social Care in a Mixed Economy.* Buckingham: Open University Press.

# 31

# Working on the Front Line: Risk Culture and Nursing in the New NHS

*Ellen Annandale*

This chapter begins with a discussion of nurses' and midwives' perceptions of the risk climate in which they work and its associations with the culture of consumerism and the new NHS. This is followed by an analysis of the effects that this climate has upon relations with colleagues and with patients. [. . .]

## The data

The data come from a study of legal accountability in nursing and midwifery that was conducted in 1994. They are drawn from two sources: a questionnaire survey of all trained nurses and midwives who were employed in one hospital trust in late 1994, and in-depth interviews with nurses working on the neurology services of a different hospital trust. [. . .]

The data extracts are presented verbatim except where the notation (. . .) is used. Where the staff designation is in parentheses (i.e. staff nurse) this indicates that the data come from the survey sample. Where interview data are used, the designation precedes the dialogue (i.e. staff nurse: . . .).

## A climate of risk

> You can't really put your finger on it, what it is. And it's like at the moment you feel you've got to watch your back all the time. That's the sort of atmosphere it is. That you can't . . . if you're talking to somebody you've got to be careful. That's the feeling: the openness has gone. (sister)

> I think nursing *is* stressful, but as far as accountability is concerned . . . you see it's something you think about *all* the time. It's not here in front of your head, it's in the *background* and I think until something comes up, a mistake has been made, then you're made aware of it; that's when you start thinking about it. (staff nurse)

Originally published in *Sociological Review*, 94(3), 1996: 416–51 (abridged).

As these comments reveal, risk surrounds practice, it is in the *background*, there is an *atmosphere*: it is always there. As one staff nurse explained, it is 'always on your mind that you may be held responsible in a legal dispute for actions or words'. Or, as one sister more graphically put it, 'litigation is the "bogey man" that stands behind my shoulder as I practise as a midwife'. This atmosphere engenders a feeling of vulnerability, a fear that you may do the 'wrong thing' or, more worryingly, that whatever you do may not be 'right'.

> You hear of others 'being held accountable' and begin to fear that whatever you say or do may not be right. And you begin to feel more alone. (staff nurse)

Feeling vulnerable or under suspicion means working under 'a constant awareness that you may be subject to criticism, quite often in an unrealistic way' (sister).

The recognition that 'since we are all human, we can all make mistakes' only adds to this vulnerability, particularly when, as one nurse put it, 'I am constantly being made aware that every little thing that is done could in the future be used against me' (staff nurse).

Feelings of vulnerability, the sense that the future haunts actions in the present, can create a fair degree of stress. Indeed, only 23 per cent of the survey sample reported that concerns with legal accountability did not cause them 'any stress at all', while 60 per cent said it caused them a 'little' and 17 per cent a 'great deal' of stress. General fears of either making a mistake, experiencing a complaint or being sued, and a general fear of the nurses or midwives' actions being used against them, were identified as the source of this stress by just over 40 per cent (others referred to more specific aspects of practice which will be discussed, below).

It could be argued that these concerns are intrinsic and long-standing to medical and nursing work. Signs and symptoms do not order themselves into neat diagnostic categories, nor do they unequivocally signal the 'correct' treatment regimen. Rather, the process of acquiring, interpreting, managing and reporting 'the disorders of human illness' is an error-ridden process (Paget, 1988: 34). Yet the nurses in the survey and interview samples felt almost without exception that the concerns that they identified were of *recent* origin. Over 55 per cent of the survey sample felt that legal accountability had become a concern over the last three years, and 37 per cent over the last five years. The sample was asked to indicate (yes/no) whether *each* of the factors listed in Table 31.1 was a reason for increased concern about legal accountability.

Clearly, the awareness of patients and their relatives, the concern of professional bodies (like the Royal College of Nursing, Unison and the UKCC), and to a lesser extent, the professionalization of nursing, and increased concern expressed by hospital trusts, all heighten

Table 31.1   *Reasons for increased concern about legal accountability (those answering 'yes')*

|                                                  | Number | %  |
|--------------------------------------------------|--------|----|
| Patients/relatives more aware of their rights    | 298    | 98 |
| Increased concern from professional bodies       | 235    | 76 |
| Professionalization of nursing                   | 156    | 50 |
| Hospital trusts/management more concerned        | 185    | 60 |
| Other                                            | 38     | 12 |

concern. However, a much clearer hierarchy emerges from the sample when they are asked to indicate the *main* reason for increased concern. Here the increased awareness of patients/relatives was the predominant factor by far, mentioned by 65 per cent. The concern of professional bodies (12 per cent), the professionalization of nursing (11 per cent) and the concern of trusts/management (6 per cent) were seen as far less significant. [. . .]

The fact that some respondents referred to *both* patient awareness *and* the changing organization of hospitals (particularly managerial changes) suggests that they may have a combined, perhaps even mutually reinforcing effect, upon the climate in which nurses and midwives work:

> As the public becomes increasingly more aware, particularly with the Patient's Charter in force, and with the advent of trusts, it seems that nurses are more responsible for themselves and have less support from employers. (staff nurse)

## Consumers as risk generators

The phase 'patients are more aware of their rights' was a constant refrain in both the nurse interviews and survey data. This *awareness* seemed to be an omnipresent cloud hanging over daily practice. Although consumerism need not be viewed negatively, it was often taken to be a new and rather malevolent presence which was resented by staff:

> *Staff nurse*: The introduction of the Patient's Charter gets Joe Public to go to bat. It's quoted considerably in the hospital, people quote it to you. So there's an emphasis on 'my granny needs to see a surgeon', you get quite a bit of that. You got it even *before* the Patient's Charter came out, when it was a White Paper.
> *Int.*: You mentioned talk about the White Paper around the hospital?
> *Staff nurse*: By patients and relatives. And in the community. People are more aware of what they're entitled to and expect standards to be higher than they used to be. Whether it's through the media, I don't know. But I've found that; they're very articulate.
> *Int.*: What about?
> *Staff nurse*: Nursing care, waiting lists: 'My mother's not been seen.'

The notion of 'patient awareness', which is really a summary term for an assemblage of concerns, is perceived as something that is imported into the hospital from without. Thus, as illustrated in the preceding dialogue, it is seen as motivated by the Patient's Charter. Broader social changes are also seen as culpable.

> People are becoming more aware of their rights, and appear to be more concerned with mistakes and unreliability in all aspects of life unfortunately. (staff nurse)

They know more, want and expect more information:

> Before, I think people used to sit back and say Oh, they're in hospital and, you know, 'let the doctors and nurses get on with it, they know what they're doing.' But with erm, there's so much hype, so much information from the media, they tend to question things because they're more aware of the things that *could* go wrong. (staff nurse)

The consumerist attitudes that are expressed in a desire for information can become particularly hard to take when they also involve a desire to blame someone for a 'bad outcome'. This is something that was particularly to the forefront of midwives' concerns:

> People generally have high, unrealistic expectations and think pregnancy, birth and newborns should be planned and perfect in line with their ideals. When it doesn't, they sue the pants off professionals. (sister)

The sense that patients and relatives are 'looking over the nurse's shoulder' undoubtedly generates personal vigilance over the nurse or midwife's actions and the actions of others:

> I think with the press, people are more aware of their rights and things like that . . . Whereas before people, if they weren't happy with something, say they had a complaint to make, they perhaps wouldn't make it. Whereas now, I think they're more eager to because they're more aware of their rights from that point of view and you need to be *aware* of what you're doing more and more. I suppose you've always *been* accountable, *even more* so now because you need to document things more and be more aware of . . . it's always in the back of your head, you know, that you've got to be careful what you do because patients, you know patients are more likely to complain. (staff nurse)

But since patients' awareness is an awareness of nurses' and midwives' practice, it can also be experienced as a form of threat and a lack of trust:

> Although at the time you feel you have done the right thing, often people, mainly relatives, interfere and question if you have given the right treatment in an attempt to intimidate you by suggesting they will take further action. (staff midwife)

[. . .]

Patient-consumers are expected, incited even, to secure their rights under a contractual model of social relations in the NHS, something which is made quite clear in the Citizen's and Patient's Charters

(Walsh, 1994). If they feel that their rights and expectations are not being met patients are encouraged to complain to the relevant authority, which is reflected in the notable rise in NHS complaints over recent years. The 1994 Health Service Commissioner's report revealed a record 1,384 complaints for 1993–4, a 13 per cent increase over the previous year. Most strikingly, hospital complaints in England took a massive leap from 32,996 in 1990/1 to 44,680 for 1991/2 (DoH, 1994). Medical malpractice litigation has also increased markedly over the last decade, contributing to fears that a trust could find itself unable to pay if faced with a series of major damages over a short period. Indeed, Health Authority spending on awards for clinical negligence rose from £53 million in 1990/1 to an estimated £125 million in 1993/4 (Harris, 1994). In response to these concerns a Special Health Authority has been set up to manage a pooled Central Fund for Clinical Negligence.

Evidently a sense of moral panic has been created by a fear of complaints and litigation (Dingwall, 1994). As we have seen, some nurses and midwives see the Patient's Charter as a catalyst for the assertion of patients' 'rights'. Yet surveys suggest that up to 40 per cent of the population may not even have *heard of* the Charter (Cohen, 1994; Mahon et al., 1994). Similarly, while informal complaints may be increasing, there are as yet few examples of litigation against nurses in Britain. Very few of the respondents in the current research actually said that they had been involved in a formal complaint. Moreover, only a minority of those who were asked in interview were aware of what would happen in the hospital if a complaint was made against them, nor were they aware of the legal definition of mal-practice. In their minds informal complaints, formal complaints and litigation seemed to merge to form an undifferentiated whole. There is, then, a sense in which the new consumerism may be more apparent than real. Perhaps, in line with findings for physicians in the US (Ennis and Vincent, 1994), nurses and midwives overestimate the *true* risk of experiencing a complaint or a malpractice suit. [. . .]

A good part of nurses' and midwives' concern seems to derive from the perception of *individual* responsibility and accountability to patients. As Hugman (1994: 215) remarks, 'market consumerism in health and welfare can be seen as the attempt to promote the patron-age model of professionalism' and to extend the power of service users over professionals. This is part and parcel of what Dingwall (1994: 47) has called a new mode of governmentality which 'segments indi-viduals into bundles of discrete interests pursued through specific and limited agreements'. Sanctified by the individualistic model of the law, this new mode of governmentality has the effect of directing health care providers away from the holistic care of the individual towards 'the servicing of human bodies under a series of specific agreements between purchaser, provider and consumer, an auto-mechanic's model of medicine' (Dingwall, 1994: 60). Clearly, the 'accountability' that the health care provider now owes to her or his client is individualized. This was clearly recognized by respondents who stressed that 'errors and inaccuracies come back on the individual more' and consequently, 'at the end of the day, it's your neck on the line'. Nurses' individual responsibility is enshrined in the UKCC Code of Conduct (1992). Indeed, the UKCC's assistant registrar for standards and ethics explains that while previously, the Code only said that *each* nurse was accountable, 'the 1992 document explicitly says that "you are personally accountable"'. This was changed, he states, to emphasize that nurses have a 'direct-personal accountability' for their practice (Pyne, 1994). Codes of professional conduct, then, are couched in the language of professionalism with duties and obligations described as 'individual ownership and responsibility for nursing actions' (Kendrick, 1995: 267).

But it is precisely this sense of ownership of one's own work that seems to be missing in the accounts that we have looked at so far. [. . .]

## Working in the new NHS

The radical changes set in train by the NHS and Community Care Act of 1990 (DoH, 1989) have gained so much momentum that the formal structure of health care now bears little resemblance to that which existed even a decade before. These changes were premised on the vision of a costly and inefficient service marked by stultifying bureaucracy and driven more by the needs of professionals than the provision of quality care to patients. The internal market has sought to introduce accountability into the system at every level, making clinical and financial decision-making more visible through contracting, standard setting and audit mechanisms. In line with broader changes in the economy, this shift has been accompanied by new '"leaner and flatter" managerial structures, decentralised cost centres, devolved budgets, the use of performance indicators and output measurement, localised bargaining, performance-related pay, and customer-oriented quality service' (Pinch, 1994: 207). On the face of it, this new organizational context would seem to cohere well with nursing's professionalizing strategy. Yet devolved authority 'does not in itself guarantee that the staff who are "close to the customer" will gain greater control over decision-making' (Walby et al., 1994: 16). As the following discussion will demonstrate, nurses feel that they have responsibility, but sometimes little control. In this context individual accountability can be experienced more as downward pressure than personal autonomy:

> I feel there is less support from management. More putting the blame on individuals. (staff nurse)

I'm concerned because management won't back you up, and someone is always singled out to take the blame. What if someone sues me? (staff nurse)

We feel that our numbers are more at risk than ever before and authorities use personal accountability to free themselves of responsibility. (staff nurse)

Apparently, in the nurses' and midwives' opinions it is '*individuals* who are blamed', 'someone is always *singled* out', authorities use '*personal* accountability'. The fact that many nurses and midwives may conceive of individual accountability as a management tool does little to lessen its impact on their day-to-day experience. [. . .]

Some nurses made a direct link between what they saw as the hospital trust's fear of the costs of litigation and downward pressure on them as individuals. For example,

Trusts will shift blame on to individuals so as not to incur heavy claims for damages. (sister)

This may be bound up with the fear of actually losing one's job or professional registration:

*Staff nurse*: In the present climate, I think everyone wants to keep their job. And everyone is so aware that jobs that were once secure now aren't. And I think that's the one thing that frightens most nurses more than anything.
*Int.*: Why has that changed?
*Staff Nurse*: Because of the economic climate of the Health Service and because . . . you know, *no one* in my group who I qualified with has got a permanent contract. So it's a matter of keeping your nose clean, otherwise you don't get your contract extended. And it's the same with a lot of other staff as well; they *can* be replaced. There are so many nurses out there.

The problem for many of the respondents was that in their opinion management expected them to assume responsibility as individuals, but consequently failed to provide a safe environment in which they could work. Ironically, in the minds of a number of nurses, this only served to increase the likelihood that mistakes would occur. This is made clear in the following remarks:
[. . .]

Lack of resources; equipment, manpower, time and finance, are taking their toll on the sort of service we can provide. People are given wonderful choices and they are disappointed when they are let down – they complain, quite rightly so. But we don't have the resources to back up the choices they are told they are entitled to. (sister)

## References

Cohen, P. (1994) 'Passing the buck?' *Nursing Times*, 90(13): 28–9.
DoH (Department of Health) (1989) *Working for Patients*. London: HMSO.

DoH (1994) *Being Heard, The Report of a Review Committee on NHS Complaints Procedures* (The Wilson Report). London: DoH.

Dingwall, R. (1994) 'Litigation and the threat to medicine', in J. Gabe, D. Kelleher and G. Williams (eds), *Challenging Medicine*. London: Routledge. pp. 46–64.

Ennis, M. and Vincent, C. (1994) 'The effects of medical accidents and litigation on doctors and patients', *Law and Social Policy*, 16(2): 97–121.

Harris, J. (1994) 'The price of failure', *Health Service Journal*, 14 April: pp. 6–10.

Hugman, R. (1994) 'Consuming health and welfare', in R. Kent, N. Whitley and N. Abercrombie (eds) *The Authority of the Consumer*. London: Routledge. pp. 207–22.

Kendrick, K. (1995) 'Nurses and doctors: a problem of partnership', in K. Soothill, L. Mackay and C. Webb (eds), *Interprofessional Relations in Health Care*. London: Edward Arnold. pp. 239–52.

Mahon, A., Wilkin, D. and Whitehouse, C. (1994) 'Choice of hospitals for elective surgery referrals: GPs' and patients' views', in R. Robinson and J. Le Grand (eds) *Evaluating the NHS Reforms*. London; Kings' Fund. pp. 108–29.

Paget, M.A. (1988) *The Unity of Mistakes. A Phenomenological Interpretation of Medical Work*. Philadelphia: Temple University Press.

Pinch, S. (1994) 'Labour flexibility and the changing welfare state: is there a post-Fordist model?', in R. Burrows and B. Loader (eds), *Towards a Post-Fordist Welfare State?* London: Routledge. pp. 203–22.

Pyne, R. (1994) 'Accountability'. Presentation to West Midlands Regional Health Authority, Advanced Nurse Practitioner Working Groups. 9 August.

Walby, S. and Greenwell, J. with Mackay, L. and Soothill, K. (1994) *Medicine and Nursing*. London: Sage.

Walsh, K. (1994) 'Citizens, charters and contracts', in R. Keat, N. Whitley and N. Abercrombie (eds), *The Authority of the Consumer*. London: Routledge. pp. 189–206.

# 32

# Learning Disabilities: a Service in Jeopardy

*R. Hadley and R. Clough*

The county Social Services department (SSD) was divided into geographical divisions, each of which was virtually a mini-Social Services department embracing field, domiciliary, day and residential care. Fieldwork was organized in area teams each of which consisted of three sub-teams dealing with children, mental health and learning disabilities, elderly people and physical disabilities. While all ongoing work was covered by the specialist teams, initial referrals were received by duty officers, drawn in turn from these teams. The duty officers were expected to have the generic skills to take any immediate action needed on referrals and, if appropriate, then pass them for further work to the relevant specialist team. In the case study team leader's (TL) area, such referrals were normally in the hands of the senior of the appropriate team by the end of the day in which they came in.

## The work of the mental health/learning disabilities team

While the team was responsible for both kinds of clients, over the years there was an increasing emphasis on specialization, with different workers concentrating on mental health and on learning disabilities (LD).

When a referral of someone with learning disabilities was made to the team, the social worker to whom the case was allocated did an initial assessment and plan.

> With our clients there was seldom any immediate rationing based on rigid eligibility criteria. There was clarification of the department's role and the initial assessment would go on over some weeks because LD clients are a lifetime commitment. You are not into spot provision. You are into a life plan.

Social workers had increasing discretion in setting about finding appropriate services. Assessment was seen as an ongoing activity,

---

From R. Hadley and R. Clough (1991) *Care in Chaos*. London: Cassell. pp. 111–21 (abridged).

taking place alongside provision. Where that provision involved other professionals such as community nurses or day care staff, it could take on a multidisciplinary character. The work of finding appropriate placements and building or supporting care systems for people with learning disabilities, was aided by a growing co-operation between different parts of the Social Services department and with different agencies with responsibilities in the field; by an increased devolution of responsibilities and access to resources by workers and carers; and by the creativity of workers encouraged by these developments.

Inside the Social Services department the specialist learning disability services in field, residential and day sections were becoming more cohesive, aided by the appointment of a manager for learning disabilities at divisional level. Work with the health service was enhanced by a joint strategy at the local level and common membership of the community mental handicap team. At the individual level, workers from different agencies routinely worked together on the same cases. There was also considerable co-working with private and voluntary homes in seeking to adapt the care provided to individual needs.

Intra- and inter-organizational co-operation was made easier by the increasing devolution of decision-making to the social workers and operational managers such as day centre managers. Social workers negotiated directly with day services and hostels for places. Once regular short-term care was agreed and set up, carers could themselves take on arrangements for hostel stays or family support, within an agreed limit.

Relations with senior management tended to be positive. At the divisional level managers regarded the LD services as 'the flagship' of the development of needs-led services aimed at developing potential and minimizing dependency. Further, while the team did not control access to scarce outside resources, it did at least have a voice in decisions made about their use. For example, the county succeeded in freeing some of its resources, previously used to support LD clients in out-of-county placements, to facilitate creative and imaginative work by social workers to support clients and their carers in their own homes and to access community facilities for them.

Further, the team leader said, sometimes management would find ways round the rules, for example making it possible to switch money from a residential establishment to support work in the community.

> Now management would say that the old management colluded improperly with the workers to make these things happen. From the perception of the workers, management was being supportive, creative and actually using their common sense about delivering a good service. It's funny how we yearn for those nice people in division! We used to mutter about them then!

These positive aspects of work in the LD field were, nevertheless, offset to a considerable extent by the inheritance from the very different approach of the old mental handicap services. Many resources were tied up in existing buildings and services, and controlled under rigid budget heads. Old ways of working often persisted, too. In addition, there was a lack of the range of appropriate specialist services needed if the aims of making it possible for LD clients to live in the community in small groups or on their own were to be realized. In particular, the department's home help service could seldom provide the services needed by LD clients, objecting that they were too difficult, or required specialist skills, or needed help at the wrong time of the day.

## Advantages and disadvantages

The team leader felt that there was much that was positive about the LD services in his area before the changes. There was a strong feeling that they were steadily improving as increased specialization was introduced, co-operation with other agencies was strengthened, more decisions were devolved to the team, and workers were becoming increasingly creative in shaping needs-led services. The frustrations facing the team focused centrally on the legacy of the bricks and mortar approach of the past and the lack of appropriate services to allow the full development of normalization. In that context, the community care legislation with its emphasis on supporting clients in their own homes and freeing up the resources for such needs-led services was seen as holding positive promise.

## The team leader's personal experience of the job

The TL got considerable enjoyment from his job, particularly prizing the feeling that he had his own territory, that he understood the world he was operating in, and felt that he had his place in it. He could say then

> I've got my manor. I know the people who I'm serving. I've got an overview and most of the people I know personally and I know I can often respond to them because I know a lot. It was the individuality and flexibility, the feeling about the relationships with a relatively small group of clients.

Having his place in this world, he said, 'gave me a certain degree of power and I knew where to go for the next bit of power'. The frustrations of the job were related to the difficulty, in the bricks and mortar culture, of freeing up the resources the team needed to help its clients, his own personal dislike of the generic work he had to do in the area team whenever it was his turn to do intake duty, and the at times overwhelming workload.

He felt secure in his work and able to speak out freely in the organization. He was not aware of pressures to conform and noted that even this bureaucratic department was prepared to tolerate eccentrics whose administrative work might be poor but whose work for clients had wide respect. [. . .]

## The organizational changes

The early implementation papers following the 1990 Act suggested different ways of introducing a purchaser/provider split in SSDs. This county chose the most radical, implementing the split at the front line by separating the assessment of cases and decisions about what provision should be made, from the provision of service itself. The authority was divided into separate purchasing and providing sections for all services except childcare. All existing staff were required to apply for jobs in the new organization and there was no guarantee that they would be able to keep the same kind of work as they had been doing.

The county was subdivided into divisions. Each was headed by a purchasing manager who deployed a number of assessment teams. Many of the social work staff, especially in the elderly and physically disabled teams, were transferred to roles as social work assessors in these teams or as care managers. The bulk of the other front-line staff of the authority – in the residential, day care, field and domiciliary services – were transferred to provider teams, within a different organizational structure.

Learning disabilities was preserved as a provider service. The TL was appointed to head a social work team specializing in LD, covering territory previously served by two area teams. Other LD specialist services from the department as well as from health were also located in the same building. [. . .]

## After the changes

During the first year following the changes the experience of the new LD team was a mixture of positives and negatives. On the downside, the team had to contend with a complex and unhelpful referral process. Specialist long-term social work was to be commissioned following assessment by a social worker in one of the case assessment teams (purchasing). If a client required a complex package of care he or she was to be referred to care management (purchasing) instead. If clients were under 18 they were to be the responsibility of the special needs children's service. [. . .]

Early in the second year, the real implications of the new system became increasingly apparent to the TL. This was partly a result of the full operationalization of the new structure but the whole process of change was given a violent impetus by the financial crisis which hit the department, along with other shire counties. [. . .] The new organizational structure had to rapidly find means of cutting several millions of pounds from its budget. It was in this context that the LD team became sharply aware of the deficiencies and contradictions of the new system in which it found itself confronting a management that had once seemed sympathetic and friendly, if paternalistic, but which was now recast almost as an opponent to be fought and out-witted in the struggle to provide clients with a decent service.

Key issues identified by the TL are the problems of the purchaser/provider split, the damage to inter-agency relationships, the side-lining of social work, and the character and behaviour of the new management.

## Contradictions of the purchaser/provider split

For the TL

> the division of the department into purchasers and providers has virtually resulted in two departments. There has been little common agreement about service objectives and principles. At times there seems to have been more effort put into fighting each other than in providing a service. Since the purchasers hold the purse-strings, specialist provider social work has little influence.

The concept of separating assessment from intervention is, in his view, 'fundamentally flawed'. Its contradictions are particularly clearly illustrated in the case of LD clients for whom a long-term and holistic perspective is usually required. Ironically, the introduction of quasi-separate assessment has not resulted in needs-led, individually designed services. Instead.

> people have been 'slotted in' and subjected to disabling and limiting generic regulations far worse than before the Community Care Act. Case assess-ment social workers have usually little specialist knowledge or under-standing of learning disabilities and have little time to carry out an assessment which they were generally expected to complete in a single visit.

The result, from the point of view of clients and carers, is that services are

> complicated, fragmented, and delayed by the split between case assessment, care management, and social work. They are left confused and irritated. It is even worse for a child transferring to adult services. Enormous amounts of time, effort and paper go into just making the system work rather than providing a service.

Further, the hoped-for new specialized services for people with LD have not emerged. Support available through the care management section of the department is limited to providing strictly personal care and is not available to help clients to develop independence. Independent sector alternatives have not materialized and are unlikely to since the 'ceilings' imposed by the department's purchasing managers on hourly rates of pay and the price of total packages remove any incentive to potential providers with appropriate expertise to become involved.

### The decline of inter-agency co-operation

The purchaser/provider split, which has taken place in the health service as well as in Social Services and the separate assessment of social care needs

> has colossally undermined formal inter-agency working. Colleagues in health feel excluded from assessment and planning. There is now a major social/health care argument with little of the mutual help and co-operation that existed before. Clients are losing out on services as a result.

The old flexibility in which workers from different departments or services co-operated to support and cover for each other in working with a client is no longer possible:

> A community nurse might only be allowed to do things to do with the maintenance of someone's health through advice on diet and personal hygiene in contrast to the system before the changes when she might call in to see if they are OK and perhaps advise them how to manage their bills. Supposing the social worker was on leave, the community nurse might cover all the things the social worker had been doing. In return the social worker might check the medication was being taken. Now they are not supposed to do it.

### Marginalizing social work

These processes have had the effect that, in the TL's words, 'social work has been totally sidelined'. Its status is reduced to 'counselling' which 'should occasionally be used to render some of the more difficult customers a bit easier to manage. If they are still difficult, the social worker has failed.' The social workers in LD are now labelled providers and are not responsible for decisions as to whether clients should get a service or not.

However, when the TL pointed out to a purchasing manager that he didn't believe, therefore, that his team should be expected to say 'no' to a client,

> The manager got really angry at that point and said 'Yes it is, it's social workers' responsibility to say no. That's exactly what it is.' The catchphrase in the department is 'the providers should own the department's budget'. The purchasing manager says: 'The trouble with your team is that they don't own the budget.' Owning the department's budget means, apparently, not advocating for your clients' needs.

Advocating for resources for a client, or even drawing attention to unmet need, which once would have been accepted as the job of the social worker (whether or not the resources were available to help), are now, according to the team leader, likely to be seen as hostile acts.

> Nowadays they say you are disloyal. It's as though they have no respect for your judgement. In the past people respected that you were making a professional judgement and giving them your advice on your considered view and they received that in that spirit. Then they said 'yea' or 'nay'. Nowadays they resent us making such requests and are in effect saying 'What the hell are you doing coming up here and saying this to us? What you are saying to us is absolutely subversive and a sacking offence.'

Most recently, the whole future of the LD teams in the county appears to be in doubt as it has become known that the director feels there is no longer a need for a specialist provider service and would like to see the social workers in the existing teams remustered as generic care managers in the purchasing part of the department.

## The making of macho management

These interchanges with management are typical of the much more abrasive style of leadership that began to surface at the beginning of the changes. 'It was as though they had been briefed to suddenly introduce that kind of style to Social Services management.'

It became increasingly clear that a new culture was developing in the management of the department which was driven first and foremost by the budget and the need to balance the books, and which was to be delivered in a new management style, wrapped in the language and style of a commercial business. Behind it all was an overriding demand that appearances should be maintained, and that the department should present a picture of an organization that was coping. [. . .]

The team leader's overall view of the impact of the Act on his organization was extremely negative. There was decreasing recognition of specialist needs: decreasing co-operation between workers and external agencies; decreasing emphasis on needs-led, individualized services; a concentration of power and decision-making in the hands of the purchasing managers; services were finance-led 'to an astonishing degree'; no value was placed on professional judgement which was being replaced by rules and 'tick the box' evaluations. The result was an extremely demoralized staff. [. . .]

## For the future

In the TL's view planning is essential in the provision of LD services but is currently virtually impossible with the purchaser/provider split.

Providers are not supposed to do it and purchasers are totally taken up with the 'here and now'. Planning and preparing for the future is the absolute core of what most LD social work is about and is the central dilemma for most families with an LD member. Individual personal plans have virtually been abandoned as 'useless' to purchasers and the multi-agency approach is also largely seen as irrelevant.

The team leader would like to see the return to a *whole-hearted* service for people with learning disabilities. A crucial element in this would be the development of close collaboration in joint planning with health. But even more important, in his view, is to make it possible for professionals to get on and do what they know how to do. 'It could be done *now* if they *trusted* us.'

# 33

# Evaluating Market Principles in Health Care

*Linda J. Jones*

How successful have the changes in the National Health Service been? One problem to face is that it is too early to come to any final conclusions. It is also clear that the 1990 reforms exposed and accelerated trends in health care already apparent in the 1980s. The decline in acute beds, for example, was a marked feature of the 1980s, fuelled by changes in medical technology which increased minimally invasive surgery and day surgery. Any judgement about the 1990 reforms must acknowledge that rapid change was already taking place in health care. It must also acknowledge that market principles have not been allowed free rein in the health service, and that government direction and control of the market is still very evident. [. . .]

On the political left the creation of NHS trusts and general practice fundholders was met with deep scepticism and seen as a way of distracting attention from the real issue in health care: its chronic underfunding. There is now less antipathy to trusts, providing they can be brought to heel by tough purchaser health authorities, but suspicion about fundholding endures. General practitioners are not necessarily to be regarded as the most suitable defenders of patients' interests, as the Conservative government has cast them. Let's begin with a provisional evaluation of the 1990 government reforms which introduced quasi-markets and contractualism.

## Hospital trusts

The first wave of 57 NHS trusts mainly consisted of acute general hospitals, but district community services, mental health and handicap services, specialist hospitals and ambulance services all contributed some candidates. In April 1992 a second wave of 99 NHS trusts opted out of district health authority control, and this has been followed by further waves. Each trust is run by a board of

---

From Linda J. Jones (1994) *The Social Context of Health and Health Work.* London: Macmillan. pp. 521–30 (abridged).

directors as an independent business, free to acquire and dispose of
assets and to determine staffing, pay, working conditions and skill
mix, although output levels are negotiated with purchasing authorities (Bartlett and Harrison, 1993). The cost of trust status – the
board, staffing, business planning and so on – is high, estimated at
between £500,000 and £750,000 a year for acute trusts and £250,000 for
community trusts. Most of these costs would have been met regionally
or centrally before 1990. The high costs of trust status and the high
fixed costs of running hospitals, together with rapid technological
change, have made acute trusts vulnerable in the new internal
marketplace. The loss of even small contracts, when fundholding GPs
or purchaser district health authorities (DHAs) decide to move
business elsewhere, can mean the difference between breaking even
and running at a loss. Of the first wave of 57 trusts eight failed to
achieve the required return on capital and two did not manage to
break even (Newchurch and Co., 1993).

To date most of the contracts that have been negotiated by the
DHAs with the trusts have been *block contracts*: in other words, a
contract in which the purchaser agrees to pay the provider trust an
annual amount in return for using a broad range of agreed services.
Only a minority of NHS trusts have become involved in *cost-per-case
contracts*, in which prices are set for each type of treatment (NAHAT,
1993a). This is mainly because very little information currently exists
about the cost of individual treatment (Bartlett and Harrison, 1993).
However, this type of contract is widely used in the United States and
undoubtedly will be adopted here. It would have the effect of making
health care costs more transparent and would enable the construction
of competitive 'league tables' of costs of treatments in different trusts
– a process which the New Right would claim as extending consumer
sovereignty. The extension of cost-per-case contracts will also put
acute trusts under greater pressure to cut costs, resulting in mergers
and in the disappearance of some trusts altogether.

Mergers of acute hospital trusts are already a marked feature of
health care in the 1990s, and the drive to reduce costs by lowering
labour costs has been evident. The impact on staffing has been
significant, with redundancies and changes in skill mix threatening
nursing in particular. But the mergers and closures are not just cost-
cutting exercises. They are also evidence of the impact of technological change, in particular the rapid rise in day surgery, in new
surgical techniques which are less traumatic and do not require long
hospitalization, and in out-patient care. In Birmingham, for example,
43 per cent of planned surgery is already done on a day case basis. It
has been argued that even with the loss of far more acute beds the
average district general hospital will be able to serve a population 50–
100 per cent bigger by the end of the 1990s (Newchurch & Co., 1993),
and projections are that as few as 28 high-technology hospitals,

supported by locality hospitals for day cases, could provide all UK secondary and tertiary care (*Guardian*, 3 January 1994). It was on this basis that the Tomlinson Report (DoH, 1993) recommended rationalization of hospitals and a shift of funds to primary and community health services in London, but such changes are now being planned over all Britain. They will not, however, get through without enormous difficulty, partly because of public distaste for hospital closure but also because waiting lists have soared above one million and bed crises and treatment failures hit the headlines daily. It is difficult to justify closing hospitals which are breaking even and treating more patients than ever before, and where the level of need is evidently high. Hospital staff, faced with transferral or redundancy, have made common cause with patient and consumer groups to resist closures. Behind all this is the fear that freed resources will not be transferred into primary care but seen as 'efficiency savings' which must be used to meet NHS running costs.

## General practice and community trusts

Community trusts have lower management costs, but the entry costs for newcomers are much less and competition between the trusts is getting fierce. This may be one area where the private sector will make inroads in the 1990s. Technological and policy change is rapidly expanding the range of services that will be delivered by these trusts – through 'hospital-at-home' schemes, local treatment options and the extension of domiciliary care. They are coming under some pressure from GP fundholders, who have been encouraged by the new legislation to expand from being small businesses into large-scale enterprises and who want a flexible and responsive community trust to fit in with practice requirements. Some new models of primary–community linkage are emerging, such as the Lyme Community Care Unit model (Ham et al., 1993). In this instance two non-fundholding GP practices took over the management of community health services staff for their area and provided services for 8,000 patients under contract to Dorset.

GP fundholding involved nearly 20 per cent of GP practices and over 20 per cent of the population by 1993, and single-handed practitioners and smaller practices are being encouraged to form consortia and move into fundholding on a joint basis. Fundholders have real power in the market, not just as purchasers of care packages for their patients but as strategic players in the shift to primary-focused health care. An increasing number are contracting into their practices new services such as chiropody and occupational therapy and are undertaking some surgical procedures. Practice nurses' roles are being expanded and may engulf some of the work of the community nursing services hitherto carried out by health visitors, whose numbers are being cut back (*Guardian*, 6 October 1993). [. . .] A recent study concluded that 'GPs appear to have replaced hospital doctors and managers as the key advisers to DHAs' (Ham et al., 1993). Important initiatives are the use of GP surgeries for minor surgery and as centres in which to locate secondary care services. Physiotherapy, audiology, dermatology, child psychiatry and dietetics are specialities now being offered in some GP practices in some DHAs, such as Stockport, Dorset, Hampshire and Wirral (NAHAT, 1993a).

There seems to be a real possibility that community nursing could wither away as the opportunities for practice nurses expand. The result could be that community nurses are integrated into general practice, working under GPs. This may be hastened by the process of competitive tendering, in which the local community nursing service may not necessarily be awarded the contract to provide the local nursing service. If the link between nurses and the local community is broken, it will be very tempting for doctors to develop comprehensive, in-house nursing services. Added to this is the issue of community nurse identity in the future, in particular whether district nurses, health visitors and practice nurses should continue to be trained for distinct occupations. Some observers have highlighted the need for 'radical changes in working practices' and the 'removal of intra-professional boundaries' – which are linked with the need to reduce labour costs – as major priorities for the 1990s (Newchurch & Co. 1993).

### Evaluating the purchaser–provider split

Perhaps the biggest shake-up of all has taken place in the purchaser DHAs, squeezed by spending cuts and rising demands for health care. By 1993 mergers between DHAs were becoming commonplace, bringing economies of scale and aiding the drive to develop coherent health strategies based on significant populations. In Oxford Region, for example, the number of DHAs fell from nine to five, in North East Thames from 15 to seven, in Yorkshire from 16 to seven, in East Anglia from eight to a projected five by April 1994. This has resulted in increasing co-terminosity (shared boundaries) between DHAs and family health services authorities (FHSAs), such that enabling legislation has been called for to allow DHAs and FHSAs to merge (Ham et al., 1993). This would mean that one body performed all the work of purchasing, in association with GP fundholders, and could overcome some of the current fragmentation. Even without legislation a few DHAs and FHSAs have begun to work in close co-operation, just as DHAs and GP fundholders are forming new alliances to plan purchasing. [. . .]

In spite of such innovations the general picture is of much slower changes to traditional working relationships. Bartlett and Harrison's

(1993) study of the introduction of the quasi-market in health in Bristol and Weston Health Authority indicates that it 'will fail to operate in a competitive fashion in many local areas':

> The absence of a range of suppliers, and the likelihood of services being purchased almost exclusively by a single purchaser, suggests that competition does not exist in any real sense of the word. The potential for altering these conditions rests in part with the DoH and regional health authorities, but at a local level it may be argued that it is equally important for the purchasers of services to be willing to stimulate a range of suppliers, as to draw up well-structured contracts for the purchase of services. (Bartlett and Harrison, 1993)

From other studies, which looked at the potential for competition, it seems that quasi-markets may be able to operate, but this will depend on a number of factors such as population density and the readiness of patients to travel further (Appleby et al., 1991; Le Grand and Bartlett, 1993). GP fundholders are better placed to use a range of providers than health authorities, but the question remains whether this will benefit their patients. The creation of alternative suppliers is not likely to come about in the short term, and it is arguably not an efficient use of resources to spend money on creating competitors rather than improving existing services. To date there is a lack of evidence that trusts have enhanced patient choice. It is not patients who get to make choices about which hospitals are used, but GPs or health authority purchasers.

The development of comprehensive needs assessment strategies for their populations by DHAs, however, may enable them to improve standards of health care in the longer term and to shift the balance towards prevention and health promotion. [. . .] Le Grand and Bartlett (1993) conclude that further decentralization of purchasing may improve the operation of quasi-markets by making them more efficient and responsive and by enhancing choice. On the other hand they acknowledge that 'cream-skimming' by GP fundholders – that is, being more selective in choosing patients so that the old and chronic sick are excluded – is difficult to control and would lead to greater inequity in health care. They also note the large transition costs and, we might add, the considerable growth in health service bureaucracy – an estimated 40 per cent increase since 1990.

## Accountability

The lack of democratic accountability that now characterizes the new NHS, from government-appointed regional chairs through to the boards of hospital trusts and the role of the GPs, is perhaps the most worrying aspect of the changes. [. . .] There is no accountability at local level, apart from such monitoring as the community health councils (CHCs) are able to do. The NHS, the biggest employer of labour in the world with over a million workers, is of course democratically accountable to Parliament, via the Secretary of State for Health. The minister can be questioned, and the running of the NHS is scrutinized by the Select Committee on Health, the Public Accounts Committee and the Audit Commission. But this is the same minister who agrees the appointment of the chairs of the DHAs and FHSAs, appoints the chair and non-executive directors of the NHS trust boards and has until now been appointing the chair and non-executive members of regional health authorities – who in their turn have overseen the appointment of district chairs and managers. The opportunity for patronage in the health service, and for making 'political' appointments, has enormously expanded.

This has given rise to a fierce debate about accountability. While some have argued that DHAs should be brought under the control of local authorities (Harrison et al., 1990) others have pointed to the successive decisions by politicians over the last 50 years to keep the NHS under national and central control (NAHAT, 1993b). They point to the difficulties there would be in persuading FHSAs and GPs to work under local authorities and the problems inherent in any realignment of the purchaser–provider split. On the other hand the safeguards for the public in the present quasi-market system (apart from accountability to Parliament and CHC monitoring) rest almost entirely on the extent to which DHAs and trusts are prepared to allow their work to be scrutinized. NAHAT (1993b) has called for openness in board selections and dealings, for ethical behaviour and for links with the local community. But in a market system, where trusts are in increasing competition for patients and funding levels are not growing fast enough, it seems unlikely that widespread consultation with local residents and open door access to meetings and committees will be seen as a priority unless there is overwhelming pressure to do so. [. . .]

It is, of course, still very early to make any final judgements. [. . .] But as many critics have argued, equity and equality could be endangered by the restructuring of health and community care. The spectre of a 'two-tier' service developing in health care – as represented in the United States by an impoverished public sector and an immensely wealthy, highly expensive and interventionist private sector – is not a reassuring one.

On the other hand those on the New Right would argue that greater efficiency, effectiveness and choice can be promoted without damaging equity; indeed the New Right philosophy of personal freedom and natural inequality rests on the assumption that choice and equity are closely related. The notion of the sovereign consumer proposes that individuals make free and untrammelled choices in the marketplace of health or social care; since supply will balance demand, everyone – in theory – gets what they want. The fact that different entry points, resources and opportunities mean that everyone doesn't get a fair share is seen as natural and inevitable. The market provides a better way than any other of ensuring that everyone gets closest to gaining an equitable share. Critics of this view point to the inefficiencies of the free market in regulating the economy and argue that too high a price must be paid by some – through unemployment, poverty and lack of access – for the choice and personal freedom gained by others (Wilding, 1992). The assumption that everyone can participate in the free market of health care is mistaken; for example, most users lack the knowledge and information on which to base informed choices about their treatment and care.

## References

Appleby, J. et al. (1991) *Implementing the Reforms: a Survey of Unit General Managers in the West Midlands Region* (Monitoring Managed Competition, Project Paper 5). Birmingham: NAHAT.

Bartlett, W. and Harrison, L. (1993) 'Quasi-markets and the National Health Service reforms', in J. Le Grand and W. Bartlett (eds), *Quasi-Markets and Social Policy*. London: Macmillan.

Department of Health (1993) *The Tomlinson Report on London's Hospitals*. London: HMSO.

Ham, C., Scholefield, D. and Williams, J. (1993) *Partnerships in Purchasing*. Birmingham: NAHAT.

Harrison, S., Hunter, D. and Pollitt, C. (1990) *The Dynamics of British Health Policy*. London: Unwin.

Le Grand, J. and Bartlett, W. (1993) *Quasi-Markets and Social Policy*. London: Macmillan.

National Association of Health Authorities and Trusts (NAHAT) (1993a) *Purchasing for a Healthy Population*. Birmingham: NAHAT.

National Association of Health Authorities and Trusts (1993b) *Securing Public Accountability in the NHS*. Birmingham: NAHAT.

Newchurch & Company (1993) *Strategic Change in the NHS – Unleashing the Market*. London: Newchurch & Co.

Wilding, P. (1992) 'The public sector in the 1980s', in N. Manning and R. Page (eds), *Social Policy Review 4*. London: Social Policy Association.

# 34

# Principles of Reform

*David Marsland*

Radical reform is essential. Recent reforms, designed to target assistance more effectively, and to introduce competition, local management
and consumer choice within the existing state monopoly framework,
may secure some real improvement in the wasteful extravagance, gross
inefficiency and bureaucratic sclerosis of the welfare state. They are
unlikely, however, to provide adequate long-term, permanent answers
to the deep-seated problems of state welfare. For example, even after
the implementation of radical structural reforms in education and
health care, it seems certain that pressures for yet bigger increases in
resources will continue, and even escalate. Standards are improving,
but they are a long way short of adequate. Nothing less than the
disestablishment of state welfare, it seems, will suffice to produce the
levels of efficiency and effectiveness we have the right to expect from
these crucial services.

## Principles of reform

[. . .] I suggest that all those who are committed to freedom and to
genuine improvement in the real welfare of the British people ought
to speak up unapologetically for:

- a gradual but substantial expansion of the area of freedom and
  choice in welfare;
- a diminution of local and central state control in education,
  health, pensions and housing;
- a serious effort at targeting welfare help more purposefully and
  precisely;
- measures designed to strengthen the family, and to restore to it
  those rights and responsibilities for looking after its own which
  the welfare state has expropriated;

From David Marsland (1996) *Welfare or Welfare State?* Basingstoke: Macmillan. pp. 157–
60 (abridged).

- a continuing campaign to present to the public the positive attractions of enterprise, initiative and self-reliance, and to scotch the enervating influence of the poverty lobby and other friends of state power.

In the context of these objectives, welfare reform should be guided by three working assumptions. Together they define a principled approach to progress beyond state welfare.

First, genuine welfare depends entirely on economic progress and national prosperity. This in turn requires hard work and enterprising attitudes on the part of the population, and constant revivification of a dynamic enterprise culture. Anything which hinders economic progress threatens prosperity, or stifles enterprise is an impediment to genuine welfare. These impediments include: the remaining nationalized industries; bureaucratic big business; anti-competitive professional associations and trade unions; excessive tax levels; wage regulation; local government extravagance; and egalitarian social policies. No one who defends any of this collectivist baggage can be genuinely concerned about welfare whatever they may pretend.

Second, any compromise with the poverty lobby has to be avoided. Its arguments and influence have to be faced and answered. This largely state-financed network of academics, pressure groups and media operators is a powerful negative factor in any attempt at improving real welfare. Its spokesmen constantly exaggerate the extent of poverty. They disseminate misunderstandings of its nature and its causes. They deliberately paint the bleakest possible picture of social conditions. They peddle outdated bureaucratic-collectivist remedies to largely imaginary problems. I sometimes find it difficult to be sure whether they are being less than honest or worse than stupid. Unless their power, here at home and especially and increasingly on the European front, is controlled, we shall be dragged down before long to the levels of beggary from which the socialist world is only now seeking escape.

My third basic assumption involves trusting the British people. For despite what is often alleged, the British much prefer self-reliance and self-help – and the independence which accompany them – to state handouts. *They* know, even if the intellectuals and the mandarins do not, that socialism with a human face is a squared circle, that the welfare state is a treacherous, if tempting, snare, and that the world is a tough sort of place, with free lunches about as common as wasps that don't sting. Polling research which apparently reveals widespread support for state welfare and economic equalization is highly suspect, to put it no more strongly (Saunders and Harris, 1990: Harris and Seldon, 1987).

Beyond these three assumptions – no progress, no welfare; treat the poverty lobby with contempt; trust the people's independence of spirit

– there are a number of further principles which should guide the transformation of the welfare state into a genuinely free society.

First, welfare services should be provided by independent, competing suppliers – schools, colleges, doctors, clinics, hospitals, pension and insurance companies, building societies and so on – to the choice of consumers, and paid for either directly out of consumers' pockets, or by means of commercial insurance. The welfare state has done much to destroy the British people's traditional prudence. It will have to be restored, and linked to lifetime planning for self and family. The insurance industry and voluntary mutual associations will need encouragement to provide the essential mechanisms of self-reliance in a free society (Green, 1984). Why should not most people be responsible for their own insurance against employment, sickness and so on, and provide for their own positive needs, for education and housing for example, by the same means (Bell et al., 1994)?

Second, if the people are to take back responsibility for their own and their family's welfare, they will need relieving of a substantial proportion of the tax burden to which they have been unjustly subjected for 50 years to pay for the wasteful machinery of the welfare state. This has to mean serious reductions in income tax across the board, promised clearly and definitively beforehand, and delivered on time. It should also involve, on top of this, substantial tax rebates along the lines of the allowances introduced as part of the current health care reforms for private insurance of elderly parents. This aspect of welfare reform is necessary, and at the same time a source of potentially powerful support for its effective implementation. Real tax cuts could be even more attractive to voters in large numbers than were council house sales discounts or privatization share sales – both of them big vote winners.

Third, timing and phasing of the introduction of such radical reforms will be crucial to their success or failure. No one currently protected – or rather apparently protected – by state welfare provision should be compelled to exit, or find a service he or she has been taking for granted suddenly withdrawn. Detailed planning will be required, indicating plainly the phasing in of the various alternatives over a period of years.

Fourth and last, but by no means least, the principles governing social assistance for the – mainly temporary and fluctuating – minority of those needing special help will require very careful elucidation. It was to help this minority that the welfare state was first established. We have let it expand absurdly for no good reason at all, considering that standards of living have been improving rapidly and consistently during the period of its growth. We must at all costs prevent this recurring, or the whole reform process will be undermined. The crux is to avoid confusing disadvantage with inequality. There is no adequate reason for believing that even the relatively disadvantaged necessarily need long-term assistance. What they want is positive support, designed to restore them to self-reliance expeditiously.

The command economy of socialism is almost everywhere regarded today as an impediment to progress and prosperity, and a threat to freedom. Yet its precise equivalent in the sphere of those services we have been encouraged by socialists to define as 'welfare' remains entrenched in Britain and in much of the otherwise free world. We should let this 'command society' of the welfare state, this spurious community of bureaucratic rules and mechanically routinized practices, go the same way into the dustbin of history – and for the same reasons. It doesn't work, and it enslaves the people. We have to shift beyond 'welfare' towards a genuinely free society of self-reliance and enterprising initiative if real welfare is to be assured.

### References

Bell, M. et al. (1994) *The End of the Welfare State*. London: Adam Smith Institute.

Green, D.G. (1984) *Mutual Aid or Welfare State*? London: Allen & Unwin.

Harris, R. and Seldon, A. (1987) *Welfare without the State: a Quarter Century of Repressed Public Choice*. London: Institute of Economic Affairs.

Saunders, P. and Harris, C. (1990) 'Privatization and the consumer', *Sociology*, 24(1).

# 35

# Alternative Futures

## Roger Hadley and Roger Clough

The fundamental issues at the heart of community care are, in fact, first and foremost value issues. How do we define and respond to the vulnerability of the human condition? The way we answer this question relates to the way we define society and relationships within it. Women, for instance, provide by far the larger part of both informal and formal community care. The weakness of statutory support for informal carers and poor financial reward of most formal carers reflects and confirms their lower status. Community care must be looked at as part of society, not as a matter of alternative technologies. The systems in which we live and work are consequent on beliefs about people and their relationships, the nature of a good society and, at a level of greater detail, the very motivation for work.

## The neo-liberal project

Underlying the whole of the neo-liberal or Thatcherite project is a view of the nature of human beings and the dynamics of an effective economy. The substance and limits of this view are evident in all the major initiatives of the administration including the health and community care reforms.

At the core of this philosophy is the notion of the self-interested individual pursuing his or her own maximum good. Given the existence of a free market, the expression of individual needs and preferences will result in the greatest good for the greatest number. That greatest good is largely defined in terms of material wealth, and what it can buy. More complex definitions of social bonds such as 'society' have little meaning. The role of the state is to ensure the liberty of the subject and the free operation of the market. Public services beyond such functions, where politically realistic, should be purely residual, run on scientific management lines and designed to maintain the minimum level of existence required to ensure sufficient

---

From Roger Hadley and Roger Clough (1991) *Care in Chaos*. London: Cassell. pp. 206–11 (abridged).

social cohesion for the 'failures' in the system. People who devote their careers to public service for larger reasons are hard to understand in this perspective except as saints or charlatans. Inequality is an essential element in the dynamics of such a society, and relative poverty will always be with us. Money is the measure of all things.

This compressed view of the neo-liberal perspective necessarily fails to capture its subtleties and the extent to which it is subject to compromise in practice. But, in so far as it represents the underlying direction pursued by the administration, it helps to explain both the inadequate resourcing of the community care reforms and the contradictions in their structure and operation. The first is explained by the policy of residualism: the second can be attributed at least in part to mere indifference. [. . .]

At best, we believe, the neo-liberal view captures only a part of the human potential. Human beings are social animals. They are defined by their relations with each other. Conflict and competition are matched by co-operation and mutuality. 'Fraternity', 'sorority', 'sisterhood', 'interdependence', 'humanity' – all represent wider elements of our loyalties and concern for others (Beedell, 1989: 93) perhaps best captured in the term 'mutuality'. Such mutuality, meaning 'the recognition of mutual obligations to others, stemming from the acceptance of a common kinship' (Holman, 1993: 57) is an essential ingredient in some of the most important parts of our lives.

The very basis of the informal systems of care, which provide by far the largest part of care in the community, is just such mutuality: a complex set of interrelationships founded on a multitude of motives including love, empathy and obligation (e.g. Wenger, 1990, 1993), and in which direct material reward is certainly not the major force. Important though the satisfaction of basic material needs must be, people clearly have many more ways of realizing themselves than through accumulation and consumption alone, and the central institutions of our society such as the family, education, politics and religion bear witness to that fact.

It follows that if we are to work towards a society that recognizes this richness and variety in human beings and regards it as a strength, not a liability, it will be necessary to develop institutions more sensitive to diversity and the needs of the different groups it represents than any commercial market can be. [. . .]

The report of the Commission on Human Justice (Borrie, 1994) goes some way towards this but lacks clarity on the financing of community care. We believe that social care, as far as possible, should be financed collectively and be free at the point of use. How this might be achieved is a matter for national debate and decision.

Important as such a development would be, the problems that lead people to want and need support will not wither away. Fairer financing will mean that many people will be in a position where they will not need to call on the state for assistance. But the problems of dependency are not just those of money: they relate to the tensions and vulnerabilities that exist when, as adults, we are unable to cope. These are matters which take us back to the nature of society and the responsibility of one person for another.

Neither the market nor scientific management is compatible with a synergistic approach to collective action in the provision of community care. Public resources available for community care, in our view, should and could be significantly increased, but in the end they will always be finite. The issue of finding the most effective ways of using these resources remains. This calls for a continuing dialogue in every locality between all the contributors to such care and the ability to respond flexibly and creatively to any decisions which result, untrammelled by the rules of competition or the 'managers must manage' credo. We suggest that the following are likely to be required ingredients in developing a creative relationship between the different interests involved.

- *A national debate to determine the values and the objectives for community care.* Everyone should have the opportunity to be involved in the debate and it is essential to get as near as possible to a system based on shared values. From this *a nationally agreed framework* would define overarching objectives, financial resources, rights to services and information, and responsibilities and standards.
- *Locality control over resources and systems*, enabling their deployment in ways that reflect local priorities and maximize the development of local initiatives and creativity. Particular systems, such as the separation of purchaser and provider, should no longer be requirements. This demands an acceptance by central government, of whatever party, that the consequence of local citizen involvement will be local difference.
- *Service user and citizen involvement* to share in decisions over local strategies for community care and their implementation.
- *A new professionalism* based on the framework for effective service provision in community care, acknowledging a primary responsibility to users (e.g. Clough, 1990; Hugman, 1991) and aimed at making specialist help and advice available wherever it is needed.
- *A new managerialism*, drawing on the example of new wave management and giving priority to creating and supporting the conditions for a synergistic service culture.
- *Common regulations governing the support and operation of public and independent service providers*, thus dispensing with the current discrimination against the public sector.

One of the lessons to be learned from the systems imposed on public services by the Conservatives is that collaboration and co-operation cannot be taken for granted when changes are imposed. They are by-products of wider systems in which people find that it is worthwhile and possible to work with others. Trust is an essential element in such relationships but it cannot be decreed or demanded by managers; it grows from common commitments and understandings, and from experience. Sadly, trust has been one of the greatest casualties of the 1990 Act, victim of competition, secrecy and macho-managerialism. Only a new context, of the kind we have sketched above, and the opening of a dialogue at all levels, can provide the conditions for its revival. [. . .]

There are obviously many obstacles in the way of such changes. They imply a society in which power is far more decentralized, in which the intrusion of the market and neo-Taylorist management into the public sector have been curbed, and a general confidence re-established in the potential of public service. These in turn probably require constitutional reforms to reduce the overweening power of central government and its executive and to establish a more plural-istic and devolved form of government throughout the country. [. . .]

It is through local initiatives and in accessible and user-friendly settings that the basis for synergistic policy and practice is most likely to be established (e.g. Holman, 1993). There is already a history of pioneering practice in small-scale projects and schemes in which service providers have established close links with local communities in the shaping of the local personal social services (e.g. Hadley et al., 1987; Smale and Bennett, 1989; Bayley et al., 1989; Hadley and Young, 1990; Darvill and Smale, 1990; Martinez-Brawley and Delevan, 1993). These were mostly extinguished by the effects of the community care reforms but their example and experience offer a starting point for the development of policies of the kind we have described and stand as a reminder that innovation does not have to wait on grand reforms.

If this alternative future is ever to become a reality it is likely that it will begin with initiatives in the front line, where people know what the issues and problems are and have the vision and energy to tackle them in innovative ways.

## References

Bayley, M. et al. (1989) *Local Health and Welfare: Is Partnership Possible?* Aldershot: Gower.
Beedell, C. (1989) 'Investments in being looked after: an ideological commentary', in R. Clough and P. Parsloe, *Squaring the Circle? Being Cared for and Caring after Firth, Griffiths and Wagner*, Bristol: University of Bristol.
Borrie, G. (1994) *Social Justice: Strategies for Social Renewal.* London: Vintage.
Clough, R. (1990) *Practice, Politics and Power in Social Services Departments.* Aldershot: Gower.
Darvill, G. and Smale, G. (eds) (1990) *Partners in Empowerment: Networks of Innovation in Social Work.* London: NISW.

Hadley, R. and Young, K. (1990) *Creating a Responsive Public Service*. Hemel Hempstead; Harvester Wheatsheaf.

Hadley, R. et al. (1987) *A Community Social Worker's Handbook*. London: Tavistock.

Holman, B. (1993) *A New Deal for Social Welfare*. Oxford: Lion.

Hugman, R. (1991) *Power in the Caring Professions*. Basingstoke: Macmillan.

Martinez-Brawley, E. with Delevan, S. (1993) *Transferring Technology in the Personal Social Services*. Washington D.C.: National Association of Social Workers.

Smale, G. and Bennett, B. (1989) *Pictures of Practice, Vol. I: Community Social Work in Scotland*. London: NISW.

Wenger, G.C. (1990) 'Social support: the leaven in a changing world?' Introduction to special issue as guest editor, *Journal of Aging Studies*, 4(4): 375–89.

Wenger, G.C. (1993) 'The formation of social networks: self-help, mutual aid and older people in contemporary Britain', *Journal of Aging Studies*, 7(1): 25–40.

# Index

abuse, 173–4
  within the family,
    of children, 210, 246–57
    of elderly people, 173, 211, 258–61
  within institutional care, 209–10,
    212–28, 230–5
    of children, 209, 212, 214–16, 217,
      218–19, 222, 226, 227
    of elderly people, 218, 226, 230–5
access, rights of, in residential homes, 85
accountability
  lack of, 224–5, 264
  and the NHS, 299–301
  in nursing, 279–85
Action on Elder Abuse, 258, 259
acute hospital care, 272–3
Adams, Mary, 14
adolescent groups, house meetings for
    hostel residents, 111, 145–53
affluent society, and concept of
    community, 108–9
Aguilera, D.C., 275
Ahmad, B., 214, 218
Ahmad, S., 214, 216
Aitken, K., 179
All Wales Strategy, 202
almshouses, 65
alternative medicine, 97–8
Andover Union, 63
Annandale, Ellen, 264, 279–85
anonymity, in residential homes, 82–3
Anthony, James, 152–3
Appleby, J., 299
Arnell, Jane (case study), 136–7, 138
Arney, W.R., 123
asylums, 66–7
Atkin, K., 2
Atkins, Ernest (Tom), 14–16
attachment, and children from ethnic
    minorities, 100
attitudes
  towards ethnic minorities, 185–9
  see also racism

autonomy, in residential homes, 83–4
auxiliary nurses, bedroom abuse by, 230–5
Aveline, M., 145

Baldock, John, 263, 266–71
Baldwin, N., 60
Baldwin, S., 109, 164
Baldwin, Stanley, 106
Banta, D., 125
Barn, R., 214
Barnard, D., 119
Barnes, Marian, 113, 198–207
Barron, David, 16–18
Bartlett, W., 296, 298–9
'batch living', 71
Battle, J., 157
Bauman, Zygmunt, 213, 214, 226
Bayley, M., 309
bedroom abuse, 230–5
Beedell, C., 307
behavioural programmes, for children
    from ethnic minorities, 187–8
Bell, D., 107
Bell, M., 304
Benner, P., 4, 8, 56–8, 242, 243
Bennett, B., 309
Bennis, W.G., 152
Benzeval, M., 158
bereavement, and loss of one's home, 75
Beresford, P., 202, 203
Berry, A., 237
Bibbings, Annie, 112, 171–81
Biggs, Simon, 211, 258–61
Billingham, K., 155
Bilsborrow, S., 176
'binary management', 71–2
Bion, W.R., 153
Birmingham Community Care Special
    Action Project, 203
black and ethnic minorities
  children from see under children
  and health care, 97–8
  informal (unpaid) carers among, 177
  and residential care, 60–1, 91–103
  stereotyping of, 112, 183, 184–6, 214, 216

body care
  and nursing practice, 236–45, 275–6
  *see also* touching
Bonnerjea, L., 2
Booth, Charles, 64
Bornat, Joanna, 9–24, 111, 139–43
Borrie, G., 307
Braye, S., 203
Brettel, Caroline B., 34
Brisenden, Simon, 167
Brookwood Hospital, 223
Brotchie, J., 141
Brown, Hilary, 209–11
Browne, B., 78
Browne, K., 256
Bryar, R., 161
Bulmer, M., 106, 107, 108
bureaucracy, 214, 226
Burnside, I., 141
Butcher, T., 274
Butler, Robert, 139, 140–1
Bytheway, B., 3

Caesarean section, 126, 127
Calnan, K., 158
Campbell, C., 275
Campbell, R., 123
Canter, D. and Canter, S., 86
care plans, 99–100
Carers National Association, 2, 163, 173,
  177, 181
Carers (Recognition and Services) Act
  (1995), 2, 200
Carpenter, M., 201
Central Council for Education and
  Training in Social Work (CCETSW),
  112
certification, 66, 67
Chalmers, I., 125
Chard, T., 124, 127
Charlesworth, A., 2, 177
childbirth, 111, 123–7
children
  abuse of,
    within the family, 210, 246–57
    in residential care, 209, 212, 214–16,
      217, 218–19, 222, 226, 227
  as carers, 3, 176–7
  custody of, 67–8
  from black and ethnic minorities,
    disabled, 112, 182–9
  education of, 101
  residential care of, 94–5, 100, 101, 216,
    218–19
  *see also* adolescent groups

Children Act (1989), 100, 246, 252, 255
Church Hill House Hospital, 223
clientalism, 266, 269–70
clinical negligence, 283
closure, hospital, 297
Clough, R., 264, 287–94, 306–9
Cohen, P., 283
Coleman, P.G., 141–3
collective empowerment, 205–7
collective responsibility, 194
Commission on Human Justice, 307
commitment, of health professionals, 195
communication
  problems of, 186
  *see also* language
community
  concept of, 61, 104–10
  sociological approaches to, 106–10
community care, 3, 7–8, 11–13, 163, 164,
  266–71, 306–9
  *see also* family; health visiting; informal
    (unpaid) carers; social workers
Community Health House, 155–62
'community liberated', 108
community lost thesis, 107
community saved thesis, 107
community trusts, 297–8
complaints, hospital, 282
compulsory detention, 66–8
Connelly, N., 198
consultation
  with informal (unpaid) carers, 180–1
  with service users, 203, 308
consumerism, 266, 267–8
  as risk generator in nursing practice,
    264, 281–4
continuum model of abuse, 251
contractualism, 296
corruption of care *see* abuse
Coulter, A., 158
counselling, genetic, 187
covering tactics, for Parkinson's Disease
  sufferers, 115–16
Crick, Malcolm, 34
Croft, S., 203
Crossman, R.H.S., 220
Crowther, M.A., 64
cultural identity, 96
Custody of Children Act (1891), 67

Dalley, Gillian, 3, 164, 200
Dartington Social Research Unit,
  246–57
Darvill, G., 309
Davies, Celia, 1–5, 111–13, 190–6, 263–5

Davies, J., 158
Davis, F., 239
Delevan, S., 309
dementia, life-history work for people
  with, 111, 130–8
dependence, 166–8, 265, 308
depersonalization, 213, 214, 232
detention, compulsory, 66–8
deterrent purposes of institutions, 62, 63,
  65
Dingwall, R., 283
disabled people
  children from ethnic minorities, 112,
    182–9
  women, 112, 164–5, 168–9
  *see also* learning disabled
discrimination, 183, 184
  against informal (unpaid) carers, 177
disengagement theory, 143
district health authorities (DHAs), 298,
  299, 300
Dobroff, Rose, 139–40
Doyal, Lesley, 111, 123–7, 181
drug treatment, for Parkinson's Disease
  sufferers, 119–21
Dryden, W., 145
Duffy, Bernadette, 111, 145–53
Dunlop, M., 275–6

Ebersole, P., 141
economics *see* finance
economy, informal, 108
education, of children in care, 101
Edwards, Albert (case study), 132–4,
  137–8
efficiency, institutional, 221–2
Elbourne, D., 124
Elder, G.H., 142
elderly people, 204
  abuse of, 173, 211, 218, 226, 230–5,
    258–61
  life-history work (reminiscence) with,
    130–8, 139–43
  relocation of, 76–9
  in residential homes, 64, 76–7, 80–9, 218,
    226, 230–5
  and touching, 275
electronic foetal monitoring (EFM), 126,
  127
Elias, N., 236, 245
Ellis, K., 200
Ely Hospital, 220
emotional control, 241–4
'emotional labour', 4, 241
emotional neglect, 246, 254, 255, 257

emotional support, for informal (unpaid)
  carers, 173–4
employment
  casualization of, 108
  of disabled women, 168
  opportunities for unpaid carers, 175–6
empowerment, 109, 113, 198–207
enclosed organizations, 222–4
Ennis, M., 283
environment, of residential homes for the
  elderly, 80–9
episiotomies, 125
Equal Opportunities Commission (EOC),
  2, 3
equality, for informal (unpaid) carers, 177
Erikson, Erik, 141
Esping-Andersen, G., 272
Estes, Carol, 258
ethical considerations, 33
ethnic minorities *see* black and ethnic
  minorities
Evers, A., 273
exploitation, of informal (unpaid) carers,
  210

Faden, R., 125
Families Association, 156
family, 3
  abuse within the, 210, 211, 246–57,
    258–61
  and ethnic minorities, 98–9
  support from, 160–1
  *see also* informal (unpaid) carers
family health services authorities
  (FHSAs), 298, 300
Farleigh Hospital, 219, 223
Farmer, E., 251
Farrant, W., 158
femininity, 191, 192
Fever, Fred, 19
Fido, Rebecca, 13–14
finance
  and unpaid carers, 172
  *see also* resourcing of services
Finch, J., 3, 109, 163–4, 259
Fisher, J.D., 274
Fisher, M., 202
Fisk, Lyn, 111, 155–62
food, and ethnic minorities, 98
Foreman, David, 216
Foucault, M., 216, 261
Foulkes, S.H., 153
Fowles, A.J., 60, 70–4
fundholding in general practice, 295,
  297–8, 299

Gans, H., 107
Garcia, J., 123, 124, 125
Garforth, S., 125
*Gemeinschaft/Gesellschaft*, 106–7
gender
  of health care workers, 201
  and images of professionalism, 191–2
  inequalities of, 201, 217
  and touch, 274
general practice, 8, 48–55, 300
  fundholding in, 295, 297–8, 299
genetic counselling, 187
Ghate, Deborah, 253
Gibbons, Jane, 252
Gilleard, C., 174
Glasser, W., 146
Glendenning, F., 259
Glendinning, C., 273
Glennerster, H., 274
Glouberman, Sholom, 20–1
Goffman, Erving, 60, 70–4, 212, 215, 221, 227, 230
Goodwin, S., 155
Graham, H., 3, 158, 165
Grant, A., 126, 127
Grant, G., 200, 201
Green, D.G., 304
Gregson, N., 276
grief, at loss of one's home, 75
Griffin, C., 215
Grocke, M., 248, 249
group meetings, in hostels for adolescent girls, 111, 145–53
Groves, D., 3, 109, 164
Gutman, G.M., 76

Hadley, R., 264, 287–94, 306–9
Haight, B.K., 141
Hale, Susan, 140
Halsey, A., 106
Ham, C., 297, 298
Harris, C., 303
Harris, J., 283
Harris, R., 303
Harrison, L., 296, 298–9
Harrison, S., 300
Harvey, D., 108–9
Hastings, Clare, 56–8
health, determinants of, 158–9
health visiting, 111–12, 155–62, 297–8
Heath, C., 275
Heller, Tom, 8, 48–55
Hendrix, S., 141
Henley, N.M., 274
Herbert, C.P., 76

hierarchical structures, and corruption of care, 225
Hillery, G.A., 106
Hochschild, A.R., 4, 241
Hollenbach, M., 275
Hollinghurst, Val, 7, 36–9
Holman, B., 307, 309
Holocaust, 213
home, loss of one's, 75–9
Homer, A., 174
hospital admission
  compulsory *see* compulsory detention
  of elderly people, 77–9
hospital closures, 297
hospital trusts, 295–7
Hughes, M., 77
Hugman, Richard, 195, 283, 308
humiliation, 214, 215, 217

identity
  cultural, 96
  loss of, 72–3
Ignatieff, M., 62
Illich, I., 273
illness, lived experience of, 56–8
independence, 166–8
Independent Living Movement, 3, 166–8
induction of births, 126–7
informal (unpaid) carers, 2, 7–8, 36–47, 163–4, 171–81, 200–1, 210, 306, 307
  *see also* family
informalization, of economy and employment, 108
information, provision of, for informal carers, 174–5
informed consent, 33
Institute of Child Health, 248, 249
institutional care, 7, 9–24, 26–35, 59–68
  abuse within, 209–10, 212–28, 230–5
  *see also* life-history work; residential care; total institutions
institutional racism, 112, 183
Invalid Care Allowance, 172
isolation
  involuntary, 215
  professional, 220

James, N., 4, 195
Jamieson, Jessie (case study), 134–6
Janowitz, B., 127
Jeffrey, P., 126
Jeffreys, Margot, 23–4
Jews, 213
Johnson, J., 3
Johnson, M.R.D., 216

Jones, K., 60, 70–4
Jones, Linda J., 264, 295–301
Jourard, S.M., 274

Kahn, B., 212, 214, 216, 217, 221, 222, 228
Kantor, R.E., 86
Keady, J., 201
Keirse, M., 123
Keith, L., 3, 164, 165
Kellaher, L., 60, 80–9
Kelman, H., 213
Kempe, C., 246
Kendrick, K., 284
key workers, 99, 100
Kiernat, I.M., 141
Killick, John, 111, 130–8
Kitzinger, J., 193
Kitzinger, Sheila, 124, 125
knowledge, and professionalism, 194, 196

language
    and care of ethnic minorities, 96–7,
        186
    in nursing care, 244–5
Latin America, 127
Lawler, Jocelyn, 210, 236–45
Lawrence, R.J., 80
Lawton, M.P., 81
learning disabled
    as carers, 40–7
    institutional care for, 13–14
        *see also* Lennox Castle Hospital
    social services and the, 264, 287–94
    *see also* mentally disordered
Lee-Treweek, Geraldine, 209–10, 230–5
Lees, S., 215
Le Grand, J., 299
Lennox Castle Hospital, 7, 26–35
Lesemann, F., 273
Levy, A., 212, 214, 216, 217, 221, 222, 228
Lewis, C.N., 141
Lewis, J., 2, 46, 274
Lewis, M.I., 141
Liddiard, P., 158
Lieberman, M.A., 76–7
life-history work (reminiscence), 111,
    130–8, 139–43
Lightfoot, J., 276
Lipman, A., 83
litigation, medical malpractice, 283
local initiatives, 308, 309
long-term care, 272, 273–4
    *see also* institutional care
Lonnqvist, Bo, 34
Lowe, M., 276

Lummis, Trevor, 29
Lyme Community Care Unit, 297
Lynne (case study), 40–7

McCarthy, Brian, 111, 145–53
McCorkle, R., 275
Macfarlane, A., 123, 126
McGrath, M., 202
McLaughlin, E., 273
McMahon, A.W., 141
Mahon, A., 283
management
    'binary', 71–2
    failure of, 219–22
market principles, within the NHS, 263,
    284, 295–301
marriage, and disability among ethnic
    minorities, 188
Marris, Peter, 75–6
Marsh, P., 202
Marsland, David, 265, 302–5
Martin, C., 273
Martin, J.P., 212, 220, 221, 222, 223
Martinez-Brawley, E., 309
Marxism, and the concept of community,
    108–9
Mary Dendy Hospital, 222
masculinity, as embodiment of
    professionalism, 191–2, 193
Mason, J., 259
Mason, Philip, 167
Mayo, Marjorie, 61, 104–10
medical model of care, 4, 273
medical profession, 190–6
    *see also* general practice; nurses and
        nursing practice
medical/social boundary, 264, 272–7
medication, for Parkinson's Disease
    sufferers, 119–21
medicine, alternative/traditional, 97–8
Mental Health Act (1959), 67
mental hospitals, 66–7
mentally disordered
    abuse of, 218, 219, 226
    institutionalization of, 66–7
    *see also* learning disabled
Meredith, B., 2, 46
mergers
    of acute hospital trusts, 296–7
    between district health authorities
        (DHAs), 298
Milton Keynes Needs project, 158
Mitchell, Howard, 7, 26–35
mobility, ease of, 86–8
Montagu, A., 275

moral concerns, neutralization of, 213–16
moral support, for informal (unpaid)
 carers, 173–4
Morris, Jenny, 3, 112, 163–9, 273
Mountford, Dora, 10–13
Mugford, M., 126
mutuality, 105, 265, 307

NAHAT (National Association of Health
 Authorities and Trusts), 296, 298, 300
nakedness
 and nursing care, 236–41, 244–5
 within families, 249
National Institute for Social Work
 (NISW), 59, 91
negligence, clinical, 283
Netherlands, 123, 127
neutralization, of normal moral concerns,
 213–16
Newchurch and Co., 296, 298
Newpin befriending system, 160
Newson, J. and Newson, E., 248
NHS, market principles within the, 263,
 284, 295–301
NHS and Community Care Act (1990), 113,
 163, 203, 258, 263, 270
NHS trusts, 295–7
Nissel, M., 2
Nolan, M., 201
Nolan, Peter, 20
Norman, A., 60, 75–9
Normansfield Inquiry, 221
nurses and nursing practice, 4, 56–8,
 190–1, 194, 195, 196, 210, 236–45, 275–6
 community, 297–8
 and culture of consumerism, 264, 279–85
 see also auxiliary nurses; health visiting

Oakley, A., 123, 124
obstetrics, 111, 123–7
old people see elderly people
Oliver, M., 167, 273
Opportunities for Women, 175
organizational structures, and corruption
 of care, 225–6
orientation, problems of, in residential
 homes, 86
Owen, M., 251

Page, R.W., 176
Paget, M.A., 280
Parker, R.A., 59–60, 62–8
Parkinson's Disease, 111, 114–22
Parry, G., 160
Parsloe, P., 203

Patient's Charter, 281, 282, 283
pauperism, 66
Peace, Sheila, 59–61, 80–9
Pennell, I., 273
Perls, F., 151
personal development, and empowerment,
 198–9, 202
personalization, in residential homes, 84
Phillips, A., 127
Phillipson, C., 259
physical environment, of residential
 homes for the elderly, 80–9
Pierson, C., 272
Pillemer, K., 260
Pinch, S., 284
Pinder, Ruth, 111, 114–22
pindown regime, 209, 212, 214–16, 217, 222,
 224, 225, 227
Placek, P., 127
Plant, R., 206
politics, community, 105
Poor Law system, 62–3, 65, 66
Porter, S., 195
Potts, Maggie, 13–14
Pound, A., 160
poverty, 108, 303
 feminization of, 109
power, 109
 abuse of, 216–18
 and group development, 152
powerlessness, 216–18
Poyner, B., 77
prejudice, 183–4
Preston-Shoot, M., 203
Prior, D., 200, 202
privatism, 266, 268–9
professionalism, 112, 190–6, 308
 and corruption of care, 225
professionals
 conflict between informal (unpaid)
  carers and, 178–9
 see also medical profession
public/private spatial distinction, and
 residential care, 80–3
purchase of services, 267–8, 276
 see also consumerism
purchaser/provider split
 in the NHS, 298–9
 and services for the learning disabled,
  291–2, 293–4
Pyne, R., 284

Race Equality Unit (REU), 91
racism, 61, 91, 94, 95, 96, 214, 216
 institutional, 112, 183

Rakusen, J., 127
Rapoport, A., 80, 86
Rapp, R., 125
Raynes, N., 217
RCN (Royal College of Nursing), 196
reality therapy, 146-7
recognition, of informal (unpaid) carers, 171-2
reflective practice, 194
Reformatory and Industrial Schools Act (1891), 67
Reid, M., 124
Reitz, H.J., 152
religion, 99
relocation, 60, 75-9
reminiscence *see* life-history work
residential care
  for adolescent girls, 111, 145-53
  black perspectives on, 91-103
  for the elderly, 64, 76-7, 80-9, 218, 226, 230-5
  public/private spatial distinction in, 80-3
  *see also* institutional care
resourcing of services, 205
  *see also* market principles
respite care, 175
responsibility, 204-5
  collective, 194
  individual, of nurses, 283, 284, 285
Rhudick, P.I., 141
Richards, M., 124, 127
rights of patients, awareness of, 281-3
risk culture, and nursing, 264, 279-85
Robb, Martin, 1-5, 111-13
Roberge, L., 246
Roberts, Robert, 65, 213
Rose, M.E., 62
Rosenfeld, H.M., 274
Rosow, I., 81-2
Roszack, T., 275
Royal Commission on the Aged Poor (1895), 65
Royal Commission on the Law Relating to Mental Illness and Mental Deficiency (1954-7), 67
Rubin, J.E., 274
Russell, J., 158
Ruzek, S., 127
Ryan, J., 219, 273

Sadock, B.J., 152
safety, of residents in care, 88-9
Safier, G., 141
St Augustine's Hospital, 223

Salem, R., 77
Samuel, R., 106
Saqi, S., 256
Saunders, P., 303
Scally, Margaret, 31
Schechter, M., 246
Schwartz, E., 125
Seldon, A., 303
self-esteem, 160
self-reliance, 265, 303-4, 305
service, community as, 106
sexual abuse, 246, 250, 251, 253, 257
Shah, Robina, 112, 182-9
Shepard, H.A., 152
Simkin, P., 126
Smale, G., 309
Smith, Marjorie, 248, 249, 250, 251
Smith, P.B., 153
social workers, and services for learning disabled, 264, 287-94
social/medical boundary, 264, 272-7
Spencer, Liz, 253
spirituality, 99
Spitz, H., 152
Stacey, Margaret, 3, 195
staffing, and residential care of black and ethnic minorities, 99-101
Stafford, R., 127
state, community as the, 106
stereotyping, cultural, 112, 183, 184-6, 214, 216
Stevenson, Olive, 203, 211
stigmatization, 64, 65, 66
support
  emotional and moral, 173-4
  from family, 160-1
Sussman, N.M., 274
Synnott, A., 274

Tavistock Institute of Human Relations, 77
taxes, 304
Teamcare Valleys (TCV) initiative, 111, 157
technological change, 296-7
Thacker, S., 125
Thoburn, J., 254
Thomas Coram Research Unit, 248, 249
Thomas, F., 219, 273
Thompson, Paul, 29
Thornton, S., 141
Thursz, D., 199
Tizard, B., 217
Tocqueville, Alexis de, 266
Toennies, F., 104-5, 106-7

tokenism, 184
Tomlinson Report, 297
total institutions, Goffman's concept of, 60, 70–4
touching, 274–7
  *see also* body care
Townsend, Peter, 7, 9–10, 64, 213
traditional medicines, 97–8
trust, 309
  and empowerment, 202
trusts
  community, 297–8
  hospital, 295–7
Tuckman, B.W., 152
Twigg, J., 2, 109, 164, 179, 200, 264, 272–7

UKCC (United Kingdom Central Council for Nursing, Midwifery and Health Visiting), 196, 284
unemployment, 108
Ungerson, Clare, 2, 109, 263, 266–71
United States, 127
unpaid carers *see* informal (unpaid) carers

Victor, C., 142
Vincent, C., 283

Waerness, K., 3
Wagner Committee, 59, 60
Wagner Development Group, Black Perspectives Sub-Group, 60, 91–103
Walby, S., 284
Walker, Alan, 113, 198–207
Walmsley, Jan, 7–8, 40–7, 165, 194
Walsh, K., 282
Wardhaugh, Julia, 209, 212–28
Warren, C.A.B., 238
Waterhouse, L., 254
welfarism, 266, 269

Wellman, B., 108
Wenger, G.C., 307
Westin, A., 82
Whitbeck, C., 125
Whitcher, J.S., 274
Whittingham Hospital, 223
Wilcocks, D., 230
Wilding, Paul, 209, 212–28, 301
will-breaking, 214, 215
Willcocks, D., 60, 80–9
Williams, Patricia, 50
Williams, Raymond, 104, 105
Williams, Ted, 18–19
Willmott, P., 75, 106, 107
Winterton Hospital, 222–3
Wistow, G., 200, 203, 274
Wolf, R., 260
women
  caring responsibilities of, 3, 109–10, 163–4, 168
  and childbirth, 123–7
  disabled, 112, 164–5, 168–9
  and poverty, 109
workhouses, 62–4, 65
working class, and the workhouse, 65
World Health Organization, 125, 126, 155
  Conference on Primary Health Care (1978), 155
Wrubel, J., 4, 8, 56–8, 242, 243

Yalom, I.D., 152
Yeo, E. and Yeo, S., 105
Young, K., 309
Young, M., 75, 107
young people
  as carers, 3, 176–7
  *see also* adolescent groups; children